Stanley Gibbo
Stamp Catalog

Hong Kong

7th Edition 2025

STANLEY
GIBBONS
THE HOME OF STAMP COLLECTING

By Appointment to
His Majesty The King
Philatelists
Stanley Gibbons
London

Published by Stanley Gibbons
Editorial, Publication and Sales Offices:
Suite 4, Endeavour House, Crow Arch Lane,
Ringwood, Hants BH24 1HP

© Stanley Gibbons 2025

British Library Cataloguing in Publication Data.
A catalogue record for this book is available from the British Library.

1st Edition - 2004
2nd Edition - 2008
3rd Edition - 2010
4th Edition - 2013
5th Edition - 2015
6th Edition - 2018
7th Edition - 2025

Errors and omissions excepted
the colour reproduction of stamps is only as
accurate as the printing process will allow.

ISBN-13: 978-1-83654-452-4

Item No. R2877-25

Printed by
Halstan, Amersham

Contents

Stanley Gibbons Baldwin's Auctions
399 Strand, London WC2R 0LX
Tel: +44 (0)208 092 5856
E-mail: auctions@SGBaldwins.com
Website: www.SGBaldwins.com

Monday–Saturday 9.30 a.m. to 6 p.m..

**Stanley Gibbons Publications,
Mail Order, Gibbons Stamp Monthly**
Suite 4, Endeavour House,
Crow Arch Lane, Ringwood,
Hampshire BH24 1HP.
Tel: +44 (0)1425 472363
E-mail: support@stanleygibbons.com

Monday–Friday 8.30 a.m. to 5 p.m.

**Stanley Gibbons Publications
Overseas Representation**
Stanley Gibbons Publications are
represented overseas by the following

Australia
Renniks Publications PTY LTD
Unit 6, 30 Perry St, Matraville,
NSW 2036, Australia
Tel: +612 9695 7055
Website: www.renniks.com

Canada
Unitrade Associates
99 Floral Parkway, Toronto,
Ontario M6L 2C4, Canada
Tel: +1 416 242 5900
Website: www.unitradeassoc.com

Canada
F.v.H. Stamps
102-340 West Cordova Street,
Vancouver, BC, V6B 1E8, Canada
Tel: +1 604 684 8408
Website: www.fvhstamps.com

Canada
Armstrong's
PO Bos 261,
Bright's Grove
Ontario, Canada N0N 1C0
Tel: +519 464 2688
Website: www.armstrongsstamps.ca

Denmark
Nordfrim A/S
Kvindevadet 42,
Otterup DK-5450, Denmark
Tel: +45 64 82 1256
Website: www.nordfrim.com

Japan
Japan Philatelic
PO Box 2, Suginami-Minami,
Tokyo 168-8081, Japan
Tel: +81 3330 41641
Website: www.yushu.co.jp

Netherlands
Uitgeverij Davo BV
PO Box 411, Ak Deventer, 7400
Netherlands
Tel: +3188 0284300
Website: www.davo.nl

New Zealand
Mowbray Collectables
Private Bag 63000
Wellington
New Zealand

New Zealand
Philatelic Distributors
PO Box 863
15 Mount Edgecumbe Street
New Plymouth 4615, New Zealand
Tel: +6 46 758 65 68
Website: www.stampcollecta.com

Singapore
C S Philatelic Agency
Peninsula Shopping Centre #04-29
3 Coleman Street, 179804, Singapore
Tel: +65 6337-1859
Website: www.cs.com.sg

General Philatelic Information and Guidelines to the Scope of Stanley Gibbons Commonwealth Catalogues

These notes reflect current practice in compiling the Stanley Gibbons Commonwealth Catalogues.

The Stanley Gibbons Stamp Catalogue has a very long history and the vast quantity of information it contains has been carefully built up by successive generations through the work of countless individuals. Philately is never static and the Catalogue has evolved and developed over the years. These notes relate to the current criteria upon which a stamp may be listed or priced. These criteria have developed over time and may have differed somewhat in the early years of this catalogue. These notes are not intended to suggest that we plan to make wholesale changes to the listing of classic issues in order to bring them into line with today's listing policy, they are designed to inform catalogue users as to the policies currently in operation.

PRICES

The prices quoted in this Catalogue are the estimated selling prices of Stanley Gibbons at the time of publication. They are, unless it is specifically stated otherwise, for examples in fine condition for the issue concerned. Superb examples are worth more; those of a lower quality considerably less.

All prices are subject to change without prior notice and Stanley Gibbons may from time to time offer stamps below catalogue price. Individual low value stamps sold at 399 Strand are liable to an additional handling charge. Purchasers of new issues should note the prices charged for them contain an element for the service rendered and so may exceed the prices shown when the stamps are subsequently catalogued. Postage and handling charges are extra.

No guarantee is given to supply all stamps priced, since it is not possible to keep every catalogued item in stock. Commemorative issues may, at times, only be available in complete sets and not as individual values.

Quotation of prices. The prices in the left-hand column are for unused stamps and those in the right-hand column are for used.

A dagger (†) denotes that the item listed does not exist or is not believed to exist in that condition and a blank, or dash, that it exists, or may exist, but we are unable to quote a price.

We welcome information concerning items which are currently unpriced; such assistance may lead to them being priced in future editions.

Prices are expressed in pounds and pence sterling. One pound comprises 100 pence (£1 = 100p).

The method of notation is as follows: pence in numerals (e.g. 10 denotes ten pence); pounds and pence, up to £100, in numerals (e.g. 4.25 denotes four pounds and twenty-five pence); prices above £100 are expressed in whole pounds with the '£' sign shown.

Unused stamps. Great Britain and Commonwealth: the prices for unused stamps of Queen Victoria to King George V are for lightly hinged examples. Unused prices for King Edward VIII, King George VI, Queen Elizabeth and King Charles III issues are for unmounted mint or 'mint never hinged' (MNH).

Some stamps from the King George VI period are often difficult to find in unmounted mint condition. In such instances we would expect that collectors would need to pay a high proportion of the price quoted to obtain mounted mint examples. Generally speaking lightly mounted mint stamps from this reign, issued before 1945, are in considerable demand.

Used stamps. The used prices are normally for stamps fine postally used, which for the vast majority of those issued since 1900 refers to cancellation with a clear circular or oval dated postmark. It may also include stamps cancelled to order, where this practice exists, or with commemorative or 'first day' postmarks.

A pen-cancellation on early issues can sometimes correctly denote postal use. Instances are individually noted in the Catalogue in explanation of the used price given.

Prices quoted for bisects on cover or large piece are for those dated during the period officially authorised.

Stamps not sold unused to the public (e.g. some official stamps) are priced used only.

The use of 'unified' designs, that is stamps inscribed for both postal and fiscal purposes, results in a number of stamps of very high face value. In some instances these may not have been primarily intended for postal purposes, but if they are so inscribed we include them. The used prices shown refer to postally used examples, although prices for fiscally used may be shown within brackets. Collectors should be careful to avoid stamps with fiscal cancellations being offered as 'postal fiscals' and also fiscally used stamps that have had their cancellations removed and fraudulent postmarks applied.

Cover prices. To assist collectors, cover prices are quoted for issues up to 1945 at the beginning of each country.

The system gives a general guide in the form of a factor by which the corresponding used price of the basic loose stamp should be multiplied when found in fine average condition on cover.

Care is needed in applying the factors and they relate to a cover which bears a single of the denomination listed; if more than one denomination is present the most highly priced attracts the multiplier and the remainder are priced at the simple figure for used singles in arriving at a total.

The cover should be of non-philatelic origin; bearing the correct postal rate for the period and distance involved and cancelled with the markings normal to the offices concerned. **Purely philatelic items have a cover value only slightly greater than the catalogue value for the corresponding used stamps.** This applies generally to those high-value stamps used philatelically rather than in the normal course of commerce. Low-value stamps, e.g. ¼d. and ½d., are desirable when used as a single rate on cover and merit an increase in 'multiplier' value.

First day covers in the period up to 1945 are not within the scope of the system and the multiplier should not be used. As a special category of philatelic usage, with wide variations in valuation according to scarcity, they require separate treatment.

Oversized covers, difficult to accommodate on an album page, should be reckoned as worth little more than the corresponding value of the used stamps. The condition of a cover also affects its value. Except for 'wreck covers', serious damage or soiling reduce the value where the postal markings and stamps are ordinary ones. Conversely, visual appeal adds to the value and this can include freshness of appearance, important addresses, old-fashioned but legible hand-writing, historic town-names, etc.

The multipliers are a base on which further value would be added to take account of the cover's postal historical importance in demonstrating such things as unusual, scarce or emergency cancels, interesting routes, significant postal markings, combination usage, the development of postal rates, and so on.

Minimum price. The minimum catalogue price quoted is 10p. For individual stamps prices between 10p. and 95p. are provided as a guide for catalogue users. The lowest price charged for individual stamps or sets purchased from Stanley Gibbons is £1.

Set prices. Set prices are generally for one of each value, excluding shades and varieties, but including major colour changes. Where there are alternative shades, etc., the cheapest is usually included. The number of stamps in the set is always stated for clarity. The prices for sets containing *se-tenant* pieces are based on the prices quoted for such combinations, and not on those for the individual stamps.

Varieties. Where plate or cylinder varieties are priced in used condition the price quoted is for a fine used example with the cancellation well clear of the listed flaw.

Specimen stamps. The pricing of these items is explained under that heading.

Stamp booklets. Prices are for complete assembled booklets in fine condition with those issued before 1945 showing normal wear and tear. Incomplete booklets and those which have been 'exploded' will, in general, be worth less than the figure quoted.

Repricing. Collectors will be aware that the market factors of supply and demand directly influence the prices quoted in this Catalogue. Whatever the scarcity of a particular stamp, if there is no one in the market who wishes to buy, it cannot be expected to achieve a high price. Conversely, the same item actively sought by numerous potential buyers may cause the price to rise.

All the prices in this Catalogue are examined during the preparation of each new edition by the expert staff of Stanley Gibbons and repriced as necessary. They take many factors into account, including supply and demand, and are in close touch with the international stamp market and the auction world.

Commonwealth cover prices and advice on postal history material originally provided by Edward B Proud.

GUARANTEE

All stamps are guaranteed originals in the following terms:

If not as described, and returned by the purchaser, we undertake to refund the price paid to us in the original transaction. If any stamp is certified as genuine by the Expert Committee of the Royal Philatelic Society, London, or by BPA Expertising Ltd, the purchaser shall not be entitled to make any claim against us for any error, omission or mistake in such certificate.

Consumers' statutory rights are not affected by the above guarantee.

The recognised Expert Committees in this country are those of the Royal Philatelic Society, 15 Abchurch Lane, London EC4 7BW, and BPA Expertising Ltd, PO Box 1141, Guildford, Surrey GU5 0WR. They do not undertake valuations under any circumstances and fees are payable for their services.

MARGINS ON IMPERFORATE STAMPS

| Superb | Very fine | Fine | Average | Poor |

GUM

| Unmounted | Very lightly mounted | Lightly mounted | Mounted/ large part original gum (o.g.). | Heavily mounted small part o.g. |

CENTRING

| Superb | Very fine | Fine | Average | Poor |

CANCELLATIONS

| Superb | Very fine | Fine | Average | Poor |

Superb   Very fine

Fine   Average   Poor

CONDITION GUIDE

To assist collectors in assessing the true value of items they are considering buying or in reviewing stamps already in their collections, we now offer a more detailed guide to the condition of stamps on which this catalogue's prices are based.

For a stamp to be described as 'Fine', it should be sound in all respects, without creases, bends, wrinkles, pin holes, thins or tears. If perforated, all perforation 'teeth' should be intact, it should not suffer from fading, rubbing or toning and it should be of clean, fresh appearance.

Margins on imperforate stamps: These should be even on all sides and should be at least as wide as half the distance between that stamp and the next. To have one or more margins of less than this width, would normally preclude a stamp from being described as 'Fine'. Some early stamps were positioned very close together on the printing plate and in such cases 'Fine' margins would necessarily be narrow. On the other hand, some plates were laid down to give a substantial gap between individual stamps and in such cases margins would be expected to be much wider.

An 'average' four-margin example would have a narrower margin on one or more sides and should be priced accordingly, while a stamp with wider, yet even, margins than 'Fine' would merit the description 'Very Fine' or 'Superb' and, if available, would command a price in excess of that quoted in the catalogue.

Gum: Since the prices for stamps of King Edward VIII, King George VI, Queen Elizabeth and King Charles III are for 'unmounted' or 'never hinged' mint, even stamps from these reigns which have been very lightly mounted should be available at a discount from catalogue price, the more obvious the hinge marks, the greater the discount.

Catalogue prices for stamps issued prior to King Edward VIII's reign are for mounted mint, so unmounted examples would be worth a premium. Hinge marks on 20th century stamps should not be too obtrusive, and should be at least in the lightly mounted category. For 19th century stamps more obvious hinging would be acceptable, but stamps should still carry a large part of their original gum—'Large part o.g.'—in order to be described as 'Fine'.

Centring: Ideally, the stamp's image should appear in the exact centre of the perforated area, giving equal margins on all sides. 'Fine' centring would be close to this ideal with any deviation having an effect on the value of the stamp. As in the case of the margins on imperforate stamps, it should be borne in mind that the space between some early stamps was very narrow, so it was very difficult to achieve accurate perforation, especially when the technology was in its infancy. Thus, poor centring would have a less damaging effect on the value of a 19th century stamp than on a 20th century example, but the premium put on a perfectly centred specimen would be greater.

Cancellations: Early cancellation devices were designed to 'obliterate' the stamp in order to prevent it being reused and this is still an important objective for today's postal administrations. Stamp collectors, on the other hand, prefer postmarks to be lightly applied, clear, and to leave as much as possible of the design visible. Dated, circular cancellations have long been 'the postmark of choice', but the definition of a 'Fine' cancellation will depend upon the types of cancellation in use at the time a stamp was current—it is clearly illogical to seek a circular datestamp on a Penny Black.

'Fine', by definition, will be superior to 'Average', so, in terms of cancellation quality, if one begins by identifying what 'Average' looks like, then one will be half way to identifying 'Fine'. The illustrations will give some guidance on mid-19th century and mid-20th century cancellations of Great Britain, but types of cancellation in general use in each country and in each period will determine the appearance of 'Fine'.

As for the factors discussed above, anything less than 'Fine' will result in a downgrading of the stamp concerned, while a very fine or superb cancellation will be worth a premium.

Self-adhesive stamps: The majority of used self-adhesive stamps cannot easily be removed from postal items and are therefore best collected intact or 'on-piece'. In the latter case, we recommend that stamps are carefully trimmed from envelopes with straight, even margins all round, taking care not to cut into the stamp itself. A margin of 2mm all round is ideal.

Combining the factors: To merit the description 'Fine', a stamp should be fine in every respect, but a small deficiency in one area might be made up for in another by a factor meriting an 'Extremely Fine' description.

Some early issues are so seldom found in what would normally be considered to be 'Fine' condition, the catalogue prices are for a slightly lower grade, with 'Fine' examples being worth a premium. In such cases a note to this effect is given in the catalogue, while elsewhere premiums are given for well-centred, lightly cancelled examples.

In the 21st century many postal administrations seem to feel that there is little need for stamps to be legibly cancelled and ink-jet markings, heavy obliterations and pen cancellations are very much the order of the day, while a large proportion of stamps are left without a postal marking of any kind. Used stamps of this type are of very little value and the prices shown in this catalogue are for clear circular operational date stamps or appropriate commemorative cancellations, although the latter are also frowned upon by many collectors.

Stamps graded at less than fine remain collectable and, in the case of more highly priced stamps, will continue to hold a value. Nevertheless, buyers should always bear condition in mind.

The Catalogue in General

Contents. The Catalogue is confined to adhesive postage stamps, including miniature sheets. For particular categories the rules are:

(a) Revenue (fiscal) stamps are listed only where they have been expressly authorised for postal duty.

(b) Stamps issued only precancelled are included, but normally issued stamps available additionally with precancel have no separate precancel listing unless the face value is changed.

(c) Stamps prepared for use but not issued, hitherto accorded full listing, are nowadays foot-noted with a price (where possible).

(d) Bisects (trisects, etc.) are only listed where such usage was officially authorised.

(e) Stamps issued only on first day covers or in presentation packs and not available separately are not listed but may be priced in a footnote.

(f) New printings are only included in this Catalogue where they show a major philatelic variety, such as a change in shade, watermark or paper. Stamps which exist with or without imprint dates are listed separately; changes in imprint dates are mentioned in footnotes.

(g) Official and unofficial reprints are dealt with by footnote.

(h) Stamps from imperforate printings of modern issues which occur perforated are covered by footnotes, but are listed where widely available for postal use.

Exclusions. The following are excluded:

(a) non-postal revenue or fiscal stamps;

(b) postage stamps used fiscally (although prices are now given for some fiscally used high values);

(c) local carriage labels and private local issues;

(d) bogus or phantom stamps;

(e) railway or airline letter fee stamps, bus or road transport company labels or the stamps of private postal companies operating under licence from the national authority;

(f) cut-outs;

(g) all types of non-postal labels and souvenirs;

(h) documentary labels for the postal service, e.g. registration, recorded delivery, air-mail etiquettes, etc.;

(i) privately applied embellishments to official issues and privately commissioned items generally;

(j) stamps for training postal officers.

Full listing. 'Full listing' confers our recognition and implies allotting a catalogue number and (wherever possible) a price quotation.

In judging status for inclusion in the catalogue broad considerations are applied to stamps. They must be issued by a legitimate postal authority, recognised by the government concerned, and must be adhesives valid for proper postal use in the class of service for which they are inscribed. Stamps, with the exception of such categories as postage dues and officials, must be available to the general public, at face value, in reasonable quantities without any artificial restrictions being imposed on their distribution.

For errors and varieties the criterion is legitimate (albeit inadvertent) sale through a postal administration in the normal course of business. Details of provenance are always important; printers' waste and deliberately manufactured material are excluded.

Certificates. In assessing unlisted items due weight is given to Certificates from recognised Expert Committees and, where appropriate, we will usually ask to see them.

Date of issue. Where local issue dates differ from dates of release by agencies, 'date of issue' is the local date. Fortuitous stray usage before the officially intended date is disregarded in listing.

Catalogue numbers. Stamps of each country are catalogued chronologically by date of issue. Subsidiary classes are placed at the end of the country, as separate lists, with a distinguishing letter prefix to the catalogue number, e.g. D for postage due, O for official and E for express delivery stamps.

The catalogue number appears in the extreme left-column. The boldface Type numbers in the next column are merely cross-references to illustrations.

A catalogue number with a suffix will normally relate to the main number, so 137a will be a variant of No. 137, unless the suffix appears as part of the number in the left-hand column such as Great Britain No. 20a, in which case that should be treated as the main number. A number with multiple suffixes will relate to the first letter or letters of that suffix, so 137ab will be a variant of 137a and 137aba a variant of 137ab. The exception is an 'aa' suffix, which will precede an 'a' and always refers to the main number, so 137aa relates to 137, not 137a.

Once published in the Catalogue, numbers are changed as little as possible; really serious renumbering is reserved for the occasions when a complete country or an entire issue is being rewritten. The edition first affected includes cross-reference tables of old and new numbers.

Our catalogue numbers are universally recognised in specifying stamps and as a hallmark of status.

'Missing' numbers. Following rewriting it is frequently the case that individual or series of numbers become redundant. Apparent gaps in the numbering, such as, New Zealand 472/543 or St Helena 102 do not indicate that a stamp or stamps are omitted, but that an earlier revision has been made to the listing.

Illustrations. Stamps are illustrated at three-quarters linear size. Stamps not illustrated are the same size and format as the value shown, unless otherwise indicated. Stamps issued only as miniature sheets have the stamp alone illustrated but sheet size is also quoted. Overprints, surcharges, watermarks and postmarks are normally actual size. Illustrations of varieties are often enlarged to show the detail. Stamp booklet covers are illustrated half-size, unless otherwise indicated.

The colour illustrations of stamps are intended as a guide only, they may differ in shade from the originals.

Designers. Designers' names are quoted where known, though space precludes naming every individual concerned in the production of a set. In particular, photographers supplying material are usually named only where they also make an active contribution in the design stage; posed photographs of reigning monarchs are, however, an exception to this rule.

CONTACTING THE CATALOGUE EDITOR

The editor is always interested in hearing from people who have new information which will improve or correct the Catalogue. As a general rule he must see and examine the actual stamps before they can be considered for listing; although a high-resolution scan, particularly if supported by a certificate provided by a reliable authority may provide sufficient evidence.

Submissions should be made in writing to the Catalogue Editor, Stanley Gibbons Publications at the Ringwood office or via email to thecatalogueeditor@stanleygibbons.com. For items submitted by post the cost of return postage would be appreciated, and this should include the registration fee if required.

Where information is solicited purely for the benefit of the enquirer, the editor cannot undertake to reply if the answer is already contained in these published notes or if return postage is omitted. Written communications are greatly preferred to enquiries by telephone or e-mail and the editor regrets that he or his staff cannot see personal callers without a prior appointment being made. Correspondence may be subject to delay during the production period of each new edition.

The editor welcomes close contact with study circles and is interested, too, in finding reliable local correspondents who will verify and supplement official information in countries where this is deficient.

> We regret we do not give opinions as to the genuineness of stamps, nor do we identify stamps or number them by our Catalogue.

TECHNICAL MATTERS

The meanings of the technical terms used in the catalogue will be found in our *Philatelic Terms Illustrated*. References below to (more specialised) listings are to be taken to indicate, as appropriate, the Stanley Gibbons *Great Britain Specialised Catalogue* or the *Great Britain Concise Catalogue*.

1. Printing

Printing errors. Errors in printing are of major interest to the Catalogue. Authenticated items meriting consideration would include: background, centre or frame inverted or omitted; centre or subject transposed; error of colour; error or omission of value; double prints and impressions; printed both sides; and so on.

Apparent 'double prints' including overprints, on stamps printed by offset litho arising from movement of the rubber 'blanket' involved in this process are however, outside the scope of this catalogue, although they may be included in more specialised listings.

Designs *tête-bêche*, whether intentionally or by accident, are listable. *Se-tenant* arrangements of stamps are recognised in the listings or footnotes. Gutter pairs (a pair of stamps separated by blank margin) are not included in this volume. Colours only partially omitted are

not listed. Stamps with embossing omitted are reserved for our more specialised listings.

Printing varieties. Listing is accorded to major changes in the printing base which lead to completely new types. In recess-printing this could be a design re-engraved; in photogravure or photolithography a screen altered in whole or in part. It can also encompass flat-bed and rotary printing if the results are readily distinguishable.

To be considered at all, varieties must be constant.

Early stamps, produced by primitive methods, were prone to numerous imperfections; the lists reflect this, recognising re-entries, retouches, broken frames, misshapen letters, and so on. Printing technology has, however, radically improved over the years, during which time photogravure and lithography have become predominant. Varieties nowadays are more in the nature of flaws and these, being too specialised for this general catalogue, are almost always outside the scope.

In no catalogue, however, do we list such items as: dry prints, kiss prints, doctor-blade flaws, colour shifts or registration flaws (unless they lead to the complete omission of a colour from an individual stamp), lithographic ring flaws, and so on. Neither do we recognise fortuitous happenings like paper creases or confetti flaws.

'Varieties of varieties'. We no longer provide individual listings for combinations of two or more varieties; thus a plate variety or overprinting error will not be listed for various watermark orientations.

Overprints (and surcharges). Overprints of different types qualify for separate listing. These include overprints in different colours; overprints from different printing processes such as litho and typo; overprints in totally different typefaces, etc. Major errors in machine-printed overprints are important and listable. They include: overprint inverted or omitted; overprint double (treble, etc.); overprint diagonal; overprint double, one inverted; pairs with one overprint omitted, e.g. from a radical shift to an adjoining stamp; error of colour; error of type fount; letters inverted or omitted, etc. If the overprint is hand-stamped, few of these would qualify and a distinction is drawn. We continue, however, to list pairs of stamps where one has a handstamped overprint and the other has not, unless it is known that such items were created deliberately at the request of purchasers (see note below Zanzibar 394/413).

Albino prints or double prints, one of them being albino (i.e. showing an uninked impression of the printing plate) are listable unless they are particularly common in this form (see the note below Travancore No. 32fa, for example). We do not, however, normally list reversed albino overprints, caused by the accidental or deliberate folding of sheets prior to overprinting (British Levant Nos. 51/8).

Varieties occurring in overprints will often take the form of broken letters, slight differences in spacing, rising spaces, etc. Only the most important would be considered for listing or footnote mention.

Sheet positions. If space permits we quote sheet positions of listed varieties and authenticated data is solicited for this purpose.

De La Rue plates. The Catalogue classifies the general plates used by De La Rue for printing British Colonial stamps as follows:

VICTORIAN KEY TYPE

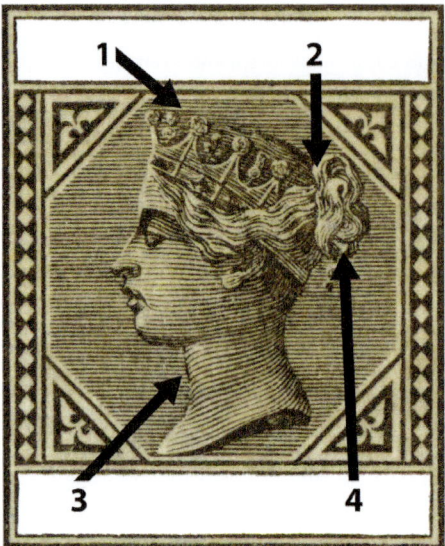

Die I

1. The ball of decoration on the second point of the crown appears as a dark mass of lines.
2. Dark vertical shading separates the front hair from the bun.
3. The vertical line of colour outlining the front of the throat stops at the sixth line of shading on the neck.
4. The white space in the coil of the hair above the curl is roughly the shape of a pin's head.

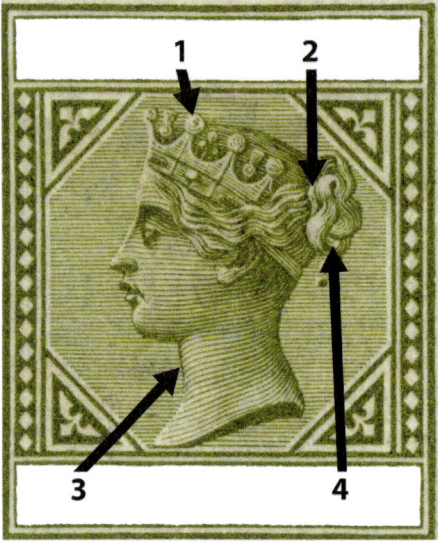

Die II

1. There are very few lines of colour in the ball and it appears almost white.
2. A white vertical strand of hair appears in place of the dark shading.
3. The line stops at the eighth line of shading.
4. The white space is oblong, with a line of colour partially dividing it at the left end.

Plates numbered 1 and 2 are both Die I. Plates 3 and 4 are Die II.

GEORGIAN KEY TYPE

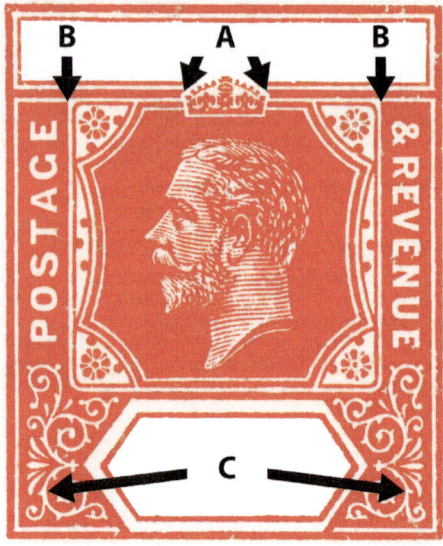

Die I

A. The second (thick) line below the name of the country is cut slanting, conforming roughly to the shape of the crown on each side.
B. The labels of solid colour bearing the words 'POSTAGE' and '& REVENUE' are square at the inner top corners.
C. There is a projecting 'bud' on the outer spiral of the ornament in each of the lower corners.

Die II

A. The second line is cut vertically on each side of the crown.
B. The labels curve inwards at the top.
C. There is no 'bud' in this position.

Unless otherwise stated in the lists, all stamps with watermark Multiple Crown CA (w **8**) are Die I while those with watermark Multiple Crown Script CA (w **9**) are Die II. The Georgian Die II was introduced in April 1921 and was used for Plates 10 to 22 and 26 to 28. Plates 23 to 25 were made from Die I by mistake.

2. Paper

All stamps listed are deemed to be on (ordinary) paper of the wove type and white in colour; only departures from this are normally mentioned.

Types. Where classification so requires we distinguish such other types of paper as, for example, vertically and horizontally laid; wove and laid bâtonné; card(board); carton; cartridge; glazed; granite; native; pelure; porous; quadrillé; ribbed; rice; and silk thread.

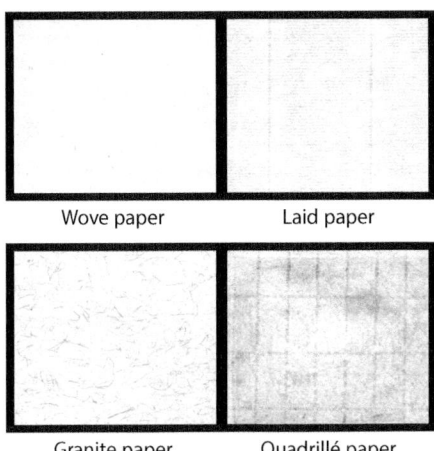

Wove paper	Laid paper
Granite paper	Quadrillé paper

Burelé band

The various makeshifts for normal paper are listed as appropriate. The varieties of double paper and joined paper are recognised. The security device of a printed burelé band on the back of a stamp, as in early Queensland, qualifies for listing.

Descriptive terms. The fact that a paper is handmade (and thus probably of uneven thickness) is mentioned where necessary. Such descriptive terms as 'hard' and 'soft'; 'smooth' and 'rough'; 'thick', 'medium' and 'thin' are applied where there is philatelic merit in classifying papers.

Coloured, very white and toned papers. A coloured paper is one that is coloured right through (front and back of the stamp). In the Catalogue the colour of the paper is given in italics, thus:

black/*rose* = black design on rose paper.

Papers have been made specially white in recent years by, for example, a very heavy coating of chalk. We do not classify shades of whiteness of paper as distinct varieties. There does exist, however, a type of paper from early days called toned. This is off-white, often brownish or buffish, but it cannot be assigned any definite colour. A toning effect brought on by climate, incorrect storage or gum staining is disregarded here, as this was not the state of the paper when issued.

'Ordinary' and 'Chalk-surfaced' papers. The availability of many postage stamps for revenue purposes made necessary some safeguard against the illegitimate re-use of stamps with removable cancellations. This was at first secured by using fugitive inks and later by printing on paper surfaced by coatings containing either chalk or china clay, both of which made it difficult to remove any form of obliteration without damaging the stamp design.

This catalogue lists these chalk-surfaced paper varieties from their introduction in 1905. Where no indication is given, the paper is 'ordinary'.

The 'traditional' method of indentifying chalk-surfaced papers has been that, when touched with a silver wire, a black mark is left on the paper, and the listings in this catalogue are based on that test. However, the test itself is now largely discredited, for, although the mark can be removed by a soft rubber, some damage to the stamp will result from its use.

The difference between chalk-surfaced and pre-war ordinary papers is fairly clear: chalk-surfaced papers being smoother to the touch and showing a characteristic sheen when light is reflected off their surface. Under good magnification tiny bubbles or pock marks can be seen on the surface of the stamp and at the tips of the perforations the surfacing appears 'broken'. Traces of paper fibres are evident on the surface of ordinary paper and the ink shows a degree of absorption into it.

Initial chalk-surfaced paper printings by De La Rue had a thinner coating than subsequently became the norm. The characteristics described above are less pronounced in these printings.

During and after the Second World War, substitute papers replaced the chalk-surfaced papers, these do not react to the silver test and are therefore classed as 'ordinary', although differentiating them without recourse to it is more difficult, for, although the characteristics of the chalk-surfaced paper remained the same, some of the ordinary papers appear much smoother than earlier papers and many do not show the watermark clearly. Experience is the only solution to identifying these, and comparison with stamps whose paper type is without question will be of great help.

Another type of paper, known as 'thin striated' was used only for the Bahamas 1s. and 5s. (Nos. 155a, 156a, 171 and 174) and for several stamps of the Malayan states. Hitherto these have been described as 'chalk-surfaced' since they gave some reaction to the silver test, but they are much thinner than usual chalk-surfaced papers, with the watermark showing clearly. Stamps on this paper show a slightly 'ribbed' effect when the stamp is held up to the light. Again, comparison with a known striated paper stamp, such as the 1941 Straits Settlements Die II 2c. orange (No. 294) will prove invaluable in separating these papers.

Glazed paper. In 1969 the Crown Agents introduced a new general-purpose paper for use in conjunction with all current printing processes. It generally has a marked glossy surface but the degree varies according to the process used, being more marked in recess-printing stamps. As it does not respond to the silver test this presents a further test where previous printings were on chalky paper. A change of paper to the glazed variety merits separate listing.

Green and yellow papers. Issues of the First World War and immediate postwar period occur on green and yellow papers and these are given separate Catalogue listing. The original coloured papers (coloured throughout) gave way to surface-coloured papers, the stamps having 'white backs'; other stamps show one colour on the front and a different one at the back. Because of the numerous variations a grouping of colours is adopted as follows:

Yellow papers

(1) The original *yellow* paper (throughout), usually bright in colour. The gum is often sparse, of harsh consistency and dull-looking. Used 1912–1920.

(2) The *white-backs*. Used 1913–1914.

(3) A bright lemon paper. The colour must have a pronounced greenish tinge, different from the 'yellow' in (1). As a rule, the gum on stamps using this lemon paper is plentiful, smooth and shiny, and the watermark shows distinctly. Care is needed with stamps printed in green on yellow paper (1) as it may appear that the paper is this lemon. Used 1914–1916.

(4) An experimental *orange-buff* paper. The colour must have a distinct brownish tinge. It is not to be confused with a muddy yellow (1) nor the misleading appearance (on the surface) of stamps printed in red on yellow paper where an engraved plate has been insufficiently wiped. Used 1918–1921.

(5) An experimental *buff* paper. This lacks the brownish tinge of (4) and the brightness of the yellow shades. The gum is shiny when compared with the matt type used on (4). Used 1919–1920.

(6) A *pale yellow* paper that has a creamy tone to the yellow. Used from 1920 onwards.

Green papers

(7) The original 'green' paper, varying considerably through shades of blue-green and yellow-green, the front and back sometimes differing. Used 1912–1916.

(8) The *white backs*. Used 1913–1914.

(9) A paper blue-green on the surface with *pale olive* back. The back must be markedly paler than the front and this and the pronounced olive tinge to the back distinguish it from (7). Used 1916–1920.

(10) Paper with a vivid green surface, commonly called *emerald-green*; it has the olive back of (9). Used 1920.

(11) Paper with *emerald-green* both back and front. Used from 1920 onwards.

3. Perforation and Rouletting

Perforation gauge. The gauge of a perforation is the number of holes in a length of 2 cm. For correct classification the size of the holes (large or small) may need to be distinguished; in a few cases the actual number of holes on each edge of the stamp needs to be quoted.

Measurement. The Gibbons *Instanta* gauge is the standard for measuring perforations. The stamp is viewed against a dark background with the transparent gauge put on top of it. Though the gauge measures to decimal accuracy, perforations read from it are generally quoted in the Catalogue to the nearest half. For example:

Just over perf 12¾ to just under 13¼ = perf 13
Perf 13¼ exactly, rounded up = perf 13½
Just over perf 13¼ to just under 13¾ = perf 13½
Perf 13¾ exactly, rounded up = perf 14

However, where classification depends on it, actual quarter-perforations are quoted.

It should be noted that there were sometimes slight variations in the spacing of the pins along the length of a perforator, giving rise to small differences in the resulting measurements. Since they come from the same perforators and the measurements are generally within the same '½' band on the Instanta gauge we ignore these differences.

Notation. Where no perforation is quoted for an issue it is imperforate. Perforations are usually abbreviated (and spoken) as follows, though sometimes they may be spelled out for clarity. This notation for rectangular stamps (the majority) applies to diamond shapes if 'top' is read as the edge to the top right.

P 14: perforated alike on all sides (read: 'perf 14').
P 14×15: the first figure refers to top and bottom, the second to left and right sides (read: 'perf 14 by 15'). This is a compound perforation. For an upright triangular stamp the first figure refers to the two sloping sides

and second to the base. In inverted triangulars the base is first and the second figure to the sloping sides.

P 14–15 or 14 to 15: perforation measuring anything between 14 and 15: the holes are irregularly spaced, thus the gauge may vary along a single line or even along a single edge of the stamp (read: 'perf 14 to 15').

P 14 *irregular*: perforated 14 from a worn perforator, giving badly aligned holes irregularly spaced (read: 'irregular perf 14').

P *comp(ound)* 14×15: two gauges in use but not necessarily on opposite sides of the stamp. It could be one side in one gauge and three in the other; or two adjacent sides with the same gauge. (Read: 'perf compound of 14 and 15'.) For three gauges or more, abbreviated as 'P 12, 14½, 15 *or compound*' for example.

P 14, 14½: perforated approximately 14¼ (read: 'perf 14 or 14½'). It does *not* mean two stamps, one perf 14 and the other perf 14½. This obsolescent notation is gradually being replaced in the Catalogue.

Imperf: imperforate (not perforated)

Imperf×P 14: imperforate at top ad bottom and perf 14 at sides.

P 14×*imperf*: perf 14 at top and bottom and imperforate at sides.

Imperf×perf

Such headings as 'P 13×14 (*vert*) and P 14×13 (*horiz*)' indicate which perforations apply to which stamp format—vertical or horizontal.

Some stamps are additionally perforated so that a label or tab is detachable; others have been perforated for use as two halves. Listings are normally for whole stamps, unless stated otherwise.

Other terms. Perforation almost always gives circular holes; where other shapes have been used they are specified, e.g. square holes; lozenge perf. Interrupted perfs are brought about by the omission of pins at regular intervals. Perforations merely simulated by being printed as part of the design are of course ignored. With few exceptions, privately applied perforations are not listed.

In the 19th century perforations are often described as clean cut (clean, sharply incised holes), intermediate or rough (rough holes, imperfectly cut, often the result of blunt pins).

Perforation errors and varieties. Authenticated errors, where a stamp normally perforated is accidentally issued imperforate, are listed provided no traces of perforation (blind holes or indentations) remain. They must be provided as pairs, both stamps wholly imperforate, and are only priced in that form.

Note that several postal administrations and their agencies are now deliberately releasing imperforate versions of issued stamps in restricted quantities and at premium prices. These are not listable, but, where possible, their existance will be noted.

In recent years a growing number of imperforates have been released from printers' archives. These are not listable but they are so widespread that it is not practical to note all of them. Collectors are warned against confusing such releases with genuine errors.

Stamps imperforate between stamp and sheet margin are not listed in this catalogue, but such errors on Great Britain stamps will be found in the *Great Britain Specialised Catalogue*.

Pairs described as 'imperforate between' have the line of perforations between the two stamps omitted.

Imperf between (horiz pair): a horizontal pair of stamps with perfs all around the edges but none between the stamps.

Imperf between (vert pair): a vertical pair of stamps with perfs all around the edges but none between the stamps.

| Imperf between (vertical pair) | Imperf horizontally (vertical pair) |

Where several of the rows have escaped perforation the resulting varieties are listable. Thus:

Imperf vert (horiz pair): a horizontal pair of stamps perforated top and bottom; all three vertical directions are imperf—the two outer edges and between the stamps.

Imperf horiz (vert pair): a vertical pair perforated at left and right edges; all three horizontal directions are imperf—the top, bottom and between the stamps.

Straight edges. Large sheets cut up before issue to post offices can cause stamps with straight edges, i.e. imperf on one side or on two sides at right angles. They are not usually listable in this condition and are worth less than corresponding stamps properly perforated all round. This does not, however, apply to certain stamps, mainly from coils and booklets, where straight edges on various sides are the manufacturing norm affecting every stamp. The listings and notes make clear which sides are correctly imperf.

Malfunction. Varieties of double, misplaced or partial perforation caused by error or machine malfunction are not listable, neither are freaks, such as perforations placed diagonally from paper folds, nor missing holes caused by broken pins.

Types of perforating. Where necessary for classification, perforation types are distinguished.
These include:
Line perforation from one line of pins punching single rows of holes at a time.
Comb perforation from pins disposed across the sheet in comb formation, punching out holes at three sides of the stamp a row at a time.
Harrow perforation applied to a whole pane or sheet at one stroke.
Rotary perforation from toothed wheels operating across a sheet, then crosswise.
Sewing machine perforation. The resultant condition, clean-cut or rough, is distinguished where required.
Pin-perforation is the commonly applied term for pin-roulette in which, instead of being punched out, round holes are pricked by sharp-pointed pins and no paper is removed.

Mixed perforation occurs when stamps with defective perforations are re-perforated in a different gauge.

Different printings of the same stamp were sometimes perforated using different machines, e.g., line or comb. Unless these involve different gauges of perforation, they are not separately listed; however, in some cases these differences can help identify listed printings, such as Falkland Islands Nos. 60/63 and 116/122.

The differences between line and comb perforations are most easily seen in blocks of four or larger, where, ideally, comb perforation will show a single perforation hole at the meeting point of four stamps, while line perforation will show a double hole at this point. Very occasionally, line perforation holes will coincide exactly, but never on all four corners of a stamp.

Care needs to be exercised where, due to a slight irregularity in the 'beat' of the machine, double holes can sometimes occur in comb perforation and, especially where there is a significant difference in the price (e.g., Jamaica 132a), accurate measurement of the perforations and reference to the relevant footnotes is essential.

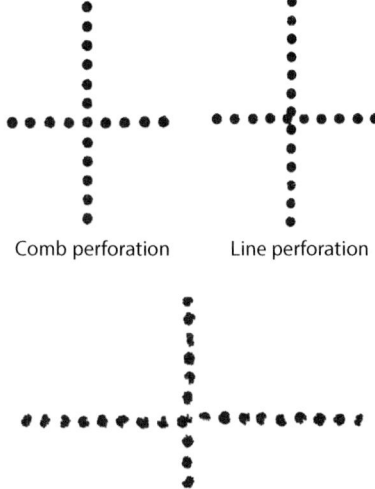

| Comb perforation | Line perforation |

Comb perforation. In spite of the double hole at the intersection, this cannot be line perforated as the horizontal perforations are not in a straight line

Die-cut. Self-adhesive stamps are not perforated in the traditional way, but are die-cut in order to facilitate their removal from the backing paper. Such die-cutting may be 'free-form', to match the design of the stamp, with straight edges, or, most frequently, with simulated 'perforations' or undulating edges. Such 'perforations' or undulations are measured in the same way as conventional perforations.

Punctured stamps. Perforation holes can be punched into the face of the stamp. Patterns of small holes, often in the shape of initial letters, are privately applied devices against pilferage. These (perfins) are outside the scope except for Australia, Canada, Cape of Good Hope, Papua and Sudan where they were used as official stamps by the national administration. Identification devices, when officially inspired, are listed or noted; they can be shapes, or letters or words formed from holes, sometimes converting one class of stamp into another.

Rouletting. In rouletting the paper is cut, for ease of separation, but none is removed. The gauge is measured, when needed, as for perforations. Traditional French terms descriptive of the type of cut are often used and types include:

Arc roulette (percé en arc). Cuts are minute, spaced arcs, each roughly a semicircle.

Cross roulette (percé en croix). Cuts are tiny diagonal crosses.

Line roulette (percé en ligne or en ligne droite). Short straight cuts parallel to the frame of the stamp. The commonest basic roulette. Where not further described, 'roulette' means this type.

Rouletted in colour or coloured roulette (percé en lignes colorées or en lignes de coleur). Cuts with coloured edges, arising from notched rule inked simultaneously with the printing plate.

Saw-tooth roulette (percé en scie). Cuts applied zigzag fashion to resemble the teeth of a saw.

Serpentine roulette (percé en serpentin). Cuts as sharply wavy lines.

Zigzag roulette (percé en zigzags). Short straight cuts at angles in alternate directions, producing sharp points on separation. US usage favours 'serrate(d) roulette' for this type.

Pin-roulette (originally *percé en points* and now *perforés trous d'epingle*) is commonly called pin-perforation in English.

4. Gum

All stamps listed are assumed to have gum of some kind; if they were issued without gum this is stated. Original gum (o.g.) means that which was present on the stamp as issued to the public. Deleterious climates and the presence of certain chemicals can cause gum to crack and, with early stamps, even make the paper deteriorate. Unscrupulous fakers are adept in removing it and regumming the stamp to meet the unreasoning demand often made for 'full o.g.' in cases where such a thing is virtually impossible.

The gum normally used on stamps has been gum arabic until the late 1960s when synthetic adhesives were introduced. Harrison and Sons Ltd for instance use *polyvinyl alcohol*, known to philatelists as PVA. This is almost invisible except for a slight yellowish tinge which was incorporated to make it possible to see that the stamps have been gummed. It has advantages in hot countries, as stamps do not curl and sheets are less likely to stick together. Gum arabic and PVA are not distinguished in the lists except that where a stamp exists with both forms this is indicated in footnotes. Our more specialised catalogues provide separate listing of gums for Great Britain.

Self-adhesive stamps are issued on backing paper, from which they are peeled before affixing to mail. Unused examples are priced as for backing paper intact, in which condition they are recommended to be kept. Used examples are best collected on cover or on piece.

5. Watermarks

Stamps are on unwatermarked paper except where the heading to the set says otherwise.

Detection. Watermarks are detected for Catalogue description by one of four methods: (1) holding stamps to the light; (2) laying stamps face down on a dark background; (3) adding a few drops of petroleum ether 40/60 to the stamp laid face down in a watermark tray; (4) by use of the Stanley Gibbons Detectamark Spectrum, or other equipment, which work by revealing the thinning of the paper at the watermark. (Note that petroleum ether is highly inflammable in use and can damage photogravure stamps.)

Listable types. Stamps occurring on both watermarked and unwatermarked papers are different types and both receive full listing.

Single watermarks (devices occurring once on every stamp) can be modified in size and shape as between different issues; the types are noted but not usually separately listed. Fortuitous absence of watermark from a single stamp or its gross displacement would not be listable.

To overcome registration difficulties the device may be repeated at close intervals (*a multiple watermark*), single stamps thus showing parts of several devices. Similarly, a *large sheet watermark* (or *all-over watermark*) covering numerous stamps can be used. We give informative notes and illustrations for them. The designs may be such that numbers of stamps in the sheet automatically lack watermark: this is not a listable variety. Multiple and all-over watermarks sometimes undergo modifications, but if the various types are difficult to distinguish from single stamps notes are given but not separate listings.

Papermakers' watermarks are noted where known but not listed separately, since most stamps in the sheet will lack them. Sheet watermarks which are nothing more than officially adopted papermakers' watermarks are, however, given normal listing.

Marginal watermarks, falling outside the pane of stamps, are ignored except where misplacement caused the adjoining row to be affected, in which case they may be footnoted. They usually consist of straight or angled lines and double-lined capital letters, they are particularly prevalent on some Crown CC and Crown CA watermark stamps.

Watermark errors and varieties. Watermark errors are recognised as of major importance. They comprise stamps intended to be on unwatermarked paper but issued watermarked by mistake, or stamps printed on paper with the wrong watermark. Varieties showing letters omitted from the watermark are also included, but broken or deformed bits on the dandy roll are not listed unless they represent repairs.

Watermark positions. The diagram shows how watermark position is described in the Catalogue. Paper has a side intended for printing and watermarks are usually impressed so that they read normally when looked through from that printed side. However, since philatelists customarily detect watermarks by looking at the back of the stamp the watermark diagram also makes clear what is actually seen.

Illustrations in the Catalogue are of watermarks in normal positions (from the front of the stamps) and are actual size where possible.

Differences in watermark position are collectable varieties. This Catalogue now lists inverted, sideways inverted and reversed watermark varieties on Commonwealth stamps from the 1860s onwards except where the watermark position is completely haphazard or, due to the method of printing, appear in equal quantities upright and inverted (e.g. Papua Nos. 47/83) In such cases it should be assumed that the price is the same, either way.

Where a watermark comes indiscriminately in various positions our policy is to cover this by a general note: we do not give separate listings because the watermark position in these circumstances has no particular philatelic importance.

Sideways watermarks. A review of the sideways watermarks listed in this catalogue has shown that, while in Great Britain it is fair to say that the 'normal' sideways watermark shows the top of the device (as shown in its illustration) pointing to the left as seen from the front and to the right as seen from the back of the stamp, the opposite is very often the case on Crown Agents colonial issues.

We have therefore adopted the policy of clearly stating whether the normal sideways watermark points to the left or to the right for all issues up to 1970. Where the normal watermark is upright and the sideways variant constitutes a rare error it has not always been possible to confirm its orientation, so we welcome the assistance of collectors in 'filling in the gaps' in these cases.

We repeat here the watermark diagram which has appeared in these introductory notes for many years, with the caveat that, while valid for Great Britain, individual listings should be consulted for the normal orientation of other sideways watermark issues.

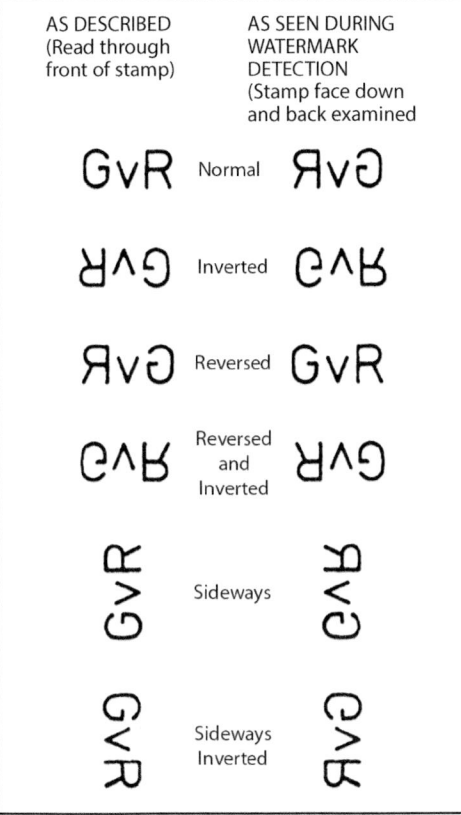

AS DESCRIBED (Read through front of stamp)		AS SEEN DURING WATERMARK DETECTION (Stamp face down and back examined
GvR	Normal	ЯvƆ
ЯʌƆ	Inverted	ƆʌЯ
ЯvƆ	Reversed	GvR
ƆʌЯ	Reversed and Inverted	ЯʌƆ
GvR (sideways)	Sideways	ƆʌЯ (sideways)
GvR (sideways)	Sideways Inverted	ЯvƆ (sideways)

Standard types of watermark. Some watermarks have been used generally for various British possessions rather than exclusively for a single colony. To avoid repetition the Catalogue classifies 11 general types, as under, with references in the headings throughout the listings being given either in words or in the form ('W w 9') (meaning 'watermark type w 9'). In those cases where watermark illustrations appear in the listings themselves, the respective reference reads, for example, W **153**, thus indicating that the watermark will be found in the normal sequence of illustrations as (type) **153**.

The general types are as follows, with an example of each quoted.

W	Description	Example
w **1**	Large Star	St Helena No. 1
w **2**	Small Star	Turks Is. No. 4
w **2a**	Small Truncated Star	Queensland No. 59
w **3**	Broad (pointed) Star	Grenada No. 24
w **4**	Crown (over) CC, small stamp	Antigua No. 13
w **5**	Crown (over) CC, large stamp	Antigua No. 31
w **6**	Crown (over) CA, small stamp	Antigua No. 21
w **7**	Crown CA (CA over Crown), large stamp	Sierra Leone No. 54

w **8**	Multiple Crown CA	Antigua No. 41
w **9**	Multiple Script CA	Seychelles No. 158
w **9a**	do. Error	Seychelles No. 158a
w **9b**	do. Error	Seychelles No. 158b
w **10**	V over Crown	Queensland No. 265
w **11**	Crown over A	Queensland No. 282

CC in these watermarks is an abbreviation for 'Crown Colonies' and CA for 'Crown Agents'. Watermarks w **1**, w **2** and w **3** are on stamps printed by Perkins, Bacon; w **4** onwards on stamps from De La Rue and other printers.

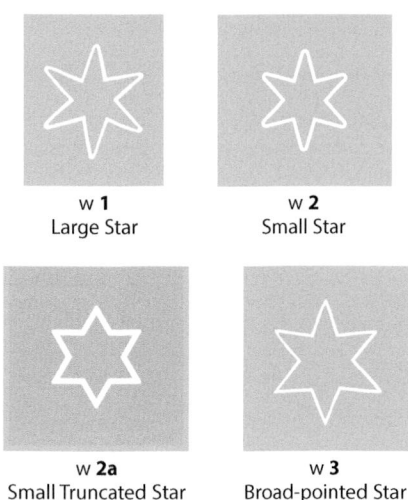

w **1** Large Star	w **2** Small Star
w **2a** Small Truncated Star	w **3** Broad-pointed Star

Watermark w **1**, *Large Star*, measures 15 to 16 mm across the star from point to point and about 27 mm from centre to centre vertically between stars in the sheet. It was made for long stamps like Ceylon 1857 and St Helena 1856.

Watermark w **2**, *Small Star* is of similar design but measures 12 to 13½mm from point to point and 24 mm from centre to centre vertically. It was for use with ordinary-size stamps such as Grenada 1863–1871.

When the Large Star watermark was used with the smaller stamps it only occasionally comes in the centre of the paper. It is frequently so misplaced as to show portions of two stars above and below and this eccentricity will very often help in determining the watermark.

Watermark w **2a**, *Small Truncated Star*, only used for Queensland stamps of 1868–1874.

Watermark w **3**, *Broad-pointed Star*, resembles w **1** but the points are broader.

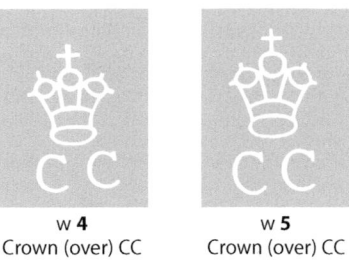

w **4** Crown (over) CC	w **5** Crown (over) CC

Two Crown (over) CC watermarks were used: w **4** was for stamps of ordinary size and w **5** for those of larger size. It is known that the latter was sometimes used for stamps of ordinary size but since the differences are difficult to identify on single stamps we do not list them separately.

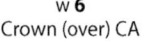

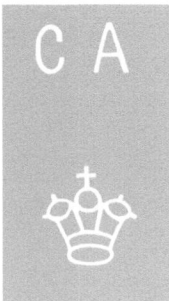

w 6
Crown (over) CA

w 7
CA over Crown

Two watermarks of *Crown CA* type were used, w **6** being for stamps of ordinary size. The other, w **7**, is properly described as *CA over Crown*. It was specially made for paper on which it was intended to print long fiscal stamps: that some were used postally accounts for the appearance of w **7** in the Catalogue. The watermark occupies twice the space of the ordinary Crown CA watermark, w **6**. Stamps of normal size printed on paper with w **7** watermark show it *sideways*; it takes a horizontal pair of stamps to show the entire watermark (e.g. Labuan Nos. 1/4).

w 8
Multiple Crown CA

w 9
Multiple Script CA

Multiple watermarks began in 1904 with w **8**, *Multiple Crown CA*, changed from 1921 to w **9**, *Multiple Script CA*. On stamps of ordinary size portions of two or three watermarks appear and on the large-sized stamps a greater number can be observed. The change to letters in script character with w **9** was accompanied by a Crown of distinctly different shape.

It seems likely that there were at least two dandy rolls for each Crown Agents watermark in use at any one time with a reserve roll being employed when the normal one was withdrawn for maintenance or repair.

Both the Mult Crown CA and the Mult Script CA types exist with one or other of the letters omitted from individual impressions. It is possible that most of these occur from the reserve rolls as they have only been found on certain issues. The MCA watermark experienced such problems during the early 1920s and the Script over a longer period from the early 1940s until 1951.

During the 1920s damage must also have occurred on one of the Crowns on the Multiple Crowns CA paper as a substituted Crown has been found on certain issues. This is smaller than the normal and consists of an oval base joined to two upright ovals with a circle positioned between their upper ends. The upper line of the Crown's base is omitted, as are the left and right-hand circles at the top and also the cross over the centre circle (e.g. Barbados No. 201c).

Substituted Crown

The *Multiple Script CA* watermark, w **9**, is known with two errors, recurring among the 1950–1952 printings of several territories. In the first a crown has fallen away from the dandy-roll that impresses the watermark into the paper pulp. It gives w **9a**, *Crown missing*, but this omission has been found in both 'Crown only' (*illustrated*) and 'Crown CA' rows. The resulting faulty paper was used for Bahamas, Johore, Seychelles and the postage due stamps of nine colonies

w **9a**: Error, Crown missing

w **9b**: Error, St Edward's Crown

When the omission was noticed a second mishap occurred, which was to insert a wrong crown in the space, giving w **9b**, St Edward's Crown. This produced varieties in Bahamas, Perlis, St. Kitts-Nevis and Singapore and the incorrect crown likewise occurs in (Crown only) and (Crown CA) rows.

w 10
V over Crown

w 11
Crown over A

Resuming the general types, two watermarks found in issues of several Australian States are: w **10**, *V over Crown*, and w **11**, *Crown over A*.

w 12
Multiple St Edward's
Crown Block CA

w 13
Multiple PTM

The *Multiple St Edward's Crown Block CA* watermark, w **12**, was introduced in 1957 and besides the change in the Crown (from that used in Multiple Script CA, w **9**) the letters reverted to block capitals. The new watermark began to appear sideways in 1966 and these stamps are generally listed as separate sets.

The watermark w **13**, *Multiple PTM*, was introduced for new Malaysian issues in November 1961.

w 14
Multiple Crown CA Diagonal

By 1974 the two dandy-rolls the 'upright' and the 'sideways' for w **12** were wearing out; the Crown Agents therefore discontinued using the sideways watermark one and retained the other only as a stand-by. A new dandy-roll with the pattern of w **14**, *Multiple Crown CA Diagonal*, was introduced and first saw use with some Churchill Centenary issues.

The new watermark had the design arranged in gradually spiralling rows. It was improved in design to allow smooth passage over the paper (the gaps between letters and rows had caused jolts in previous dandy-rolls) and the sharp corners and angles, where fibres used to accumulate, were eliminated by rounding.

This watermark had no 'normal' sideways position amongst the different printers using it. To avoid confusion our more specialised listings do not rely on such terms as 'sideways inverted' but describe the direction in which the watermark points.

w 15
Multiple POST OFFICE

During 1981 w **15**, *Multiple POST OFFICE* was introduced for certain issues prepared by Philatelists Ltd, acting for various countries in the Indian Ocean, Pacific and West Indies.

w 16
Multiple Crown Script CA Diagonal

A new Crown Agents watermark was introduced during 1985, w **16**, *Multiple Crown Script CA Diagonal*. This was very similar to the previous w **14**, but showed 'CA' in script rather than block letters. It was first used on the omnibus series of stamps commemorating the Life and Times of Queen Elizabeth the Queen Mother.

w 17
Multiple CARTOR

Watermark w **17**, *Multiple CARTOR*, was used from 1985 for issues printed by this French firm for countries which did not normally use the Crown Agents watermark.

w 18

In 2008, following the closure of the Crown Agents Stamp Bureau, a new Multiple Crowns watermark, w **18** was introduced.

In recent years the use of watermarks has, to some extent, been superseded by fluorescent security markings. These are often more visible from the reverse of the stamp (Cook Islands from 1970 onwards), but have occurred printed over the design (Hong Kong Nos. 415/430). In 1982 the Crown Agents introduced a new stock paper, without watermark, known as 'C-Kurity' on which a fluorescent pattern of blue rosettes is visible on the reverse, beneath the gum. This paper was used for issues from Gambia and Norfolk Island.

6. Colours

Stamps in two or three colours have these named in order of appearance, from the centre moving outwards. Four colours or more are usually listed as multicoloured.

In compound colour names the second is the predominant one, thus:

orange-red = a red tending towards orange;
red-orange = an orange containing more red than usual.

Standard colours used. The 200 colours most used for stamp identification are given in the Stanley Gibbons Stamp Colour Key. The Catalogue has used the Stamp Colour Key as standard for describing new issues for some years. The names are also introduced as lists are rewritten, though exceptions are made for those early issues where traditional names have become universally established.

Determining colours. When comparing actual stamps with colour samples in the Stamp Colour Key, view in a good north daylight (or its best substitute; fluorescent 'colour matching' light). Sunshine is not recommended. Choose a solid portion of the stamp design; if available, marginal markings such as solid bars of colour or colour check dots are helpful. Shading lines in the design can be misleading as they appear lighter than solid colour. Postmarked portions of a stamp appear darker than normal. If more than one colour is present, mask off the extraneous ones as the eye tends to mix them.

Errors of colour. Major colour errors in stamps or overprints which qualify for listing are: wrong colours; one colour inverted in relation to the rest; albinos (colourless impressions), where these have Expert Committee certificates; colours completely omitted, but only on unused stamps (if found on used stamps the information is footnoted) and with good credentials, missing colours being frequently faked.

Colours only partially omitted are not recognised, Colour shifts, however spectacular, are not listed.

Shades. Shades in philately refer to variations in the intensity of a colour or the presence of differing amounts of other colours. They are particularly significant when they can be linked to specific printings. In general, shades need to be quite marked to fall within the scope of this Catalogue; it does not favour nowadays listing the often numerous shades of a stamp, but chooses a single applicable colour name which will indicate particular groups of outstanding shades. Furthermore, the listings refer to colours as issued; they may deteriorate into something different through the passage of time. Collectors are warned against according any significance to colours which may have been altered by immersion in water or exposure to sunlight, but time, alone will sometimes cause colours to change, notably some of the letterpress De la Rue stamps of the late 19th and early 20th centuries.

Modern colour printing by lithography is prone to marked differences of shade, even within a single run, and variations can occur within the same sheet. Such shades are not listed.

Aniline colours. An aniline colour meant originally one derived from coal-tar; it now refers more widely to colour of a particular brightness suffused on the surface of a stamp and showing through clearly on the back.

Colours of overprints and surcharges. All overprints and surcharges are in black unless stated otherwise in the heading or after the description of the stamp.

7. Specimen Stamps

Originally, stamps overprinted SPECIMEN were circulated to postmasters or kept in official records, but after the establishment of the Universal Postal Union supplies were sent to Berne for distribution to the postal administrations of member countries.

During the period 1884 to 1928 most of the stamps of British Crown Colonies required for this purpose were overprinted SPECIMEN in various shapes and sizes by their printers from typeset formes. Some locally produced provisionals were handstamped locally, as were sets prepared for presentation. From 1928 stamps were punched with holes forming the word SPECIMEN, each firm of printers using a different machine or machines. From 1948 the stamps supplied for UPU distribution were no longer punctured, although receiving authorities sometimes applied SPECIMEN markings of their own.

Stamps of some other Commonwealth territories were overprinted or handstamped locally, while stamps of Great Britain and those overprinted for use in overseas postal agencies (mostly of the higher denominations) bore SPECIMEN overprints and handstamps applied by the Inland Revenue or the Post Office.

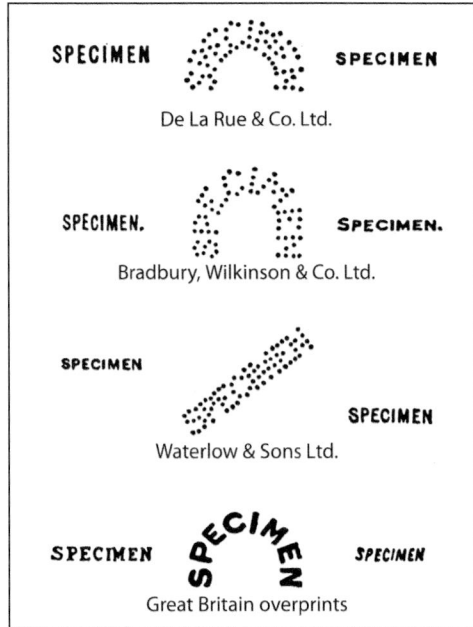

De La Rue & Co. Ltd.

Bradbury, Wilkinson & Co. Ltd.

Waterlow & Sons Ltd.

Great Britain overprints

Some of the more common types of overprints or punctures are illustrated here. Collectors are warned that dangerous forgeries of the punctured types exist.

The *Stanley Gibbons Commonwealth Catalogues* record those Specimen overprints or perforations intended for distribution by the UPU to member countries and we are grateful to James Bendon, author and publisher of *UPU Specimen Stamps, 1878 - 1961*, a much expanded edition of which was published in 2015, for his assistance with these listings. The Specimen overprints of Australia and its dependent territories, which were sold to collectors by the Post Office, are also included.

All other Specimens are outside the scope of this volume.

In specifying type of specimen for individual high-value stamps, 'H/S' means handstamped, 'Optd' is overprinted and 'Perf' is punctured. Some sets occur mixed, e.g. 'Optd/Perf'. If unspecified, the type is apparent from the date or it is the same as for the lower values quoted as a set.

Prices. Prices for stamps up to £1 are quoted in sets; higher values are priced singly. Where specimens exist in more than one type the price quoted is for the cheapest. Specimen stamps have rarely survived even as pairs; these and strips of three, four or five are worth considerably more than singles.

Various Perkins Bacon issues exist obliterated with a 'CANCELLED' within an oval of bars handstamp.

Perkins Bacon 'CANCELLED'
Handstamp

This was applied to six examples of those issues available in 1861 which were then given to members of Sir Rowland Hill's family. 75 different stamps (including four from Chile) are recorded with this handstamp although others may possibly exist. The unauthorised gift of these 'CANCELLED' stamps to the Hill family was a major factor in the loss of the Agent General for the Crown Colonies (the forerunner of the Crown Agents) contracts by Perkins Bacon in the following year. Where examples of these scarce items are known to be in private hands the catalogue provides a price.

For full details of these stamps see *CANCELLED by Perkins Bacon* by Peter Jaffé (published by Spink in 1998).

8. Luminescence

Machines which sort mail electronically have been introduced in recent years. In consequence some countries have issued stamps on fluorescent or phosphorescent papers, while others have marked their stamps with phosphor bands.

The various papers can only be distinguished by ultraviolet lamps emitting particular wavelengths. They are separately listed only when the stamps have some other means of distinguishing them, visible without the use of these lamps. Where this is not so, the papers are recorded in footnotes or headings.

For this catalogue we do not consider it appropriate that collectors be compelled to have the use of an ultraviolet lamp before being able to identify stamps by our listings. Some experience will also be found necessary in interpreting the results given by ultraviolet. Collectors using the lamps, nevertheless, should exercise great care in their use as exposure to their light is potentially dangerous to the eyes.

Phosphor bands are listable, since they are visible to the naked eye (by holding stamps at an angle to the light and looking along them, the bands appear dark). Stamps existing with or without phosphor bands or with differing numbers of bands are given separate listings. Varieties such as double bands, bands omitted, misplaced or printed on the back are not listed.

Detailed descriptions appear at appropriate places in the listings in explanation of luminescent papers; see, for example, Australia above No. 363, Canada above Nos. 472 and 611, Cook Is. above 249, etc.

For Great Britain, where since 1959 phosphors have played a prominent and intricate part in stamp issues, the main notes above Nos. 599 and 723 should be studied, as well as the footnotes to individual listings where appropriate. In general the classification is as follows.

Stamps with phosphor bands are those where a separate cylinder applies the phosphor after the stamps are printed. Issues with 'all-over' phosphor have the 'band' covering the entire stamp. Parts of the stamp covered by phosphor bands, or the entire surface for 'all-over' phosphor versions, appear matt. Stamps on phosphorised paper have the phosphor added to the paper coating before the stamps are printed. Issues on this paper have a completely shiny surface.

Further particularisation of phosphor – their methods of printing and the colours they exhibit under ultraviolet – is outside the scope. The more specialised listings should be consulted for this information.

9. Coil Stamps

Stamps issued only in coil form are given full listing. If stamps are issued in both sheets and coils the coil stamps are listed separately only where there is some feature (e.g. perforation or watermark sideways) by which singles can be distinguished. Coil stamps containing different stamps *se-tenant* are also listed.

Coil join pairs are too random and too easily faked to permit of listing; similarly ignored are coil stamps which have accidentally suffered an extra row of perforations from the claw mechanism in a malfunctioning vending machine.

10. Stamp Booklets

Stamp booklets are fully listed in this catalogue.

Single stamps from booklets are listed if they are distinguishable in some way (such as watermark or perforation) from similar sheet stamps.

Booklet panes are listed where they contain stamps of different denominations *se-tenant*, where stamp-size labels are included, or where such panes are otherwise identifiable. Booklet panes are placed in the listing under the lowest denomination present and are only priced in unused condition.

Particular perforations (straight edges) are covered by appropriate notes.

Prior to the 1970s, the majority of stamp booklets were made up from normal sheets and panes may be bound upright or inverted and booklets may be stapled or stitched at either the left or right-hand side. Unless specifically mentioned in the listings, such variations do not command a price premium.

Only items supplied pre-folded are listed as booklets. Panes supplied flat are not listed thus, even if it is clearly intended that they should be subsequently folded in order to create a 'booklet'. Such panes are included in the main listing only.

11. Miniature Sheets and Sheetlets

We distinguish between 'miniature sheets' and 'sheetlets' and this affects the catalogue numbering. An item in sheet form that is postally valid, containing a single stamp, pair, block or set of stamps, with wide, inscribed and/or decorative margins, is a miniature sheet if it is sold at post offices as an indivisible entity. As such the Catalogue allots a single **MS** number and describes what stamps make it up. The sheetlet or small sheet differs in that the individual stamps are intended to be purchased separately for postal purposes. For sheetlets, all the component postage stamps are numbered individually and the composition explained in a footnote. Note that the definitions refer to post office sale—not how items may be subsequently offered by stamp dealers.

12. Forgeries and Fakes

Forgeries. Where space permits, notes are considered if they can give a concise description that will permit unequivocal detection of a forgery. Generalised warnings, lacking detail, are not nowadays inserted, since their value to the collector is problematic.

Forged cancellations have also been applied to genuine stamps. This catalogue includes notes regarding those manufactured by 'Madame Joseph', together with the cancellation dates known to exist. It should be remembered that these dates also exist as genuine cancellations.

For full details of these see *Madame Joseph Forged Postmarks* by Derek Worboys (published by the Royal Philatelic Society London and the British Philatelic Trust in 1994) or *Madame Joseph Revisited* by Brian Cartwright (published by the Royal Philatelic Society London in 2005).

Fakes. Unwitting fakes are numerous, particularly 'new shades' which are colour changelings brought about by exposure to sunlight, soaking in water contaminated with dyes from adherent paper, contact with oil and dirt from a pocketbook, and so on. Fraudulent operators, in addition, can offer to arrange: removal of hinge marks; repairs of thins on white or coloured papers; replacement of missing margins or perforations; reperforating in true or false gauges; removal of fiscal cancellations; rejoining of severed pairs, strips and blocks; and (a major hazard) regumming. Collectors can only be urged to purchase from reputable sources and to insist upon Expert Committee certification where there is any kind of doubt.

The Catalogue can consider footnotes about fakes where these are specific enough to assist in detection.

ACKNOWLEDGEMENTS

We are grateful to individual collectors, members of the philatelic trade and specialist societies and study circles for their assistance in improving and extending the Stanley Gibbons range of catalogues.

The address of the society relevant to this volume is:

Hong Kong Study Circle
Membership Secretary — Mr R. Newton
Email: newtons100@gmail.com

Abbreviations

Printers

A.B.N. Co.	American Bank Note Co, New York.
B.A.B.N.	British American Bank Note Co. Ottawa
B.D.T.	B.D.T. International Security Printing Ltd, Dublin, Ireland
B.W.	Bradbury Wilkinson & Co, Ltd.
Cartor	Cartor S.A., La Loupe, France
C.B.N.	Canadian Bank Note Co, Ottawa.
Continental	Continental Bank Note Co. B.N. Co.
Courvoisier	Imprimerie Courvoisier S.A., La-Chaux-de-Fonds, Switzerland.
D.L.R.	De La Rue & Co, Ltd, London.
Enschedé	Joh. Enschedé en Zonen, Haarlem, Netherlands.
Format	Format International Security Printers Ltd., London
Harrison	Harrison & Sons, Ltd. London
J.W.	John Waddington Security Print Ltd., Leeds
L.M.G.	Lowe Martin Group, Ottawa, Canada
P.B.	Perkins Bacon Ltd, London.
Questa	Questa Colour Security Printers Ltd, London
Walsall	Walsall Security Printers Ltd
Waterlow	Waterlow & Sons, Ltd, London.

General Abbreviations

Alph	Alphabet
Anniv	Anniversary
Comp	Compound (perforation)
Des	Designer; designed
Diag	Diagonal; diagonally
Eng	Engraver; engraved
F.C.	Fiscal Cancellation
H/S	Handstamped
Horiz	Horizontal; horizontally
Imp, Imperf	Imperforate
Inscr	Inscribed
L	Left
Litho	Lithographed
mm	Millimetres
MS	Miniature sheet
N.Y.	New York
Opt(d)	Overprint(ed)
P or P-c	Pen-cancelled
P, Pf or Perf	Perforated
Photo	Photogravure
Pl	Plate
Pr	Pair
Ptd	Printed
Ptg	Printing
R	Right

R.	Row
Recess	Recess-printed
Roto	Rotogravure
Roul	Rouletted
S	Specimen (overprint)
Surch	Surcharge(d)
T.C.	Telegraph Cancellation
T	Type
Typo	Typographed
Un	Unused
Us	Used
Vert	Vertical; vertically
W or wmk	Watermark
Wmk s	Watermark sideways

(†) = Does not exist

(–) (or blank price column) = Exists, or may exist, but no market price is known.

/ between colours means 'on' and the colour following is that of the paper on which the stamp is printed.

Colours of Stamps

Bl (blue); blk (black); brn (brown); car, carm (carmine); choc (chocolate); clar (claret); emer (emerald); grn (green); ind (indigo); mag (magenta); mar (maroon); mult (multicoloured); mve (mauve); ol (olive); orge (orange); pk (pink); pur (purple); scar (scarlet); sep (sepia); turq (turquoise); ultram (ultramarine); verm (vermilion); vio (violet); yell (yellow).

Colour of Overprints and Surcharges

(B.) = blue, (Blk.) = black, (Br.) = brown, (C.) = carmine, (G.) = green, (Mag.) = magenta, (Mve.) = mauve, (Ol.) = olive, (O.) = orange, (P.) = purple, (Pk.) = pink, (R.) = red, (Sil.) = silver, (V.) = violet, (Vm.) or (Verm.) = vermilion, (W.) = white, (Y.) = yellow.

Arabic Numerals

As in the case of European figures, the details of the Arabic numerals vary in different stamp designs, but they should be readily recognised with the aid of this illustration.

٠	١	٢	٣	٤	٥	٦	٧	٨	٩
0	1	2	3	4	5	6	7	8	9

International Philatelic Glossary

English	French	German	Spanish	Italian
Agate	Agate	Achat	Agata	Agata
Air stamp	Timbre de la poste aérienne	Flugpostmarke	Sello de correo aéreo	Francobollo per posta aerea
Apple Green	Vert-pomme	Apfelgrün	Verde manzana	Verde mela
Barred	Annulé par barres	Balkenentwertung	Anulado con barras	Sbarrato
Bisected	Timbre coupé	Halbiert	Partido en dos	Frazionato
Bistre	Bistre	Bister	Bistre	Bistro
Bistre-brown	Brun-bistre	Bisterbraun	Castaño bistre	Bruno-bistro
Black	Noir	Schwarz	Negro	Nero
Blackish Brown	Brun-noir	Schwärzlichbraun	Castaño negruzco	Bruno nerastro
Blackish Green	Vert foncé	Schwärzlichgrün	Verde negruzco	Verde nerastro
Blackish Olive	Olive foncé	Schwärzlicholiv	Oliva negruzco	Oliva nerastro
Block of four	Bloc de quatre	Viererblock	Bloque de cuatro	Bloco di quattro
Blue	Bleu	Blau	Azul	Azzurro
Blue-green	Vert-bleu	Blaugrün	Verde azul	Verde azzuro
Bluish Violet	Violet bleuâtre	Bläulichviolett	Violeta azulado	Violtto azzurrastro
Booklet	Carnet	Heft	Cuadernillo	Libretto
Bright Blue	Bleu vif	Lebhaftblau	Azul vivo	Azzurro vivo
Bright Green	Vert vif	Lebhaftgrün	Verde vivo	Verde vivo
Bright Purple	Mauve vif	Lebhaftpurpur	Púrpura vivo	Porpora vivo
Bronze Green	Vert-bronze	Bronzegrün	Verde bronce	Verde bronzo
Brown	Brun	Braun	Castaño	Bruno
Brown-lake	Carmin-brun	Braunlack	Laca castaño	Lacca bruno
Brown-purple	Pourpre-brun	Braunpurpur	Púrpura castaño	Porpora bruno
Brown-red	Rouge-brun	Braunrot	Rojo castaño	Rosso bruno
Buff	Chamois	Sämisch	Anteado	Camoscio
Cancellation	Oblitération	Entwertung	Cancelación	Annullamento
Cancelled	Annulé	Gestempelt	Cancelado	Annullato
Carmine	Carmin	Karmin	Carmín	Carminio
Carmine-red	Rouge-carmin	Karminrot	Rojo carmín	Rosso carminio
Centred	Centré	Zentriert	Centrado	Centrato
Cerise	Rouge-cerise	Kirschrot	Color de ceresa	Color Ciliegia
Chalk-surfaced paper	Papier couché	Kreidepapier	Papel estucado	Carta gessata
Chalky Blue	Bleu terne	Kreideblau	Azul turbio	Azzurro smorto
Charity stamp	Timbre de bienfaisance	Wohltätigkeitsmarke	Sello de beneficenza	Francobollo di beneficenza
Chestnut	Marron	Kastanienbraun	Castaño rojo	Marrone
Chocolate	Chocolat	Schokolade	Chocolate	Cioccolato
Cinnamon	Cannelle	Zimtbraun	Canela	Cannella
Claret	Grenat	Weinrot	Rojo vinoso	Vinaccia
Cobalt	Cobalt	Kobalt	Cobalto	Cobalto
Colour	Couleur	Farbe	Color	Colore
Comb-perforation	Dentelure en peigne	Kammzähnung, Reihenzähnung	Dentado de peine	Dentellatura e pettine
Commemorative stamp	Timbre commémoratif	Gedenkmarke	Sello conmemorativo	Francobollo commemorativo
Crimson	Cramoisi	Karmesin	Carmesí	Cremisi
Deep Blue	Blue foncé	Dunkelblau	Azul oscuro	Azzurro scuro
Deep bluish Green	Vert-bleu foncé	Dunkelbläulichgrün	Verde azulado oscuro	Verde azzurro scuro
Design	Dessin	Markenbild	Diseño	Disegno

English	French	German	Spanish	Italian
Die	Matrice	Urstempel. Type, Platte	Cuño	Conio, Matrice
Double	Double	Doppelt	Doble	Doppio
Drab	Olive terne	Trüboliv	Oliva turbio	Oliva smorto
Dull Green	Vert terne	Trübgrün	Verde turbio	Verde smorto
Dull purple	Mauve terne	Trübpurpur	Púrpura turbio	Porpora smorto
Embossing	Impression en relief	Prägedruck	Impresión en relieve	Impressione a relievo
Emerald	Vert-eméraude	Smaragdgrün	Esmeralda	Smeraldo
Engraved	Gravé	Graviert	Grabado	Inciso
Error	Erreur	Fehler, Fehldruck	Error	Errore
Essay	Essai	Probedruck	Ensayo	Saggio
Express letter stamp	Timbre pour lettres par exprès	Eilmarke	Sello de urgencia	Francobollo per espresso
Fiscal stamp	Timbre fiscal	Stempelmarke	Sello fiscal	Francobollo fiscale
Flesh	Chair	Fleischfarben	Carne	Carnicino
Forgery	Faux, Falsification	Fälschung	Falsificación	Falso, Falsificazione
Frame	Cadre	Rahmen	Marco	Cornice
Granite paper	Papier avec fragments de fils de soie	Faserpapier	Papel con filamentos	Carto con fili di seta
Green	Vert	Grün	Verde	Verde
Greenish Blue	Bleu verdâtre	Grünlichblau	Azul verdoso	Azzurro verdastro
Greenish Yellow	Jaune-vert	Grünlichgelb	Amarillo verdoso	Giallo verdastro
Grey	Gris	Grau	Gris	Grigio
Grey-blue	Bleu-gris	Graublau	Azul gris	Azzurro grigio
Grey-green	Vert gris	Graugrün	Verde gris	Verde grigio
Gum	Gomme	Gummi	Goma	Gomma
Gutter	Interpanneau	Zwischensteg	Espacio blanco entre dos grupos	Ponte
Imperforate	Non-dentelé	Geschnitten	Sin dentar	Non dentellato
Indigo	Indigo	Indigo	Azul indigo	Indaco
Inscription	Inscription	Inschrift	Inscripción	Dicitura
Inverted	Renversé	Kopfstehend	Invertido	Capovolto
Issue	Émission	Ausgabe	Emisión	Emissione
Laid	Vergé	Gestreift	Listado	Vergato
Lake	Lie de vin	Lackfarbe	Laca	Lacca
Lake-brown	Brun-carmin	Lackbraun	Castaño laca	Bruno lacca
Lavender	Bleu-lavande	Lavendel	Color de alhucema	Lavanda
Lemon	Jaune-citron	Zitrongelb	Limón	Limone
Light Blue	Bleu clair	Hellblau	Azul claro	Azzurro chiaro
Lilac	Lilas	Lila	Lila	Lilla
Line perforation	Dentelure en lignes	Linienzähnung	Dentado en linea	Dentellatura lineare
Lithography	Lithographie	Steindruck	Litografía	Litografia
Local	Timbre de poste locale	Lokalpostmarke	Emisión local	Emissione locale
Lozenge roulette	Percé en losanges	Rautenförmiger Durchstich	Picadura en rombos	Perforazione a losanghe
Magenta	Magenta	Magentarot	Magenta	Magenta
Margin	Marge	Rand	Borde	Margine
Maroon	Marron pourpré	Dunkelrotpurpur	Púrpura rojo oscuro	Marrone rossastro
Mauve	Mauve	Malvenfarbe	Malva	Malva
Multicoloured	Polychrome	Mehrfarbig	Multicolores	Policromo
Myrtle Green	Vert myrte	Myrtengrün	Verde mirto	Verde mirto
New Blue	Bleu ciel vif	Neublau	Azul nuevo	Azzurro nuovo
Newspaper stamp	Timbre pour journaux	Zeitungsmarke	Sello para periódicos	Francobollo per giornali
Obliteration	Oblitération	Abstempelung	Matasello	Annullamento
Obsolete	Hors (de) cours	Ausser Kurs	Fuera de curso	Fuori corso
Ochre	Ocre	Ocker	Ocre	Ocra

English	French	German	Spanish	Italian
Official stamp	Timbre de service	Dienstmarke	Sello de servicio	Francobollo di
Olive-brown	Brun-olive	Olivbraun	Castaño oliva	Bruno oliva
Olive-green	Vert-olive	Olivgrün	Verde oliva	Verde oliva
Olive-grey	Gris-olive	Olivgrau	Gris oliva	Grigio oliva
Olive-yellow	Jaune-olive	Olivgelb	Amarillo oliva	Giallo oliva
Orange	Orange	Orange	Naranja	Arancio
Orange-brown	Brun-orange	Orangebraun	Castaño naranja	Bruno arancio
Orange-red	Rouge-orange	Orangerot	Rojo naranja	Rosso arancio
Orange-yellow	Jaune-orange	Orangegelb	Amarillo naranja	Giallo arancio
Overprint	Surcharge	Aufdruck	Sobrecarga	Soprastampa
Pair	Paire	Paar	Pareja	Coppia
Pale	Pâle	Blass	Pálido	Pallido
Pane	Panneau	Gruppe	Grupo	Gruppo
Paper	Papier	Papier	Papel	Carta
Parcel post stamp	Timbre pour colis postaux	Paketmarke	Sello para paquete postal	Francobollo per pacchi postali
Pen-cancelled	Oblitéré à plume	Federzugentwertung	Cancelado a pluma	Annullato a penna
Percé en arc	Percé en arc	Bogenförmiger Durchstich	Picadura en forma de arco	Perforazione ad arco
Percé en scie	Percé en scie	Bogenförmiger Durchstich	Picado en sierra	Foratura a sega
Perforated	Dentelé	Gezähnt	Dentado	Dentellato
Perforation	Dentelure	Zähnung	Dentar	Dentellatura
Photogravure	Photogravure, Heliogravure	Rastertiefdruck	Fotograbado	Rotocalco
Pin perforation	Percé en points	In Punkten durchstochen	Horadado con alfileres	Perforato a punti
Plate	Planche	Platte	Plancha	Lastra, Tavola
Plum	Prune	Pflaumenfarbe	Color de ciruela	Prugna
Postage Due stamp	Timbre-taxe	Portomarke	Sello de tasa	Segnatasse
Postage stamp	Timbre-poste	Briefmarke, Freimarke, Postmarke	Sello de correos	Francobollo postale
Postal fiscal stamp	Timbre fiscal-postal	Stempelmarke als Postmarke verwendet	Sello fiscal-postal	Fiscale postale
Postmark	Oblitération postale	Poststempel	Matasello	Bollo
Printing	Impression, Tirage	Druck	Impresión	Stampa, Tiratura
Proof	Épreuve	Druckprobe	Prueba de impresión	Prova
Provisionals	Timbres provisoires	Provisorische Marken. Provisorien	Provisionales	Provvisori
Prussian Blue	Bleu de Prusse	Preussischblau	Azul de Prusia	Azzurro di Prussia
Purple	Pourpre	Purpur	Púrpura	Porpora
Purple-brown	Brun-pourpre	Purpurbraun	Castaño púrpura	Bruno porpora
Recess-printing	Impression en taille-douce	Tiefdruck	Grabado	Incisione
Red	Rouge	Rot	Rojo	Rosso
Red-brown	Brun-rouge	Rotbraun	Castaño rojizo	Bruno rosso
Reddish Lilac	Lilas rougeâtre	Rötlichlila	Lila rojizo	Lilla rossastro
Reddish Purple	Poupre-rouge	Rötlichpurpur	Púrpura rojizo	Porpora rossastro
Reddish Violet	Violet rougeâtre	Rötlichviolett	Violeta rojizo	Violetto rossastro
Red-orange	Orange rougeâtre	Rotorange	Naranja rojizo	Arancio rosso
Registration stamp	Timbre pour lettre chargée (recommandée)	Einschreibemarke	Sello de certificado lettere	Francobollo per raccomandate
Reprint	Réimpression	Neudruck	Reimpresión	Ristampa
Reversed	Retourné	Umgekehrt	Invertido	Rovesciato
Rose	Rose	Rosa	Rosa	Rosa
Rose-red	Rouge rosé	Rosarot	Rojo rosado	Rosso rosa
Rosine	Rose vif	Lebhaftrosa	Rosa vivo	Rosa vivo
Roulette	Percage	Durchstich	Picadura	Foratura
Rouletted	Percé	Durchstochen	Picado	Forato
Royal Blue	Bleu-roi	Königblau	Azul real	Azzurro reale
Sage green	Vert-sauge	Salbeigrün	Verde salvia	Verde salvia
Salmon	Saumon	Lachs	Salmón	Salmone

English	French	German	Spanish	Italian
Scarlet	Écarlate	Scharlach	Escarlata	Scarlatto
Sepia	Sépia	Sepia	Sepia	Seppia
Serpentine roulette	Percé en serpentin	Schlangenliniger Durchstich	Picado a serpentina	Perforazione a serpentina
Shade	Nuance	Tönung	Tono	Gradazione de colore
Sheet	Feuille	Bogen	Hoja	Foglio
Slate	Ardoise	Schiefer	Pizarra	Ardesia
Slate-blue	Bleu-ardoise	Schieferblau	Azul pizarra	Azzurro ardesia
Slate-green	Vert-ardoise	Schiefergrün	Verde pizarra	Verde ardesia
Slate-lilac	Lilas-gris	Schierferlila	Lila pizarra	Lilla ardesia
Slate-purple	Mauve-gris	Schieferpurpur	Púrpura pizarra	Porpora ardesia
Slate-violet	Violet-gris	Schieferviolett	Violeta pizarra	Violetto ardesia
Special delivery stamp	Timbre pour exprès	Eilmarke	Sello de urgencia	Francobollo per espressi
Specimen	Spécimen	Muster	Muestra	Saggio
Steel Blue	Bleu acier	Stahlblau	Azul acero	Azzurro acciaio
Strip	Bande	Streifen	Tira	Striscia
Surcharge	Surcharge	Aufdruck	Sobrecarga	Soprastampa
Tête-bêche	Tête-bêche	Kehrdruck	Tête-bêche	Tête-bêche
Tinted paper	Papier teinté	Getöntes Papier	Papel coloreado	Carta tinta
Too-late stamp	Timbre pour lettres en retard	Verspätungsmarke	Sello para cartas retardadas	Francobollo per le lettere in ritardo
Turquoise-blue	Bleu-turquoise	Türkisblau	Azul turquesa	Azzurro turchese
Turquoise-green	Vert-turquoise	Türkisgrün	Verde turquesa	Verde turchese
Typography	Typographie	Buchdruck	Tipografia	Tipografia
Ultramarine	Outremer	Ultramarin	Ultramar	Oltremare
Unused	Neuf	Ungebraucht	Nuevo	Nuovo
Used	Oblitéré, Usé	Gebraucht	Usado	Usato
Venetian Red	Rouge-brun terne	Venezianischrot	Rojo veneciano	Rosso veneziano
Vermilion	Vermillon	Zinnober	Cinabrio	Vermiglione
Violet	Violet	Violett	Violeta	Violetto
Violet-blue	Bleu-violet	Violettblau	Azul violeta	Azzurro violetto
Watermark	Filigrane	Wasserzeichen	Filigrana	Filigrana
Watermark sideways	Filigrane couché	Wasserzeichen liegend	Filigrana acostado	Filigrana coricata
Wove paper	Papier ordinaire, Papier uni	Einfaches Papier	Papel avitelado	Carta unita
Yellow	Jaune	Gelb	Amarillo	Giallo
Yellow-brown	Brun-jaune	Gelbbraun	Castaño amarillo	Bruno giallo
Yellow-green	Vert-jaune	Gelbgrün	Verde amarillo	Verde giallo
Yellow-olive	Olive-jaunâtre	Gelboliv	Oliva amarillo	Oliva giallastro
Yellow-orange	Orange jaunâtre	Gelborange	Naranja amarillo	Arancio giallastro
Zig-zag roulette	Percé en zigzag	Sägezahnartiger Durchstich	Picado en zigzag	Perforazione a zigzag

A **Country of Issue** – When a country changes its name, the catalogue listing changes to reflect the name change, for example Namibia was formerly known as South West Africa, the stamps in the Stanley Gibbons *Southern Africa Catalogue* are all listed under Namibia, but split into South West Africa and then Namibia.

B **Country Information** – Brief geographical and historical details for the issuing country.

C **Currency** – Details of the currency, and dates of earliest use where applicable, on the face value of the stamps.

D **Illustration** – Generally, the first stamp in the set. Stamp illustrations are reduced to 75%, with overprints and surcharges shown actual size.

E **Illustration or Type Number** – These numbers are used to help identify stamps, either in the listing, type column, design line or footnote, usually the first value in a set. These type numbers are in a bold type face – **123**; when bracketed (**123**) an overprint or a surcharge is indicated. Some type numbers include a lower-case letter – **123a**, this indicates they have been added to an existing set.

F **Date of issue** – This is the date that the stamp/set of stamps was issued by the post office and was available for purchase. When a set of definitive stamps has been issued over several years the Year Date given is for the earliest issue. Commemorative sets are listed in chronological order. Stamps of the same design, or issue are usually grouped together, for example some of the New Zealand landscapes definitive series were first issued in 2003 but the set includes stamps issued to May 2007.

G **Number Prefix** – Stamps other than definitives and commemoratives have a prefix letter before the catalogue number.
Their use is explained in the text: some examples are A for airmail, D for postage due and O for official stamps.

H **Footnote** – Further information on background or key facts on issues.

I **Stanley Gibbons Catalogue number** – This is a unique number for each stamp to help the collector identify stamps in the listing. The Stanley Gibbons numbering system is universally recognised as definitive.
Where insufficient numbers have been left to provide for additional stamps to a listing, some stamps will have a suffix letter after the catalogue number (for example 214a). If numbers have been left for additions to a set and not used they will be left vacant.
The separate type numbers (in bold) refer to illustrations (see **E**).

J **Colour** – If a stamp is printed in three or fewer colours then the colours are listed, working from the centre of the stamp outwards (see **R**).

K **Design line** – Further details on design variations.

L **Key Type** – Indicates a design type on which the stamp is based. These are the bold figures found below each illustration, for example listed in Cameroon, in the *West Africa Catalogue*, is the Key type A and B showing the ex-Kaiser's yacht *Hohenzollern*. The type numbers are also given in bold in the second column of figures alongside the stamp description to indicate the design of each stamp. Where an issue comprises stamps of similar design, the corresponding type number should be taken as indicating the general design. Where there are blanks in the type number column it means that the type of the corresponding stamp

is that shown by the number in the type column of the same issue. A dash (–) in the type column means that the stamp is not illustrated. Where type numbers refer to stamps of another country, e.g. where stamps of one country are overprinted for use in another, this is always made clear in the text.

M **Coloured Papers** – Stamps printed on coloured paper are shown – e.g. 'brown/*yellow*' indicates brown printed on yellow paper.

N **Surcharges and Overprints** – Usually described in the headings. Any actual wordings are shown in bold type. Descriptions clarify words and figures used in the overprint. Stamps with the same overprints in different colours are not listed separately. Numbers in brackets after the descriptions are the catalogue numbers of the non-overprinted stamps. The words 'inscribed' or 'inscription' (generally abbreviated as 'inscr') refer to the wording incorporated in the design of a stamp and not surcharges or overprints.

O **Face value** – This refers to the value of each stamp and is the price it was sold for at the Post Office when issued. Some modern stamps do not have their values in figures but instead it is shown as a letter, for example Great Britain use 1st or 2nd on their stamps as opposed to the actual value.

P **Catalogue Value** – Mint/Unused. Prices quoted for Queen Victoria to King George V stamps are for lightly hinged examples.

Q **Catalogue Value** – Used. Prices generally refer to fine postally used examples. For certain issues they are for cancelled-to-order.

Prices
Prices are given in pence and pounds. Stamps worth £100 and over are shown in whole pounds:

Shown in Catalogue as	Explanation
10	10 pence
1·75	£1·75
15.00	£15
£150	£150
£2300	£2300

Prices assume stamps are in 'fine condition'; we may ask more for superb and less for those of lower quality. The minimum catalogue price quoted is 10p and is intended as a guide for catalogue users. The lowest price for individual stamps purchased from Stanley Gibbons is £1.
Prices quoted are for the cheapest variety of that particular stamp. Differences of watermark, perforation, or other details, often increase the value. Prices quoted for mint issues are for single examples, unless otherwise stated. Those in *se-tenant* pairs, strips, blocks or sheets may be worth more. Where no prices are listed it is either because the stamps are not known to exist (usually shown by a †) in that particular condition, or, more usually, because there is no reliable information on which to base their value.
All prices are subject to change without prior notice and we cannot guarantee to supply all stamps as priced. Prices quoted in advertisements are also subject to change without prior notice.

R **Multicoloured** – Nearly all modern stamps are multicoloured (more than three colours); this is indicated in the heading, with a description of the stamp given in the listing.

S **Perforations** – Please see the 'Information and Guidelines' section for a detailed explanation of perforations.

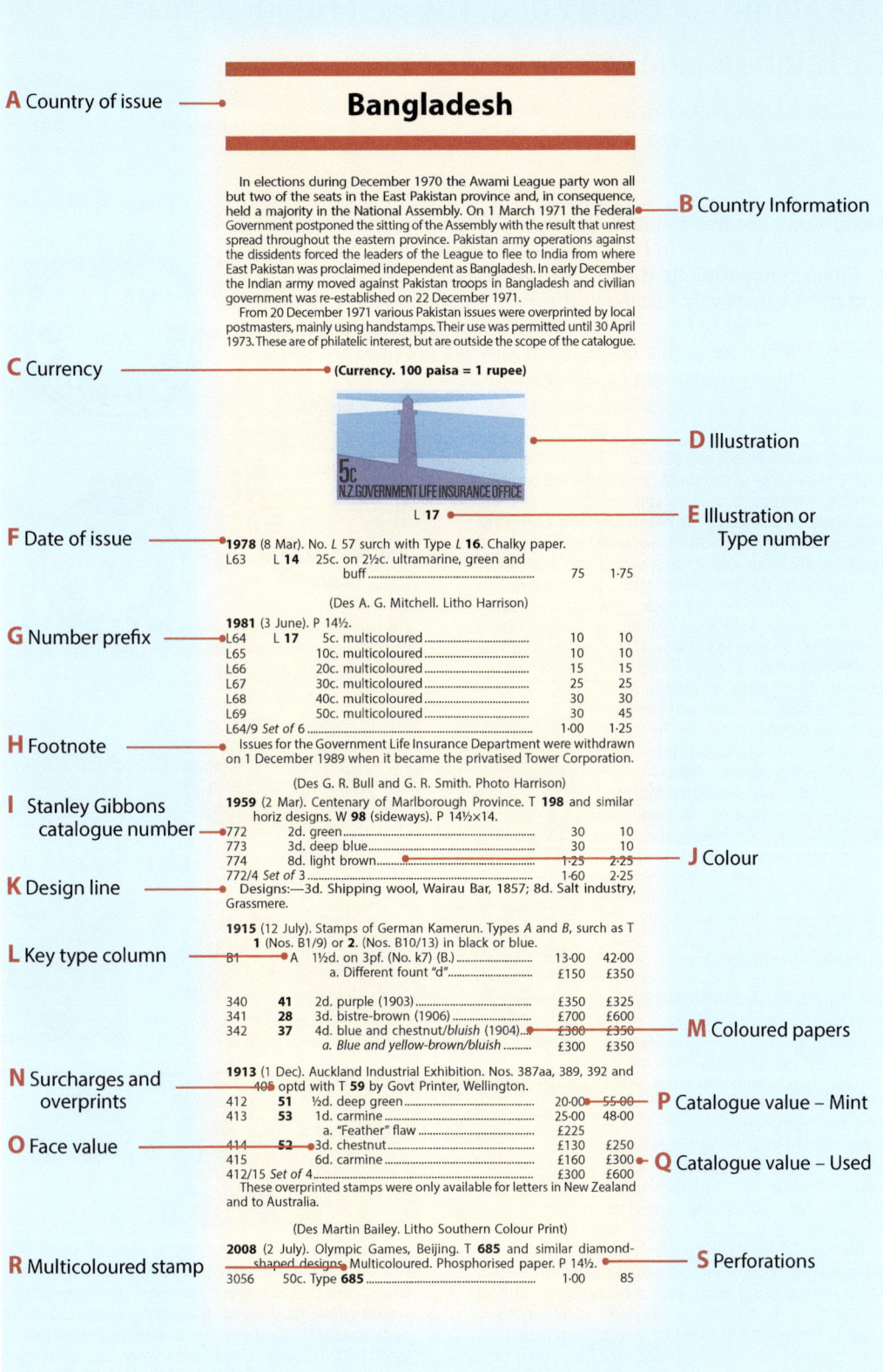

A Country of issue

Bangladesh

B Country Information

In elections during December 1970 the Awami League party won all but two of the seats in the East Pakistan province and, in consequence, held a majority in the National Assembly. On 1 March 1971 the Federal Government postponed the sitting of the Assembly with the result that unrest spread throughout the eastern province. Pakistan army operations against the dissidents forced the leaders of the League to flee to India from where East Pakistan was proclaimed independent as Bangladesh. In early December the Indian army moved against Pakistan troops in Bangladesh and civilian government was re-established on 22 December 1971.

From 20 December 1971 various Pakistan issues were overprinted by local postmasters, mainly using handstamps. Their use was permitted until 30 April 1973. These are of philatelic interest, but are outside the scope of the catalogue.

C Currency

(Currency. 100 paisa = 1 rupee)

D Illustration

5c
N.Z.GOVERNMENT LIFE INSURANCE OFFICE

L **17**

E Illustration or Type number

F Date of issue

1978 (8 Mar). No. *L* 57 surch with Type *L* **16**. Chalky paper.

L63	L **14**	25c. on 2½c. ultramarine, green and buff		75	1·75

(Des A. G. Mitchell. Litho Harrison)

G Number prefix

1981 (3 June). P 14½.

L64	L **17**	5c. multicoloured		10	10
L65		10c. multicoloured		10	10
L66		20c. multicoloured		15	15
L67		30c. multicoloured		25	25
L68		40c. multicoloured		30	30
L69		50c. multicoloured		30	45
L64/9 *Set of 6*				1·00	1·25

H Footnote

Issues for the Government Life Insurance Department were withdrawn on 1 December 1989 when it became the privatised Tower Corporation.

(Des G. R. Bull and G. R. Smith. Photo Harrison)

I Stanley Gibbons catalogue number

1959 (2 Mar). Centenary of Marlborough Province. T **198** and similar horiz designs. W **98** (sideways). P 14½×14.

772	2d. green		30	10
773	3d. deep blue		30	10
774	8d. light brown		1·25	2·25
772/4 *Set of 3*			1·60	2·25

J Colour

K Design line

Designs:—3d. Shipping wool, Wairau Bar, 1857; 8d. Salt industry, Grassmere.

L Key type column

1915 (12 July). Stamps of German Kamerun. Types *A* and *B*, such as T **1** (Nos. B1/9) or **2**. (Nos. B10/13) in black or blue.

B1	A	1½d. on 3pf. (No. k7) (B.)	13·00	42·00
		a. Different fount "d"	£150	£350

340	**41**	2d. purple (1903)	£350	£325
341	**28**	3d. bistre-brown (1906)	£700	£600
342	**37**	4d. blue and chestnut/*bluish* (1904)	£300	£350
		a. Blue and yellow-brown/*bluish*	£300	£350

M Coloured papers

N Surcharges and overprints

1913 (1 Dec). Auckland Industrial Exhibition. Nos. 387aa, 389, 392 and 405 optd with T **59** by Govt Printer, Wellington.

412	**51**	½d. deep green	20·00	55·00
413	**53**	1d. carmine	25·00	48·00
		a. "Feather" flaw	£225	
414	**52**	3d. chestnut	£130	£250
415		6d. carmine	£160	£300
412/15 *Set of 4*			£300	£600

P Catalogue value – Mint

O Face value

These overprinted stamps were only available for letters in New Zealand and to Australia.

Q Catalogue value – Used

(Des Martin Bailey. Litho Southern Colour Print)

R Multicoloured stamp

2008 (2 July). Olympic Games, Beijing. T **685** and similar diamond-shaped designs. Multicoloured. Phosphorised paper. P 14½.

3056	50c. Type **685**		1·00	85

S Perforations

The Stamps of Hong Kong: The First Hundred Years
By Hugh Jefferies

Hong Kong became a British Colony 175 years ago this month and issued its first stamps in December 1862. From then, until its return to China in July 1997, its stamp issues were some of the most popular and most extensively studied in the 'Part 1' Catalogue. It was one of the first countries to have its own specialist study circle and has a vast philatelic literature. In this article, Hugh Jefferies provides an overview of one of his own favourite collecting areas.

European trade with China dates from the early 16th century, with Portugal establishing a base in Macao in 1557. The majority of this trade was carried out through Canton, where a European settlement was set up, ultimately dominated by the British East India Company. Trade with China was difficult, however, and there were many restrictions, restrictions which the East India Company turned to their advantage by importing opium into China from India. This trade grew rapidly until, in 1839 the Chinese authorities ordered the British to leave Canton, first moving to Macao and then to the relatively under-developed island of Hong Kong, which had the benefit of an excellent harbour. After some fighting, the island was formally ceded to Britain under the Treaty of Chuenpi on 26 January 1841, ratified by the Treaty of Nanking in 1843.

The colony was expanded into the Kowloon Peninsula in 1860 and by the 1898 Treaty of Peking the New Territories were acquired under a 99-year lease. In September 1984 the British government agreed to restore Hong Kong to China from 1 July 1997 and on 30 June of that year 135 years of British rule came to an end.

EARLY POSTAL MARKINGS AND THE FIRST STAMPS

A post office was opened at Victoria during 1841 using a locally made ornate circular, handstamp inscribed 'POST OFFICE/HONG KONG/1841', followed from 1843 by the familiar crowned-circle types, with Hong Kong hyphenated (*Fig 1*). At this time the post office was under the GPO in London, but it was transferred to local control on 1 May 1860.

Shortly afterwards, the governor, Sir Hercules Robinson, requested a supply of British stamps to be used in Hong Kong, but his request was refused on the grounds that, now it was under local control, it is up to the colony to make its own arrangements for the supply of stamps. Eventually, on 8 December 1862 the first Hong Kong stamps appeared. Printed by De La

Fig 1 *The Crowned Circle handstamps—in use before the first stamps were issued*

Fig 2 *The 1863–71 Crown CC set—almost! I'm still missing the 18c.*

Rue on unwatermarked paper, there were seven values from 2c. to 96c. Strangely, although all contemporary postal markings showed Hong Kong in two words, or occasionally hyphenated, the stamps showed it as one word 'HONGKONG'. The stamps were cancelled by a British-type numeral handstamp 'B62'.

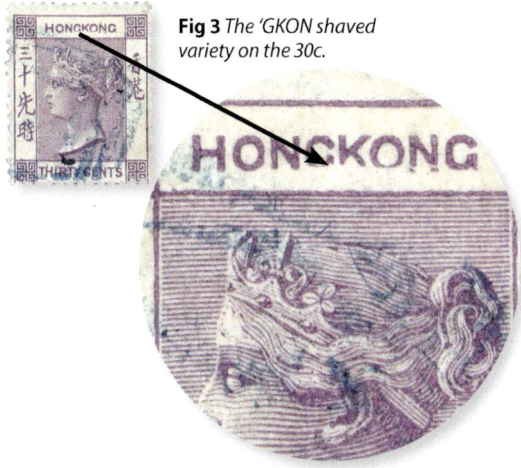

Fig 3 *The 'GKON shaved variety on the 30c.*

Fig 4 *A selection of Spiro forgeries— all perf 12½*

Fig 5 *The original wide and subsequent narrower Queen Victoria stamps*

For many years the Stanley Gibbons Catalogue listed certain British stamps cancelled with the B62 obliterator but that listing has since been removed as the stamps were never on sale in the colony and were, presumably, postmarked on arrival.

The unwatermarked stamps had only a short life and began to be replaced less than a year later by the same designs printed on Crown CC paper (*Fig 2*). There is a considerable range of shades in this set and all values exist with watermark varieties—inverted, reversed or inverted and reversed—which, since they are invariably quite easy to see are well worth checking for. There are also numerous minor plate flaws to look out for, the best-known of which is the catalogue-listed 'GKON' of HONGKONG' damaged at foot (*Fig 3*) on the 30c. (both vermilion and mauve versions), which occurred at R9/5 of the lower right pane from plate 1. Other things to look out for are the 4c. slate perf 12½ which is a bit of a mystery stamps and the distinctive 96c. olive-bistre, which had a short life and is a real rarity unused and quite a good stamp used.

EARLY WARNINGS
It is necessary to give a couple of warnings here; firstly, that there are Spiro forgeries of the entire set complete with 'B62' cancellations, and they are all perf 12½. So if you come across a perf 12½ 4c. slate do check that it has a watermark before you buy—the Spiro forgeries were on unwatermarked paper (*Fig 4*).

The second point is that for many years, the SG catalogue included a note to say that prices were for 'average' examples and that fine specimens were rarely met with and are worth considerably more. The note has now been dropped, so the current prices are for stamps in fine condition—it stands to reason that examples in 'average' condition should be substantially discounted in price, but I have to say that I have seen some quite scruffy stamps being offered at substantial proportions of catalogue—these are to be avoided! On the other hand, if you are prepared to be a bit 'forgiving' of the odd short perforation tooth or tone spot, you can build up a good showing of these stamps at reasonable cost.

Interestingly the design area of the stamp was narrowed slightly, for the new values introduced with the Crown CC watermark, so the 2c., 8c., 16c., 24c., 48c. and 96c. are 19½mm wide, but all subsequent values were only 18½mm between the left and right frames, presumably to make them easier to perforate (*Fig 5*). For those first seven values the wide-frame designs were retained for the rest of the reign, which is why they often appear to be off-centre.

SURCHARGES AND NEW VALUES

As with many other colonies in the mid-to-late 19th century, difficulties in communicating with sources of supply in the UK and shipping times back to the local post office meant that temporary shortages and the need for new values as a result of postal rate changes had to be met by resorting to local surcharging.

A number of these were prepared by local printers Noronha and Sons between 1876 and 1880, with 5c. surcharges on the 18c. and 24c., 10c. on the 12c. 16c. and 24c., 16c. on the 18c. and 28c. on the 30c. mauve. Inevitably, varieties occurred and are worth looking out for, but even the basic surcharges may take some time to find with used catalogue prices for those mentioned now ranging between £50 and £150 (Fig 6). New values (5c., 10c. and 16c.) and colour changes for the 2c. and 48c. also appeared on Crown CC paper, before the change to Crown CA began 1882.

By this time the B62 obliterators were giving way to circular datestamp cancellations, so finding nice-looking examples is easier, but many commercial firms at this time were handstamping their stamps to prevent theft. Most collectors view these stamps with firms' 'chops' as being undesirable, but the Hong Kong Study Circle Journal carries frequent articles on them as they develop into a new collecting area. That is the great thing about Hong Kong philately—as soon as one area of collecting seems to price itself out of the range of most collectors, they are ready to seize upon something else to study.

Returning to the Queen Victoria Crown CA stamps, the Stanley Gibbons Catalogue lists them in two sets, those issued between 1882 and 1896 and those issued to conform with the UPU colour scheme in 1900. The earlier set contains another 'Mystery stamp', the 2c. rose-pink, perf 12 of which only a handful of examples are known and which is currently priced at £75,000 unused or used. This stamp was controversial for many years, with some experts considering it to be a privately perforated proof, but it has now established itself as one of Hong Kong's great rarities.

De La Rue surcharged three values (20c. on 30c. 50c. on 48c. and $1 on 96c.) with new values in English only so these had to be handstamped individually with the Chinese value. During the same period more local surcharges were prepared by Noronha and Sons. The 7c. on 10c. and 14c. on 30c. both include a listed variety, 'Antique "t" in "cents"' at R1/1, which is not illustrated in the catalogue. The normal stamp shows a sharply uplifted 'tail' to the 't' but the antique 't' tail is almost flat. There is also a normal 't' with short tail which can be mistaken for the antique 't' so care should be taken when purchasing this variety.

THE FIRST COMMEMORATIVE

In 1891 the Hong Kong post office celebrated the 50th anniversary of the Colony by overprinting the current 2c. carmine with a four-line slogan; '1841/Hong Kong/JUBILEE/1891'. It received a total printing of only 50,000 and a stated on-sale period of only three days. This very early commemorative stamp (Fig 7) was a good item from the start, compounded by the fact that there are a number of major and minor varieties, which make it even more interesting than it might otherwise have been. To this it should be added that it has now been established that there were two settings

Fig 6 *The Hong Kong Post Office frequently had to resort to surcharging during the mid-to-late 19th century*

Fig 7 *The first commemorative issue from 1891*

Fig 8 *Postal fiscal stamps provided the higher values throughout Queen Victoria's reign*

of the overprint. Needless to say, there are also forgeries, some of which are quite good.

Throughout Queen Victoria's reign, the highest face value postage stamp was $1, higher postage rates being covered by the use of larger size 'Stamp Duty' adhesives, listed as 'postal fiscals' in the catalogue (Fig 8). The main concern with these is to ensure that you are buying stamps that have done postal, rather than fiscal duty. Here, it is better to have stamps with the ubiquitous 'B62' obliterator than the neat black 'Hong Kong/Paid All' cancellation, which, in black, was only used fiscally.

KING EDWARD VII

For the King Edward VII stamps, first issued in 1903, a more ornate design was chosen, with most values being printed in two colours, giving a much more colourful aspect to the album page than could be achieved by the rather drab Victorian stamps which preceded them (Fig 9).

As with most colonies, the initial Edward VII set was printed on Crown CA paper, but these began to be replaced by new printings on Multiple Crown CA the following year. Then, in 1906, most values were reissued on chalk-surfaced Multiple Crown CA paper, and then from 1907 some were re-issued in new colours, giving, in effect four different sets for the ten-year reign.

Fig 9 *King Edward VII brought a change of style—and to a certain extent, a change of name, with Hong Kong now written as two words*

Fig 10 *The King George V 'Broken flower'—a nice positional flaw*

Fig 11 *The Silver Jubilee 3c. with 'Lightning conductor' variety*

The watermarks are generally quite easy to see on the ordinary paper stamps (Crown CA or MCA), but much more difficult on the MCA stamps on chalk-surfaced paper, so this is a good identification feature of the latter stamps. It is well known that De La Rue's original chalk-surfaced paper had only a thin coating, but that they soon realised that better results could be achieved with a thicker application. Some Hong Kong stamps can be found with both thick and thin chalk-surfaced papers, but I have not studied this in any depth.

KING GEORGE V

The design of the Edward VII definitives, which was retained for the George V set first appearing in 1912, had the country name clearly in two words 'HONG KONG'. The 1912–21 set was on Multiple Crown CA and all values except the top $10 value were reissued on Multiple Script CA paper between 1921 and 1937 with a couple of colour changes in the early Script period resulting in scarce low values.

Much of the interest in this set lies in the plate flaws of which there are quite a few minor ones and three which have made it to the catalogue. It may seem odd that the cheapest of the three, by quite a long way, is on the most expensive basic stamp; the 'Broken flower' on the 25c. Multiple Script CA (126a) (*Fig 10*). This is because it occurred on the stamp next to the top marginal plate number and was therefore

saved in quantity, while the others, the Broken crown on the 1c. and the Broken character on the 4c. both occurred mid-sheet, so fewer have been preserved. The Broken character on the 4c., by the way, may be found in varying states. Look out also for Broken Crown flaw on the 2c., whose position is currently not known (as far as I am aware). One day that too might make it into the catalogue.

Talking of making it into the catalogue. I recall in my student days going into a stamp shop and being offered the 2c. green Multiple Script with inverted watermark for a shilling. Inverted watermarks were not listed in the catalogue at the time, but I remember thinking that a shilling would only buy me half a pint of 'best' so I'd take the risk. Now it's catalogued at £110—so who says stamps aren't a good investment!

George V's reign came to a close with the Silver Jubilee set, the Hong Kong issue being printed by Bradbury Wilkinson and therefore having the potential to find that printer's plate flaws. So far, only the 5c. value is known with the 'Extra flagstaff', but the 'Lightning conductor can be found on both the 3c. and the 5c. (*Fig 11*).

KING GEORGE VI

For the George VI definitive the Hong Kong Post Office went back to the Queen Victoria design, with 'HONGKONG' in one word, substituting the head of the new King in the place of his great grandmother. This set has been studied in considerable depth and a fine

Fig 12 *King George VI plate flaws on the 15c. and 50c.*

study was published by the Hong Kong Study Circle in 1992, written by former *GSM* author, Nick Halewood (now editor of the *HKSC Journal*) and David Antscherl, which should be the first source of reference for those interested in delving deeper into this fascinating set. Suffice it to say here that there are numerous printings and shades and a number of plate flaws, not all of which are catalogue listed (*Fig 12*).

During its currency of course Hong Kong was occupied by Japan and most of the stamps were safely hidden until liberation. The dollar values were looted, however, and were replaced by stamps in new colours after the war to ensure that the Post Office was not out of pocket! In fact, the colours were just shuffled around with the old $1 colour moving to the $10 and all the others moving down one, so the old $2 colours became the new $1, the old $5, the $2 and so on.

Prior to the issue of the George VI stamps there was a shortage of 5c. stamps (at that time the George V 5c. violet, No. 121), so the 5c. revenue stamp was authorised for postal use between 11 and 20 January 1938 (*Fig 13*). Needless to say, there was considerable demand for this stamp used 'in period' and local forgers were happy to supply. The SG catalogue mentions one Victoria 'first day' postmark without side bars between the rings, but there is another one, also 'Victoria 11 JA' in which the left stroke of the 'V' of 'VICTORIA' is not parallel with the top of the left-hand side bar. There are a number of other differences too, but I think this is the most obvious.

JAPANESE OCCUPATION

The Japanese attacked Hong Kong on the night of 15/16 December 1941 and the colony finally surrendered on Christmas Day, the 25th. When the post office reopened on 22 January, Japanese stamps were on sale. As the catalogue explains, the postmarks on Japanese stamps used in Hong Kong may be identified by a combination of light horizontal bars in the segments either side of the date panel and three stars in the lower part of the datestamp. The only catalogue listed stamps are the three surcharges prepared specifically for Hong Kong and issued in April 1945 (*Fig 14*).

The Japanese surrendered on 30 August 1945 and initially mail was carried free with an octagonal

Fig 13 *Postal use of the 5c. fiscal stamp in 1938 (Reduced)*

handstamp inscribed 'HONG KONG/1945/POSTAGE PAID' (*Fig 15*). Stamps were reintroduced on 28 September, including the perf 14½×14 emergency printings of the 2c., 4c., 5c., 30c. and 50c., which had been done by Harrison (4c.) and Bradbury Wilkinson, using De La Rue's plates following the bombing of the De La Rue works and distributed to the London trade in 1941.

MORE COMMEMORATIVES

George VI commemoratives for Hong Kong comprised the typical Coronation set of three, a very attractive set of six pictorials to mark the centenary of British occupation in 1941 (*Fig 16*) and the very far from typical Victory pair, now credited to El Wynne-Jones and WE Jones, who had worked on the design while interned by the Japanese. This was followed by the standard Silver Wedding pair and the UPU set of four.

The Silver Wedding $10 was the subject of heavy speculation in the late 1980s and is still by some way the most expensive stamp in the omnibus set. At the time of the greatest demand, buying advertisements appeared in the philatelic press for other Silver Wedding high values in the same carmine colour as the Hong Kong stamp (such as Montserrat and Seychelles). Presumably these were being 'doctored' to turn them into Hong Kong stamps, but I have never seen an example of one. It's something to be aware of though.

Before leaving King George VI it is worth mentioning the varieties which are worth looking out for. There are a number of unlisted minor flaws on the definitives as well as those which have achieved catalogue status. The extra stroke flaws on the Victory pair and the 'Spur on "N"' on the 10c. Silver Wedding can be found if you look, but the 'Crack in rock' on the UPU 80c. is a real rarity, which I am still looking for.

QUEEN ELIZABETH II

All of these, along with the 1953 Coronation stamp of 1954 showed 'HONG KONG' in two words, but when the first Queen Elizabeth set appeared it was back to a single word, as in the George VI set for which the duty plates had been retained, albeit reformatted to suit a new sheet size, changing from two panes of 60 to a single sheet of 100.

Fig 14 *Japanese occupation set on cover, showing the distinctive Hong Kong postmark (Reduced)*

Fig 15 *Liberation cover (Reduced)*

Fig 16 *The attractive Centenary set and the Silver Wedding 10c. showing the 'Spur on "N"' variety*

Again these letterpress stamps are deserving of greater study than is possible to demonstrate here, but I must just sneak in a mention of their replacements, showing the Annigoni portrait of Her Majesty which appeared in 1962. In my opinion Hong Kong is the only Commonwealth Country which issued its most attractive set of definitives in the 1960s (*Fig 17*).

Fig 17 *Queen Elizabeth stamps of 1954 and 1962*

BACK OF THE BOOK

Hong Kong also has one of the more extensive 'back of the book' listings in Part 1. Apart from the postal fiscals and Japanese occupation stamps already mentioned, there were stamps surcharged in 1879 by Noronha and Sons for use on postcards (*Fig 18*); the booklets containing Edward VII and George V stamps are comprehensively listed in the catalogue and the postage due stamps are of an attractive design not used anywhere else (*Fig 19*), although, as John Griffith-Jones' recent book shows, they were at least considered for Zanzibar.

Fig 18 *The 3c. on 16c. yellow postcard stamp*

The most extensive listing, however, is of Hong Kong stamps used in the British Post Offices in China and Japan (*Fig 20*), but these are well covered in the Catalogue and many were illustrated in an article on Hong Kong Postmarks, published here a few years ago.

Fig 19 *Hong Kong's distinctive postage due design*

For many years Hong Kong stamps were sold at these post offices at the local rate of exchange, but the Chinese Dollar devalued in relation to Hong Kong currency, making it possible to purchase Hong Kong stamps more cheaply in China and bring them back to the colony to sell at a profit. To overcome this, the entire set on Multiple Crown CA paper was overprinted 'CHINA' for sale at the treaty ports (*Fig 21*). The

Fig 20 *A selection of Treaty Port cancels on Hong Kong adhesives*

set on Multiple Script CA paper was issued in March 1922, but in November the offices closed, leaving the British naval base at Wei Hai Wei as the only place they remained on sale, until that office also closed in 1930. Thus the Script CA 'CHINA' overprints used at offices other than Wei Hai Wei are worth looking out for and keep an eye on the 'CHINA' 50c. in particular, catalogued from £1.50 on Multiple Crown CA paper, but £300 on Multiple Script.

FURTHER POSSIBILITIES

I hope this brief run through the stamps of Hong Kong has shown that it is a subject worthy of greater attention. The early postal history has been priced out of reach of most of us, but it is still possible to put together a representative used collections, provided that you are not too fastidious about condition, while always trying to find the best you can afford.

If you have been inspired, the first job is to buy a copy of the latest *Stanley Gibbons Hong Kong Catalogue* and join the excellent Hong Kong Study Circle, then try to obtain a copy of the standard work on the colony by F W Webb, reprinted a few years ago by James Bendon with helpful additional features. For the postmark enthusiast, *The Postal History of Hong Kong* by Ted Proud is also a 'must have' guide.

With all this information available, you might well wonder whether there are still opportunities for the

newcomer, but new discoveries are constantly being made and while outgoing correspondence has become prohibitively expensive, letters addressed to Hong Kong can be picked up much more cheaply (*Fig 22*), and, with its huge commercial mail outgoing covers of the Elizabethan period are plentiful, still relatively inexpensive and full of potential (*Fig 23*).

Further information and reading

The Hong Kong Study Circle: Membership secretary, Robert Newton, newtons100@gmail.com

F W Webb OBE FRPSL, *The Philatelic and Postal History of Hong Kong and the Treaty Ports of China and Japan*, reprint with additions, James Bendon, Limassol, 1991.

EB Proud, *The Postal History of Hong Kong, 1841-1997*, Proud Bailey, 2004.

Nick Halewood and David Antscherl, *A Study of the Hong Kong Definitive Adhesives of King George VI*, Hong Kong Study Circle, 1992.

This article first appeared in *Gibbons Stamp Monthly*, February 2016.

Fig 21 *The 'CHINA' overprints introduced in 1917*

Fig 22 *'Inwards' covers are still within reach – the '6' in circle handstamp on this cover is a postman's beat 'chop' (Reduced)*

Fig 23 *There is plenty of potential too in more modern covers (Reduced)*

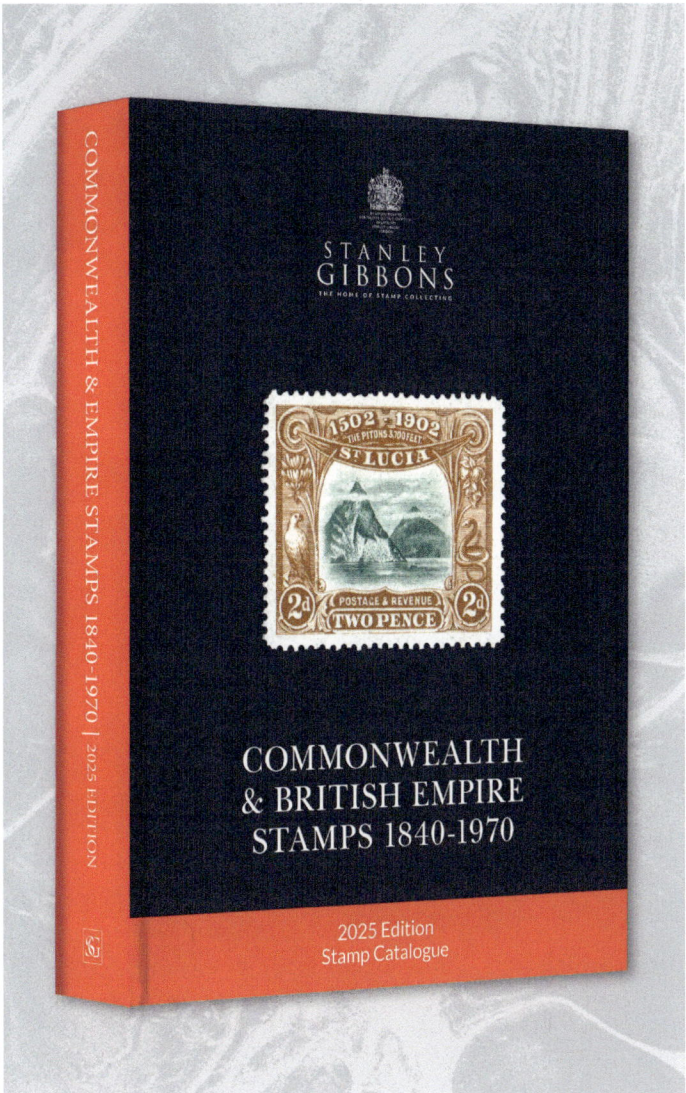

 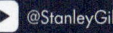

STANLEY GIBBONS

ESTABLISHED 1856

The King George VI Album Set

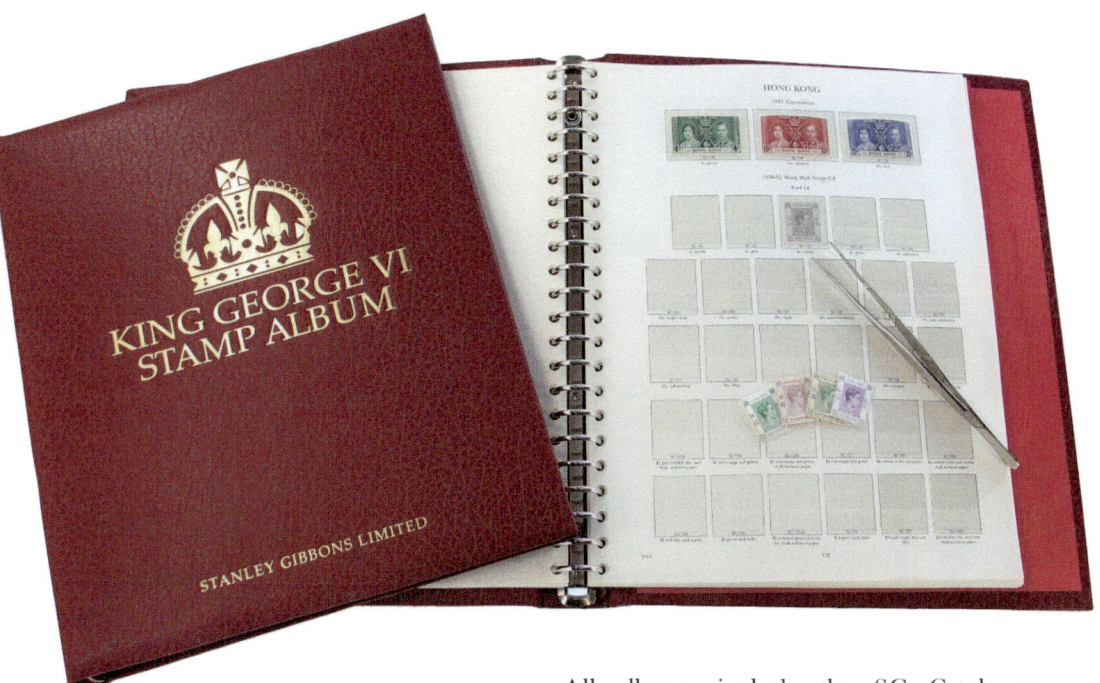

The King George VI 1936 - 1952 is presented in a six volume set of luxury padded binders, housed in three slipcases. All albums are handmade with a 22 Ring mechanism to securely hold your collection and comes supplied with a matching slipcase.

Pre-printed on cream acid free paper with spaces for all main SG numbers as per our Commonwealth and Empire stamp catalogue 1840 - 1970.

Covering all Postage, Air Due, Postal Fiscal and Offical Stamps. There are spaces for all perforation and watermark changes (including sideways but not inverted or reversed), different plates, Types and Dies, Shades and Varieties are not included.

All albums include the SG Catalogue numbers, Information Pages and many illustrations of Types and Dies are included to aid identifying the correct space for a stamp.

Indian States and Japan Occupation are not included in the main album but available separately.

All leaves are punched 22 Ring.
Leaf Size 222 x 280mm.

Available with clear mounts already affixed, or without mounts.

Product Code: RKG6
Standard (Without mounts):   £479.00
Hingeless (With mounts):   £716.00

Available from Stanley Gibbons customer service, or our distribution partners Dauwalders at www.dauwalders.co.uk

Hong Kong

CROWN COLONY

Hong Kong island was formally ceded to Great Britain on 26 January 1841. The Hong Kong Post Office was established in October 1841, when much of the business previously transacted through the Macau postal agency was transferred to the island. The first cancellation is known from April 1842, but local control of the posts was short-lived as the Hong Kong Office became a branch of the British GPO on 15 April 1843.

The colonial authorities resumed control of the postal service on 1 May 1860 although the previously established postal agencies in the Chinese Treaty Ports remained part of the British GPO system until 1 May 1868.

CROWNED-CIRCLE HANDSTAMPS

CC1   CC1b

CC3

CC1	**CC1b**	HONG KONG (R.) (17.10.1843)	Price on cover	£900
CC2	**CC1**	HONG KONG (R.) (21.8.1844)	Price on cover	£1200
CC3	**CC3**	HONG KONG (R.) (16.6.1852)	Price on cover	£550

We no longer list the Great Britain stamps with obliteration 'B62' within oval. The Government notification dated 29 November 1862 stated that only the Hong Kong stamps to be issued on 8 December would be available for postage and the stamps formerly listed were all issued in Great Britain later than the date of the notice.

(Currency. 100 cents = 1 Hong Kong dollar)

PRICES FOR STAMPS ON COVER TO 1945

Nos.	1/7	from × 6
Nos.	8/12	from × 15
No.	13	from × 6
Nos.	14/17	from × 15
No.	18	from × 50
No.	19	from × 15
Nos.	20/27	from × 10
Nos.	28/36	from × 8
Nos.	37/39	from × 12
Nos.	40/44	from × 10
Nos.	45/50	from × 15
No.	51	from × 20
No.	52	from × 10
Nos.	53/54	—
No.	55	from × 10
Nos.	56/61	from × 10
Nos.	62/99	from × 4
Nos.	100/132	from × 3
Nos.	133/136	from × 2
Nos.	137/139	from × 4
Nos.	140/168	from × 2
Nos.	P1/P3	from × 2
Nos.	D1/D12	from × 10

PRICES FOR STAMPS ON COVER TO 1945

Nos.	F1/F11	from × 20
No.	F12	from × 4

PRINTERS. All definitive issues up to 1962 were typographed by De La Rue and Co., except for some printings between 1941 and 1945.

1   2   3

1862 (8 Dec)–**63**. No wmk. Perf 14.

1	**1**	2c. brown	£550	£130
		a. *Deep brown* (1863)	£750	£170
2		8c. yellow-buff	£800	95·00
3		12c. pale greenish blue	£650	65·00
4	**3**	18c. lilac	£650	60·00
5		24c. green	£1400	£130
6		48c. rose	£3000	£400
7		96c. brownish grey	£4000	£500

'GKON' of 'HONGKONG' damaged at foot (Pl. 1 lower right pane R. 9/5)

1863 (Aug)–**71**. Wmk Crown CC. Perf 14.

8	**1**	2c. deep brown (11.64)	£375	35·00
		a. *Brown*	£150	8·50
		b. *Pale yellowish brown*	£180	14·00
		w. Wmk inverted	£800	£150
		x. Wmk reversed	—	£325
		y. Wmk inverted and reversed	†	£950
9	**2**	4c. grey	£170	22·00
		ay. Wmk inverted and reversed	†	£950
		b. *Slate*	£130	9·50
		bw. Wmk inverted	£600	£140
		c. *Deep slate*	£170	18·00
		d. *Greenish grey*	£350	55·00
		dw. Wmk inverted	†	£450
		e. *Bluish slate*	£500	28·00
		ew. Wmk inverted	£1400	£225
		f. *Perf 12½. Slate* (8.70)	£12000	£275
		fw. Wmk inverted	—	£950
10		6c. lilac	£475	21·00
		a. *Mauve*	£700	22·00
		w. Wmk inverted	£1800	£160
		x. Wmk reversed	£2000	£250
		y. Wmk inverted and reversed		
11	**1**	8c. pale dull orange (10.64)	£600	15·00
		a. *Brownish orange*	£550	18·00
		b. *Bright orange*	£500	18·00
		w. Wmk inverted	£1500	£180
		x. Wmk reversed	£1600	£350
12		12c. pale greenish blue (4.65)	£1100	45·00
		a. *Pale blue*	35·00	9·50
		b. *Deep blue*	£300	15·00
		w. Wmk inverted	—	£140
		x. Wmk reversed	—	£200
13	**3**	18c. lilac (1866)	£7000	£1100
		w. Wmk inverted	£11000	£1100
		x. Wmk reversed	£18000	£1700
		y. Wmk inverted and reversed	†	£2750
14		24c. green (10.64)	£650	12·00
		a. *Pale green*	£800	20·00
		b. *Deep green*	£1300	35·00
		w. Wmk inverted	£2750	£180
		x. Wmk reversed	£2500	£300
15	**2**	30c. vermilion	£1100	16·00
		a. *Orange-vermilion*	£900	18·00
		b. 'GKON' of 'HONGKONG' damaged at foot	—	£1900
		w. Wmk inverted	£3000	£225
		x. Wmk reversed	—	£325
16		30c. mauve (14.8.71)	£275	6·00
		a. 'GKON' of 'HONGKONG' damaged at foot	—	£600
		w. Wmk inverted	£1400	£160
		x. Wmk reversed	—	£325
17		48c. pale rose (1.65)	£1500	80·00
		a. *Rose-carmine*	£1100	42·00
		w. Wmk inverted	£2500	£225
		x. Wmk reversed	—	£400
18		96c. olive-bistre (1.65)	£80000	£800
		w. Wmk inverted	†	£5500

Dive into the world of Luxembourg crypto stamps!

Discover the unique crypto stamp
collection of POST Luxembourg

19		96c. brownish grey (1865)	£1600	80·00
		a. Brownish black	£2000	70·00
		w. Wmk inverted	£2250	£250
		y. Wmk inverted and reversed	†	£2000

There is a wide range of shades in this issue, of which we can only indicate the main groups.

No. 12 is the same shade as No. 3 without wmk, the impression having a waxy appearance.

A single used example of the 48c. in a bright claret shade is known. No other stamps in this shade, either mint or used, have been discovered.

See also Nos. 22 and 28/31.

16	**28**	**5**	**10**
cents.	**cents.**	**cents.**	**cents.**
(4)	(5)	(6)	(7)

ts .

No. 20b

1876 (Aug)–**77**. Nos. 13 and 16 surch with T **4** or T **5** by Noronha and Sons, Hong Kong.

20	3	16c. on 18c. lilac (1.4.77)	£2500	£160
		a. Space between 'n' and 't'	£8000	£900
		b. Space between 's' and stop	£8000	£900
		w. Wmk inverted	£6000	£1000
21	2	28c. on 30c. mauve	£2000	55·00
		a. 'GKON' of 'HONGKONG' damaged at foot	—	£1100

1877 (Aug). New value. Wmk Crown CC. Perf 14.

22	3	16c. yellow	£2000	70·00
		w. Wmk inverted and reversed	£4250	£500

1880 (1 Mar–Sept). Surch with T **6** or T **7** by Noronha and Sons.

23	1	5c. on 8c. bright orange (No. 11b) (9.80)	£1500	£120
		a. Surch inverted	†	£21000
		b. Surch double	†	£21000
24	3	5c. on 18c. lilac (No. 13)	£1200	75·00
		x. Wmk reversed	£2500	£1100
		y. Wmk inverted and reversed	†	£3500
25	1	10c. on 12c. pale blue (No. 12a)	£1200	60·00
		a. Blue	£1800	£120
		b. Surch double	†	£50000
26	3	10c. on 16c. yellow (No. 22) (5.80)	£4250	£160
		a. Surch inverted	—	£95000
		b. Surch double	†	£75000
		w. Wmk inverted	†	£2000
27		10c. on 24c. green (No. 14) (6.80)	£1600	£120
		w. Wmk inverted	†	£750

Three examples of No. 26b are known, all used in Shanghai.

1880 (Mar–Dec). Colours changed and new values. Wmk Crown CC. Perf 14.

28	1	2c. dull rose	£275	42·00
		a. Rose	£300	42·00
		w. Wmk inverted	†	£550
29	2	5c. blue (12.80)	£800	65·00
		w. Wmk inverted	—	£550
30		10c. mauve (11.80)	£900	21·00
		w. Wmk inverted	—	£550
31	3	48c. brown	£1500	£130

1882 (May)–**96**. Wmk Crown CA. Perf 14.

32	1	2c. rose-lake (7.82)	£300	42·00
		a. Rose-pink	£300	38·00
		ab. Perf 12	£95000	£95000
		w. Wmk inverted	—	£275
		x. Wmk reversed	†	£700
33		2c. carmine (1884)	60·00	3·00
		a. Aniline carmine	60·00	3·00
		w. Wmk inverted	—	£180
34	2	4c. slate-grey (1.4.96)	42·00	4·50
		w. Wmk inverted	—	£275
35		5c. pale blue	55·00	1·25
		a. Blue	55·00	1·25
		aw. Wmk inverted	£500	£120
		x. Wmk reversed	—	£475
36		10c. dull mauve (8.82)	£1100	25·00
		w. Wmk inverted	—	£475
37		10c. deep blue-green (1884)	£2250	50·00
		a. Green (2.84)	£190	2·25
		aw. Wmk inverted	†	£750
38		10c. purple/red (1.1.91)	45·00	1·75
		w. Wmk inverted	£750	£150
		x. Wmk reversed	£1300	£300
		y. Wmk inverted and reversed		
39		30c. yellowish green (1.1.91)	£180	50·00
		a. Grey-green	£120	32·00
38s, 39as Optd 'SPECIMEN' Set of 2			£400	

Examples of No. 39 should not be confused with washed or faded stamps from the grey-green shade which tend to turn to a very yellow-green when dampened.

For other stamps with this watermark, but in colours changed to the UPU scheme, see Nos. 56/61.

20	**50**	**1**
CENTS	**CENTS**	**DOLLAR**
(8)	(9)	(10)

1885 (Sept). As Nos. 15, 19 and 31, but wmk Crown CA, surch with Types **8** to **10** by De La Rue.

40	2	20c. on 30c. orange-red	£200	8·50
		a. Surch double	£95000	—
		w. Wmk inverted	£1600	£550
41	3	50c. on 48c. yellowish brown	£450	50·00
		w. Wmk inverted	£1600	£550
42		$1 on 96c. grey-olive	£850	£100
40s/42s Optd 'SPECIMEN' Set of 3			£1300	

For the $1 on 96c. black and grey-black see Nos. 53/53a.

7	**14**	**弍**	**五十**	**壹圓**
cents.	**cents.**			
(11)	(12)	(13) (20c.)	(14) (50c.)	(15) ($1)

1891 (1 Jan–Mar).

*(a) Nos. 16 and 37 surch with T **11** or T **12** by Noronha and Sons, Hong Kong.*

43	2	7c. on 10c. green	£100	10·00
		a. Antique 't' in 'cents' (R. 1/1)	£700	£160
		b. Surch double	£7000	£1500
44		14c. on 30c. mauve (2.91)	£250	90·00
		a. Antique 't' in 'cents' (R. 1/1)	£2750	£1000
		b. 'GKON' of 'HONGKONG' damaged at foot	£6000	£2000

*(b) As Nos. 40/42 (surch with Types **8** to **10** by De La Rue), but colours changed.*

45	2	20c. on 30c. yellowish green (No. 39)	£200	£180
		a. Grey-green (No. 39a)	£140	£170
46	3	50c. on 48c. dull purple	£350	£375
47		$1 on 96c. purple/red	£950	£400
45as/47s Optd 'SPECIMEN' Set of 3			£850	

*(c) Nos. 45/47 with further surch, Types **13/15**, in Chinese characters, handstamped locally (March).*

48	2	20c. on 30c. yellowish green	60·00	15·00
		a. Grey-green	48·00	14·00
		b. Surch double	£25000	£25000
49	3	50c. on 48c. dull purple	85·00	5·50
50		$1 on 96c. purple/red	£500	25·00
		w. Wmk inverted	£2000	

The true antique 't' variety (Nos. 43a and 44a) should not be confused with a small 't' showing a short foot. In the antique 't' the crossbar is accurately bisected by the vertical stroke, which is thicker at the top. The lower curve bends towards the right and does not turn upwards to the same extent as on the normal.

The handstamped surcharges on Nos. 48/50 were applied over the original Chinese face values. The single character for '2' was intended to convert '30c.' to '20c'. There were six slightly different versions of the '2' handstamp and three for the '50c'.

Errors of the handstamped Chinese surcharges, such as double, treble, double one inverted and surcharges on both side panels of the stamp are now omitted as being outside the scope of the catalogue. While some without doubt possess philatelic merit, it is impossible to distinguish between the genuine errors and the clandestine copies made to order with the original chops. No. 55c is retained as this represents a distinctly different chop which was used for the last part of the printing.

1841			
Hong Kong			
JUBILEE	**10**	**拾**	**拾**
1891	**CENTS**		
(16)	(17)	(18)	(19)

1891 (22 Jan). 50th Anniversary of Colony. Optd with T **16** by Noronha and Sons, Hong Kong.

51	1	2c. carmine (No. 33)	£500	£140
		a. Short 'J' in 'JUBILEE' (R. 1/6)	£900	£225
		b. Short 'U' in 'JUBILEE' (R. 1/1)	£900	£225

		c. Broken '1' in '1891' (R. 2/1)	£950	£300
		d. Tall narrow 'K' in 'Kong' (R. 1/3)	£1300	£475
		e. Opt double	£18000	£15000
		f. Space between 'O' and 'N' of 'Hong' (R. 1/5)	£1700	£750

Most of the supply of No. 51, which was only on sale for three days, was overprinted from a setting of 12 (6×2) applied five times to complete each pane. There were six printings from this setting, but a second setting, possibly of 30 or 60, was used for the seventh. Positions quoted are from the setting of 12. Most varieties only occur in some printings and many less marked overprint flaws also exist.

The prices quoted for No. 51e are for examples on which the two impressions are distinctly separated. Examples on which the two impressions are almost coincidental are worth considerably less.

1898 (1 Apr). Wmk Crown CA. Perf 14.

*(a) Surch with T **10** by D.L.R. and handstamped Chinese characters as T **15**.*

52	**3**	$1 on 96c. black	£250	30·00
		a. Grey-black	£225	30·00

*(b) Surch with T **10** only.*

53	**3**	$1 on 96c. black	£3250	£4250
		a. Grey-black	£2750	£4000
		as. Optd 'SPECIMEN'	£600	

Nos. 52/52a and 53/53a show considerable variation in shades, with some paler shades verging on grey. Nos. 53/53a should not be confused with the 1885 $1 on 96c. grey-olive (No. 42).

1898 (1 Apr).

*(a) Surch with T **17** by Noronha and Sons, Hong Kong.*

54	**2**	10c. on 30c. grey-green (No. 39a)	£650	£1300
		a. Figures '10' widely spaced (1½ mm)	£7500	£10000
		b. Surch double		

*(b) As No. 54, but with handstamped Chinese characters, T **18**, in addition.*

55	**2**	10c. on 30c. grey-green (No. 39a)	80·00	£100
		a. Yellowish green	£100	£120
		b. Figures '10' widely spaced (1½ mm)	£800	£1000
		c. Chinese character large (Type **19**)	£1000	£1100
		d. Surch Type **17** double	£12000	
		s. Handstamped 'SPECIMEN'	£140	

T **17** was applied in a horizontal setting of 12, Nos. 54a and 55b appearing on position 12 for the early printings only. The true 1½ mm wide spacing is not known on No. 55c. Examples showing spacing of 1·2 mm–1·3 mm are worth a premium over the normal prices.

1900 (Aug)–**01**. Wmk Crown CA. Perf 14.

56	**1**	2c. dull green	30·00	1·00
		w. Wmk inverted	£325	£140
57	**2**	4c. carmine (1901)	25·00	90
		w. Wmk inverted	†	—
58		5c. yellow	35·00	11·00
		w. Wmk inverted	—	£700
59		10c. ultramarine	55·00	2·75
		w. Wmk inverted	—	£140
60	**1**	12c. blue (1901)	50·00	70·00
61	**2**	30c. brown (1901)	75·00	32·00
56/61 *Set of 6*			£225	£100
56s/59s, 61s Optd 'SPECIMEN' *Set of 5*			£600	

20

21

22

23

1903 (Jan–July). Wmk Crown CA. Perf 14.

62	**20**	1c. dull purple and brown	3·00	50
63		2c. dull green (7.03)	24·00	3·00
		w. Wmk inverted	†	£1300
		y. Wmk inverted and reversed	†	£1500
64	**21**	4c. purple/red (7.03)	30·00	40
65		5c. dull green and brown-orange (7.03)	25·00	12·00

66		8c. slate and violet (12.2.03)	18·00	2·25
67	**20**	10c. purple and blue/*blue* (7.03)	70·00	1·50
68	**23**	12c. green and purple/*yellow* (12.2.03).	16·00	7·50
69		20c. slate and chestnut (6.03)	65·00	7·00
70	**22**	30c. dull green and black (21.5.03)	65·00	30·00
71	**23**	50c. dull green and magenta (6.03)	65·00	70·00
72	**20**	$1 purple and sage-green (6.03)	£130	30·00
73	**23**	$2 slate and scarlet (7.03)	£375	£400
74	**22**	$3 slate and dull blue (7.03)	£450	£450
75	**23**	$5 purple and blue-green (6.03)	£650	£650
76	**22**	$10 slate and orange/*blue* (7.03)	£1400	£500
		w. Wmk inverted	†	—
62/76 *Set of 15*			£3000	£1900
62s/76s Optd 'SPECIMEN' *Set of 15*			£2250	

No. 63w is known used at Shanghai.

1904 (4 Oct)–**06**. Wmk Mult Crown CA. Chalk-surfaced paper (8c., 12c., $3, $5) or ordinary paper (others). Perf 14.

77	**20**	2c. dull green	29·00	2·75
		a. Chalk-surfaced paper (1906)	30·00	5·50
		aw. Wmk inverted	†	£1100
78	**21**	4c. purple/red	45·00	40
		a. Chalk-surfaced paper (1906)	28·00	2·00
79		5c. dull green and brown-orange	75·00	22·00
		a. Chalk-surfaced paper (1906)	26·00	7·00
		aw. Wmk inverted	£750	
80		8c. slate and violet (1906)	22·00	2·25
81	**20**	10c. purple and blue/*blue* (3.05)	40·00	1·50
82	**23**	12c. green and purple/*yellow* (1906)	26·00	9·00
83		20c. slate and chestnut	70·00	4·75
		a. Chalk-surfaced paper (1906)	65·00	4·25
		aw. Wmk inverted	†	£1100
84	**22**	30c. dull green and black	70·00	40·00
		a. Chalk-surfaced paper (1906)	70·00	25·00
85	**23**	50c. green and magenta	£110	20·00
		a. Chalk-surfaced paper (1906)	95·00	23·00
86	**20**	$1 purple and sage-green	£200	50·00
		a. Chalk-surfaced paper (1906)	£180	50·00
87	**23**	$2 slate and scarlet	£450	£190
		a. Chalk-surfaced paper (1905)	£375	£150
88	**22**	$3 slate and dull blue (1905)	£375	£350
89	**23**	$5 purple and blue-green (1905)	£550	£500
90	**22**	$10 slate and orange/*blue* (5.05)	£1900	£1600
		aw. Wmk inverted	†	—
		b. Chalk-surfaced paper (1906)	£2000	£1400
77/90 *Set of 14*			£3250	£2250

No. 77aw is known used at Shanghai in October 1908 and 83aw at Hoihow in March 1908.

1907–**11**. Colours changed and new value. Wmk Mult Crown CA. Chalk-surfaced paper (6c. and 20c. to $2). Perf 14.

91	**20**	1c. brown (9.10)	11·00	1·10
		x. Wmk reversed	†	£2000
92		2c. deep green	48·00	1·75
		a. Green	48·00	1·50
		w. Wmk inverted	£1500	£900
93	**21**	4c. carmine-red	22·00	50
		w. Wmk inverted	†	£2000
		x. Wmk reversed	†	£2000
94	**22**	6c. orange-vermilion and purple (10.07)	48·00	9·50
95	**20**	10c. bright ultramarine	65·00	50
96	**23**	20c. purple and sage-green (3.11)	55·00	55·00
97	**22**	30c. purple and orange-yellow (3.11)	65·00	60·00
98	**23**	50c. black/*green* (3.11)	50·00	22·00
99		$2 carmine-red and black (1910)	£400	£450
91/99 *Set of 9*			£650	£500
91s, 93s/99s Optd 'SPECIMEN' *Set of 8*			£1200	

No. 91x is known used at Canton in December 1912 and January 1913, No. 92w at Shanghai in 1908 and 93x at Swatow in February 1911.

24

25

26

27

28

(A)

(B)

In Type A of the 25c. the upper Chinese character in the left-hand label has a short vertical stroke crossing it at the foot. In Type B this stroke is absent.

Crown broken at right (R. 9/2)

Broken flower at top right (Upper left pane R. 1/3)

1912 (9 Nov)–**21**. Wmk Mult Crown CA. Chalk-surfaced paper (12c. to $10). Perf 14.

100	**24**	1c. brown	7·50	55
		a. Black-brown	9·50	3·00
		b. Crown broken at right	£250	£180
101		2c. deep green	20·00	30
		a. Green	24·00	40
		w. Wmk inverted	†	£1500
		y. Wmk inverted and reversed	†	—
102	**25**	4c. carmine-red	14·00	30
		a. Scarlet (1914)	55·00	3·00
		aw. Wmk inverted		
		y. Wmk inverted and reversed	†	£2000
103	**26**	6c. yellow-orange	8·50	3·50
		a. Brown-orange	8·50	4·50
		w. Wmk inverted	£1200	£1100
		y. Wmk inverted and reversed	†	£2000
104	**25**	8c. grey	38·00	12·00
		a. Slate (1914)	50·00	8·50
105	**24**	10c. ultramarine	55·00	30
		a. Deep bright ultramarine	35·00	30
106	**27**	12c. purple/yellow	16·00	17·00
		a. White back (1914)	18·00	21·00
		as. Optd 'SPECIMEN'	£160	
107		20c. purple and sage-green	20·00	1·75
108	**28**	25c. purple and magenta (Type A) (1.14)	50·00	48·00
109		25c. purple and magenta (Type B) (8.19)	£300	95·00
		a. Broken flower	£5000	
110	**26**	30c. purple and orange-yellow	65·00	14·00
		a. Purple and orange	45·00	10·00
		w. Wmk inverted		
111	**27**	50c. black/blue-green	30·00	3·50
		a. White back (5.14)	40·00	4·50
		as. Optd 'SPECIMEN'	£180	
		b. On blue-green, olive back (1917)	£1400	40·00
		c. On emerald surface (9.19)	48·00	8·50
		d. On emerald back (7.12.21)	40·00	12·00
		ds. Optd 'SPECIMEN'	£200	
		w. Wmk inverted	£4000	
		y. Wmk inverted and reversed	†	£3750
112	**24**	$1 purple and blue/blue	75·00	6·50
		w. Wmk inverted	£350	£200
113	**27**	$2 carmine-red and grey-black	£200	80·00
114	**26**	$3 green and purple	£300	£140
115	**27**	$5 green and red/green	£725	£475
		a. White back (5.14)	£650	£425
		as. Optd 'SPECIMEN'	£450	
		b. On blue-green, olive back (1917)	£1300	£450
		bs. Optd 'SPECIMEN'	£650	
		bw. Wmk inverted	£5500	
116	**26**	$10 purple and black/red	£600	£110
100/116 Set of 17			£2000	£800
100s/116s Optd 'SPECIMEN' Set of 17			£2250	

No. 100b occurred in 1916 on R. 9/2 of the lower right pane before being retouched.

4c. Top of lower Chinese characters at right broken off (R. 9/4, lower left pane)

1921 (Jan)–**37**. Wmk Mult Script CA. Chalk-surfaced paper (12c. to $5). Perf 14.

117	**24**	1c. brown	3·50	40
118		2c. blue-green	7·00	1·00
		a. Yellow-green (1932)	32·00	3·00
		bw. Wmk inverted	£120	

118c		2c. grey (14.4.37)	25·00	15·00
119	**25**	3c. grey (8.10.31)	15·00	2·00
120		4c. carmine-rose	8·00	70
		a. Carmine-red (1932)	16·00	30
		b. Top of lower Chinese characters at right broken off	£110	85·00
121		5c. violet (16.10.31)	24·00	30
		x. Wmk reversed	†	—
122		8c. grey	28·00	48·00
123		8c. orange (7.12.21)	8·00	2·75
		w. Wmk inverted	£1400	£1000
124	**24**	10c. bright ultramarine	15·00	30
		aw. Wmk inverted	£475	
		ay. Wmk inverted and reversed	†	£1500
		b. 'A' of 'CA' missing from wmk	†	—
124c	**27**	12c. purple/yellow (3.4.33)	26·00	5·00
125		20c. purple and sage-green (7.12.21)	14·00	30
126	**28**	25c. purple and magenta (Type B) (7.12.21)	10·00	3·25
		a. Broken flower	55·00	70·00
		w. Wmk inverted	†	£900
127	**26**	30c. purple and chrome-yellow (7.12.21)	14·00	3·25
		a. Purple and orange-yellow	45·00	8·50
		w. Wmk inverted	£475	
128	**27**	50c. black/emerald (1924)	35·00	40
129	**24**	$1 purple and blue/blue (7.12.21)	50·00	1·25
130	**27**	$2 carmine-red and grey-black (7.12.21)	£140	12·00
131	**26**	$3 green and dull purple (1926)	£200	85·00
132	**27**	$5 green and red/emerald (1925)	£500	95·00
117/132 Set of 18			£1000	£225
117s/132s Optd or Perf (2c. grey, 3c., 5c., 12c.) 'SPECIMEN' Set of 18			£2250	

No. 120b occurs on R. 9/4 of the lower left pane. It is a progressive flaw, the illustration showing its most advanced state.

28a Windsor Castle

Extra flagstaff (Plate '1' R. 9/1)

Short extra flagstaff (Plate '2' R. 2/1)

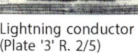

Lightning conductor (Plate '3' R. 2/5)

Flagstaff on right-hand turret (Plate '5' R. 7/1)

Double flagstaff
(Plate '6' R. 5/20)

(Des H. Fleury. Recess B.W.)

1935 (6 May). Silver Jubilee. Wmk Mult Script CA. Perf 11×12.

133	**28a**	3c. ultramarine and grey-black	4·00	3·50
		c. Lightning conductor	£375	£275
		e. Double flagstaff	£1100	
134		5c. green and indigo	8·50	2·75
		a. Extra flagstaff	£325	£300
		b. Short extra flagstaff	£425	£450
		c. Lightning conductor	£400	£300
		d. Flagstaff on right-hand turret	£650	£450
		e. Double flagstaff	£750	£650
135		10c. brown and deep blue	18·00	1·25
136		20c. slate and purple	32·00	12·00
		b. Short extra flagstaff	£900	£400
		d. Flagstaff on right-hand turret	£950	£475
		e. Double flagstaff	£1100	£500
133/136 Set of 4			55·00	18·00
133s/136s Perf 'SPECIMEN' Set of 4			£500	

28b King George VI and
Queen Elizabeth

(Des D.L.R. Recess B.W.)

1937 (12 May). Coronation. Wmk Mult Script CA. Perf 11×11½.

137	**28b**	4c. green	4·50	6·50
138		15c. carmine	8·00	3·00
139		25c. blue	10·00	5·50
137/139 Set of 3			20·00	13·50
137s/139s Perf 'SPECIMEN' Set of 3			£350	

29 King
George VI

Stop after 'CENTS' (Left pane R. 4/2)

Normal   Broken
          character
          (Left pane
          R. 6/6, later
          repaired)

Short right leg to 'R' (Right pane
R. 7/3, left pane R. 3/1)

1938–52. Wmk Mult Script CA. Chalk-surfaced paper (80c., $1 (No. 155), $2 (No. 157), $5 (No. 159), $10 (No. 161)). Perf 14.

140	**29**	1c. brown (24.5.38)	2·75	6·50
		aa. Doubly printed	£10000	
		a. Pale brown (4.2.52)	4·75	12·00
141		2c. grey (5.4.38)	2·00	1·00
		a. Perf 14½×14 (28.9.45)	1·75	7·00
142		4c. orange (5.4.38)	12·00	6·50
		a. Perf 14½×14 (28.9.45)	5·00	3·50
143		5c. green (24.5.38)	1·25	70
		a. Perf 14½×14 (28.9.45)	4·00	5·50
144		8c. red-brown (1.11.41)	1·75	3·50
		a. Imperf (pair)	£50000	—
		b. Stop after 'CENTS'	£350	£225
145		10c. bright violet (13.4.38)	50·00	1·50
		a. Perf 14½×14. Dull violet (28.9.45)	9·50	20
		b. Dull reddish violet (8.4.46)	10·00	1·75
		c. Reddish lilac (9.4.47)	25·00	25
146		15c. scarlet (13.4.38)	2·00	30
		a. Broken character	£130	50·00
147		20c. black (1.2.46)	1·50	30
148		20c. scarlet-vermilion (1.4.48)	14·00	40
		a. Rose-red (25.4.51)	28·00	5·50
149		25c. bright blue (5.4.38)	29·00	5·00
150		25c. pale yellow-olive (24.9.46)	8·50	4·75
151		30c. yellow-olive (13.4.38)	£150	4·00
		a. Perf 14½×14. Yellowish olive (28.9.45)	30·00	15·00
152		30c. blue (27.12.46)	7·00	20
153		50c. purple (13.4.38)	55·00	75
		a. Perf 14½×14. Deep magenta (28.9.45)	30·00	1·40
		ab. Printed both sides, inverted on reverse	£1100	†
		b. Reddish purple (9.4.46)	17·00	3·50
		c. Chalk-surfaced paper. Bright purple (9.4.47)	14·00	20
154		80c. carmine (2.2.48)	6·50	1·25
155		$1 dull lilac and blue (chalk-surfaced paper) (27.4.38)	10·00	4·25
		a. Short right leg to 'R'	£180	£190
		b. Ordinary paper. Pale reddish lilac and blue (28.9.45)	26·00	35·00
		ba. Short right leg to 'R'	£350	£400
156		$1 red-orange and green (8.4.46)	27·00	30
		a. Short right leg to 'R'	£275	65·00
		b. Chalk-surfaced paper (21.6.48)	55·00	2·25
		ba. Short right leg to 'R'	£450	95·00
		c. Chalk-surfaced paper. Yellow-orange and green (6.11.52)	90·00	15·00
		ca. Short right leg to 'R'	£750	£275
157		$2 red-orange and green (24.5.38)	80·00	45·00
158		$2 reddish violet and scarlet (8.4.46)	55·00	11·00
		a. Chalk-surfaced paper (9.4.47)	55·00	1·00
159		$5 dull lilac and scarlet (2.6.38)	75·00	55·00
160		$5 green and violet (8.4.46)	80·00	25·00
		a. Yellowish green and violet (8.4.46)	£600	48·00
		ab. Chalk-surfaced paper (9.4.47)	£130	5·00
161		$10 green and violet (2.6.38)	£750	£150
162		$10 pale bright lilac and blue (8.4.46)	£140	65·00
		a. Deep bright lilac and blue (8.4.46)	£325	80·00
		b. Chalk-surfaced paper. Reddish violet and blue (9.4.47)	£200	24·00
140/162 Set of 23			£1100	£275
140s/162s Perf 'SPECIMEN' Set of 23			£2750	

Following bomb damage to the De La Rue works on the night of 29 December 1940 various emergency arrangements were made to complete current requisitions for Hong Kong stamps:

No. 144a. One imperforate sheet was found and most of the stamps were sold singly to the public at a branch PO and used for postage.

Nos. 141a, 143a, 145a, 151a and 153a (all printings perforated 14½×14 except the 4c.) were printed and perforated by Bradbury Wilkinson & Co. Ltd. using De La Rue plates. These stamps are on rough-surfaced paper.

No. 142a was probably printed by Harrison & Sons, the major part of the printing being in undivided sheets of 120 (12×10) instead of the normal two panes of 60 (6×10).

Printings of the 1c. and dollar values and probably the 8c. were made by Williams, Lea & Co. using De La Rue plates.

With the exception of the 8c. it is believed that none of these printings were issued in Hong Kong before its occupation by the Japanese on 25 December 1941, although examples could be obtained in London from late 1941. The issue dates quoted are those on which the stamps were eventually released in Hong Kong following liberation in 1945.

Nos. 160/160a and 162/162a were separate printings released in Hong Kong on the same day.

30 Street Scene   **31** *Empress of Japan* (liner) and Junk

32 The University   **33** The Harbour

34 The Hong Kong Bank   **35** *Falcon* (clipper) and Short S.23 Empire C Class Flying Boat

(Des E. A. von Kobza Nagy and W. E. Jones. Recess B.W.)

1941 (26 Feb). Centenary of British Occupation. T **30/35**. Wmk Mult Script CA (sideways on horiz designs*). Perf 13½×13 (2c. and 25c.) or 13×13½ (others).

163		2c. orange and chocolate	8·00	3·00
164		4c. bright purple and carmine	9·50	5·00
165		5c. black and green	4·50	50
166		15c. black and scarlet	12·00	3·00
167		25c. chocolate and blue	20·00	10·00
168		$1 blue and orange	50·00	14·00
163/168	*Set of 6*		90·00	32·00
163s/168s Perf 'SPECIMEN' *Set of 6*			£550	

*   The sideways watermark shows Crown to left of CA, *as seen from the back of the stamp.*

Hong Kong was under Japanese occupation from 25 December 1941 until 30 August 1945. The Japanese post offices in the colony were closed from 31 August and mail was carried free, marked with cachets reading 'HONG KONG/1945/POSTAGE PAID'. Military administration lasted until 1 May 1946. Hong Kong stamps were re-introduced on 28 September 1945.

36 King George VI and Phoenix   Extra stroke (R. 1/2)

(Des E. I. Wynne-Jones and W. E. Jones. Recess D.L.R.)

1946 (29 Aug). Victory. Wmk Mult Script CA. Perf 13.

169	**36**	30c. blue and red (*shades*)	2·75	2·00
		a. Extra stroke	£140	90·00
170		$1 brown and red	3·25	75
		a. Extra stroke	£160	70·00
169s/170s Perf 'SPECIMEN' *Set of 2*			£275	

36A King George VI and Queen Elizabeth   **36b** King George VI and Queen Elizabeth

Spur on 'N' of 'KONG' (R. 2/9)

(Des and photo Waterlow (T **36a**). Design recess; name typo B.W. (T **36b**))

1948 (22 Dec). Royal Silver Wedding. Wmk Mult Script CA. Perf 14×15 (10c.) or 11½ ($10).

171	**36a**	10c. violet	3·75	1·50
		a. Spur on 'N'	£100	90·00
172	**36b**	$10 carmine	£275	£130

36c Hermes, Globe and Forms of Transport   **36d** Hemispheres, jet-powered Vickers Viking Airliner and Steamer

36e Hermes and Globe   **36f** UPU Monument

Crack in rock (R. 12/5)

(Des Waterlow (Types **36c/36f**). Design recess; name typo B.W. (Types **36d/36e**))

1949 (10 Oct). 75th Anniversary of Universal Postal Union. Wmk Mult Script CA. Perf 13½–14 (10c., 80c.) or 11×11½ (20c., 30c.).

173	**36c**	10c. violet	4·00	1·00
174	**36d**	20c. carmine-red	13·00	6·00
175	**36e**	30c. deep blue	10·00	6·00
176	**36f**	80c. bright reddish purple	30·00	4·00
		a. Crack in rock	£400	£190
173/176 *Set of 4*			50·00	15·00

37 Queen
Elizabeth II

(Des and eng B.W. Recess D.L.R.)

1953 (2 June). Coronation. Wmk Mult Script CA. Perf 13½×13.
177	**37**	10c. black and slate-lilac	4·00	30

37a Queen
Elizabeth II

$2 Normal   **$2** Short
character

$2 The top stroke in the right-hand upper character is shortened (Pl. 1-1, R. 6/4)

$1.30 Normal

$1.30 Short 'TI II' (Pl. 1·1, R. 10/10)

1954 (5 Jan)–**62**. Ordinary paper (5c. to 15c.) or chalk-surfaced paper (others). Wmk Mult Script CA. Perf 14.
178	**37a**	5c. orange	2·00	20
		a. Imperf (pair)	£2250	—
179		10c. lilac	3·00	10
		aw. Wmk inverted	£450	
		b. Reddish violet (25.1.61)	13·00	10
180		15c. green	4·00	3·75
		a. Pale green (6.12.55)	5·00	3·00
181		20c. brown	6·00	30
182		25c. scarlet	5·00	6·00
		a. Rose-red (26.6.58)	5·50	5·00
183		30c. grey	4·50	20
		a. Pale grey (26.2.58)	8·00	75
184		40c. bright blue	5·50	50
		a. Dull blue (10.1.61)	17·00	2·50
185		50c. reddish purple	6·50	20
186		65c. grey (20.6.60)	28·00	19·00
187		$1 orange and green	10·00	20
		a. Short right leg to 'R'	£180	23·00
188		$1.30 blue and red (20.6.60)	32·00	3·00
		a. Short 'THI'	£200	50·00
		b. Bright blue and red (23.1.62)	60·00	6·00
		ba. Short 'THI'	£450	90·00
189		$2 reddish violet and scarlet	16·00	1·10
		a. Short character	£200	50·00

		b. Light reddish violet and scarlet (26.2.58)	20·00	1·25
		ba. Short character	£225	50·00
190		$5 green and purple	95·00	5·00
		a. Yellowish green and purple (7.3.61)	£130	11·00
191		$10 reddish violet and bright blue	85·00	15·00
		a. Light reddish violet and bright blue (26.2.58)	£100	18·00
178/191		Set of 14	£250	45·00

No. 178a exists from two sheets, each of which had 90 stamps imperforate and ten perforated on three sides only.

The 10c. exists in coils constructed from normal sheets.

The duty plates for the King George VI issue were reformatted to reduce the sheet size from 120 (two panes of 60) to 100. In doing so, one of the 'short 'R' clichés was discarded. The other occurs on R. 10/9 of No. 187.

On Nos. 188a/188ba the duty plate appears bolder than in other positions.

38 University Arms   **39** Statue of Queen Victoria

(Des and photo Harrison)

1961 (11 Sept). Golden Jubilee of Hong Kong University. W w **12**. Perf 11½×12.
192	**38**	$1 multicoloured	10·00	2·00
		a. Gold ptg omitted	£3250	£3250

Normal   **10c.** White spot over character in lower right corner (Pl. 1A-1A, R. 1/3)

(Des Cheung Yat-man. Photo Harrison)

1962 (4 May). Stamp Centenary. W w **12**. Perf 14½.
193	**39**	10c. black and magenta	1·00	10
		a. Spot on character	10·00	
194		20c. black and light blue	5·00	2·25
195		50c. black and bistre	5·00	40
193/195		Set of 3	10·00	2·50

40 Queen Elizabeth II (after Annigoni)   **41** Queen Elizabeth II (after Annigoni)

Normal   Broken '5'

The horizontal bar of the '5' is missing (Pl. 1A, R. 3/1 and Pl. 1B, R. 2/2)

(Photo Harrison)

1962 (4 Oct)–**73**. Chalk-surfaced paper. W w **12** (upright). Perf 15×14 (5c. to $1) or 14×14½ (others).
196	**40**	5c. red-orange	75	60
		a. Broken '5'	21·00	
197		10c. bright reddish violet	1·50	10
		a. Reddish violet (19.11.71)	9·50	2·50
		ab. Glazed paper (14.4.72)	9·00	3·50

198		15c. emerald	3·25	4·25
199		20c. red-brown	2·50	2·00
		a. Brown (13.12.71).......	7·00	7·00
		ab. Glazed paper (27.9.72)..	14·00	20·00
200		25c. cerise	3·75	5·00
201		30c. deep grey-blue	2·50	10
		a. Chalky blue (19.11.71)	7·50	6·00
		ab. Glazed paper (27.9.72)..	17·00	11·00
202		40c. deep bluish green	5·00	70
203		50c. scarlet	1·75	30
		a. Vermilion (13.12.71)...	23·00	3·25
		ab. Glazed paper (27.9.72)..	10·00	4·00
204		65c. ultramarine	20·00	2·50
205		$1 sepia	24·00	40
206	**41**	$1.30 multicoloured	3·25	20
		a. Pale yellow omitted..........	65·00	
		b. Pale yellow inverted (horiz pair).......	£6500	
		c. Ochre (sash) omitted........	60·00	
		d. Glazed paper (3.2.71).......	22·00	3·00
		da. Ochre (sash) omitted.......	55·00	
		dw. Wmk inverted	40·00	
		dwa. Pale yellow omitted........	£140	
207		$2 multicoloured	6·50	1·00
		a. Pale yellow omitted†........	70·00	
		b. Ochre (sash) omitted........	60·00	
		c. Pale yellow† and ochre (sash) omitted..................	£275	
		dw. Wmk inverted	11·00	
		e. Glazed paper (1973)*......	£425	13·00
208		$5 multicoloured	15·00	1·75
		a. Ochre (sash) omitted........	60·00	
		ab. Pale yellow and ochre omitted......	£130	
		bw. Wmk inverted	42·00	
		c. Glazed paper (3.2.71).......	35·00	14·00
		cw. Wmk inverted	75·00	55·00
209		$10 multicoloured	26·00	3·00
		a. Ochre (sash) omitted........	£180	
		b. Pale yellow† and ochre (sash) omitted..................	£275	
		ba. Pale yellow† omitted........	£200	
		cw. Wmk inverted	£160	
		d. Glazed paper (1973)*......	£2250	£300
210		$20 multicoloured	65·00	32·00
		a. Ochre omitted	£325	
		w. Wmk inverted	£850	
196/210 Set of 15.....................			£160	42·00

*   These are from printings which were sent to Hong Kong in March 1973 but not released in London.
†   This results in the Queen's face appearing pinkish.
    No. 197 exists from coils.
    It is believed that No. 206b comes from the last two vertical rows of a sheet, the remainder of which had the pale yellow omitted.
    The $1.30 to $20 exist with PVA gum as well as gum arabic. The glazed paper printings are with PVA gum only.
    See also Nos. 222/236.

42 Protein Foods   **43** Red Cross Emblem

(Des M. Goaman. Photo Harrison)

1963 (4 June). Freedom from Hunger. W w **12**. Perf 14×14½.

211	**42**	$1.30 bluish green..............	30·00	4·00

(Des V. Whiteley. Litho B.W.)

1963 (2 Sept). Red Cross Centenary. W w **12**. Perf 13½.

212	**43**	10c. red and black..............	4·00	30
213		$1.30 red and blue	20·00	7·00

44 ITU Emblem   **45** ICY Emblem

(Des M. Goaman. Litho Enschedé)

1965 (17 May). ITU Centenary. W w **12**. Perf 11×11½.

214	**44**	10c. light purple and orange-yellow	3·00	25
		w. Wmk inverted............	70·00	
215		$1.30 olive-yellow and deep bluish green..........	16·00	5·00

(Des V. Whiteley. Litho Harrison)

1965 (25 Oct). International Co-operation Year. W w **12**. Perf 14½.

216	**45**	10c. reddish purple and turquoise-green....................	3·00	25
		w. Wmk inverted............	2·50	2·50
217		$1.30 deep bluish green and lavender (shades)................	12·00	3·50

 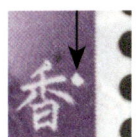

46 Sir Winston Churchill and St Paul's Cathedral in Wartime

10c. Large white dot to right of upper white Chinese character (Pl. 2B, R. 3/4).

(Des Jennifer Toombs. Photo Harrison)

1966 (24 Jan). Churchill Commemoration. Printed in black, cerise and gold and with background colours stated. W w **12**. Perf 14.

218	**46**	10c. new blue	3·00	15
		w. Wmk inverted............	26·00	
219		50c. deep green...............	5·00	30
		w. Wmk inverted............	3·00	4·00
220		$1.30 brown....................	20·00	2·00
221		$2 bluish violet	30·00	9·00
		w. Wmk inverted............	£225	
218/221 Set of 4..........................			55·00	10·00

> **WATERMARK BLOCK CA SIDEWAYS.** Unless otherwise stated, W w **12** sideways watermarks show Crown to left of CA, *as seen from the back of the stamp.*

1966 (1 Aug)–**72**. As Nos. 196/208 and 210 but W w **12** (sideways). Chalk-surfaced paper (5c. to $1) or glazed, ordinary paper ($1.30 to $20).

222	**40**	5c. red-orange (6.12.66)	65	1·25
223		10c. reddish violet (31.3.67)†	75	70
		a. Imperf (horiz pair)..........	£1100	
		b. Dot beside character..........	10·00	
		w. Wmk Crown to right of CA	£200	£170
224		15c. emerald (31.3.67)†	2·25	4·50
225		20c. red-brown	2·25	2·75
		a. Glazed, ordinary paper (14.4.72).....	8·50	16·00
226		25c. cerise (31.3.67)†	3·50	6·00
		aw. Wmk Crown to right of CA	45·00	
		b. Glazed, ordinary paper (14.4.72).....	15·00	27·00
227		30c. deep grey-blue (31.3.70)	10·00	8·00
		a. Glazed, ordinary paper (14.4.72).....	14·00	20·00
228		40c. deep bluish green (1967)	4·00	3·25
		a. Glazed, ordinary paper (14.4.72).....	14·00	23·00
229		50c. scarlet (31.3.67)†	2·75	1·25
		w. Wmk Crown to right of CA (13.5.69).................	4·00	3·00
230		65c. ultramarine (29.3.67)	7·00	13·00
		a. Bright blue (16.7.68)..........	12·00	18·00
231		$1 sepia (29.3.67)†	18·00	1·75
		w. Wmk Crown to right of CA	75·00	
232	**41**	$1.30 multicoloured (14.4.72)	15·00	3·50
		a. Pale yellow omitted..........	70·00	
		w. Wmk Crown to right of CA (17.11.72).................	18·00	4·75
233		wa. Ochre omitted..........	70·00	
		$2 multicoloured (13.12.71)	25·00	3·00
		b. Pale yellow omitted..........	75·00	
		w. Wmk Crown to right of CA (17.11.72).................	20·00	9·00
		wa. Ochre (sash) omitted..........	70·00	
234		$5 multicoloured (13.12.71)	90·00	32·00
		a. Pale yellow omitted..........	£170	
236		$20 multicoloured (14.4.72)	£180	95·00
222/236 Set of 14.....................			£300	£150

†   Earliest known postmark dates.
    The 5c. to 25c., 40c. and 50c. exist with PVA gum as well as gum arabic, but the 30c., and all stamps on glazed paper exist with PVA gum only.
    No. 223a also exists with both gums.

47 WHO Building

(Des M. Goaman. Litho Harrison)

1966 (20 Sept). Inauguration of WHO Headquarters, Geneva. W w **12** (sideways). Perf 14.

237	**47**	10c. black, yellow-green and light blue	3·00	30
238		50c. black, light purple and yellow-brown	9·00	2·25

48 'Education'   **48a** 'Science'

48b 'Culture'

1966 (1 Dec). 20th Anniversary of UNESCO. W w **12** (sideways). Perf 14. (Des Jennifer Toombs. Litho Harrison)

239	**48**	10c. slate-violet, red, yellow and orange	2·50	20
240	**48a**	50c. orange-yellow, violet and deep olive	5·50	90
241	**48b**	$2 black, light purple and orange	40·00	20·00
239/241	Set of 3		45·00	20·00

49 Rams' Heads on Chinese Lanterns

10c. White dot after '1967' (R. 2/2)

(Des V. Whiteley. Photo Harrison)

1967 (17 Jan). Chinese New Year. Year of the Ram. T **49** and similar horiz design. W w **12** (sideways). Perf 14½.

242		10c. rosine, olive-green and light yellow-olive	2·00	50
		a. Dot after '1967'	14·00	
243		$1.30 emerald, rosine and light yellow-olive..	15·00	6·50

Designs: 10c. T **49**; $1.30, Three Rams.

50 Cable Route Map

51 Rhesus Macaques in Tree. Year of the Monkey

(Des V. Whiteley. Photo Harrison)

1967 (30 Mar). Completion of Malaysia–Hong Kong Link of SEACOM Telephone Cable. W w **12**. Perf 12½.

244	**50**	$1.30 new blue and red	12·00	1·50

(Des R. Granger Barrett. Photo Harrison)

1968 (23 Jan). Chinese New Year. Year of the Monkey. T **51** and similar horiz design. W w **12** (sideways). Perf 14½.

245		10c. gold, black and scarlet	2·00	50
246		$1.30 gold, black and scarlet	15·00	6·50

Designs: 10c. T **51**; $1.30, Family of Rhesus Macaques.

52 *Iberia* (liner) at Ocean Terminal

(Des and litho D.L.R.)

1968 (24 Apr). Sea Craft. T **52** and similar horiz design. Perf 13.

247		10c. multicoloured	1·75	15
		a. Dull orange and new blue omitted	£2750	
248		20c. cobalt-blue, black and brown	2·50	1·75
249		40c. orange, black and mauve	7·50	14·00
250		50c. orange-red, black and green	5·00	75
		a. Green omitted	£1300	
251		$1 greenish yellow, black and red	7·00	8·00
252		$1.30 Prussian blue, black and pink	21·00	3·25
247/252	Set of 6		40·00	25·00

Designs: 10c. T **52**; 20c. Pleasure launch; 40c. Car ferry; 50c. Passenger ferry; $1, Sampan; $1.30, Junk.

53 *Bauhinia blakeana*

54 Arms of Hong Kong

(Des V. Whiteley. Photo Harrison)

1968 (25 Sept)–**73**. W w **12**. Perf 14×14½.

(a) Upright wmk. Chalk-surfaced paper.

253	**53**	65c. multicoloured	12·00	50
		aw. Wmk inverted	32·00	
		b. Glazed, ordinary paper (3.73)	£120	25·00
254	**54**	$1 multicoloured	12·00	40
		a. Glazed ordinary paper	£160	40·00

(b) Sideways wmk. Glazed, ordinary paper.

254b	**53**	65c. multicoloured (27.9.72)	65·00	40·00
254c	**54**	$1 multicoloured (13.12.71)	9·00	2·50

Nos. 253/254 exist with PVA gum as well as gum arabic.
Nos. 254b/254c with PVA gum only.

55 Aladdin's Lamp and Human Rights Emblem

(Des R. Granger Barrett. Litho B.W.)

1968 (20 Nov). Human Rights Year. W w **12** (sideways). Perf 13½.

255	**55**	10c. orange, black and myrtle-green	2·50	75
256		50c. yellow, black and deep reddish purple	4·00	2·50

56 Cockerel

(Des R. Granger Barrett. Photo Enschedé)

1969 (11 Feb). Chinese New Year. Year of the Rooster. T **56** and similar multicoloured design. Perf 13½.

257		10c. Type **56**	3·00	1·00
		a. Red omitted	£400	
258		$1.30 Cockerel (*vert*)	32·00	9·00

58 Arms of Chinese University

59 Earth Station and Satellite

(Des V. Whiteley. Photo Govt Ptg Bureau, Tokyo)

1969 (26 Aug). Establishment of Chinese University of Hong Kong. Perf 13½.

259	**58**	40c. violet, gold and pale turquoise-blue	6·00	3·00

(Des V. Whiteley. Photo Harrison)

1969 (24 Sept). Opening of Communications Satellite Tracking Station. W w **12**. Perf 14½.

260	**59**	$1 multicoloured	10·00	2·50

60 Chow's Head

62 Expo '70 Emblem

(Des R. Granger Barrett. Photo D.L.R.)

1970 (28 Jan). Chinese New Year. Year of the Dog. T **60** and similar design. W w **12** (sideways on $1.30). Perf 14½×14 (10c.) or 14×14½ ($1.30).

261	10c. lemon-yellow, orange-brown and black	3·00	1·00
262	$1.30 multicoloured	40·00	10·00

Designs: Vert—10c. T **60**. Horiz—$1.30, Chow standing.

(Des and litho B.W.)

1970 (14 Mar). World Fair Osaka. T **62** and similar multicoloured design. W w **12** (sideways on 25c.). Perf 13½×13 (15c.) or 13×13½ (25c.).

263	15c. Type **62**	3·50	85
264	25c. Expo '70 emblem and junks (*horiz*)	3·50	1·50

64 Plaque in Tung Wah Hospital

65 Symbol

(Des M. F. Griffith. Photo Harrison)

1970 (9 Apr). Centenary of Tung Wah Hospital. W w **12** (sideways). Perf 14½.

265	**64**	10c. multicoloured	2·00	25
266		50c. multicoloured	4·00	1·50
		w. Wmk Crown to right of CA	10·00	

(Des J. Cooter. Litho B.W.)

1970 (5 Aug). Asian Productivity Year. W w **12**. Perf 14×13½.

267	**65**	10c. multicoloured	3·00	1·00

66 Pig

(Des Kan Tai-keung. Photo Govt Ptg Bureau, Tokyo)

1971 (20 Jan). Chinese New Year. Year of the Pig. Perf 13½.

268	**66**	10c. multicoloured	2·50	90
269		$1.30 multicoloured	24·00	11·00

67 '60' and Scout Badge
68 Festival Emblem

(Des Kan Tai-keung. Litho Harrison)

1971 (23 July). Diamond Jubilee of Scouting in Hong Kong. W w **12** (sideways). Perf 14×15.

270	**67**	10c. black, scarlet and yellow	75	10
271		50c. black, green and blue	2·50	1·00
272		$2 black, magenta and bluish violet	12·00	12·00
270/272 *Set of 3*			14·00	12·00

(Litho Waddington)

1971 (2 Nov). Hong Kong Festival. T **68** and similar designs. W w **12** (sideways on 10c. and 50c.). Perf 14 (10c.) or 14½ (others).

273	**68**	10c. orange and purple	80	20
274	-	50c. multicoloured	1·25	60
275	-	$1 multicoloured	4·50	7·00
273/275 *Set of 3*			6·00	7·00

Designs: Horiz (39×23 mm)—50c. Coloured streamers. Vert (23×39 mm)—$1 'Orchid'.

69 Stylised Rat

(Des Kan Tai-keung. Photo D.L.R)

1972 (8 Feb). Chinese New Year. Year of the Rat. W w **12**. Perf 13½.

276	**69**	10c. red, gold and black	2·50	50
277		$1.30 gold, red and black	28·00	11·00
		w. Wmk inverted	50·00	38·00

70 Tunnel Entrance

(Des G. Drummond from painting by G. Baxter. Litho Harrison)

1972 (20 Oct). Opening of Cross-Harbour Tunnel. W w **12**. Perf 14×15.

278	**70**	$1 multicoloured	4·50	2·25
		a. Yellow (tunnel) missing	£3000	
		w. Wmk inverted	£110	

71 Phoenix and Dragon

72 Ox

(Des (from photograph by D. Groves) and photo Harrison)

1972 (20 Nov). Royal Silver Wedding. W w **12**. Perf 14×15.

279	**71**	10c. multicoloured	30	15
		a. Gold omitted	£1100	
280		50c. multicoloured	1·10	1·40
		a. Dull purple ('50c' 'HONG KONG' and background) double	£450	
		w. Wmk inverted	60·00	

(Des R. Granger Barrett. Photo Harrison)

1973 (25 Jan). Chinese New Year. Year of the Ox. W w **12** (sideways on 10c.). Perf 14½.

281	**72**	10c. reddish orange, brown and black..	75	50
282	–	$1.30 light yellow, yellow-orange and black	3·50	6·00
		w. Wmk inverted	28·00	

Design: $1.30 similar to 10c., but horiz.

73 Queen Elizabeth II   **74** Queen Elizabeth II

(Des from coinage. Photo ($10 and $20 also embossed) Harrison)

1973 (12 June)–**74**. W w **12** (sideways on 15c., 30c., 40c. $1.30, $2, $5, $10, $20). Perf 14½×14 (Nos. 283/291) or 14×14½ (Nos. 292/296).

283	**73**	10c. bright orange	1·25	60
		a. Wmk sideways (from coils)	1·75	2·50
284		15c. yellow-green	9·00	10·00
		w. Wmk Crown to left of CA (21.1.74)	9·50	12·00
285		20c. reddish violet	2·00	30
		w. Wmk inverted	3·50	
286		25c. lake-brown	11·00	8·50
287		30c. ultramarine	1·00	60
		w. Wmk Crown to left of CA (21.1.74)	4·50	2·50
288		40c. turquoise-blue	3·25	3·25
		a. Printed on the gummed side	£1250	
289		50c. light orange-vermilion	1·75	60
290		65c. greenish bistre	16·00	15·00
291		$1 bottle-green	2·25	80
292	**74**	$1.30 pale yellow and reddish violet	7·00	90
293		$2 pale green and reddish brown	8·00	1·25
294		$5 pink and royal blue	13·00	3·50
		a. Imperf (horiz pair)	£850	
		b. Pink omitted	£3250	
295		$10 pink and deep blackish olive	14·00	10·00
296		$20 pink and brownish black	28·00	38·00
		w. Wmk Crown to right of CA	75·00	
283/296 *Set of 14*			£100	80·00

*The normal sideways watermark shows Crown to right of CA on the 15c. and 30c., and to left of CA on 40c. and T **74**, *as seen from the back of the stamp*.

Nos. 295/296 are known with embossing omitted, but it has been reported that such errors can be faked.

No. 289 exists in coils constructed from normal sheets.

See also Nos. 311/324e and 340/353.

74a Princess Anne and Captain Mark Phillips   **75** Festival Symbols forming Chinese Character

(Des PAD Studio. Litho Questa)

1973 (14 Nov). Royal Wedding. Centre multicoloured. W w **12** (sideways). Perf 13½.

297	**74a**	50c. ochre	35	15
		w. Wmk Crown to right of CA	40·00	
298		$2 bright mauve	1·25	1·75

The normal sideways watermark shows Crown to left of CA, *as seen from the back of the stamp*.

(Des Kan Tai-keung. Litho B.W)

1973 (23 Nov). Hong Kong Festival. T **75** and similar horiz designs. W w **12**. Perf 14½.

299	**75**	10c. brownish red and bright green	40	10
		w. Wmk inverted	2·50	
300	–	50c. deep magenta and reddish orange	1·50	95
		w. Wmk inverted	6·50	
301		$1 bright green and deep mauve	3·50	4·00
299/301 *Set of 3*			4·75	4·50

Each value has the festival symbols arranged to form a Chinese character. 'Hong' on the 10c.; 'Kong' on the 50c.; 'Festival' on the $1.

76 Tiger   **77** Chinese Mask

(Des R. Granger Barrett. Litho Harrison)

1974 (8 Jan). Chinese New Year. Year of the Tiger. W w **12** (sideways* on $1.30). Perf 14½.

302	**76**	10c. multicoloured	2·00	50
		w. Wmk inverted	13·00	
303	–	$1.30 multicoloured	6·50	12·00
		w. Wmk Crown to left of CA	18·00	

Design: $1.30 Similar to T **76**, but vert.

*The normal sideways watermark shows Crown to right of CA, *as seen from the back of the stamp*.

(Des R. Hookham. Litho Enschedé)

1974 (1 Feb). Arts Festival. Vert designs as T **77** showing Chinese opera masks. W w **12** (sideways). Perf 12×12½.

304	**77**	10c. multicoloured	60	10
305	–	$1 multicoloured	2·50	3·00
306	–	$2 multicoloured	4·25	8·00
304/306 *Set of 3*			6·50	10·00
MS307 159×94 mm. Nos. 304/306. Wmk upright. Perf 14×13			28·00	35·00

78 Pigeons with Letters

(Des Kan Tai-keung. Litho Harrison)

1974 (9 Oct). Centenary of Universal Postal Union. T **78** and similar horiz designs. W w **12** (sideways* on 10 and 50c.). Perf 14½.

308		10c. light greenish blue, light yellow-green and slate-black	30	10
		aw. Wmk Crown to right of CA	3·25	
		b. No wmk	35·00	
309		50c. deep mauve, orange and slate-black	60	40
		w. Wmk Crown to right of CA	38·00	
310		$2 multicoloured	1·75	4·00
		w. Wmk inverted	13·00	
308/310 *Set of 3*			2·40	4·00

Designs: 10c. T **78**; 50c. Globe within letter; $2 Hands holding letters.

*The normal sideways watermark shows Crown to left of CA, *as seen from the back of the stamp*.

1975 (21 Jan)–**82**. New values (60c., 70c., 80c. and 90c.) or as Nos. 283/296 but W w **14** (sideways* on 10c., 20c., 25c., 50c., 65c. and $1).

311	**73**	10c. bright orange (21.2.75)	55	30
		a. Wmk upright (from coils) (10.78)	2·50	4·00
312		15c. yellow-green (21.1.75)	20·00	15·00
313		20c. reddish violet (19.3.75)	50	10
		a. *Deep reddish mauve* (21.6.77)	1·50	10
		b. *Deep reddish purple* (22.6.79)	1·50	10
		bw. Wmk Crown to right of CA	1·50	20

314		25c. lake-brown (19.3.75)	25·00	18·00
315		30c. ultramarine (9.4.75)	70	70
		a. *Deep ultramarine* (20.4.78)	1·50	70
		w. Wmk inverted	8·50	
316		40c. turquoise-blue (19.3.75)	1·25	2·50
		w. Wmk inverted	4·00	
317		50c. light orange-vermilion (19.3.75)	2·75	70
318		60c. lavender (4.5.77)	1·75	2·50
		w. Wmk inverted	11·00	
319		65c. greenish bistre (19.3.75)	30·00	13·00
320		70c. yellow (4.5.77)	1·75	1·00
		a. *Chrome-yellow* (24.1.80)	4·50	1·25
		w. Wmk inverted	11·00	
321		80c. bright magenta (4.5.77)	2·25	3·25
		a. *Magenta* (24.1.80)	3·25	3·75
		bw. Wmk inverted	8·00	
321c		90c. sepia (1.10.81)	4·00	2·75
		cw. Wmk inverted	£750	
322		$1 bottle-green (19.3.75)	3·00	75
		a. *Blackish olive* (24.1.80)	3·25	1·00
		w. Wmk Crown to right of CA	4·00	
323	**74**	$1.30 pale yellow and reddish violet (19.3.75)	2·50	30
		w. Wmk inverted	7·00	
324		$2 pale green and reddish brown (19.3.76)	3·00	1·25
		aa. Pale green omitted	£3250	
		a. *Pale green and brown* (10.5.82)	8·50	5·00
		bw. Wmk inverted	10·00	
324c		$5 pink and royal blue (20.4.78)	4·75	1·75
		ca. *Pink and deep ultramarine* (10.5.82)	17·00	4·50
		cw. Wmk inverted (10.5.82)	15·00	4·50
324d		$10 pink and deep blackish olive (20.4.78)	5·00	6·50
		dw. Wmk inverted	12·00	
324e		$20 pink and brownish black (20.4.78)	9·00	14·00
		ea. Imperf (horiz pair)	£800	
		ew. Wmk inverted	18·00	
311/324e *Set of 18*			£110	75·00

*The normal sideways watermark shows Crown to left of CA, *as seen from the back of the stamp.*

Nos. 324d/324e are known with the embossing omitted. See note after No. 296.

The 20c. and $20 from the printing released on 24 January 1980 were issued on two different papers, one ordinary and the other chalk-surfaced. All stamps from subsequent printings were also on chalk-surfaced paper. As the printed design covers the entire surface of the paper, it is not possible to identify the chalk surface on individual stamps.

79 Stylised Hare

(Des Kan Tai-keung. Litho Harrison)

1975 (5 Feb). Chinese New Year. Year of the Hare. T **79** and similar horiz design. Perf 14½.

(a) No wmk.

325	**79**	10c. silver and light red	1·00	75
326	–	$1.30 gold and light green	3·50	11·00

(b) W w 12.

327	**79**	10c. silver and light red	1·00	60
		w. Wmk inverted	45·00	
328	–	$1.30 gold and light green	3·00	5·50
		w. Wmk inverted	65·00	

Design: $1.30 Pair of Hares.

80 Queen Elizabeth II, the Duke of Edinburgh and Hong Kong Arms

(Des PAD Studio. Litho Questa)

1975 (30 Apr). Royal Visit. W w **14** (sideways). Perf 13½×14.

329	**80**	$1.30 multicoloured	2·00	1·25
330		$2 multicoloured	3·00	3·00

81 Mid-Autumn Festival   **82** Hwamei

(Des Tao Ho. Litho De La Rue, Bogota)

1975 (31 July). Hong Kong Festivals of 1975. T **81** and similar vert designs. Multicoloured. No wmk. Perf 14.

331		50c. Type **81**	2·00	50
332		$1 Dragon-boat Festival	5·50	2·50
		a. Black (oars, etc) omitted	£800	
		b. Printed on the gummed side		
333		$2 Tin Hau Festival	19·00	9·50
331/333 *Set of 3*			24·00	11·00
MS334 102×83 mm. Nos. 331/333			50·00	30·00

(Des C. Kuan. Litho Harrison)

1975 (29 Oct). Birds. T **82** and similar vert designs. Multicoloured. W w **14**. Perf 14½.

335		50c. Type **82**	2·00	50
		a. Brown omitted	£900	
		w. Wmk inverted	7·00	
336		$1.30 Chinese Bulbul	5·00	2·50
337		$2 Black-capped Kingfisher	12·00	8·50
		w. Wmk inverted	23·00	
335/337 *Set of 3*			18·00	10·50

The omission of the brown colour from No. 335a causes the bird to appear in the green underlay colour.

83 Dragon

(Des Kan Tai-keung. Litho Questa)

1976 (21 Jan). Chinese New Year. Year of the Dragon. T **83** and similar horiz design. W w **14** (sideways). Perf 14½.

338	**83**	20c. mauve, dull lake and gold	50	10
		w. Wmk Crown to right of CA	75·00	
339	–	$1.30 light yellow-green, light red and gold	3·00	2·50
		a. light red omitted	£1500	

No. 339 is as T **83** but has the design reversed.

*The normal sideways watermark shows Crown to left of CA, *as seen from the back of the stamp.*

1976 (20 Feb)–**00**. As Nos. 283, 285, 287 and 293/296 but without wmk.

340	**73**	10c. bright orange (coil stamp) (19.3.76)	28·00	12·00
342		20c. reddish violet	3·50	1·50
		a. Imperf (pair)	£750	
344		30c. ultramarine	8·00	2·75
		a. Imperf (pair)	£850	
350	**74**	$2 pale green and reddish brown	9·00	3·75
351		$5 pink and royal blue	17·00	7·00
352		$10 pink and deep blackish olive (19.3.76)	80·00	42·00
353		$20 pink and brownish black (19.3.76)	£180	65·00
340/353 *Set of 7*			£300	£120

No. 353 is known with the embossing omitted. See note after No. 296.

84 '60' and Girl Guides Badge   **20c.** Short 'N' in Hong (Plate 1B. R. 4/4)

(Des P. Ma. Photo Harrison)

1976 (23 Apr). Girl Guides Diamond Jubilee. T **84** and similar horiz design. Multicoloured. W w **12**. Perf 14½.

354	20c. Type **84**...	50	10
	a. Short 'N'..	12·00	
	w. Wmk inverted...................................	4·00	
355	$1.30 Badge, stylised diamond and '60'..........	2·50	2·50
	a. Background (light blue) omitted		
	w. Wmk inverted...................................	18·00	

85 'Postal Services' in Chinese Characters   **86** Tree Snake on Branch

(Des Tao Ho. Litho Harrison)

1976 (11 Aug). Opening of new GPO. T **85** and similar vert designs. W w **14**. Perf 14½.

356	20c. yellow-green, light greenish grey and black	75	10
	w. Wmk inverted...................................	£600	
357	$1.30 reddish orange, light greenish grey and black	2·00	1·50
358	$2 yellow, light greenish grey and black....	3·50	4·00
356/358 *Set of 3*		5·50	5·00

Designs: 20c. T **85**; $1.30, Old GPO; $2 New GPO.

(Des Jennifer Wong. Litho J.W)

1977 (6 Jan). Chinese New Year. Year of the Snake. T **86** and similar horiz design. W w **14** (sideways*). Perf 13½.

359	**86**	20c. multicoloured	50	15
360	**-**	$1.30 multicoloured	1·50	3·00
		w. Wmk Crown to left of CA	12·00	

The $1.30 shows a Snake facing left.

*The normal sideways watermark shows Crown to right of CA, *as seen from the back of the stamp.*

87 Presentation of the Orb

(Des Hong Kong Govt Services Dept; adapted J.W. Litho Harrison)

1977 (7 Feb). Silver Jubilee. T **87** and similar multicoloured designs. W w **14** (sideways on $2). Perf 14½×14 ($2) or 14×14½ (others).

361	20c. Type **87**...	40	10
	w. Wmk inverted...................................	50·00	
362	$1.30 Queen's visit, 1975	1·00	75
363	$2 The Orb (*vert*)	1·25	1·50
361/363 *Set of 3*		2·25	2·00

 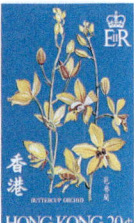

88 Tram Cars   **89** Buttercup Orchid

(Des Tao Ho. Litho J.W)

1977 (30 June). Tourism. T **88** and similar vert designs. Multicoloured. W w **14**. Perf 13½.

364	20c. Type **88**...	55	10
	w. Wmk inverted...................................	£650	£225

365	60c. Star Ferryboat	1·00	1·75
	w. Wmk inverted...................................	3·50	
366	$1.30 The Peak Railway	1·25	1·75
	w. Wmk inverted...................................	18·00	
367	$2 Junk and sampan	1·25	3·00
	w. Wmk inverted...................................	8·00	
364/267 *Set of 4*		3·50	6·00

(Des Beryl Walden. Litho Questa)

1977 (12 Oct). Orchids. T **89** and similar vert designs. Multicoloured. W w **14**. Perf 14½.

368	20c. Type **89**...	90	20
369	$1.30 Lady's Slipper Orchid........................	1·75	1·25
370	$2 Susan Orchid	3·00	3·75
368/370 *Set of 3*		5·00	4·75

90 Horse

(Des Graphic Atelier Ltd, Hong Kong. Litho Harrison)

1978 (26 Jan). Chinese New Year. Year of the Horse. W w **14** (sideways*). Perf 14½.

371	**90**	20c. magenta, yellow-olive and brown-olive	50	10
		w. Wmk Crown to left of CA	4·00	
372		$1.30 orange, yellow-brown and reddish brown	1·75	4·00

*The normal sideways watermark shows Crown to right of CA, *as seen from the back of the stamp.*

91 Queen Elizabeth II   **92** Girl and Boy holding Hands

(Des G. Vasarhelyi. Litho Harrison)

1978 (2 June). 25th Anniversary of Coronation. W w **14**. Perf 14×14½.

373	**91**	20c. magenta and ultramarine	30	10
374		$1.30 ultramarine and magenta	80	1·40
		w. Wmk inverted...................................	35·00	

(Des Annette Walker. Litho Harrison)

1978 (8 Nov). Centenary of Pa Leung Kuk (child care organisation). T **92** and similar horiz design. Multicoloured. W w **14** (sideways*). Perf 14½.

375	20c. Type **92**...	25	15
	w. Wmk Crown to left of CA	45	40
376	$1.30 Ring of children	75	1·60
	w. Wmk Crown to left of CA	1·50	2·75

*The normal sideways watermark shows the Crown to the right of CA *as seen from the back of the stamp.*

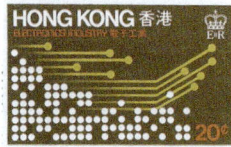

93 Electronics Industry

(Litho Harrison)

1979 (9 Jan). Industries. T **93** and similar horiz designs. W w **14** (sideways). Perf 14½.

377	20c. orange-yellow, olive-yellow and yellow-olive...	25	10
378	$1.30 multicoloured	55	1·25
379	$2 multicoloured	65	2·00
377/379 *Set of 3*		1·25	3·00

Designs: 20c. T **93**; $1.30 Toy industry; $2, Garment industry.

94 *Precis orithya*   **$2** Short right leg to 'R' (Plate 1B. R. 4/5)

(Des Jane Thatcher. Photo Harrison)

1979 (20 June). Butterflies. T **94** and similar vert designs. Multicoloured. No wmk. Perf 14½.

380	20c. Type **94**	30	10
381	$1 *Graphium sarpedon*	55	40
382	$1.30 *Heliophorus epicles*	60	70
383	$2 *Danus genutia*	75	3·00
	a. Short leg to 'R'	28·00	
380/383 *Set of 4*		2·00	3·75

95 Diagrammatic view of Railway Station

(Des Tao Ho. Litho J.W)

1979 (1 Oct). Mass Transit Railway. T **95** and similar horiz designs. Multicoloured. W w **14** (sideways*). Perf 13½.

384	20c. Type **95**	35	10
	w. Wmk Crown to left of CA	3·50	
385	$1.30 Diagrammatic view of car	55	40
	w. Wmk Crown to left of CA	13·00	
386	$2 Plan showing route of railway	65	1·40
	w. Wmk Crown to left of CA	75·00	
384/386 *Set of 3*		1·40	1·75

*The normal sideways watermark shows Crown to right of CA, *as seen from the back of the stamp.*

96 Tsui Shing Lau Pagoda   **97** Queen Elizabeth the Queen Mother

(Des D. Leonard. Litho J.W)

1980 (14 May). Rural Architecture. T **96** and similar designs. W w **14** (sideways on $1.30 and $2). Perf 13×13½ (20c.) or 13½×13 (others).

387	20c. black, magenta and yellow	25	20
	w. Wmk inverted	45·00	
388	$1.30 multicoloured	30	80
389	$2 multicoloured	65	1·75
387/389 *Set of 3*		1·25	2·50

Designs: Vert—20c. T **96**. Horiz—$1.30 Village House, Sai O; $2 Ching Chung Koon Temple.

(Des Harrison. Litho Harrison)

1980 (4 Aug). 80th Birthday of Queen Elizabeth the Queen Mother. W w **14** (sideways). Perf 14.

390	**97** $1.30 multicoloured	1·00	1·25

98 Botanical Gardens   **99** Red-spotted Grouper

(Des D. Chan. Litho J.W)

1980 (12 Nov). Parks. T **98** and similar vert designs. Multicoloured. W w **14**. Perf 13½.

391	20c. Type **98**	15	15
392	$1 Ocean Park	30	25
393	$1.30 Kowloon Park	35	35
394	$2 Country Parks	50	2·00
391/394 *Set of 4*		1·10	2·50

(Des Jane Thatcher. Litho J.W)

1981 (28 Jan). Fish. T **99** and similar horiz designs. Multicoloured. W w **14** (sideways*). Perf 13½.

395	20c. Type **99**	20	15
	w. Wmk Crown to left of CA	4·00	
396	$1 Golden Thread-finned Bream	40	35
397	$1.30 Scar-breasted Tuskfish	45	40
398	$2 Blue-barred Orange Parrotfish	55	2·00
395/398 *Set of 4*		1·40	2·50

*The normal sideways watermark shows Crown to right of CA, *as seen from the back of the stamp.*

100 Wedding Bouquet from Hong Kong   **101** Suburban Development

(Des J.W. Photo Harrison)

1981 (29 July). Royal Wedding. T **100** and similar vert designs. Multicoloured. W w **14** (sideways). Perf 14.

399	20c. Type **100**	20	10
400	$1.30 Prince Charles in Hong Kong	45	20
401	$5 Prince Charles and Lady Diana Spencer	1·00	2·00
399/401 *Set of 3*		1·50	2·00

(Des Tao Ho. Litho J.W)

1981 (14 Oct). Public Housing. T **101** and similar vert designs showing suburban development. W w **14**. Perf 13½.

402	20c. multicoloured	15	10
	a. Red (jacket and trousers) omitted	£300	
	w. Wmk inverted (pair)	£550	
403	$1 multicoloured	45	40
404	$1.30 multicoloured	50	50
405	$2 multicoloured	60	1·50
402/405 *Set of 4*		1·50	2·25
MS406 148×105 mm. Nos. 402/405. Wmk inverted		2·75	5·50
	w. Wmk upright	70·00	60·00

102 Victoria from the Harbour, *c* 1856

(Des R. Solley. Litho Questa)

1982 (5 Jan). Port of Hong Kong, Past and Present. T **102** and similar horiz designs. Multicoloured. W w **14**. Perf 14½.

407	20c. Type **102**		35	15
408	$1 West Point, Hong Kong, 1847		75	45
409	$1.30 Fleet of Junks		80	45
410	$2 Liner *Queen Elizabeth 2* at Hong Kong		1·50	1·90
407/410	*Set of 4*		3·00	2·75

103 Large Indian Civet

(Des Karen Phillipps. Litho Harrison)

1982 (4 May). Wild Animals. T **103** and similar horiz designs. W w **14** (sideways*). Perf 14½.

411	20c. black, salmon-pink and olive-bistre		20	15
	w. Wmk Crown to right of CA		25·00	
412	$1 multicoloured		35	35
413	$1.30 black, emerald and yellow-orange		40	45
	w. Wmk Crown to right of CA		35·00	
414	$5 black, orange-brown and greenish yellow		1·00	3·00
411/414	*Set of 4*		1·75	3·50

Designs: 20c. T **103**; $1 Chinese Pangolin; $1.30, Chinese Porcupine; $5 Indian Muntjac ('Barking Deer').

*The normal sideways watermark shows Crown to left of CA, *as seen from the back of the stamp.*

104 Queen Elizabeth II   **105** Queen Elizabeth II

(Des A. Hacker. Photo ($5 to $50 also embossed) Harrison)

1982 (30 Aug). W w **14** (sideways* on Nos. 427/430). Perf 14½×14 (Nos. 415/426) or 14×14½ (others).

415	**104**	10c. bright carmine, carmine and lemon	80	60
416		20c. bluish violet, violet and lavender	1·00	1·00
417		30c. bluish violet, violet and salmon	2·00	30
418		40c. vermilion and pale blue	1·50	30
419		50c. chestnut, orange-brown and sage-green	1·50	30
420		60c. bright purple and brownish grey	2·00	2·00
421		70c. deep grey-green, myrtle-green and orange-yellow	2·00	1·00
		a. Imperf (pair)	£800	
422		80c. bistre-brown, light brown and sage-green	2·00	3·00
423		90c. bottle-green, deep grey-green and pale turquoise-green	4·50	70
424		$1 reddish orange, red-orange and pale rose	2·25	30
425		$1.30 turquoise-blue and mauve	3·25	30
426		$2 ultramarine and flesh	4·00	60
427	**105**	$5 deep magenta, bright purple and olive-yellow	4·00	2·00
		w. Wmk Crown to right of CA	13·00	
428		$10 sepia and grey-brown	6·00	4·25
		w. Wmk Crown to right of CA	13·00	
429		$20 deep claret and pale blue	8·00	13·00
		w. Wmk Crown to right of CA	20·00	
430		$50 deep claret and brownish grey	23·00	28·00
		w. Wmk Crown to right of CA	45·00	
415/430		*Set of 16*	60·00	50·00

*The normal sideways watermark shows Crown to left of CA, *as seen from the back of the stamp.*

Nos. 415/430 come with a fluorescent security marking, 'Hong Kong' in Chinese characters encircled by the same in English, printed over the central oval of the design.

Nos. 415 and 424 also exist from coils.

No. 428 is known with the embossing omitted. See note after No. 296.

For similar stamps without watermark see Nos. 471/487.

106 Table Tennis   **107** Dancing

(Des A. Wong. Litho J.W)

1982 (20 Oct). Sport for the Disabled. T **106** and similar horiz designs. Multicoloured. W w **14**. Perf 14×14½.

431	30c. Type **106**		25	10
432	$1 Racing		45	60
433	$1.30 Basketball		1·50	75
434	$5 Archery		2·25	5·25
431/434	*Set of 4*		4·00	6·00

(Des Tao Ho. Litho J.W)

1983 (26 Jan). Performing Arts. T **107** and similar vert designs. W w **14** (sideways*). Perf 14½×14.

435	30c. cobalt and deep grey-blue		30	10
436	$1.30 rose and brown-purple		80	80
437	$5 bright green and deep green		2·25	4·00
435/437	*Set of 3*		3·00	4·50

Designs: 30c. T **107**; $1.30, Theatre; $5 Music.

108 Aerial View of Hong Kong

(Des local artist. Litho Enschedé)

1983 (14 Mar). Commonwealth Day. T **108** and similar horiz designs. Multicoloured. W w **14** (sideways*). Perf 14½×13.

438	30c. Type **108**		50	10
	w. Wmk Crown to right of CA		3·00	
439	$1 *Liverpool Bay* (container ship)		1·25	90
	w. Wmk Crown to right of CA		7·00	
440	$1.30 Hong Kong flag		1·25	90
	w. Wmk Crown to right of CA		8·00	
441	$5 Queen Elizabeth II and Hong Kong		2·75	5·00
438/441	*Set of 4*		5·25	6·25

*The normal sideways watermark shows Crown to left of CA, *as seen from the back of the stamp.*

109 Victoria Harbour

(Des Tao Ho. Litho Harrison)

1983 (17 Aug). Hong Kong by Night. T **109** and similar horiz designs. Multicoloured. W w **14** (sideways*). Perf 14½.

442	30c. Type **109**		1·00	15
	w. Wmk Crown to right of CA		4·50	
443	$1 Space Museum, Tsim Sha Tsui Cultural Centre		2·50	1·00
444	$1.30 Fireworks display		3·00	1·25
	a. Silver (value and inscr) omitted		£1500	
445	$5 Jumbo, floating restaurant		9·00	10·00
	a. Silver (value and inscr) omitted		£5000	
442/445	*Set of 4*		14·00	11·00

*The normal sideways watermark shows Crown to left of CA, *as seen from the back of the stamp.*

110 Old and New Observatory Buildings

(Des C. Shun Wah. Litho Harrison)

1983 (23 Nov). Centenary of Hong Kong Observatory. T **110** and similar horiz designs. W w **14** (sideways). Perf 14½.

446	40c. yellow-orange, bistre-brown and black	45	10
447	$1 reddish mauve, deep mauve and black	75	75
448	$1.30 new blue, steel-blue and black.............	80	75
449	$5 olive-yellow, brown-olive and black......	3·00	6·75
446/449 *Set of 4*..............		4·50	7·50

Designs: 40c. T **110**; $1 Wind-measuring equipment; $1.30 Thermometer; $5 Ancient and modern seismometers.

111 de Havilland DH.86 Dragon Express *Dorado* (Hong Kong Penang Service, 1936)

(Des M. Harris. Litho J.W)

1984 (7 Mar). Aviation in Hong Kong. T **111** and similar multicoloured designs. W w **14** (sideways* on 40c. to $1.30, inverted on $5). Perf 13½.

450	40c. Type **111**	75	15
	w. Wmk Crown to left of CA	7·00	
451	$1 Sikorsky S-42B flying boat *Hong Kong Clipper* (San Francisco–Hong Kong Service, 1937)................	1·00	1·00
452	$1.30 Cathay Pacific Boeing 747 jet leaving Kai Tak Airport..............	1·10	1·00
453	$5 Baldwin brothers' balloon, 1891 (*vert*)..	3·25	8·50
450/453 *Set of 4*................		5·50	9·50

*The normal sideways watermark shows Crown to right of CA, *as seen from the back of the stamp.*

112 Map by Captain E. Belcher, 1836

(Des R. Solley. Litho B.D.T)

1984 (21 June). Maps of Hong Kong. T **112** and similar horiz designs. Multicoloured. W w **14** (sideways). Perf 14.

454	40c. Type **112**........................	1·00	20
455	$1 Bartholomew map of 1929................	1·50	1·00
456	$1.30 Early map of Hong Kong waters.............	1·75	1·00
457	$5 Chinese-style map of 1819..................	8·50	11·00
454/457 *Set of 4*................		11·50	12·00

113 Cockerel

(Des J. Yim. Litho Cartor)

1984 (6 Sept). Chinese Lanterns. T **113** and similar horiz designs showing stylised animals as lanterns. Multicoloured. W w **14** (sideways*). Perf 13½x13.

458	40c. Type **113**	75	15
	w. Wmk Crown to right of CA	12·00	

459	$1 Dog.................	1·50	1·25
460	$1.30 Butterfly................	2·00	1·25
461	$5 Fish................	8·00	12·00
458/461 *Set of 4*................		11·00	13·00

*The normal sideways watermark shows Crown to left of CA, *as seen from the back of the stamp.*

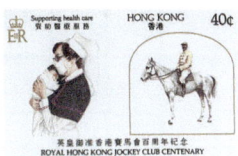

114 Jockey on Horse and Nurse with Baby ('Health Care')

(Des M. Harris. Litho Walsall)

1984 (21 Nov). Centenary of Royal Hong Kong Jockey Club. T **114** and similar horiz designs showing aspects of Club's charity work. Multicoloured. W w **14** (sideways*). Perf 14.

462	40c. Type **114**	1·25	20
463	$1 Disabled man playing handball ('Support for Disabled')	2·00	1·75
464	$1.30 Ballerina ('The Arts')................	3·00	2·00
	w. Wmk Crown to right of CA	3·00	
465	$5 Humboldt Penguins ('Ocean Park')	9·00	12·00
462/465 *Set of 4*................		14·00	14·50
MS466 178×98 mm. Nos. 462/465................		23·00	28·00

*The normal sideways watermark shows Crown to left of CA, *as seen from the back of the stamp.*

115 Hung Sing Temple

(Des M. Harris. Litho J.W)

1985 (14 Mar). Historic Buildings. T **115** and similar horiz designs. Multicoloured. Perf 13½.

467	40c. Type **115**................	40	20
468	$1 St John's Cathedral..................	70	1·00
469	$1.30 The Old Supreme Court Building...........	75	1·00
470	$5 Wan Chai Post Office	3·00	7·00
467/470 *Set of 4*................		4·25	8·00

1985 (13 June)–**87**. As Nos. 415/416, 418/430 and new value ($1.70). No wmk. Perf 14½×14 (10c. to $2) or 14×14½ (others).

471	**104**	10c. bright carmine, carmine and lemon (23.10.85)	70	1·50
472		20c. bluish violet, violet and lavender (6.87)................	25·00	22·00
474		40c. vermilion and pale blue (23.10.85)	1·00	2·00
475		50c. chestnut, orange-brown and sage green (7.4.86)	1·00	40
476		60c. bright purple and brownish grey (23.10.85)................	1·75	1·10
477		70c. deep grey-green, myrtle-green and orange-yellow (3.10.85)..........	4·50	1·00
478		80c. bistre-brown light brown and sage-green (23.10.85)	4·50	4·00
479		90c. bottle-green, deep grey-green and pale turquoise-green (23.10.85)................	7·00	75
480		$1 reddish orange, red-orange and pale rose (23.10.85)	1·75	40
		a. Imperf (horiz pair)................	2·50	45
481		$1.30 turquoise-blue and mauve	1·00	40
482		$1.70 dull ultramarine, bright blue and bright green (2.9.85)	5·00	1·50
483		$2 ultramarine and flesh (23.10.85)	3·75	1·50
484	**105**	$5 deep magenta, bright purple and olive-yellow (2.10.85)	10·00	3·75
485		$10 sepia and grey-brown (23.10.85) ...	10·00	5·00
486		$20 deep claret and pale blue (23.10.85)	14·00	7·50
487		$50 deep claret and brownish grey (23.10.85)	35·00	28·00
471/487 *Set of 16*................			£120	70·00

No. 475 was first issued in booklets (No. SB20). It was released in sheets on 23 October 1986.

116 Prow of Dragon Boat

117 The Queen Mother with Prince Charles and Prince William, 1984

(Des R. Hookham. Litho Cartor)

1985 (19 June). Tenth International Dragon Boat Festival. T **116** and similar horiz designs showing different parts of Dragon Boat. Multicoloured. Perf 13½×13.

488	40c. Type **116**	50	15
489	$1 Drummer and rowers	1·75	1·25
490	$1.30 Rowers	3·00	1·60
491	$5 Stern of boat	9·25	11·00
488/491 Set of 4		13·00	12·50
MS492 190×100 mm. Nos. 488/491. Perf 13×12		18·00	22·00

(Des C. Abbott. Litho Questa)

1985 (7 Aug). Life and Times of Queen Elizabeth the Queen Mother. T **117** and similar vert designs. Multicoloured. Perf 14½×14.

493	40c. At Glamis Castle, aged 7	50	10
494	$1 Type **117**	1·50	1·00
495	$1.30 The Queen Mother, 1970 (from photo by Cecil Beaton)	1·75	1·10
496	$5 With Prince Henry at his christening (from photo by Lord Snowdon)	3·00	4·75
493/496 Set of 4		6·00	6·25

118 Melastoma

(Des N. Jesse. Litho B.D.T)

1985 (25 Sept). Native Flowers. T **118** and similar horiz designs. Multicoloured. Perf 13½.

497	40c. Type **118**	75	20
498	50c. Chinese Lily	75	40
499	60c. Grantham's Camellia	1·00	1·75
500	$1.30 Narcissus	1·75	1·25
501	$1.70 Bauhinia	2·00	1·50
502	$5 Chinese New Year Flower	3·75	12·00
497/502 Set of 6		9·00	15·00

A limited edition prestige booklet *sold at* $35 was issued on 17 June 2000. This contained three panes each of one value with elliptical perforations in re-drawn designs as Nos. 501, 840 and 998 but all inscribed 'HONG KONG, CHINA' (*Price, £18 unused*).

119 Hong Kong Academy for Performing Arts

(Des N. Jesse. Litho Format)

1985 (27 Nov). New Buildings. T **119** and similar multicoloured designs. Perf 15.

503	50c. Type **119**	50	15
504	$1.30 Exchange Square (*vert*)	70	45
505	$1.70 Hong Kong Bank Headquarters (*vert*)	70	45
506	$5 Hong Kong Coliseum	1·25	4·50
503/506 Set of 4		2·75	5·00

120 Halley's Comet in the Solar System

120a At Wedding of Miss Celia Bowes-Lyon, 1931

(Des A. Chan. Litho Cartor)

1986 (26 Feb). Appearance of Halley's Comet. T **120** and similar horiz designs. Multicoloured. Perf 13½×13.

507	50c. Type **120**	75	20
508	$1.30 Edmond Halley and Comet	1·00	80
509	$1.70 Comet over Hong Kong	1·10	85
510	$5 Comet passing the Earth	3·75	9·00
507/510 Set of 4		6·00	9·75
MS511 135×80 mm. Nos. 507/510		13·00	25·00

(Des A. Theobald. Litho Harrison)

1986 (21 Apr). 60th Birthday of Queen Elizabeth II. T **120a** and similar vert designs. Multicoloured. Perf 14½×14.

512	50c. Type **120a**	35	10
513	$1 Queen in Garter procession, Windsor Castle, 1977	50	40
514	$1.30 In Hong Kong, 1975	60	45
515	$1.70 At Royal Lodge, Windsor, 1980 (from photo by Norman Parkinson)	65	55
516	$5 At Crown Agents Head Office, London, 1983	2·00	4·00
512/516 Set of 5		3·50	5·00

121 Mass Transit Train, Boeing 747 Airliner and Map of World

(Des Agay Ng Kee Chuen. Litho B.D.T)

1986 (18 July). Expo '86 World Fair, Vancouver. T **121** and similar horiz designs. Multicoloured. Perf 13½.

517	50c. Type **121**	70	30
518	$1.30 Hong Kong Bank Headquarters and map of world	1·25	80
519	$1.70 Container ship and map of world	1·60	1·10
520	$5 Dish aerial and map of world	3·00	7·50
517/520 Set of 4		6·00	8·75

122 Hand-liner Sampan

123 *The Second Puan Khequa* (attr Spoilum)

(Des Graphic Communications Ltd. Litho B.D.T)

1986 (24 Sept). Fishing Vessels. T **122** and similar horiz designs, each showing fishing boat and outline of fish. Multicoloured. Perf 13½.

521	50c. Type **122**	60	15
522	$1.30 Stern trawler	1·10	75
523	$1.70 Long liner junk	1·25	80
524	$5 Junk trawler	3·50	8·00
521/524 Set of 4		5·75	8·75

(Des R. Solley. Litho B.D.T)

1986 (9 Dec). 19th-century Hong Kong Portraits. T **123** and similar vert designs. Multicoloured. Perf 14×13½.

525	50c. Type **123**	35	15
526	$1.30 *Chinese Lady* (19th-century copy)	80	1·00

527	$1.70 *Lamqua* (self-portrait)	90	1·10
528	$5 *Wife of Wo Hing Qua* (attr G. Chinnery) .	2·50	6·00
525/528 *Set of 4*		4·00	7·50

124 Rabbit

(Des Kan Tai-keung. Lithe B.D.T)

1987 (21 Jan). Chinese New Year. Year of the Rabbit. T **124** and similar horiz designs showing stylised Rabbits. Perf 13½.

529	50c. multicoloured	75	15
530	$1.30 multicoloured	1·25	1·10
531	$1.70 multicoloured	1·40	1·10
532	$5 multicoloured	5·00	6·50
529/532 *Set of 4*		7·75	8·00
MS533 133×84 mm. Nos. 529/532		28·00	30·00

Nos. 530/531 have the '0' omitted from their face values.

125 *Village Square, Hong Kong Island, 1838* (Auguste Borget)

126 Queen Elizabeth II and Central Victoria

(Des J. Yim. Litho B.D.T.)

1987 (23 Apr). 19th-century Hong Kong Scenes. T **125** and similar horiz designs. Multicoloured. Perf 14.

534	50c. Type **125**	80	15
535	$1.30 *Boat Dwellers, Kowloon Bay, 1838* (Auguste Borget)	2·25	1·25
536	$1.70 *Flagstaff House, 1846* (Murdoch Bruce) .	2·75	1·40
537	$5 *Wellington Street, late 19th-century* (C. Andrasi)	7·50	11·00
534/537 *Set of 4*		12·00	12·50

Two types of Nos. 538/552.

I. Heavy shading under mouth and cheek

II. Lighter shading

(Des R. Hookham. Litho Leigh-Mardon Ltd, Melbourne)

1987 (13 July)–**88**. T **126** and similar vert designs, each showing Queen Elizabeth II and Hong Kong skyline. Perf 14½×14 (10c. to $2) or 14 ($5 to $50).

A. Shading as Type I.

538A	**126**	10c. multicoloured	80	1·00
539A		40c. multicoloured	1·75	2·50
540A		50c. multicoloured	1·00	40
541A		60c. multicoloured	2·25	1·50
542A		70c. multicoloured	2·00	1·25
543A		80c. multicoloured	2·75	2·50
544A		90c. multicoloured	2·75	1·00
545A		$1 multicoloured	2·25	70
546A		$1.30 multicoloured	3·00	80
547A		$1.70 multicoloured	3·00	80
548A		$2 multicoloured	3·00	1·25
549A	-	$5 multicoloured	8·00	1·75
550A	-	$10 multicoloured	8·50	4·50
551A	-	$20 multicoloured	13·00	13·00
552A	-	$50 multicoloured	20·00	29·00
538A/552A *Set of 15*			65·00	55·00

B. Shading as Type II (1.9.88).

538B	**126**	10c. multicoloured	75	65
539B		40c. multicoloured	1·75	2·00
540B		50c. multicoloured	1·50	60
541B		60c. multicoloured	1·75	1·25
542B		70c. multicoloured	2·00	80
543B		80c. multicoloured	2·00	2·50
544B		90c. multicoloured	2·25	1·00
545B		$1 multicoloured	8·50	2·50
546B		$1.30 multicoloured	3·50	1·25
546cB		$1.40 multicoloured	3·00	3·50
547B		$1.70 multicoloured	9·00	4·00
547cB		$1.80 multicoloured	3·00	1·75
548B		$2 multicoloured	3·50	1·25
549B	-	$5 multicoloured	5·00	2·00
550B	-	$10 multicoloured	15·00	4·50
551B	-	$20 multicoloured	20·00	10·00
552B	-	$50 multicoloured	45·00	18·00
538B/552B *Set of 17*			£120	50·00

Designs (25×31 mm): $5 Kowloon; $10 Victoria Harbour; $20 Legislative Council Building; $50 Government House.

Nos. 538/552 carry the fluorescent security markings as described beneath Nos. 415/430 with the $5 to $50 values showing an additional vertical fluorescent bar at right.

For these stamps as Type II, but with imprint dates, see Nos. 600/615.

127 Hong Kong Flag

128 Alice Ho Miu Ling Nethersole Hospital, 1887

(Des R. Hookham. Photo Enschedé)

1987 (13 July)–**92**. Coil Stamps. T **127** and similar vert designs. Perf 14½×14.

(a) Without imprint date.

553	10c. multicoloured	1·00	2·50
554	50c. bistre, lake and black	2·00	3·00

(b) With imprint date.

554a	10c. multicoloured (1.8.89)	1·25	1·00
554b	50c. bistre, lake and black (1.8.89)	1·50	1·75
554c	80c. bright mauve, deep blue-green and black (26.3.92)	2·50	5·00
554d	90c. bright blue, reddish brown and black (26.3.92)	2·50	3·00
554e	$1.80 bright emerald, royal blue and black (26.3.92)	3·00	4·00
554f	$2.30 orange-brown, deep violet and black (26.3.92)	3·50	5·50
554a/554f *Set of 6*		14·00	18·00

Design: 10c. T **127**; 50c. to $2.30, Map of Hong Kong.

Nos. 553/554f carry the fluorescent security marking as described beneath Nos. 415/430.

The printings with imprint date have every fifth stamp in the rolls of 1,000 numbered on the reverse.

Imprint dates: '1989', Nos. 554a/554b; '1990', No. 554a, '1991', Nos. 554a/554f.

(Des A. Fang. Litho Walsall)

1987 (8 Sept). Hong Kong Medical Centenaries. T **128** and similar horiz designs. Multicoloured. Perf 14½.

555	50c. Type **128**	1·25	20
556	$1.30 Matron and nurses, Nethersole Hospital, 1891	2·50	1·40
557	$1.70 Scanning equipment, Faculty of Medicine	3·00	1·40
558	$5 Nurse and patient, Faculty of Medicine	9·00	9·00
555/558 *Set of 4*		14·00	11·00

129 Casual Dress with Fringed Hem, 220–589

(Des Sumiko Davies. Litho CPE Australia Ltd, Melbourne)

1987 (18 Nov). Historical Chinese Costumes. T **129** and similar horiz designs. Multicoloured. Perf 13½.

559	50c. Type **129**	40	10
560	$1.30 Two-piece dress and wrap, 581–960	80	70
561	$1.70 Formal dress, Song Dynasty, 950–1279	90	80
562	$5 Manchu empress costume, 1644–1911	2·25	6·00
559/562 *Set of 4*		4·00	7·00

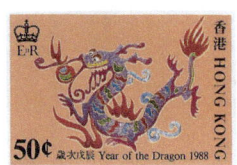

130 Dragon

131 White-breasted Kingfisher

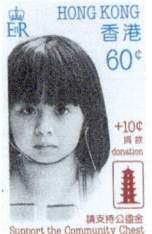

134 Hong Kong Catholic Cathedral

135 Deaf Girl

(Des Kan Tai-keung. Litho CPE Australia Ltd, Melbourne)

1988 (27 Jan). Chinese New Year. Year of the Dragon. T **130** and similar horiz designs showing Dragons. Perf 13½.

563	50c. multicoloured	50	15
564	$1.30 multicoloured	1·00	80
565	$1.70 multicoloured	1·10	85
566	$5 multicoloured	2·50	5·00
563/566 Set of 4		4·50	6·00
MS567 134×88 mm. Nos. 563/566		9·00	12·00

(Des Karen Phillipps. Litho CPE Australia Ltd, Melbourne)

1988 (20 Apr). Hong Kong Birds. T **131** and similar vert designs. Multicoloured. Perf 13½.

568	50c. Type **131**	75	30
569	$1.30 Fujian Niltava	1·00	80
570	$1.70 Black Kite	1·40	1·00
571	$5 Lesser Pied Kingfisher	2·75	5·50
568/571 Set of 4		5·50	7·00

(Des C. Buendia. Litho CPE Australia Ltd, Melbourne)

1988 (30 Sept). Centenary of Hong Kong Catholic Cathedral. Perf 14.

582	**134**	60c. multicoloured	1·00	1·50

(Des M. Tucker. Litho Harrison)

1988 (30 Nov). Community Chest Charity. T **135** and similar vert designs. Perf 14½.

583	60c.+10c. brownish black, vermilion and greenish blue	40	80
584	$1.40+20c. brownish black, vermilion and bright green	50	1·00
585	$1.80+30c. brownish black, vermilion and bright orange	65	1·25
586	$5+$1 brownish black, vermilion and yellow-brown	1·00	4·00
583/586 Set of 4		2·25	6·25

Designs: 60c. T **135**; $1.40 Elderly woman; $1.80 Blind boy using braille typewriter; $5 Mother and baby.

132 Chinese Banyan

133 Lower Terminal, Peak Tramway

(Des A. Chan. Litho B.D.T)

1988 (16 June). Trees of Hong Kong. T **132** and similar vert designs. Multicoloured. Perf 13½.

572	50c. Type **132**	30	10
573	$1.30 Hong Kong Orchid Tree	55	40
574	$1.70 Cotton Tree	65	55
575	$5 Schima	1·75	4·50
572/575 Set of 4		3·00	5·00
MS576 135×85 mm. Nos. 572/575		12·00	10·00

> A limited edition prestige booklet *sold at* $30 was issued on 21 July 2001. This contained two panes each containing two values in re-drawn designs as Nos. 572/575 but all inscribed 'HONG KONG, CHINA' (*Price*, £16 *unused*).

(Des Lilian Tang. Litho Leigh-Mardon Ltd, Melbourne)

1988 (4 Aug). Centenary of The Peak Tramway. T **133** and similar vert designs. Multicoloured. Perf 14½×15.

577	50c. Type **133**	30	10
578	$1.30 Tram on incline	60	80
579	$1.70 Peak Tower Upper Terminal	70	1·00
580	$5 Tram	2·00	4·50
577/580 Set of 4		3·25	5·75
MS581 160×90 mm. Nos. 577/580		10·00	12·00

136 Snake

(Des Kan Tai-keung. Litho Enschedé)

1989 (18 Jan). Chinese New Year. Year of the Snake. T **136** and similar horiz designs. Multicoloured. Perf 13½×14.

587	60c. Type **136**	45	15
	a. Booklet pane. Nos. 587 and 589, each×5	8·50	
588	$1.40 Snake and Fish	1·50	70
589	$1.80 Snake on branch	1·60	85
590	$5 Coiled Snake	4·50	7·25
587/590 Set of 4		7·25	8·00
MS591 135×85 mm. Nos. 587/590		12·00	10·00

137 Girl and Doll

138 *Twins* (wood carving, Cheung Yee)

(Des M. Tucker. Litho B.D.T)

1989 (4 May). Cheung Chair Bun Festival. T **137** and similar vert designs. Multicoloured. Perf 13½.

592	60c. Type **137**	40	15
593	$1.40 Girl in festival costume	85	70
594	$1.80 Paper effigy of god Tani Si Wong	90	80
595	$5 Floral gateway	2·50	5·00
592/595 Set of 4		4·25	6·00

(Des Kan Tai-keung. Litho Enschedé)

1989 (19 July). Modern Art. T **138** and similar vert designs. Multicoloured. Perf 12×12½.

596	60c. Type **138**	40	15
597	$1.40 *Figures* (acrylic on paper, Chan Luis)	80	80
598	$1.80 *Lotus* (copper sculpture, Van Lau)	90	90
599	$5 *Zen Painting* (ink and colour on paper, Lou Shou-kwan)	2·00	4·75
596/599 *Set of 4*		3·50	6·00

1989 (1 Aug)–**91**. As Nos. 538B/552B, and new values, with imprint date added to designs. Perf 14½×14 (10c. to $2.30) or 14 ($5 to $50).

A. Imprint date '1989' (1.8.89).

600A	126	10c. multicoloured	1·00	1·25
601A		40c. multicoloured	2·75	4·00
602A		50c. multicoloured	1·50	1·00
603A		60c. multicoloured	1·75	30
604A		70c. multicoloured	2·50	2·50
605A		80c. multicoloured	2·50	2·00
606A		90c. multicoloured	1·75	1·25
607A		$1 multicoloured	2·25	1·00
608A		$1.30 multicoloured	4·00	2·50
609A		$1.40 multicoloured	4·00	1·25
610A		$1.80 multicoloured	1·75	60
611A		$2 multicoloured	2·50	50
612A	-	$5 multicoloured	7·00	1·50
613A	-	$10 multicoloured	10·00	6·00
614A	-	$20 multicoloured	16·00	11·00
615A	-	$50 multicoloured	25·00	22·00

B. Imprint date '1990' (1990).

600B	126	10c. multicoloured	1·00	1·25
601B		40c. multicoloured	2·75	4·00
602B		50c. multicoloured	1·50	1·00
603B		60c. multicoloured	1·75	30
604B		70c. multicoloured	2·50	2·50
605B		80c. multicoloured	2·50	2·00
606B		90c. multicoloured	1·75	1·25
607B		$1 multicoloured	2·25	1·00
608B		$1.30 multicoloured	4·00	2·50
609B		$1.40 multicoloured	4·00	1·25
610B		$1.80 multicoloured	1·75	60
611B		$2 multicoloured	2·50	50
612B	-	$5 multicoloured	7·00	1·50
613B	-	$10 multicoloured	10·00	6·00
614B	-	$20 multicoloured	16·00	11·00
615B	-	$50 multicoloured	25·00	22·00

C. Imprint date '1991' (2.4.91).

600C	126	10c. multicoloured	1·10	1·25
602C		50c. multicoloured	2·00	1·00
603C		60c. multicoloured	2·50	30
604C		70c. multicoloured	3·50	2·50
605C		80c. multicoloured	3·50	2·50
606C		90c. multicoloured	2·50	1·25
607C		$1 multicoloured	3·25	1·00
607Ca		$1.20 multicoloured	4·00	3·75
609Ca		$1.70 multicoloured	4·00	5·00
610C		$1.80 multicoloured	1·75	60
611C		$2 multicoloured	3·50	50
611Ca		$2.30 multicoloured	4·00	3·75
612C	-	$5 multicoloured	8·50	2·00
613C	-	$10 multicoloured	12·00	6·50
614C	-	$20 multicoloured	20·00	11·00
615C	-	$50 multicoloured	20·00	22·00

For miniature sheets containing No. 613 see Nos. **MS**646, **MS**684, **MS**685 and **MS**701.

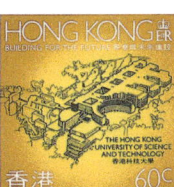

139 Lunar New Year Festivities

140 University of Science and Technology

(Des Sumiko Davies. Litho Enschedé)

1989 (6 Sept). Hong Kong People. T **139** and similar vert designs. Multicoloured. Perf 13×14½.

616	60c. Type **139**	75	10
617	$1.40 Shadow boxing and horse racing	2·00	80
618	$1.80 Foreign-exchange dealer and traditional builder	2·00	90
619	$5 Multi-racial society	4·50	8·00
616/619 *Set of 4*		8·25	8·75

For miniature sheet containing design as $5, but smaller (75×35 mm), see No. **MS**847.

(Des I. Leung. Litho CPE Australia Ltd, Melbourne)

1989 (5 Oct). Building for the Future. T **140** and similar square designs. Perf 13.

620	60c. blue-black, orange-yellow and yellow-brown	45	15
621	70c. black, pale rose and rose	50	40
622	$1.30 black, bright yellow-green and blue-green	1·00	1·00
623	$1.40 black, azure and bright blue	1·00	70
624	$1.80 brownish black, pale turquoise green and turquoise-blue	1·25	1·00
625	$5 agate, pale red-orange and orange-red	6·50	8·50
620/625 *Set of 6*		9·50	10·50

Designs: 60c. T **140**; 70c. Cultural Centre; $1.30 Eastern Harbour motorway interchange; $1.40 New Bank of China Building; $1.80 Convention and Exhibition Centre; $5 Mass Transit electric train.

141 Prince and Princess of Wales and Hong Kong Skyline

142

(Des Ng Kee-chuen. Litho Leigh-Mardon Ltd, Melbourne)

1989 (8 Nov). Royal Visit. T **141** and similar vert designs, each showing portrait and different view. Multicoloured. W **142** (sideways). Perf 14½.

626	60c. Type **141**	1·50	30
627	$1.40 Princess of Wales	3·50	1·10
628	$1.80 Prince of Wales	2·50	1·10
629	$5 Prince and Princess of Wales in evening dress	9·00	10·00
626/629 *Set of 4*		12·00	11·50
MS630 128×75 mm. No. 629		15·00	12·00

143 Horse

(Des Kan Tai-keung. Litho Enschedé)

1990 (23 Jan). Chinese New Year. Year of the Horse. T **143** and similar horiz designs. Perf 13½×12½.

631	60c. multicoloured	65	20
	a. Booklet pane. Nos. 631 and 633, each×3	6·50	
632	$1.40 multicoloured	1·60	1·25
633	$1.80 multicoloured	1·60	1·25
634	$5 multicoloured	6·00	11·00
631/634 *Set of 4*		9·00	12·00
MS635 135×85 mm. No. 631/634		14·00	12·00

144 Chinese Lobster Dish

145 Air Pollution and Clean Air

(Des N. Yung and Sumiko Davies. Litho Enschedé)

1990 (26 Apr). International Cuisine. T **144** and similar vert designs showing various dishes. Multicoloured. Perf 12½×13.

636	60c. Type **144**	60	15
637	70c. Indian	60	50

638	$1.30 Chinese vegetables............................	1·00	1·25
639	$1.40 Thai	1·00	70
640	$1.80 Japanese	1·25	95
641	$5 French	4·25	8·50
636/641 Set of 6..		8·00	11·00

(Litho Leigh-Mardon Ltd, Melbourne)

1990 (5 June). United Nations World Environment Day. T **145** and similar vert designs. Multicoloured. Perf 14½.

642	60c. Type **145**	35	15
643	$1.40 Noise pollution and music	70	60
644	$1.80 Polluted and clean water.....................	80	60
645	$5 Litter on ground and in bin...................	2·25	4·00
642/645 Set of 4..		3·50	4·75

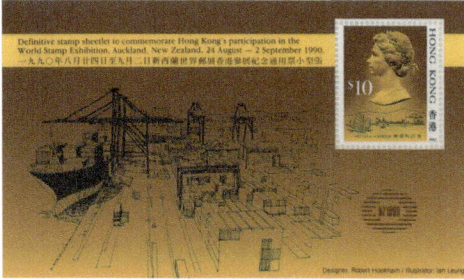

145a (*image scaled to 49% of original size*)

(Des R. Hookham and I. Leung. Litho Leigh-Mardon Ltd, Melbourne)

1990 (24 Aug). New Zealand 1990 International Stamp Exhibition, Auckland. Sheet 130×75 mm containing No. 613. Perf 14.

MS646 **145a** $10 multicoloured... 70·00   80·00

The stamp in No. **MS**646 shows the imprint date as '1990'.

146 Street Lamp and Des Voeux Road, 1890

(Des M. Tucker. Litho Leigh-Mardon Ltd, Melbourne)

1990 (2 Oct). Centenary of Electricity Supply. T **146** and similar horiz designs. Perf 14½.

647	60c. black, olive-bistre and pale orange-brown..	60	15
648	$1.40 multicoloured	1·00	80
649	$1.80 black, olive-bistre and deep cobalt.......	1·25	80
650	$5 multicoloured..	2·25	4·50
647/650 Set of 4..		4·50	5·50
MS651 155×85 mm. Nos. 648 and 650...........................		4·50	6·00

Designs: 60c. T **146**; $1.40 Street lamp and Jumbo (floating restaurant) 1940; $1.80 Street lamp and pylon, 1960; $5 Street lamp and Hong Kong from harbour, 1980.

147 Christmas Tree and Skyscrapers

(Litho Leigh-Mardon Ltd, Melbourne)

1990 (8 Nov). Christmas. T **147** and similar horiz designs. Multicoloured. Perf 14½.

652	50c. Type **147**	20	10
653	60c. Dove with Holly	20	15
654	$1.40 Firework display	55	40
655	$1.80 Father Christmas hat on sky scraper......	70	40
656	$2 Children with Father Christmas............	90	1·10
657	$5 Candy stick with bow and Hong Kong skyline..	2·25	5·50
652/657 Set of 6..		4·25	7·00

148 Ram

(Des Kan Tai-keung. Litho Enschedé)

1991 (24 Jan). Chinese New Year. Year of the Ram. T **148** and similar horiz designs. Perf 13½×12½.

658	60c. multicoloured	25	15
	a. Booklet pane. Nos. 658 and 660, each×3, with margins all round..............	4·50	
659	$1.40 multicoloured	65	60
660	$1.80 multicoloured	80	75
661	$5 multicoloured..	2·75	5·50
658/661 Set of 4..		4·00	6·25
MS662 135×85 mm. Nos. 658/661..........................		5·50	7·50

149 Letter 'A', Clock, Teddy Bear and Building Bricks (Kindergarten)   **150** Rickshaw

(Litho Enschedé)

1991 (18 Apr). Education. T **149** and similar vert designs. Multicoloured. Perf 13½×13.

663	80c. Type **149**	40	20
664	$1.80 Globe, laboratory flask and mathematical symbols (Primary and Secondary)	1·00	60
665	$2.30 Machinery (Vocational)	1·25	1·25
666	$5 Mortar board, computer and books (Tertiary)...	3·00	5·50
663/666 Set of 4..		5·00	6·75

(Des C. Tillyer. Litho B.D.T.)

1991 (6 June). Centenary of Public Transport. T **150** and similar square designs. Multicoloured. Perf 14.

667	80c. Type **150**	30	15
668	90c. Double-decker bus	70	75
669	$1.70 Harbour ferry	1·10	1·25
670	$1.80 Double-deck tram	1·40	80
671	$2.30 Mass Transit electric train	2·00	2·25
672	$5 Jetfoil...	3·50	6·50
667/672 Set of 6..		8·00	10·50

151 Victorian Pillar Box and Cover of 1888   **152** Bronze Buddha, Lantau Island

(Des H. Choi. Litho B.D.T.)

1991 (25 Aug). 150th Anniversary of Hong Kong Post Office (1st issue). T **151** and similar vert designs. Multicoloured. Perf 14.

673	80c. Type **151**	50	15
674	$1.70 Edwardian pillar box and cover............	1·00	1·00
675	$1.80 King George V pillar box and cover of 1935	1·10	75

676	$2.30 King George VI pillar box and cover of 1938..	1·50	2·00
677	$5 Queen Elizabeth II pillar box and cover of 1989..	4·00	7·50
673/677 Set of 5		7·25	10·00
MS678 130×75 mm. $10 As No. 677..................................		14·00	16·00

See also Nos. **MS**745 and **MS**899.

(Litho Questa)

1991 (24 Oct). Landmarks. T **152** and similar vert designs. Perf 14.

679	80c. rosine and black...........................	40	15
680	$1.70 bright emerald and black.................	80	1·25
681	$1.80 reddish violet and black...................	1·75	80
682	$2.30 new blue and black........................	1·00	2·00
683	$5 bright yellow-orange and black..............	2·75	7·25
679/683 Set of 5		6·00	10·00

Designs: 80c. T **152**; $1.70, Peak Pavilion; $1.80, Clocktower of Kowloon-Canton Railway Station; $2.30, Catholic Cathedral; $5 Wong Tai Sin Temple.

152a (*image scaled to 49% of original size*)

(Des Kan Tai-keung. Litho Leigh-Mardon Ltd, Melbourne)

1991 (16 Nov). Phila Nippon '91 International Stamp Exhibition, Tokyo. Sheet 130×75 mm containing No. 613. Perf 14.

MS684 $10 multicoloured.. 28·00 28·00

The stamp in No. **MS**684 shows the imprint date as '1991'.

152b (*image scaled to 49% of original size*)

(Des Li Shik-kwong. Litho Leigh-Mardon Ltd, Melbourne)

1991 (4 Dec). Olympic Games, Barcelona (1992) (1st issue). Sheet 130×75 mm. containing No. 613. Perf 14.

MS685 $10 multicoloured.. 14·00 17·00

The stamp in No. **MS**685 shows the imprint date as '1991'.
See also Nos. 696/**MS**700 and **MS**722.

153 Monkey

(Des Kan Tai-keung. Litho Leigh-Mardon Ltd, Melbourne)

1992 (22 Jan). Chinese New Year. Year of the Monkey. T **153** and similar horiz designs. Perf 14½.

686	80c. multicoloured	35	15
	a. Booklet pane. Nos. 686 and 688, each×3, with margins all round..............	5·50	
687	$1.80 multicoloured	65	70
688	$2.30 multicoloured	1·00	1·25
689	$5 multicoloured	2·25	6·50
686/689 Set of 4		3·75	7·75
MS690 135×85 mm. Nos. 686/689..........................		9·50	12·00

153a Royal Barge in Hong Kong Harbour

(Des D. Miller. Litho Leigh-Mardon Ltd, Melbourne)

1992 (11 Feb). 40th Anniversary of Queen Elizabeth II's Accession. T **153a** and similar horiz designs. Multicoloured. Perf 14½.

691	80c. Type **153a**....................................	50	15
692	$1.70 Queen watching dancing display...........	80	70
693	$1.80 Fireworks display............................	80	35
694	$2.30 Three portraits of Queen Elizabeth........	1·00	1·00
695	$5 Queen Elizabeth II............................	2·00	3·25
691/695 Set of 5		4·50	5·00

154 Running

(Des Li Shik-kwong. Litho Leigh-Mardon Ltd, Melbourne)

1992 (2 Apr). Olympic Games, Barcelona (2nd issue). T **154** and similar horiz designs. Perf 14½.

696	80c. Type **154**.....................................	30	20
697	$1.80 Swimming and javelin.......................	70	70
698	$2.30 Cycling	1·50	1·50
699	$5 High jump	1·75	5·00
696/699 Set of 4		3·75	6·75
MS700 130×75 mm. As Nos. 696/699*............................		5·50	8·50

*The stamps from No. **MS**700 show the inscriptions in different colours, instead of the black on Nos. 696/699. The designs of the $1.80 and $5 values from the miniature sheet have also been rearranged so that 'HONG KONG' and the Royal Cypher occur at the right of the inscription.

For No. **MS**700 additionally inscribed for the opening of the Games see No. **MS**722.

154a (*image scaled to 49% of original size*)

(Des Kan Tai-keung. Litho Leigh-Mardon Ltd, Melbourne)

1992 (22 May). World Columbian Stamp Expo '92 Exhibition, Chicago. Sheet 130×75 mm containing No. 613, but colours changed. Perf 14.

MS701 $10 multicoloured.. 3·00 6·50

The stamp in No. **MS**701 shows the imprint date as '1992'.

155 Queen Elizabeth II	**156** Stamps and Perforation Gauge

(Des I. Leung. Photo Enschedé)

1992 (16 June)–**96**. Perf 14½×14 (10c. to $5) or 14 ($10, $20, $50).

702	**155**	10c. magenta, black and pale cerise..........	30	50
		ap. Two phosphor bands (24.4.96)	2·00	2·50

702b	20c. black, blue-black and pale blue		
	(1.11.93)	1·00	1·75
	bp. Two phosphor bands (24.4.96)	2·50	3·00
703	50c. orange-red, black and yellow	30	30
	p. Two phosphor bands (24.4.96)	2·50	2·25
	pa. Imperf (pair)		
704	60c. greenish blue, black and light blue	2·00	2·50
705	70c. bright mauve, black and rose-lilac	2·00	1·75
706	80c. cerise, black and rose	45	45
707	90c. bronze-green, black and greenish		
	grey	45	60
708	$1 red-brown, black and orange-yellow	45	20
	ap. Two phosphor bands (24.4.96)	2·00	2·00
708b	$1.10 deep carmine, black and pale		
	salmon (1.6.95)	3·50	2·50
	bp. Two phosphor bands (24.4.96)	4·00	3·50
709	$1.20 bright violet, black and lilac	50	25
	ap. Two phosphor bands (24.4.96)	2·00	2·00
709b	$1.30 blue, brownish black and salmon		
	(1.11.93)	1·50	1·75
	bp. Two phosphor bands (24.4.96)	3·00	3·00
709c	$1.40 bright yellow-green, black and		
	greenish yellow (two phosphor		
	bands) (2.9.96)	3·25	3·00
709d	$1.50 reddish brown, black and light blue		
	(1.6.95)	3·00	3·75
	dp. Two phosphor bands (24.4.96)	3·00	3·75
709e	$1.60 light green, black and rose-lilac		
	(two phosphor bands) (2.9.96)	2·50	3·50
710	$1.70 dull ultramarine, black and pale		
	blue	1·00	1·00
711	$1.80 deep magenta, black and grey	2·00	55
711a	$1.90 deep blue-green, brownish black		
	and yellow-ochre (1.11.93)	1·50	2·00
	ap. Two phosphor bands (24.4.96)	3·00	3·50
712	$2 turquoise-blue, black and bright		
	turquoise-green	1·50	60
	ap. Two phosphor bands (24.4.96)	3·00	2·00
712b	$2.10 bright crimson, black and pale		
	turquoise-green (1.6.95)	3·00	4·00
	bp. One centre phosphor band (24.4.96)	4·00	4·00
	bq. Two phosphor bands (2.9.96)	5·00	6·50
713	$2.30 blackish brown, black and rose-pink	2·50	75
713a	$2.40 dull ultramarine, black and		
	brownish grey (1.11.93)	2·50	3·75
713b	$2.50 brown-olive, black and lemon (one		
	centre phosphor band) (2.9.96)	3·00	3·00
713c	$2.60 chocolate, black and yellow-brown		
	(1.6.95)	2·50	4·00
	cp. One centre phosphor band (24.4.96)	2·25	4·00
713d	$3.10 orange-brown, black and pale blue		
	(one centre phosphor band) (2.9.96)	2·25	1·50
714	$5 bright blue-green, black and light		
	green	2·00	1·50
	p. One centre phosphor band (24.4.96)	4·00	3·00
715	-	$10 red-brown, black and cinnamon	2·00	2·25
716	-	$20 rosine black and bright salmon	4·25	4·50
717		$50 grey-black, black and grey	8·50	11·00
702/717 Set of 28		50·00	55·00

Nos. 715/717 are as T **155**, but larger, 26×30 mm, and show a large perforation hole at each corner of the stamp.

Nos. 702/717 show 'HONG KONG' printed in yellow fluorescence as a security marking. Nos. 715/717 additionally show a horizontal line at foot in green fluorescence.

Nos. 702, 703, 706/709, 709b, 709d, 709e, 711/711a, 712b, 713/713b, 713c and 713d also exist from coils with every fifth stamp numbered on the reverse.

For stamps in this design from stamp booklets, printed in lithography without watermark or with watermark w **14**, see Nos. 757/765.

For miniature sheets containing designs as Nos. 714 and 715 see Nos. **MS**723, **MS**745, **MS**746, **MS**751, **MS**771, **MS**782, **MS**810, **MS**811, **MS**821, **MS**827, **MS**841 and **MS**842.

(Des Kan Tai-keung. Litho Leigh-Mardon Ltd, Melbourne)

1992 (15 July). Stamp Collecting. T **156** and similar horiz designs. Multicoloured. Perf 14½.

718	80c. Type **156**	30	25
719	$1.80 Handstamp of 1841, 1891 Jubilee		
	overprint and tweezers	60	75
720	$2.30 Stamps of 1946 and 1949 under		
	magnifying glass	85	1·25
721	$5 2c. of 1862 and watermark detector	2·00	4·00
718/721 Set of 4	3·25	5·50

> A limited edition prestige booklet sold at $65 was issued on 25 August 2001. This consisted of three panes, one of which contained four values in a re-drawn design as No. 719 but inscribed 'HONG KONG, CHINA'.

(Des Li Shik-kwong. Litho Leigh-Mardon Ltd, Melbourne)

1992 (25 July). Olympic Games, Barcelona (3rd issue). As No. **MS**700, but additionally inscribed 'To Commemorate the Opening of the 1992 Summer Olympic Games 25 July 1992', in English and Chinese, at foot of sheet.

MS722 130×75 mm. As Nos. 696/699 .... 3·25 6·00

156a (image scaled to 49% of original size)

(Des C. Tillyer. Litho Enschedé)

1992 (1 Sept). Kuala Lumpur '92 International Stamp Exhibition. Sheet 130×75 mm containing design as No. 715, but litho and colours changed. Perf 14.

MS723 $10 dull ultramarine, black and pale blue .... 3·00 8·00

No. **MS**723 shows 'HONG KONG' printed in yellow fluorescence with a horizontal green fluorescent line beneath as a security marking. There is a larger perforation hole at each corner of the stamp.

157 Principal Male Character

158 Hearts

(Des I. Leung. Litho Enschedé)

1992 (24 Sept). Chinese Opera. T **157** and similar vert designs. Multicoloured. Perf 13½.

724	80c. Type **157**	1·25	25
725	$1.80 Martial character	3·00	1·60
	a. Grey (face value and inscr) omitted	£2000	
726	$2.30 Principal female character	3·00	2·50
	a. Grey (face value and inscr) omitted	£2000	
727	$5 Comic character	6·00	10·00
724/727 Set of 4	12·00	13·00

Nos. 725a and 726a each occur on the bottom row of a sheet and were caused by the upward displacement of the grey colour. One example of each also exists showing the plate number from the bottom margin printed in the design.

(Des C. Tillyer. Litho Leigh-Mardon Ltd, Melbourne)

1992 (19 Nov). Greetings Stamps. T **158** and similar horiz designs. Multicoloured. Perf 14½.

728	80c. Type **158**	30	20
	a. Booklet pane. Nos. 728×3 and 729/731		
	with margins all round	4·50	
729	$1.80 Stars	55	60
730	$2.30 Presents	75	1·00
731	$5 Balloons	1·60	3·50
728/731 Set of 4	2·75	4·75

159 Cockerel

(Des Kan Tai-keung. Litho Enschedé)

1993 (7 Jan). Chinese New Year. Year of the Cock. T **159** and similar horiz designs. Perf 13½.

732	80c. multicoloured	30	20
	a. Booklet pane. Nos. 732 and 734,		
	each×3, with margins all round	4·00	
733	$1.80 multicoloured	70	80
734	$2.30 multicoloured	95	1·25
735	$5 multicoloured	1·75	4·25
732/735 Set of 4	3·25	5·75
MS736 133×84 mm. Nos. 732/735	4·00	6·50

160 Pipa

161 Central Waterfront, Hong Kong in 1954

(Des Sumiko Davies. Litho Leigh-Mardon Ltd, Melbourne)

1993 (14 Apr). Chinese String Musical Instruments. T **160** and similar vert designs. Multicoloured. Fluorescent paper. Perf 14½.

737	80c. Type **160**	30	20
738	$1.80 Erhu	55	60
739	$2.30 Ruan	65	1·00
740	$5 Gehu	1·25	3·75
737/740 Set of 4		2·50	5·00

(Des C. Tillyer. Litho Leigh-Mardon Ltd, Melbourne)

1993 (2 June). 40th Anniversary of Coronation. T **161** and similar horiz designs. Multicoloured. Fluorescent paper. Perf 14.

741	80c. Type **161**	50	20
742	$1.80 Hong Kong in 1963	1·00	60
743	$2.30 Hong Kong in 1975	1·00	1·00
744	$5 Hong Kong in 1992	2·00	3·75
741/744 Set of 4		4·00	5·00

161a (*image scaled to 49% of original size*)

(Des Julia Brown and G. Smith. Litho Enschedé)

1993 (6 July). 150th Anniversary of Hong Kong Post Office (2nd issue). Sheet 130×75 mm containing design as No. 715, but litho. Perf 14.
MS745 $10 red-brown, black and cinnamon...................... 4·50   6·00
No. **MS**745 shows 'HONG KONG' printed in yellow fluorescence with a horizontal green fluorescent line beneath as a security marking. There is a larger perforation hole at each corner of the stamp.

161b (*image scaled to 55% of original size*)

(Des Lam Bing-pui. Litho Enschedé)

1993 (12 Aug). Hong Kong '94 International Stamp Exhibition. Sheet 115×78 mm containing design as No. 715 but litho and colours changed. Perf 14.
MS746 $10 deep purple, black, bistre-yellow and greenish blue... 4·50   4·00
No. **MS**746 shows 'HONG KONG' printed in yellow fluorescence with a horizontal green fluorescent line beneath as a security marking. There is a larger perforation hole at each corner of the stamp.

162 University of Science and Technology Building and Student

(Des Lam Bing-pui. Litho Leigh-Mardon Ltd, Melbourne)

1993 (8 Sept). Hong Kong's Contribution to Science and Technology. T **162** and similar horiz designs. Multicoloured. Perf 14½.

747	80c. Type **162**	25	20
748	$1.80 Science Museum building and energy machine exhibit	40	40
749	$2.30 Governor's Award and circuit board	60	90
750	$5 Dish aerials and world map	1·25	3·50
747/750 Set of 4		2·25	4·50

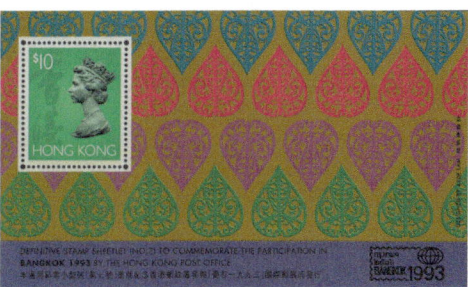

162a (*image scaled to 49% of original size*)

(Des Lam Bing-pui. Litho Enschedé)

1993 (6 Oct). Bangkok '93 International Stamp Exhibition. Sheet 131×76 mm containing design as No. 715, but litho and colours changed. Perf 14.
MS751 $10 bright emerald, blackish green and bright blue-green.. 2·50   3·50
No. **MS**751 shows 'HONG KONG' printed in yellow fluorescence with a horizontal green fluorescent line beneath as a security marking. There is a larger perforation hole at each corner of the stamp.

163 Red Calico Egg-fish

(Des N. Young. Litho Leigh-Mardon Ltd, Melbourne)

1993 (17 Nov). Goldfish. T **163** and similar horiz designs. Multicoloured. Perf 14½.

752	$1 Type **163**	35	20
753	$1.90 Red Cap Oranda	60	40
754	$2.40 Red and White Fringetail	70	1·00
755	$5 Black and Gold Dragon-eye	1·25	4·00
752/755 Set of 4		2·50	5·00
MS756	130×75 mm. Nos. 752/755	5·00	7·00

1993 (14 Dec)–**97**. As Nos. 702, 708, 709, 709bp, 709e, 710/712, 712b, 713a and 714, but printed in lithography by Leigh-Mardon Ltd (Nos. 757, 758, 759 and 760/765) or Enschedé (others). Perf 14½×14.

(a) No wmk.

757	**155**	$1 red-brown, black and orange-yellow	80	80
		a. Booklet pane. No. 757x10 with margins all round	7·50	
757b		$1.20 bright violet, black and lilac (1.6.95)	70	1·75
		ba. Booklet pane. No. 757bx10 with margins all round	6·50	
757c		$1.30 blue, deep brown and salmon (two phosphor bands) (2.9.96)	50	1·00

	ca. Booklet pane. No. 757c×10 with margins all round	4·50	
	cc. Booklet pane. As No. **MS**872a, but with enlarged margins at left and foot (14.2.97)	9·00	
757d	$1.60 light green, black and rose-lilac (two phosphor bands) (14.2.97)	1·25	2·50
	db. Booklet pane. As No. **MS**872a, but with enlarged margins at left and foot	9·00	
758	$1.90 deep blue-green, brownish black and yellow-ochre (28.12.93)	1·00	1·75
	a. Booklet pane. No. 758×10 with margins all round	9·00	
758b	$2.10 deep claret, black and turquoise-green (1.6.95)	1·00	2·50
	ba. Booklet pane. No. 758b×10 with margins all round	8·50	
	bb. Two phosphor bands (14.2.97)	1·00	2·50
	bd. Booklet pane. As No. **MS**872c, but with enlarged margins at left and foot	9·00	
759	$2.40 dull ultramarine, black and brownish grey (28.12.93)	1·10	1·75
	a. Booklet pane. No. 759×10 with margins all round	9·50	
759b	$2.50 bistre, black and lemon (one centre phosphor band) (2.9.96)	60	1·75
	ba. Booklet pane. No. 759b×10 with margins all round	5·50	
759c	$2.60 deep chocolate, black and brown (1.6.95)	1·00	2·75
	ca. Booklet pane. No. 759c×10 with margins all round	8·50	
759d	$3.10 orange-brown, black and pale blue (one centre phosphor band) (2.9.96)	60	2·25
	da. Booklet pane. No. 759d×10 with margins all round	5·50	
759e	$5 bright blue-green, black and light green (one centre phosphor band) (14.2.97)	1·50	3·25
757/759e Set of 11		9·00	20·00

(b) W w **14** (12.1.94).

760	**155**	10c. magenta, black and pale cerise	3·00	6·50
		a. Booklet pane. Nos. 760 and 764×5 with margins all round	7·00	
761		$1 red-brown, black and orange-yellow	60	1·25
		a. Booklet pane. No. 761×5 and 765 with margins all round	7·00	
762		$1.70 dull ultramarine, black and pale blue	3·00	6·50
		a. Booklet pane. No. 762 and 763×5 with margins all round	7·00	
763		$1.80 deep magenta, black and grey	60	1·25
764		$2 turquoise-blue and bright turquoise-green	60	1·25
765		$5 bright blue-green, black and light green	4·00	10·00
760/765 Set of 6			10·50	24·00

Nos. 757/765 show 'HONG KONG' printed in yellow fluorescence as a security marking, although Nos. 757, 758 and 759 have all been seen without this feature.

Nos. 757/759d come from definitive booklets and Nos. 760/765 from the Prestige booklet issued to commemorate the 130th anniversary of Hong Kong stamps.

For miniature sheets containing stamps from this series see Nos. **MS**872a, **MS**872b and **MS**872c.

164 Dog

(Des Kan Tai-keung. Litho Leigh-Mardon Ltd, Melbourne)

1994 (27 Jan). Chinese New Year. Year of the Dog. T **164** and similar horiz designs. Perf 14½.

766	$1 multicoloured	30	20
	a. Booklet pane. Nos. 766 and 768, each×3, with margins all round	5·50	
767	$1.90 multicoloured	50	55
768	$2.40 multicoloured	70	1·00
769	$5 multicoloured	1·75	4·00
766/769 Set of 4		2·75	5·00
MS770 133×84 mm. Nos. 766/769		5·50	8·00

164a *(image scaled to 49% of original size)*

(Des Lam Bing-pui. Litho Leigh-Mardon Ltd, Melbourne)

1994 (18 Feb). Hong Kong '94 International Stamp Exhibition. Sheet 130×75 mm containing design as No. 714, but litho. Perf 14½×14.
MS771 $5 bright blue-green, black and light green...... 2·50 4·50

No. **MS**771 shows 'HONG KONG' printed in yellow fluorescence as a security marking.

165 Modern Police Constables on Traffic Duty

166 Dragon Boat Festival

(Des Li Shik-kwong. Litho Enschedé)

1994 (4 May). 150th Anniversary of Royal Hong Kong Police Force. T **185** and similar horiz designs. Multicoloured. Perf 13½.

772	$1 Type **165**	50	20
773	$1.20 Marine policeman with binoculars	75	50
774	$1.90 Police uniforms of 1950	75	75
775	$2 Tactical firearms unit officer with sub-machine gun	1·00	1·25
776	$2.40 Early 20th-century police uniforms	1·50	1·25
777	$5 Sikh and Chinese constables of 1900	3·00	4·25
772/777 Set of 6		7·00	7·50

(Des Li Shik-kwong. Litho Questa)

1994 (8 June). Traditional Chinese Festivals. T **166** and similar vert designs. Multicoloured. Perf 14½.

778	$1 Type **166**	30	20
779	$1.90 Lunar New Year	50	75
780	$2.40 Seven Sisters Festival	75	1·00
781	$5 Mid-Autumn Festival	1·25	4·00
778/781 Set of 4		2·50	5·50

166a *(image scaled to 47% of original size)*

(Des C. Tillyer. Litho Enschedé)

1994 (16 Aug). Conference of Commonwealth Postal Administrations, Hong Kong. Sheet 134×83 mm, containing design as No. 715, but litho. Perf 14.
MS782 $10 red-brown, black and cinnamon.................. 4·50 7·50

No. **MS**782 shows 'HONG KONG' printed in yellow fluorescence with a horizontal green fluorescent line beneath as a security marking. There is a larger perforation hole at each corner of the stamp.

167 Swimming

(Des C. Tillyer. Litho Walsall)

1994 (26 Aug). 15th Commonwealth Games, Victoria Canada. T **167** and similar horiz designs. Multicoloured. Perf 14½.

783	$1 Type **167**	20	20
784	$1.90 Bowls	30	55
785	$2.40 Gymnastics	40	70
786	$5 Weightlifting	70	3·00
783/786 Set of 4		1·40	4·00

168 Dr. James Legge and Students

169 *Alcyonium* Coral

(Des Lai Wai-kwan. Litho Leigh-Mardon Ltd, Melbourne)

1994 (5 Oct). Dr. James Legge (Chinese scholar) Commemoration. Perf 14½.

787	**168**	$1 multicoloured	1·00	1·00

(Des Brushstroke Design. Litho Questa)

1994 (17 Nov). Corals. T **169** and similar square designs. Multicoloured. Perf 14.

788	$1 Type **169**	20	20
789	$1.90 Zoanthus	30	60
790	$2.40 Tubastrea	40	75
791	$5 *Platygyra*	70	3·00
788/791 Set of 4		1·40	4·00
MS792 130×75 mm. Nos. 788/791		3·50	7·50

170 Pig

(Des Kan Tai-keung. Litho Leigh-Mardon Ltd, Melbourne)

1995 (17 Jan). Chinese New Year. Year of the Pig. T **170** and similar horiz designs. Perf 14½.

793	$1 multicoloured	30	30
	a. Booklet pane. Nos. 793 and 795, each×3, with margins all round	4·00	
794	$1.90 multicoloured	60	80
795	$2.40 multicoloured	60	1·10
796	$5 multicoloured	1·25	4·00
793/796 Set of 4		2·50	5·50
MS797 130×84 mm. Nos. 793/796		4·25	6·50

171 Hong Kong Rugby Sevens

(Des Kan Tai-keung and Roxy Lou Sze-wan. Litho Leigh-Mardon Ltd, Melbourne)

1995 (22 Mar). International Sporting Events in Hong Kong. T **171** and similar horiz designs. Multicoloured. Perf 14½.

798	$1 Type **171**	1·00	20
799	$1.90 The China Sea Yacht Race	1·00	80
800	$2.40 International Dragon Boat Races	1·50	1·10
801	$5 Hong Kong International Horse Races	3·00	4·25
798/801 Set of 4		6·00	5·75

172 Tsui Shing Lau Pagoda

173 Regimental Badge

(Des I. Leung. Recess and litho Enschedé)

1995 (24 May). Hong Kong Traditional Rural Buildings. T **172** and similar horiz designs. Multicoloured. Perf 13½.

802	$1 Type **172**	20	25
803	$1.90 Sam Tung Uk Village	35	50
804	$2.40 Lo Wai Village	45	80
805	$5 Man Shek Tong house	1·00	3·25
802/805 Set of 4		1·75	4·25

(Des Lam Bing-pui. Litho Leigh-Mardon Ltd, Melbourne)

1995 (16 Aug). Disbandment of the Royal Hong Kong Regiment. T **173** and similar multicoloured designs. Perf 14½.

806	$1.20 Type **173**	45	25
807	$2.10 Regimental guidon (*horiz*)	55	75
808	$2.60 Colour of Hong Kong Volunteer Defence Corps, 1928 (*horiz*)	55	85
809	$5 Cap badge of Royal Hong Kong Defence Force, 1951	85	3·50
806/809 Set of 4		2·25	4·75

173a (*image scaled to 49% of original size*)

(Des C. Tillyer and Valerie Carter. Litho Enschedé)

1995 (1 Sept). Singapore '95 International Stamp Exhibition. Sheet 130×75 mm, containing design as No. 715, but litho and colours changed. Perf 14.

MS810 **173a** $10 deep magenta, yellow-olive, yellow and brown-lilac		4·00	8·00

No. **MS**810 shows 'HONG KONG' printed in yellow fluorescence with a horizontal green fluorescent line beneath as a security marking. There is a larger perforation hole at each corner of the stamp.

173b (*image scaled to 49% of original size*)

(Des D. Lai. Litho Enschedé)

1995 (9 Oct). 50th Anniversary of End of Second World War. Sheet 130×75 mm, containing design as No. 715, but litho. Perf 14.

MS811 $10 red-brown, black and cinnamon		4·75	9·00

No. **MS**811 shows 'HONG KONG' printed in yellow fluorescence with a horizontal green fluorescent line beneath as a security marking. There is a larger perforation hole at each corner of the stamp.

174 Bruce Lee

(Des Lau Siu-hang and Wong Kum. Litho Enschedé)

1995 (15 Nov). Hong Kong Film Stars. T **174** and similar horiz designs. Multicoloured. Perf 13½.

812	$1.20 Type **174**	2·00	75
813	$2.10 Leung Sing-par	3·50	1·50
814	$2.60 Yam Kim-fai	4·00	1·75
815	$5 Lin Dai	6·00	5·00
812/815 *Set of 4*		14·00	8·00

175 Rat

(Des Kan Tai-keung. Litho Enschedé)

1996 (31 Jan). Chinese New Year. Year of the Rat. T **175** and similar horiz designs. Perf 13½.

816	$1.20 multicoloured	25	30
	a. Booklet pane. Nos. 816 and 818,		
	each×3, with margins all round	2·50	
817	$2.10 multicoloured	50	55
818	$2.60 multicoloured	50	65
819	$5 multicoloured	1·50	1·75
816/819 *Set of 4*		2·50	3·00
MS820 133×83 mm. Nos. 816/819		3·50	5·00

175a (*image scaled to 49% of original size*)

(Des Lam Bing-pui. Litho Enschedé)

1996 (23 Feb). Visit HONG KONG '97 Stamp Exhibition (1st issue). Sheet 130×80 mm, containing designs as No. 715, but litho and colours changed. Perf 14.

MS821 **175a** $10 yellow-orange, black and bright green		3·25	8·00

No. **MS**821 shows 'HONG KONG' printed in yellow fluorescence with a horizontal green fluorescent line beneath as a security marking. There is a large perforation hole at each corner of the stamp.

See also Nos. **MS**827, **MS**841, **MS**872, and **MS**873.

176 Rhythmic Gymnastics

(Des B. Kwan. Litho Ashton-Potter America Inc, New York)

1996 (20 Mar). Olympic Games, Atlanta. T **176** and similar vert designs. Multicoloured with Royal Cypher and face values in black and Olympic Rings multicoloured (Nos. 822/825). Two phosphor bands ($1.20) or one side phosphor band (others). Perf 13½.

822	$1.20 Type **176**	20	20
823	$2.10 Diving	30	50
824	$2.60 Athletics	35	60
825	$5 Basketball	1·50	3·25
822/825 *Set of 4*		2·10	4·00
MS826 130×75 mm. As Nos. 822/825, but Royal Cypher and Olympic Rings in gold and face values in black (medal in bottom sheet margin)		2·10	6·00

For these designs with Royal Cypher and Olympic Rings in gold see Nos. 832/836.

176a (*image scaled to 49% of original size*)

(Des A. Lam. Litho Enschedé)

1996 (18 May). Visit HONG KONG '97 Stamp Exhibition (2nd issue). Sheet 130×80 mm, containing design as No. 715, but litho and colours changed. Perf 14.

MS827 **176a** $10 bright emerald, greenish black and bluish violet		2·50	6·00

No. **MS**827 shows 'HONG KONG' printed in yellow fluorescence with a horizontal green fluorescent line beneath as a security marking. There is a large perforation hole at each corner of the stamp.

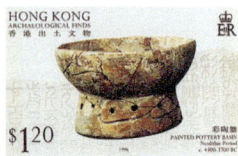

177 Painted Pottery Basin, *c.* 4500–3700 BC

(Des I. Leung. Litho Enschedé)

1996 (26 June). Archaeological Discoveries. T **177** and similar horiz designs. Multicoloured. Two phosphor bands ($1.20) or one side band (others). Perf 13½.

828	$1.20 Type **177**	35	25
829	$2.10 Stone 'yue' (ceremonial axe), *c.* 2900–2200	40	1·00
830	$2.60 Stone 'ge' (halberd), *c.* 2200–1500 BC	45	1·00
831	$5 Pottery tripod, *c.* 25–220 AD	80	3·00
828/831 *Set of 4*		1·75	5·00

(Des B. Kwan,. Litho Ashton-Potter America Inc, New York)

1996 (19 July). Opening of Centennial Olympic Games, Atlanta. Designs as Nos. 822/825, but with Royal Cypher and Olympic Rings in gold and face values in colours quoted. Two phosphor bands ($1.20) or one side band (others). Perf 14½.

832	$1.20 Type **176** (bright magenta)	20	25
833	$2.10 As No. 823 (deep ultramarine)	30	1·00
834	$2.60 As No. 824 (light green)	30	2·00
835	$5 As No. 825 (orange-vermilion)	1·00	3·50
832/835 *Set of 4*		1·60	6·00
MS836 130×75 mm. As No. **MS**826, but with medal in top margin. P 13½		2·25	5·50

The stamps in Nos. **MS**826 and **MS**836 are similar. The miniature sheets differ in the marginal inscriptions and illustrations. No. **MS**826 is inscribed '1996 OLYMPIC GAMES' and has a Gold Medal in the bottom margin. No. **MS**836 is inscribed 'TO COMMEMORATE THE OPENING OF THE CENTENNIAL OLYMPIC GAMES 19 JULY 1996' and has the medal in the top margin.

178 Pat Sin Leng Mountain

(Des Lam Bing-pui. Litho Harrison)

1996 (24 Sept). Mountains. T **178** and similar multicoloured designs. Two phosphor bands ($1.30) or one side phosphor band (others). Perf 13½×14½ ($1.30), 14×14½ ($2.50), 14½×14 ($3.10) or 14½×13½ ($5).

837	$1.30 Type **178**	45	35
838	$2.50 Ma On Shan (40×35 mm)	65	1·50
839	$3.10 Lion Rock (35×40 mm)	85	2·00
840	$5 Lantau Peak (25×46½ mm)	1·10	4·00
837/840 Set of 4		2·75	7·00

178a (*image scaled to 49% of original size*)

(Des A. Lam. Litho Enschedé)

1996 (16 Oct). Visit HONG KONG '97 Stamp Exhibition (3rd issue). Sheet 130×80 mm, containing design as No. 715 but litho and colours changed. Perf 14½×14.

MS841 $10 apple-green, black and rose-carmine............ 2·50 4·50

No. **MS**841 shows 'HONG KONG' printed in yellow fluorescence with a horizontal green fluorescent line beneath as a security marking. There is a larger perforation hole at each corner of the stamp.

178b (*image scaled to 49% of original size*)

(Des B. Kwan. Litho Enschedé)

1996 (29 Oct). Hong Kong Team's Achievements at Atlanta Olympic Games. Sheet 130×75 mm, containing design as No. 715 but litho. Perf 14½×14.

MS842 $10 red-brown, black and cinnamon.................... 2·50 3·25

No. **MS**842 shows 'HONG KONG' printed in yellow fluorescence with a horizontal green fluorescent line beneath as a security marking. There is a larger perforation hole at each corner of the stamp.

179 Main Building, University of Hong Kong, 1912

180 Part of Hong Kong Skyline

(Des T. Li. Recess and litho Ashton-Potter America Inc, New York)

1996 (26 Nov). Urban Heritage. T **179** and similar horiz designs. Multicoloured. Two phosphor bands ($1.30) or one phosphor band (others). Perf 13½.

843	$1.30 Type **179**	30	70
844	$2.50 Western Market, 1906	50	85
845	$3.10 Old Pathological Institute, 1905	55	1·00
846	$5 Flagstaff House, 1846	70	2·25
843/846 Set of 4		1·75	4·25

(Des A. Lam. Litho Walsall)

1996 (4 Dec). Serving the Community. Sheet 130×75 mm, containing design as No. 619, but smaller, 25×35 mm. Multicoloured. One phosphor band. Perf 13½×13½.

MS847 $5 Multi-racial society................................. 1·00 1·25

(Des Kan Tai-keung)

1997 (26 Jan). T **180** and similar vert designs showing different sections of Hong Kong skyline. Two phosphor bands (10c. to $2.10), one centre phosphor band ($2.50 to $5) or phosphorised paper ($10).

(a) Sheet stamps. Litho Ashton-Potter Canada. Perf 13½×13 (10c. to $5) or 14×13½ ($10, $20, $50).

848	10c. purple and rose-pink	15	30
849	20c. purple-brown and orange-red	30	30
850	50c. deep green and bright orange	20	40
851	$1 greenish blue and orange-yellow	30	20
852	$1.20 deep dull green and olive-yellow	30	50
853	$1.30 deep violet and apple green	30	25
	a. Booklet pane. No. 853×10 with margins all round	3·25	
854	$1.40 maroon and bright green	30	50
855	$1.60 deep purple and bright blue-green	30	60
856	$2 deep olive and greenish blue	40	50
857	$2.10 deep turquoise-blue and bright blue	40	60
858	$2.50 violet and bright mauve	50	1·00
	a. Booklet pane. No. 858×10 with margins all round	4·75	
859	$3.10 purple and cerise	60	70
	a. Booklet pane. No. 859×10 with margins all round	5·00	
860	$5 deep magenta and bright orange	1·25	1·00
861	$10 multicoloured (28×32 mm)	2·00	2·50
862	$20 multicoloured (28×32 mm)	3·50	5·00
863	$50 multicoloured (28×32 mm)	8·00	11·00
848/863 Set of 16		17·00	22·00
MS864 273×53 mm. Nos. 848/857, and as Nos. 858/860 each with one side phosphor band		3·50	6·50
MS865 95×72 mm. Nos. 861/863		13·00	16·00

(b) Coil stamps. Designs as Nos. 849, 851, 853, 856 and Nos. 859/860, but photo Enschedé. Perf 14½×14.

866	10c. purple and rose-pink	20	1·00
867	50c. deep green and bright orange	25	1·00
868	$1.30 deep violet and apple-green	45	1·00
869	$1.60 deep purple and bright blue-green	45	1·00
870	$2.50 violet and bright mauve	70	1·50
871	$3.10 purple and cerise	75	2·00
866/871 Set of 6		2·50	8·00

Nos. 848/871 show 'HONG KONG' printed in yellow fluorescence and Nos. 861 and 862 have also been reported on 'all-over' fluorescent paper. The perforations on Nos. 848/865 show alternate small and large holes.

Nos. 866/871 were printed in coils with every fifth stamp numbered on the reverse.

For miniature sheets containing No. 861 see Nos. **MS**872, **MS**873, **MS**898 and **MS**968.

For miniature sheets containing Nos. 856/859 see **MS**954.

> A limited edition prestige booklet *sold at* $65 was issued on 25 August 2001. This consisted of three panes, one of which contained two values as No. 859 and two values as No. 984 but perf 13½×14 (*Price*, £30 *unused*).

180a (*image scaled to 50% of original size*)

(Des Kan Tai-keung. Litho Ashton-Potter America Inc, New York)

1997 (12 Feb). Visit HONG KONG '97 Stamp Exhibition (4th issue). Sheet 130×80 mm containing design as No. 861 but ordinary paper, and with marginal illustration in bluish violet. Perf 14×13.

MS872 **180a** $10 multicoloured.. 2·00   4·50

No. **MS**872 shows 'HONG KONG' in yellow fluorescence. The perforations show alternate small and large holes.

180e (*image scaled to 50% of original size*)

(Des Kan Tai-keung. Litho Ashton-Potter America Inc, New York)

1997 (16 Feb). Visit HONG KONG '97 Stamp Exhibition (5th issue). Sheet 130×80 mm, containing design as No. 861, but ordinary paper, and with marginal illustration in chestnut. Perf 14×13.

MS873 **180e** $10 multicoloured.. 2·00   7·00

No. **MS**873 shows 'HONG KONG' in yellow fluorescence. The perforations show alternate small and large holes.

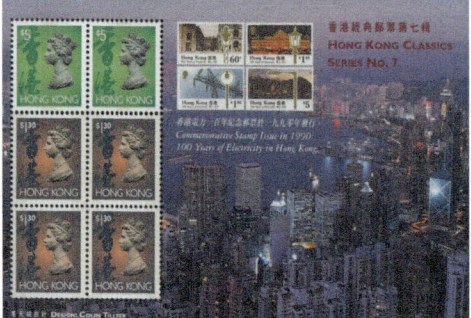

180b (*image scaled to 50% of original size*)

181 Ox

(Des Kan Tai-keung)

1997 (27 Feb). Chinese New Year. Year of the Ox. T **181** and similar horiz designs. Two phosphor bands ($1.30) or one phosphor band (others).

(a) Litho Ashton-Potter America Inc, New York. Perf 14½.

874	$1.30 multicoloured	25	25
875	$2.50 multicoloured	40	55
876	$3.10 multicoloured	55	90
877	$5 multicoloured	85	2·00
874/877	Set of 4..	1·75	3·25
MS878	133×84 mm. Nos. 874/877..................	1·75	3·00

(b) Litho Enschedé. Perf 13½.

879	$1.30 multicoloured	25	25
	a. Booklet pane. Nos. 879 and 881		
	each×3	6·00	
880	$2.50 multicoloured	40	55
881	$3.10 multicoloured	55	90
882	$5 multicoloured	85	2·50
879/882	Set of 4..	1·75	3·25
MS883	133×84 mm. Nos. 879/882..................	2·00	3·50

180c (*image scaled to 50% of original size*)

182 Yellow-breasted Bunting

(Des Shek Tak-sheun. Litho Enschedé)

1997 (27 Apr). Migratory Birds. T **182** and similar horiz designs. Multicoloured. Two phosphor bands ($1.30) or one phosphor band (others). Perf 13½.

884	$1.30 Type **182**...................................	40	35
885	$2.50 Great Knot	50	55
886	$3.10 Falcated Teal	65	90
887	$5 Black-faced Spoonbill...................	85	2·00
884/887	Set of 4..	2·25	3·25

180d (*image scaled to 50% of original size*)

1997 (14 Feb). 'Hong Kong Classics Series' Nos. 7, 8 and 9. Sheets 130×85 mm. Litho. Perf 14½×14.

MS872a **180b**	$10.20 No. 757cx4; No. 759ex2..................	4·50	8·00
MS872b **180c**	$15.60 No. 757dx2; No. 759dx4..................	4·50	8·00
MS872c **180d**	$14.20 No. 758bx2; No. 759bx4..................	4·25	8·00

A limited edition prestige booklet *sold at* $25 was issued on 30 September 2000. This contained two panes each consisting of one *se-tenant* pair (values $1.30 and $2.50 or $3.10 and $5) with elliptical perforations in re-drawn designs as Nos. 884/887 but all inscribed 'HONG KONG, CHINA' (*Price*, £14.50 *unused*).

183 Hong Kong Stadium

(Des M. Chan)

1997 (18 May). Modern Landmarks. T **183** and similar horiz designs. Multicoloured. Two phosphor bands ($1.30) or one phosphor band (others).

(a) Litho Enschedé. Perf 13½.

888	$1.30 Type **183**	30	25
889	$2.50 Peak Tower	60	55
890	$3.10 Hong Kong Convention and Exhibition Centre	85	1·10
891	$5 Lantau Bridge	1·40	5·00
888/891	*Set of 4*	2·75	6·50
MS892	130×76 mm. No. 891	1·00	2·50

(b) Photo Walsall. Perf 14×14½.

893	$1.30 Type **183**	75	25
894	$2.50 Peak Tower	1·25	1·00
895	$3.10 Hong Kong Convention and Exhibition Centre	1·25	1·50
896	$5 Lantau Bridge	2·50	6·00
893/896	*Set of 4*	5·50	8·00
MS897	130×76 mm. No. 896	1·00	2·50

183a (*image scaled to 49% of original size*)

(Des G. Lai and Leung Ka-shun. Litho Ashton-Potter America Inc, New York)

1997 (1 June). Paralympic Games, Atlanta (1996). Sheet 130×75 mm containing design as No. 861 but on ordinary paper. Perf 14×13.

MS898	$10 multicoloured	1·25	3·00

No. **MS**898 shows 'HONG KONG' printed in yellow fluorescence. The perforations show alternate small and large holes.

(Des A. Lam. Photo Courvoisier)

1997 (30 June). History of the Hong Kong Post Office. Sheet 130×75 mm containing design as No. 677, but redrawn smaller, 22×38 mm. One phosphor band. Perf 11½.

MS899	$5 multicoloured	1·00	2·00

Details of the Post Office buildings depicted on the miniature sheet are printed on the reverse.

> Hong Kong became a Special Administrative Region of the People's Republic of China on 1 July 1997 when all previous stamp issues with the exception of Nos. 848/871 were withdrawn and invalidated.

CHINESE SPECIAL REGION

184 House of Sam Tung Uk

185 Graphs and Hong Kong Bank (Finance and Banking)

(Litho Postage Stamp Ptg Wks, Peking)

1997 (1 July). Establishment of Hong Kong as Special Administrative Region of People's Republic of China. T **184** and similar vert designs. Multicoloured. Two phosphor bands ($1.30, $1.60) or one phosphor band (others). Perf 12×12½.

900	$1.30 Type **184**	40	40
901	$1.60 Hong Kong Bank and vehicles	50	50
902	$2.50 Buildings and Hong Kong Convention and Exhibition Centre	65	80
903	$2.60 Container Terminal	75	85
904	$3.10 Junks and Dolphins	90	95
905	$5 Bauhinia flower and clouds	1·40	1·50
900/905	*Set of 6*	4·25	4·50
MS906	131×75 mm. No. 905	1·50	2·00

(Des C. Tillyer. Litho Ashton-Potter Canada)

1997 (21 Sept). World Bank Group and International Monetary Fund Annual Meetings. T **185** and similar horiz designs. Multicoloured. Two phosphor bands ($1.30) or one band (others). Perf 14½.

907	$1.30 Type **185**	40	40
908	$2.50 Share prices and Stock Exchange (Investment)	65	65
909	$3.10 Map on printed circuit and dish aerial (Trade and Telecommunications)	75	75
910	$5 Satellite image and road junctions (Infrastructure and Transport)	1·40	1·50
907/910	*Set of 4*	3·00	3·00

186 Clam

187 Tiger

(Des Li Shik-kwang. Photo Enschedé)

1997 (9 Nov). Sea Shells. T **186** and similar vert designs. Multicoloured. Two phosphor bands ($1.30) or one band (others). Perf 13½.

911	$1.30 Type **186**	50	40
912	$2.50 Cowrie	90	80
913	$3.10 Cone	1·25	95
914	$5 Murex	2·00	1·50
911/914	*Set of 4*	4·25	3·25

(Des Kan Tai-keung. Litho Ashton-Potter Canada)

1998 (4 Jan). Chinese New Year. Year of the Tiger. T **187** and similar horiz designs. Two phosphor bands ($1.30) or one band (others). Perf 13½.

915	$1.30 multicoloured	65	40
	a. Perf 14½. Booklets	90	50
	ab. Booklet pane. Nos. 915a×6 and 917a×6	18·00	
916	$2.50 multicoloured	1·00	90
917	$3.10 multicoloured	1·25	1·10
	a. Perf 14½. Booklets	2·00	1·25
918	$5 multicoloured	1·75	1·60
915/918	*Set of 4*	4·25	3·50
MS919	133×84 mm. Nos. 915/918	7·75	7·50

188 Star, 1900s

(Des J. Wong Chun-wing. Photo Enschedé)

1998 (26 Apr). Centenary of Star Ferry. T **188** and similar horiz designs. Multicoloured. Two phosphor bands ($1.30) or one band (others). Perf 13½.

920	$1.30 Type **188**	50	40
921	$2.50 Star, 1910s–1920s	1·10	95
922	$3.10 Star, 1920s–1950s	1·40	1·10
923	$5 Star, 1950s onwards	2·10	1·75
920/923	*Set of 4*	4·50	3·75

Nos. 920/923, but perf 14½ were also issued in a premium booklet No. SP1 containing one example of each stamp and *sold at $25 (Price, £45 unused)*. The booklet was sold only at Australia 99 International Stamp Exhibition.

189 Observation Lounge

(Des B. Kwan. Litho German State Ptg Wks, Berlin)

1998 (5 July). Inauguration of Hong Kong International Airport, Chek Lap Kok. T **189** and similar horiz designs. Multicoloured. Two phosphor bands (Nos. 924/925) or one band (others). Perf 14.

924	$1.30 Type **189**	50	40
	a. Block of 6. Nos. 924/929	6·75	
925	$1.60 Couple boarding train	65	60
926	$2.50 Train and suspension bridge	90	80
927	$2.60 Concourse and mail vans at Airmail Centre	1·00	85
928	$3.10 Aircraft in bays	1·25	95
929	$5 Aeroplane taking off	2·10	1·50
924/929	Set of 6	5·75	4·50
MS930	145×79 mm. No. 929	3·25	3·00

Nos. 924/929 were issued both in separate sheets of 25 stamps and together in *se-tenant* blocks of six within sheets of 24 stamps.

A limited edition premium booklet No. SP6 *sold at* $65 was issued on 25 August 2001.

This consisted of three panes, one of which contained four values as No. 927.

190 de Havilland DH.86 Dragon Express *Dorado* (Hong Kong–Penang Service, 1936)

(Des A. Lam. Photo Enschedé)

1998 (5 July). Closure of Kai Tak Airport. Sheet 130×75 mm. One phosphor band. Perf 13½.

MS931	**190** $5 multicoloured	6·00	6·00

T **190** is a redrawn version of T **111**.

191 Grasshopper and Cub Scouts and Knot

192 Graphic Design

(Des G. Lai. Litho German State Ptg Wks, Berlin)

1998 (26 July). 85th Anniversary of Hong Kong Scout Association. T **191** and similar vert designs. Multicoloured. Two phosphor bands ($1.30) or one band (others). Perf 14.

932	$1.30 Type **191**	80	50
933	$2.50 Two scouts, knot, watchtower and tents	1·40	85
934	$3.10 Two venture scouts, knot, sailing dinghies and helicopter	1·75	1·25
935	$5 Rover scout and adult leader, knot and buildings	2·75	1·80
932/935	Set of 4	6·00	4·00

(Des J. Au. Litho Enschedé)

1998 (20 Sept). Hong Kong Designs. T **192** and similar vert designs. Multicoloured. Two phosphor bands ($1.30) or one band (others). Perf 13½.

936	$1.30 Type **192**	80	50
937	$2.50 Product design	1·40	90
938	$3.10 Interior design	1·75	1·10
939	$5 Fashion design	2·75	1·75
936/939	Set of 4	6·00	3·75

193 Dragonfly Kite   **194** Rabbit

(Des Wong Chun-hong. Litho Ashton-Potter Canada)

1998 (15 Nov). Kites. T **193** and similar vert designs. Multicoloured. Two phosphor bands ($1.30) or one band (others). Perf 13½.

940	$1.30 Type **193**	80	50
941	$2.50 Dragon kite	1·40	1·00
942	$3.10 Butterfly kite	1·75	1·25
943	$5 Goldfish kite	2·75	1·90
940/943	Set of 4	6·00	4·25
MS944	135×85 mm. Nos. 940/943	6·00	5·50

(Des B. Kwan. Photo Enschedé)

1999 (31 Jan). Chinese New Year. Year of the Rabbit. T **194** and similar vert designs. Multicoloured. Three phosphor bands ($1.30) or one band (others). Perf 13½.

945	$1.30 Type **194**	80	50
946	$2.50 Rabbit and scroll	1·40	90
947	$3.10 Rabbit and tangerine	1·75	1·10
948	$5 Rabbit and sweet tray	2·75	1·80
945/948	Set of 4	6·00	3·75

The gold part of the designs can be scratched off to reveal a greeting in Chinese characters. Each stamp in a sheetlet of ten shows a different message.

The phosphor bands on the $1.30 consist of one band running the full length of the stamp and two short bands.

195 Rabbit

(Des Kan Tai-keung. Recess and litho Enschedé)

1999 (21 Feb). Chinese Lunar Cycle. Sheet 250×148 mm containing similar designs to 1987–1998 New Year issues but with inscriptions changed as in T **195** and some face values altered. Multicoloured. Two phosphor bands on each stamp. Perf 13½.

MS949 $1.30 As Type **175**; $1.30 As Type **181**; $1.30 As Type **187**; $1.30 Type **195**; $1.30 As Type **170**; $1.30 As Type **130**; $1.30 As No. 768; $1.30 As Type **136**; $1.30 As No. 735; $1.30 As Type **153**; $1.30 As Type **148**; $1.30 As Type **143**	16·00 18·00

196 Calligraphy   **197** An An

(Des G. So. Litho Walsall)

1999 (14 Mar). International Year of the Elderly. T **196** and similar vert designs. Multicoloured. Two phosphor bands ($1.30) or one band (others). Perf 14½.

950	$1.30 Type **196**	1·00	50
951	$2.50 Holding bird cage	1·75	90
952	$3.10 Playing chess	2·50	1·25
953	$5 Holding walking stick (voluntary services)	3·50	1·80
950/953	Set of 4	8·00	4·00

(Des T. Ho. Litho Enschedé)

1999 (27 Mar). Hong Kong Team's Achievements at 13th Asian Games, Bangkok (1998). Sheet 135×85 mm. Two phosphor bands ($2, $2.10) or one band (others). Perf 13½×13.

MS954	Nos. 856/859.	6·00	5·00

(Des T. Ho. Litho Ashton-Potter Canada)

1999 (25 Apr). Presentation of Giant Pandas An An and Jia Jia to Hong Kong. Sheet 132×78 mm. Perf 14.

MS955	**197** $10 multicoloured.	8·00	8·50

Uncut collector's sheets containing ten examples of No. **MS**955 were also available.

198 Bus

199 Hong Kong seen from Victoria Harbour

(Des Jan Adams. Litho Walsall Security Printers Ltd)

1999 (23 May). Public Transport. T **198** and similar horiz designs. Multicoloured. Two phosphor bands ($1.30) or one band (others). Perf 14½.

956	$1.30 Type **198**.	90	55
957	$2.40 Minibus.	1·75	1·10
958	$2.50 Tram.	1·75	1·10
959	$2.60 Taxi.	1·75	1·25
960	$3.10 'Airport Express' train.	2·50	1·75
956/960 *Set of 5*.		8·00	5·00

(Des A. Lam. Litho Banknote Corporation of America Inc, Browns Summit, North Carolina)

1999 (1 July). Hong Kong and Singapore Tourist Sights. T **199** and similar square designs. Multicoloured. Two phosphor bands (Nos. 961/962) or one band (others). Perf 13½.

961	$1.20 Type **199**.	60	40
962	$1.30 Singapore skyline.	65	50
963	$2.50 Great Buddha, Lantau Island, Hong Kong.	1·25	85
964	$2.60 Merlion statue, Sentosa Island, Singapore.	1·25	90
965	$3.10 Street scene, Hong Kong.	1·75	1·25
966	$5 Bugis Junction, Singapore.	2·75	1·90
961/966 *Set of 6*.		7·25	5·25
MS967 133×76 mm. Nos. 961/966.		9·00	6·50

(Des Li Shik-kwong. Litho Enschedé)

1999 (21 Aug). China 1999 International Stamp Exhibition, Peking. Sheet 130×75 mm. Perf 14×13.

MS968	No. 861.	6·00	8·00

No. **MS**968 shows 'HONG KONG' in yellow fluorescence.

200 Hong Kong and People's Republic Flags and Hong Kong

201 Museum of Tea Ware

(Des T. Ho. Litho Southern Colour Print, Dunedin, New Zealand)

1999 (1 Oct). 50th Anniversary of People's Republic of China. T **200** and similar horiz designs. Multicoloured. Two phosphor bands ($1.30) or one band (others). Granite paper. Perf 14½ (with one elliptical hole on each vert side).

969	$1.30 Type **200**.	90	70
	a. Block or strip of 4. Nos. 969/972.	7·00	
970	$2.50 *Bauhinia blakeana* and Hong Kong harbour.	1·50	1·25
971	$3.10 Chinese Dragon Dance.	1·75	1·25
972	$5 Firework display over Hong Kong.	2·75	2·25
969/972 *Set of 4*.		6·25	5·00

The magenta and yellow colours are fluorescent.

Nos. 969/972 were issued both in separate sheets of 25 stamps and together in *se-tenant* strips of four stamps within sheets of 16.

(Des C. Tillyer. Photo Enschedé)

1999 (18 Oct)–**02**. Hong Kong Landmarks and Tourist Attractions. T **201** and similar vert designs. Multicoloured. Two phosphor bands (10c. to $2.10) or one band (others). Granite paper.

(a) Perf 13×14 (10c. to $5) or 13½×13 (others) (all with one elliptical hole on each vert side).

973	10c. Type **201**.	30	25
974	20c. St John's Cathedral.	30	25
975	50c. Legislative Council building.	30	25
976	$1 Tai Fu Tai.	45	25
977	$1.20 Wong Tai Sin Temple.	55	30
978	$1.30 Victoria Harbour.	60	30
	a. Booklet pane. No. 978×10.	6·25	
979	$1.40 Hong Kong Railway Museum.	60	30
	a. Booklet pane. No. 979×10 (1.4.02).	6·25	
980	$1.60 Tsim Sha Tsui clocktower.	70	35
980a	$1.80 Hong Kong Stadium (1.4.02).	85	35
980b	$1.90 Western Market (1.4.02).	90	40
981	$2 Happy Valley racecourse.	1·10	50
982	$2.10 Kowloon–Canton Railway.	3·25	50
982a	$2.40 Repulse Bay (1.4.02).	3·25	60
	ab. Booklet pane. No. 982a×10 (1.4.02).	14·50	
983	$2.50 Chi Lin Nunnery, Kowloon.	1·40	60
	a. Booklet pane. No. 983×10.	14·50	
983b	$3 The Peak Tower (1.4.02).	1·75	95
	bc. Booklet pane. No. 983b×10 (1.4.02).	19·00	
984	$3.10 Giant Buddha, Po Lin Monastery, Lantau Island.	1·75	95
	a. Booklet pane. No. 984×10.	19·00	
985	$5 Pagoda, Aw Boon Haw Gardens.	2·25	1·25
986	$10 Tsing Ma bridge (26×31 mm).	3·75	2·40
986a	$13 Hong Kong Cultural Centre (26×31 mm) (1.4.02).	6·75	4·25
987	$20 Hong Kong Convention and Exhibition Centre (26×31 mm).	8·25	6·00
988	$50 Hong Kong International Airport (26×31 mm).	21·00	16·00
973/988 *Set of 21*.		50·00	33·00
MS989 210×153 mm. Nos. 973/980, 981/982, 983, 984/985.		10·00	10·00
MS990 118×89 mm. Nos. 986 and 987/988.		36·00	36·00

(b) Coil stamps. Size 20×24 mm. Perf 14×13½ (Nos. 991/993, 994) or 15×13½ (Nos. 993a, 994a/994d) (all with one elliptical hole on each vert side).

991	10c. Type **201**.	1·40	1·10
	a. Perf 15×13½.	90	50
992	50c. As No. 975.	1·40	1·10
	a. Perf 15×13½.	1·25	55
993	$1.30 As No. 978.	3·00	2·40
	aa. Perf 15×13½.	2·10	60
993a	$1.40 As No. 979 (1.4.02).	2·10	60
994	$1.60 As No. 980.	3·00	1·75
	aa. Perf 15×13½.	2·25	65
994a	$1.80 As No. 980a (1.4.02).	2·75	95
994b	$2.40 As No. 982a (1.4.02).	3·00	1·25
994c	$2.50 As No. 983.	4·50	3·50
	ca. Perf 15×13½.	3·00	1·25
994d	$3 As No. 983b (1.4.02).	3·75	1·75
994e	$3.10 As No. 984.	6·00	3·50
	ea. Perf 15×13½.	3·75	2·00
991a/994ea *Set of 10 (cheapest)*.		22·00	9·00

The booklet panes have their top and bottom edges imperforate, giving stamps with one side imperf.

A premium booklet No. SP2 containing Nos. 973/985 in 13 single-stamp panes, to the value of $22, was *sold at* $35.

For miniature sheets containing No. 986 see Nos. **MS**1011, **MS**1012, **MS**1017, **MS**1038, **MS**1066, **MS**1111, **MS**1112 and **MS**1113.

For miniature sheets containing No. 985 see Nos. **MS**1061 and **MS**1085.

Nos. 991/994 were issued in coils with every fifth stamp numbered on the back.

See Nos. 1214/1234 for Nos. 973/988, with new face values.

A limited edition premium booklet No. SP6 *sold at* $65 was issued on 25 August 2001. This consisted of three panes, one of which contained two values as No. 984 but perf 13½×14 and two values as No. 859 *(Price, £30 unused)*.

202 Dolphins

203 Dragon Boat Race (fire) and City Skyline (metal)

(Des C. Tillyer. Litho Walsall Security Printers Ltd)

1999 (14 Nov). Endangered Species. The Indo-Pacific Hump-backed Dolphin ('Chinese White Dolphin'). T **202** and similar vert designs. Two phosphor bands ($1.30) or one band (others). Granite paper. Perf 14½.

995	$1.30 Type **202**	1·00	70
996	$2.50 multicoloured	1·75	1·25
997	$3.10 multicoloured	2·50	1·50
998	$5 multicoloured	3·50	2·10
995/998 *Set of 4*		8·00	5·00
MS999 150×80 mm. Nos. 995/998		10·00	8·75

A limited edition premium booklet No. SP3 *sold at* $35 was issued on 17 June 2000. This contained three panes each of one value in re-drawn designs as Nos. 501, 840 and 998 (*Price, £18 unused*).

(Des A. Lam. Photo Courvoisier)

1999 (31 Dec). New Millennium (1st issue). The Five Elements. Sheet 130×75 mm containing T **203** and similar horiz design. Multicoloured. One phosphor band. Granite paper. Perf 14½ (with one elliptical hole on each vert side).

MS1000 $5 Type **203**; $5 Tsing Ma bridge (wood) and birds flying over Mai Po Marshes (water)	7·00	5·75

204 Victoria Harbour

2000. New Millennium (2nd issue). Embossed and litho. Perf 13½.

1001	**204**	$50 multicoloured	32·00	32·00

No. 1001 is embossed with 22 carat gold.

205 Scales on Globe (Au Chung-yip)   **206** Dragon

(Des T. Ho. Photo Courvoisier)

2000. New Millennium (3rd issue). Winning Entries in Children's Millennium Stamp Design Competition. T **205** and similar horiz designs. Multicoloured. Granite paper. Two phosphor bands ($1.30) or one band (others). Perf 14½ (with one elliptical hole on each vert side).

1002	$1.30 Type **205**	70	50
1003	$2.50 Globe, space shuttle, houses and children watering tree (Cheung Hang).	1·25	95
1004	$3.10 Planets (Valerie Teh)	1·50	1·10
1005	$5 Planets, spacecraft and satellite (Tsui Ming-yin)	2·50	1·75
1002/1005 *Set of 4*		5·50	4·00

(Des B. Kwan. Litho Walsall Security Printers Ltd)

2000 (23 Jan). Chinese New Year. Year of the Dragon. T **206** and similar vert designs showing Dragons. Granite paper. Two phosphor bands ($1.30) or one band (others). Perf 14½ (with one elliptical hole on each vert side).

1006	$1.30 multicoloured	1·00	50
1007	$2.50 multicoloured	1·60	95

1008	$3.10 multicoloured	1·75	1·10
1009	$5 multicoloured	2·75	1·75
1006/1009 *Set of 4*		6·50	4·00
MS1010 Two sheets, each 135×85 mm. (a) Nos. 1006/1009. (b) $5 No. 1009. Imperf		29·00	30·00

(Des B. Kwan. Photo Courvoisier)

2000 (31 Jan). Establishment of the Certification Authority. Sheet 140×90 mm containing design as No. 986. Perf 14×14½ (with one elliptical hole on each vert side).

MS1011 $10 multicoloured	6·00	6·50

(Des C. Tillyer and A. Lam. Photo Courvoisier)

2000 (10 Feb). Visit HONG KONG 2001 Stamp Exhibition (1st issue). Sheet 130×74 mm containing design as No. 986, and with marginal illustration showing birds. Perf 14×14½ (with one elliptical hole on each vert side).

MS1012 $10 multicoloured	6·00	6·50

See also Nos. **MS**1017, **MS**1028, **MS**1037, **MS**1051 and **MS**1052.

207 Hong Kong Heritage Museum, Sha Tin

(Des F. Lau. Litho Questa)

2000 (26 Mar). Museums and Libraries. T **207** and similar triangular designs. Multicoloured. Granite paper. Two phosphor bands ($1.30) or one band (others). Perf 14×14½ ($1.30, $3.10) or 14½×14 (others).

1013	$1.30 Type **207**	90	70
	a. Block of 4. Nos. 1013/1016	7·50	
1014	$2.50 Central Library, Causeway Bay	1·75	1·25
1015	$3.10 Museum of Coastal Defence, Shau Kei Wan	1·75	1·40
1016	$5 Museum of History, Tsim Sha Tsui East	2·75	2·25
1013/1016 *Set of 4*		6·50	5·00

Nos. 1013/1016 were issued separately in large sheets and together in *se-tenant* blocks of four stamps.

(Des C. Tillyer and A. Lam. Photo Enschedé)

2000 (15 Apr). Visit HONG KONG 2001 Stamp Exhibition (2nd issue). Sheet 130×75 mm containing design as No. 986, and with marginal illustration showing flowers. Perf 13½×13 (with one elliptical hole on each vert side).

MS1017 $10 multicoloured	6·00	6·50

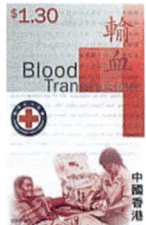

208 Patient and Nurse (Blood Transfusion)   **209** Lantern Fly (*Pyrops candelarius*)

(Des B. Kwan. Photo Courvoisier)

2000 (7 May). 50th Anniversary of Hong Kong Red Cross. T **208** and similar vert designs. Multicoloured. Granite paper. Two phosphor bands ($1.30) or one band (others). Perf 14½ (with one elliptical hole on each vert side).

1018	$1.30 Type **208**	75	60
1019	$2.50 Doctor and child (Special Education and Care for the Disabled)	1·40	1·10
1020	$3.10 Man distributing blankets (Disaster relief)	1·50	1·25
1021	$5 Volunteer and young man (Youth and Voluntary services)	2·75	2·10
1018/1021 *Set of 4*		5·75	4·50
MS1022 130×75 mm. Nos. 1018/1021		7·25	6·75

(Des C. Wong. Litho Enschedé)

2000 (16 July). Insects. T **209** and similar vert designs. Multicoloured. Granite paper. Two phosphor bands ($1.30) or one band (others). Perf 13½ (with one elliptical hole on each vert side).

1023	$1.30 Type **209**	95	80
1024	$2.50 Yellow-spotted Emerald (*Macromidia ellenae*)	1·60	1·25
1025	$3.10 Hong Kong Birdwing (butterfly) (*Troides helena spilotia*)	1·75	1·40
1026	$5 Red-cap Tortoise Beetle (*Chiridopsis bowringi*)	3·00	2·25
1023/1026 Set of 4		6·50	7·00
MS1027 130×75 mm. Nos. 1023/1026		6·50	5·50

210 Lion Rock **211** Cycling and Tennis

(Des A. Lam. Photo Enschedé)

2000 (12 Aug). Visit HONG KONG 2001 Stamp Exhibition (3rd issue). Sheet 130×75 mm. One phosphor band. Granite paper. Perf 13½×13 (with one elliptical hole on each vert side).

MS1028 **210** $10 multicoloured.......................... 6·50 7·00

(Des M. Miller. Litho Walsall Security Printers Ltd)

2000 (27 Aug). Olympic Games, Sydney. T **211** and similar vert designs. Multicoloured. Two phosphor bands ($1.30) or one band (others). Granite paper. P 14½ (with one elliptical hole on each vert side).

1029	$1.30 Type **211**	80	65
1030	$2.50 Table tennis and running	1·40	1·25
1031	$3.10 Wrestling and rowing	1·75	1·40
1032	$5 Diving and wind surfing	2·75	2·25
1029/1032 Set of 4		6·00	5·00

For Wetlands and Birds Paradise booklet panes, issued 30 September 2000, see note below Nos. 884/887.

212 View of Street (Establishment of Chamber, 1900) **213** Corals

(Des T. Ho. Litho Enschedé)

2000 (22 Oct). Centenary of the General Chamber of Commerce. T **212** and similar square designs. Multicoloured. Granite paper. Two phosphor bands ($1.30) or one band (others). Perf 14 (with one elliptical hole on each vert side).

1033	$1.30 Type **212**	80	65
1034	$2.50 Old and new headquarters (relocation, 1922)	1·40	1·25
1035	$3.10 Victims of Pak Tin village fire receiving aid	1·75	1·40
1036	$5 Man using abacus and hand using mouse	2·75	2·25
1033/1036 Set of 4		6·00	5·00

(Des A. Lam. Photo Enschedé)

2000 (25 Nov). Visit HONG KONG 2001 Stamp Exhibition (4th issue). Sheet 129×75 mm. One phosphor band. Granite paper. Perf 13½×13 (with one elliptical hole on each vert side).

MS1037 **213** $10 multicoloured.......................... 8·50 7·50

(Des C. Tillyer and T. Ho. Photo Courvoisier)

2000 (2 Dec). ITU Telecom, Asia 2000. Sheet 130×75 mm, containing design as No. 986. Perf 14×14½ (with one elliptical hole on each vert side).

MS1038 $10 multicoloured.................................. 8·50 7·50

214 Hong Kong Convention and Exhibition Centre **215** Snake

(Des C. Tillyer and Liliane Tsui. Litho and holography Cartor)

2000 (31 Dec). New Millennium. Sheet 91×151 mm. Perf 13½×13.

MS1039 **214** $20 multicoloured......................... 12·00 13·00

(Des B. Kwan. Photo Courvoisier)

2001 (1 Jan). Chinese New Year. Year of the Snake. T **215** and similar vert designs showing Snakes. Two phosphor bands ($1.30) or one band (others). Granite paper. Perf 14½ (with one elliptical hole on each vert side).

1040	$1.30 multicoloured	80	65
1041	$2.50 multicoloured	1·40	1·25
1042	$3.10 multicoloured	1·75	1·40
1043	$5 multicoloured	2·75	2·25
1040/1043 Set of 4		6·00	5·00
MS1044 Two sheets, each 135×85 mm. (a) Nos. 1040/1043. (b) $5 No. 1043. Imperf		14·00	12·00

216 Leaves and Pebbles ('Happy Memories') **217** Dragon. Year of the Dragon

(Des A. Lam. Photo Courvoisier)

2001 (1 Feb). Greetings Stamps. T **216** and similar horiz designs. Multicoloured. Two phosphor bands ($1.30, $1.60) or one band (others). Granite paper. Perf 14½ (with one elliptical hole on each vert side).

1045	$1.30 Type **216**	80	50
1046	$1.60 Swans ('Happy Valentine's Day')	1·00	65
1047	$2.50 Chicks ('Happy Birthday')	1·60	1·25
1048	$2.60 Cherry blossom ('Happy New Year')	1·90	1·25
1049	$3.10 Bamboo ('A Successful Year')	2·25	1·60
1050	$5 Poinsetta ('Merry Christmas')	3·50	2·25
1045/1050 Set of 6		10·00	6·75

Nos. 1045/1050 were each issued with a *se-tenant* half stamp-size label inscribed with the appropriate greeting.

No. 1045/1050 were re-issued for Beijing 2001 on 12 June 2001, printed by Questa, with *se-tenant* half size labels showing athletes and entertainment personalities. Entitled 'My wish', the two sheetlets of 18 (face value $46.80) were issued to promote Beijing's bid for the 2008 Olympic Games and cost $120.

(Des B. Kwan. Litho and embossed Cartor)

2001 (1 Feb). Visit HONG KONG 2001 Stamp Exhibition (5th issue). Sheet 135×90 mm. Perf 13½.

MS1051 $50 Type **217**; $50 Snake. Year of the Snake....... 50·00 48·00

No. **MS**1051 has the Dragon and the Snake embossed in gold and silver foil, and was issued in a commemorative folder.

218 Schima Tree

219 Tai Tam Tuk
Reservoir

(Des B. Kwan. Photo Courvoisier)

2001 (2–5 Feb). Visit HONG KONG 2001 Stamp Exhibition (6th issue). Sheet 130×75 mm. One phosphor band. Granite paper. Perf 14½ (with one elliptical hole on each vert side).

MS1052 $5 multicoloured. As T **218**. (a) with new blue border. (b) with new blue and yellow border. (c) with new blue, yellow and magenta borders. (d) with multicoloured border. *Set of 4 sheets*................. 13·00 13·00

No. **MS**1052 was issued on four consecutive days of the exhibition.

(Des E. Chan. Litho and embossed Walsall Security Printers Ltd)

2001 (18 Mar). 150th Anniversary of Hong Kong's Public Water Supply. T **219** and similar vert designs. Multicoloured. Two phosphor bands ($1.30) or one band (others). Granite paper. Perf 14½ (with one elliptical hole on each vert side).

1053	$1.30 Type **219**........................	80	65
	a. Block of 4. Nos. 1053/1056	7·00	
1054	$2.50 Plover Cove Reservoir	1·40	1·25
1055	$3.10 Guangdong to Hong Kong water pipeline	1·75	1·40
1056	$5 Water monitoring equipment and chemical symbols........................	2·75	2·25
1053/1056 *Set of 4*........................		6·00	5·00

Nos. 1053/1056 were issued together in *se-tenant* blocks of four stamps within the sheet.

220 Ng Cho-fan and Pak Yin

(Des Lee Chow-ming. Litho Enschedé)

2001 (8 Apr). Hong Kong Film Stars. T **220** and similar horiz designs. Multicoloured. Two phosphor bands ($1.30) or one band (others). Granite paper. Perf 13½×14½ (with one elliptical hole on each vert side).

1057	$1.30 Type **220**........................	80	65
	a. Block of 4. Nos. 1057/1060	7·00	7·00
	b. Sheetlet. Nos. 1057/1060	28·00	
1058	$2.50 Sun Ma Si-tsang and Tang Bik-wan ...	1·40	2·00
1059	$3.10 Cheung Wood-yau and Wong Man-lei..	1·75	2·00
1060	$5 Mak Bing-wing and Fung Wong-nui......	2·75	3·00
1057/1060 *Set of 4*........................		7·00	7·00

Nos. 1057/1060 were additionally perforated 13 in curved lines around the design.

Nos. 1057/1060 were issued separately in sheets of 25 stamps or together in *se-tenant* blocks of four stamps within sheets of 16.

(Des C. Tillyer and Li Shik-kwong. Photo Enschedé)

2001 (21 Apr). Ninth National Games, Guangzhou, People's Republic of China. Preliminary Contest for Sanda (discipline in National Games), Hong Kong. Sheet 130×75 mm containing design as No. 985 and with marginal illustration showing boxing gloves. Perf 13×14 (with one elliptical hole on each vert side).

MS1061 $5 multicoloured........................ 4·50 3·50

 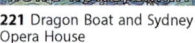 

221 Dragon Boat and Sydney Opera House

222 Emblem

(Des Kan Tai-keung and Chan Kau On. Litho SNP Ausprint, Australia)

2001 (25 June). Dragon Boat Racing. T **221** and similar horiz design. Multicoloured. One phosphor band. Granite paper. Perf 14×14½.

1062	$5 Type **221**........................	2·75	2·25
1063	$5 Dragon boat racing and Hong Kong Convention and Exhibition Centre.........	2·75	2·25
MS1064 106×70 mm. Nos. 1062/1063........................		7·50	7·50

Stamps in similar designs were issued by Australia.

(Des A. Lam. Photo Postage Stamp Printing Works, Beijing)

2001 (14 July). Choice of Beijing, China as 2008 Olympic Host City. Two phosphor bands. Perf 13×13½.

1065 **222** $1.30 multicoloured........................ 1·60 1·25

No. 1065 was issued in sheetlets comprising two blocks of six stamps and six *se-tenant* half stamp-size labels, separated by an enlarged label showing the Hong Kong skyline.

(Des C. Tillyer and B. Kwan. Photo Enschedé)

2001 (1 Aug). PHILA NIPPON 2001 World Stamp Exhibition, Tokyo. Sheet 130×75 mm containing design as No. 986. Perf 13½×13 (with one elliptical hole on each vert side).

MS1066 $10 multicoloured........................ 9·00 7·00

223 Pouring Tea (Gongfu tea)

224 Centella asiatica

(Des T. Ho. Litho Questa)

2001 (9 Sept). Tea Culture. T **223** and similar vert designs. Multicoloured. Granite paper. Two phosphor bands ($1.30) or one bands (others). Perf 14½ (with one elliptical hole on each vert side).

1067	$1.30 Type **223**........................	80	65
1068	$2.50 Hong Kong style tea	1·40	1·25
1069	$3.10 Pouring water (Yum Cha and Dim Sum)	1·90	1·60
1070	$5 Pouring hot water into tea pot	3·00	2·25
1067/1070 *Set of 4*........................		6·50	5·25

(Des C. Yick. Litho Questa)

2001 (7 Oct). Medicinal Herbs. T **224** and similar vert designs. Multicoloured. Two phosphor bands ($1.30) or one band (others). Granite paper. Perf 14½ (with one elliptical hole on each vert side).

1071	$1.30 Type **224**........................	80	65
1072	$2.50 *Lobelia chinensis*	1·40	1·25
1073	$3.10 *Gardenia jasminoides*	1·90	1·60
1074	$5 *Scutellaria indica*........................	3·00	2·25
1071/1074 *Set of 4*........................		6·50	5·25

225 Child dressed as Bear

226 Horse

(Des Kan Tai-keung. Litho Enschedé)

2001 (18 Nov). Children's Stamps. T **225** and similar vert designs. Two phosphor bands ($1.30) or one band (others). Granite paper. Self-adhesive gum. Die-cut perf 14×13½ (with one elliptical hole on each vert side).

1075	$1.30 Type **225**........................	80	65
1076	$2.50 Child dressed as Duck	1·40	1·25
1077	$3.10 Child dressed as pot plant........	1·90	1·60

1078	$5 Child dressed as Bee	3·00	2·25
1075/1079	Set of 4	6·50	5·25
MS1079	130×92 mm. Nos. 1075/1078.	7·25	7·00

The stamps had portions of the design left white for users to colour as they wished.

Such embellishments did not affect the postal validity of the stamps.

(Des B. Kwan. Litho Questa)

2002 (13 Jan). Chinese New Year. Year of the Horse. T **226** and similar vert designs showing Horses. Two phosphor bands ($1.30) or one band (others). Granite paper. Perf 14½ (with one elliptical hole on each vert side).

1080	$1.30 multicoloured	80	65
1081	$2.50 multicoloured	1·40	1·25
1082	$3.10 multicoloured	1·90	1·60
1083	$5 multicoloured	3·00	2·25
1080/1083	Set of 4	6·50	5·25
MS1084	Two sheets, each 135×85 mm. (a) Nos. 1080/1083. (b) No. 1083. Imperf.	12·00	12·50

(Des C. Tillyer and T. Ho. Photo Enschedé)

2002 (19 Jan). Serving the Community Festival, 2002. Sheet 75×130 mm containing design as No. 985 and with marginal illustration showing paper sculpture by Rebecca Leung of community activities. Perf 13×14 (with one elliptical hole on each vert side).

MS1085	$5 multicoloured	5·00	5·50

 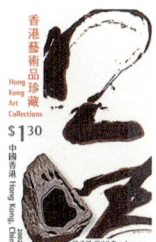

227 Snake   **228** *Lines in Motion* (detail, Chui Tze-hung)

(Des B. Kwan. Litho and embossed Cartor)

2002 (9 Feb). Chinese New Year. Year of the Snake. Sheet 135×90 mm. Perf 13½.

MS1086	$50 Type **227**; $50 Horse. Year of the Horse.	55·00	55·00

No. **MS**1086 has the Snake and the Horse embossed in gold and silver foil.

(Des C. Yick. Litho Questa)

2002 (24 Feb). Modern Art. T **228** and similar vert designs. Two phosphor bands ($1.30) or one band (others). Granite paper. Perf 14½ (with one elliptical hole on each vert side).

1087	$1.30 Type **228**	80	65
	a. Block or strip of 4. Nos. 1087/1090	6·00	
1088	$2.50 *Volume and Time* (detail, Hon Chi-fun)	1·40	1·25
1089	$3.10 *Bright Sun* (sculpture, detail, Aries Lee)	1·75	1·40
1090	$5 *Midsummer* (detail, Irene Chou)	2·75	2·25
1087/1090	Set of 4	6·00	5·00

Nos. 1087/1090 were issued separately in sheets of 25 stamps and together in *se-tenant* sheetlets of 16.

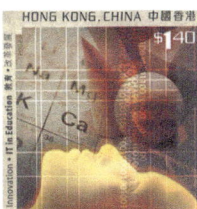 

229 Face and Periodic Table (Education)   **230** Player and Football

(Des A. Lam. Litho Questa)

2002 (14 Apr). Information Technology. T **229** and similar horiz designs. Multicoloured. Two phosphor bands (No. 1091) or one band (others). Granite paper. Perf 14 (with one elliptical hole on each vert side).

1091	$1.40 Type **229**	90	65
	a. Horiz or vert strip of 4. Nos. 1091/1094	6·75	
1092	$2.40 Face, world map and internet symbols (communications)	1·40	1·00

1093	$3 Face, film and musical notes (entertainment)	1·75	1·25
1094	$5 face, buildings and city (commerce)	3·00	2·25
1091/1094	Set of 4	6·25	4·75

Nos. 1091/1094 were issued both in individual sheets of 25 stamps and in horizontal or vertical *se-tenant* strips of four within sheetlets of 16.

A limited edition premium booklet No. SP7 *sold at* $30 was issued on 14 April 2002. This contained two panes each consisting of one pair of stamps (values $1.40 and $3 or $2.40 and $5).

(Des B. Kwan. Photo Postage Stamp Printing Works, Beijing)

2002 (16 May). World Cup Football Championship. Japan and South Korea. T **230** and similar horiz design. Multicoloured. Two phosphor bands. Paper with fluorescent fibres. Perf 12 (with one elliptical hole on each vert side).

1095	$1.40 Type **230**	1·10	90
	a. Horiz pair. Nos. 1095/1096, plus central label	2·25	1·90
1096	$1.40 Players tackling and crowd	1·10	90

Nos. 1095/1096 were issued together in horizontal pairs in sheetlets of ten stamps, five of each design, and a central vertical row of half stamp-sized labels featuring Group C teams and matches.

A special miniature sheet, 160×227 mm, containing one example of each pair of stamps issued by Hong Kong, Chinese People's Republic and Macau was available in a presentation folder.

231 North Atlantic Pink Tree Coral, Pacific Orange Cup Coral and North Pacific Horn Coral

(Des, Signals Design Group (Nos. 1097/1098), B. Kwan (others). Litho Enschedé)

2002 (19 May). Corals. T **231** and similar horiz designs. Multicoloured. Two phosphor bands (No. 1097) or one phosphor band (others). Granite paper. Perf 14 (with one elliptical hole on each vert side).

1097	$1.40 Type **231**	1·50	65
1098	$2.40 North Atlantic Giant Orange Tree Coral and Black Coral	2·00	1·00
1099	$3 *Dendronephthya gigantea* and *Dendronephthya*	3·25	1·25
1100	$5 *Tubastrea* and *Echinogorgia* and island	4·25	2·25
1097/1100	Set of 4	10·00	4·75
MS1101	161×85 mm. Nos. 1097/1100.	10·00	9·00

Stamps in similar designs were issued by Canada.

A limited edition premium booklet No. SP8 *sold at* $25 was issued on 10 May 2003. This contained two panes both inscribed 'Hoi Ha Wan MARINE PARK', each containing one pair of stamps as Nos. 1097/1098 and 1099/1100 (*Price*, £14.50 *unused*).

232 Hong Kong Buildings and Train

(Des A. Cao. Litho Southern Colour Print, Dunedin, New Zealand)

2002 (9 June). Fifth Anniversary of Beijing–Kowloon Through Train Service. T **232** and similar horiz designs. Multicoloured. Two phosphor bands (No. 1102) or one band (others). Granite paper. Perf 14½ (with one elliptical hole on each vert side).

1102	$1.40 Type **232**	80	65
	a. Horiz strip of 4. Nos. 1102/1105	6·75	
1103	$2.40 Wuhan–Changjiang Bridge and train	1·25	1·00
1104	$3 Pagodas, Shaolin Monastery, Zhengzhou and train	1·60	1·25
1105	$5 Temple of Heaven, Beijing and front of train	2·75	2·25
1102/1105	Set of 4	5·75	4·75

Nos. 1102/1105 were issued both in separate sheets of 25 stamps and together in horizontal strips of four stamps, each strip forming a composite design of a train.

The strips were each separated by a gutter.

233 Chinese White Dolphins and Coral

(Des B. Lau. Litho Walsall Security Printers Ltd)

2002 (1 July). Fifth Anniversary of Hong Kong's Status as Special Administrative Region of People's Republic of China. T **233** and similar horiz designs. Multicoloured. Two phosphor bands (No. 1106) or one band (others). Granite paper. Perf 14½ (with one elliptical hole on each vert side).

1106	$1.40 Type **233**	80	65
1107	$2.40 Schoolchildren and *bauhinia* flowers	1·25	1·00
1108	$3 Birds in flight over Hong Kong airport	1·60	1·25
1109	$5 Flags of China and Hong Kong, buildings and fireworks	2·75	2·25
1106/1109 *Set of 4*		5·75	4·75
MS1110 135×85 mm. Nos. 1106/1109		6·75	6·50

(Des C. Tillyer and P. Lung. Photo Enschedé)

2002 (27 July). PHILAKOREA 2002 World Stamp Exhibition, Seoul, South Korea. Sheet 131×75 mm containing design as No. 986. One phosphor band. Granite paper. Perf 13½×13 (with one elliptical hole on each vert side).

MS1111 $10 multicoloured		6·50	6·25

(Des C. Tillyer and F. Li. Photo Enschedé)

2002 (24 Aug). AMPHILEX 2002 World Stamp Exhibition, Amsterdam. Sheet 130×75 mm containing design as No. 986. One phosphor band. Granite paper. Perf 13½×13 (with one elliptical hole on each vert side).

MS1112 $10 multicoloured		6·50	6·25

(Des C. Tillyer and A. Lam. Photo Enschedé)

2002 (7 Sept). Hukou Waterfall Shanxi, People's Republic of China. Sheet 140×90 mm containing design as No. 986. One phosphor band. Granite paper. Perf 13½×13 (with one elliptical hole on each vert side).

MS1113 $10 multicoloured		6·50	6·25

234 Ping Chau

235 Radar Signal and Luopan (fengshui compass)

(Des Ken Li Shik Kwong. Litho and thermography Cartor)

2002 (15 Sept). Geology of Hong Kong. T **234** and similar horiz designs. Multicoloured. One phosphor band. Perf 13×13½ (with one elliptical hole on each vert side).

1114	$1.40 Type **234**	80	65
1115	$2.40 Port Island	1·25	1·00
1116	$3 Po Pin Chau	1·90	1·60
1117	$5 Lamma Island	4·00	3·25
1114/1117 *Set of 4*		7·25	5·75
MS1118 136×81 mm. Nos. 1114/1117		10·00	9·50

(Photo Enschedé)

2002 (14 Oct). Cultural Diversity. T **235** and similar horiz designs. Multicoloured. Granite paper.

(a) Two phosphor bands. Perf 13 (one elliptical hole on each vert side).

1119	10c. Type **235**	30	25
	a. Imperf sheet of 50	£2000	
	b. Booklet pane. Nos. 1119/1130	9·75	
1120	20c. Calculator and abacus	30	25
1121	50c. Incense coils and stained-glass window	30	25
1122	$1 Chair and Luohan (bed)	50	40
1123	$1.40 Dim Sum (dumplings) and loaves of bread	65	50
	a. Booklet pane. No. 1123×10	6·75	
1124	$1.80 Cutlery and chopsticks	80	65
1125	$1.90 Canned drinks and tea caddies	90	70
1126	$2 European and oriental wedding cakes	95	80
1127	$2.40 Erhu (stringed instrument) and violin	1·10	90
	a. Booklet pane. No. 1127×10	11·50	
1128	$2.50 Oriental letter box and internet symbol	1·25	1·00
1129	$3 Yachts and Dragon boat	1·40	1·25
	a. Booklet pane. No. 1129×10	14·50	
1130	$5 Traditional tiled roof and modern office block	2·40	2·00
1119/1130 *Set of 12*		9·75	8·00
MS1130a 210×150 mm. Nos. 1119/1130		11·00	10·50

(b) One phosphor band. Perf 14½×14 (one elliptical hole on each vert side).

1131	$10 Ballet dancers and Chinese opera character	4·75	2·50
1132	$13 Chess pieces and Xiangqi pieces (Chinese chess)	6·00	4·00
1133	$20 Christmas lights and Mid-autumn Festival lantern	9·50	5·25
1134	$50 Sculptures Oval with points (Henry Moore) and *Tai Chi series: Single Whip* (Ju Ming)	24·00	13·00
1131/1134 *Set of 4*		40·00	22·00
MS1135 122×101 mm. Nos. 1131/1134		45·00	44·00

(c) Coil stamps. 22×19 mm. Perf 13½×14½.

1136	$1.40 Dim Sum (dumplings) and loaves of bread	1·90	1·25
1137	$1.80 Cutlery and chopsticks	2·25	1·60
1138	$2.40 Erhu (stringed instrument) and violin	3·50	2·50
1139	$3 Yachts and Dragon boat	4·75	3·50
1136/1139 *Set of 4*		11·00	8·00

Nos. 1140/1145 are vacant.

236 Christmas Tree

237 Train and Station (Main Street)

(Des Ken Li Shik Kwong. Litho and die-stamped Enschedé)

2002 (24 Nov). Christmas. T **236** and similar vert designs. Multicoloured. Two phosphor bands ($1.40) or one phosphor band (others). Granite paper. Perf 13½ (with one elliptical hole on each vert side).

1146	$1.40 Type **236**	65	50
	a. Block or strip of 4. Nos. 1146/1149	5·50	
1147	$2.40 Bauble	1·10	90
1148	$3 Snowman	1·60	1·25
1149	$5 Bell	2·40	2·00
1146/1149 *Set of 4*		5·25	4·25

Nos. 1146/1149 were perforated around the designs.

Nos. 1146/1149 were issued separately in sheets of 25 and together, each×4, in sheetlets of 16 stamps comprising four se-tenant blocks of four.

(Litho and embossed Questa)

2003 (12 Jan). Disneyland Hong Kong. T **237** and similar square designs. Multicoloured. Two phosphor bands ($1.40) or one phosphor band (others). Granite paper. Perf 14 (with one elliptical hole on each vert side).

1150	$1.40 Type **237**	80	65
1151	$2.40 Castle (Fantasyland)	1·25	1·00
1152	$3 Tree house (Adventureland)	1·60	1·25
1153	$5 Pylons (Tomorrowland)	2·50	2·10
1150/1153 *Set of 4*		5·50	4·50
MS1154 135×85 mm. Nos. 1150/1153		6·50	6·25

Nos. 1150/**MS**1154 each have an embossed figure of Mickey Mouse in the lower left corner.

238 Argali Ram

239 Letter Writing

(Des B. Kwan)

2003 (19 Jan). New Year. Year of the Ram. T **238** and similar vert designs. Multicoloured.

(a) Two phosphor bands ($1.40) or one phosphor band (others). Granite paper. Imperf (No. MS1159(b)) or perf 14 (with one elliptical hole on each vert side) (others). Litho Questa.

1155	$1.40 Type **238**	80	65
1156	$2.40 Sheep	1·25	1·00
1157	$3 Tahr Ram	1·60	1·25
1158	$5 Gazelia Ram	2·50	2·10
1155/1158 *Set of 4*		5·50	4·50
MS1159 Two sheets, each 135×85 mm. (a) Nos. 1155/1158; (b) $5 No. 1158		12·00	12·00

(b) One phosphor band. Flocked paper. Perf 13. Litho Cartor.

1160	$10 As No. 1008 Year of the Dragon	4·75	4·00
	a. Block of 4. Nos. 1160/1163	20·00	
1161	$10 As No. 1042 Year of the Snake	4·75	4·00
1162	$10 As No. 1081 Year of the Horse	4·75	4·00
1163	$10 As No. 1158 Year of the Ram	4·75	4·00
1160/1163 *Set of 4*		17·00	14·50

(c) Size 38×51 mm. Ordinary paper. Perf 13½. Litho embossed and foil stamped Cartor.

MS1164 135×90 mm. $50 As No. 1162 Year of the Horse; $50 As. No. 1157		45·00	42·00

Nos. 1160/1163 were issued in *se-tenant* blocks of four stamps within sheets of 16.

No. **MS**1164 has the Horse and Ram embossed with gold and silver foil.

(Des M. Fung. Litho Enschedé)

2003 (13 Mar). Traditional Trades and Crafts. T **239** and similar multicoloured designs. Two phosphor bands ($1.40, $1.80) or one phosphor band (others). Granite paper. Perf 13½×14½ (horiz) or 14½×13½ (vert) (with one elliptical hole on each vert side).

1165	$1.40 Type **239**	80	65
1166	$1.80 Bird cage maker (*vert*)	1·00	85
1167	$2.40 Qipao tailoring (women's clothes)	1·25	1·00
1168	$2.50 Hairdressing (*vert*)	1·40	1·10
1169	$3 Making dough figures (*vert*)	1·60	1·25
1170	$5 Olive seller	2·50	2·10
1165/1170 *Set of 6*		7·75	6·25
MS1171 219×123 mm. Nos. 1165/1170		8·50	8·25

240 Hong Kong Skyline

(Des J. Chum. Litho Enschedé)

2003 (8 Apr). Hong Kong 2004 International Stamp Exhibition (1st issue). Sheet 135×85 mm. One phosphor band. Granite paper. Perf 13½×13 (with one elliptical hole on each vert side).

MS1172 **240** $10 multicoloured		6·50	7·00

See also Nos. **MS**1190, **MS**1213 and 1214/1234.

241 The Master-of-Nets Garden, Suzhou

(Des A. Lam. Litho Enschedé)

2003 (27 June). Mainland Scenery (1st issue). Sheet 140×90 mm. One phosphor band. Perf 13 (with one elliptical hole on each vert side).

MS1173 **241** $10 multicoloured		5·50	6·50

See also Nos. **MS**1243, **MS**1324, **MS**1349, **MS**1447, **MS**1495, **MS**1543, **MS**1594 and **MS**1671/**MS**1672.

242 Fukien Tea (semi-cascade)

(Des S. Check. Photo Enschedé)

2003 (17 July). Miniature Landscapes. T **242** and similar multicoloured designs. Two phosphor bands ($1.40) or one phosphor band (others). Granite paper. Perf 14×13 (horiz) or 13×14 (vert) (with one elliptical hole on each vert side).

1174	$1.40 Type **242**	80	65
1175	$2.40 Hedge Sageretia (informal upright)	1·25	1·00
1176	$3 Fire-thorn (cascade) (*vert*)	1·60	1·25
1177	$5 Chinese Hackberry (root on rock) (*vert*)	2·50	2·10
1174/1177 *Set of 4*		5·50	4·50

243 Ear-spot Angelfish

(Des J. Chum. Photo Walsall)

2003 (7 Aug). Aquarium Fish. T **243** and similar horiz designs. Multicoloured. Two phosphor bands ($1.40) or one phosphor band (others). Granite paper. Perf 14½ (with one elliptical hole on each vert side).

1178	$1.40 Type **243**	80	65
	a. Block of 4. Nos. 1178/1181	6·50	
1179	$2.40 Copper-banded Butterflyfish	1·25	1·00
1180	$3 Dwarf Gourami	1·60	1·25
1181	$5 Red Discus	2·50	2·10
1178/1181 *Set of 4*		5·50	4·50

Nos. 1178/1181 had either one ($5), two ($1.40, $3) or three ($2.40) fish-shaped cut-outs, and were each issued individually in sheets of 25 and together in *se-tenant* blocks of four within sheets of 16 stamps with an enlarged illustrated margin.

244 Bottles and Man holding Firework ('Celebrations')

245 Pied Avocet

(Des A. Lam. Litho Enschedé)

2003 (10 Sept). Greetings Stamps. With service indicator. T **244** and similar square design. Two phosphor bands ($1.40) or one phosphor band ($3). Multicoloured. Granite paper. Perf 14 (with one elliptical hole on each vert side).

(a) Inscr 'Local Mail Postage'.

1182	($1.40) Type **244**	80	65
1183	($1.40) Man and heart-shaped tree ('Care and Love')	80	65

(b) AIR. Inscribed 'Air Mail Postage'.

1184	($3) No. 1182	1·60	1·25
1185	($3) No. 1183	1·60	1·25
1182/1185 *Set of 4*		4·25	3·50

Nos. 1182/1183 were for use on letters up to 30 grams within Hong Kong and Nos. 1184/1185 were for use on airmail letters up to 20 grams to addresses outside Hong Kong.

Nos. 1182/1185, respectively, were each issued individually together in vertical *se-tenant* pairs, each stamp with a label attached at right, within sheets of 16 stamps.

The stamps were arranged with one horizontal row of four stamps and labels at top, two rows at bottom and a single stamp plus label at either side of a central label.

The stamps could be personalised by the addition of a photograph.

(Des A. Lam. Eng C. Slania. Recess and litho Swedish Stamp Printing Office, Stockholm)

2003 (4 Oct). Water Birds. T **245** and similar horiz designs. Multicoloured. Granite paper. Two phosphor bands ($1.40) or one phosphor band (others). Perf 12½ (with one elliptical hole on each vert side).

1186	$1.40 Type **245**	80	65
	a. Booklet pane. Nos. 1186/1189	6·25	
1187	$2.40 Horned Grebe	1·25	1·00
1188	$3 Great Crested Grebe	1·60	1·25
1189	$5 Black-throated Diver	2·50	2·10
1186/1189 Set of 4		5·50	4·50

Stamps of the same design were issued by Sweden.

246 Sha Tin Park

(Des J. Chum. Litho Enschedé)

2003 (14 Oct). Hong Kong 2004 International Stamp Exhibition (2nd issue). Sheet 135×85 mm. One phosphor band. Granite paper. Perf 13½×13 (with one elliptical hole on each vert side).

MS1190 **246** $10 multicoloured .... 5·50 6·50

247 Astronaut and Satellite

(Des Wang Huming and Liu Xiangping. Litho)

2003 (16 Oct). First Chinese Manned Space Flight. T **247** and similar horiz designs. Multicoloured. Two phosphor bands. Fluorescent markings. Granite paper. Perf 13×13½.

1191	$1.40 Type **247**	1·25	1·00
	a. Pair. Nos. 1191/1192	2·75	2·10
1192	$1.40 Shenzhou-5 space craft	1·25	1·00

Nos. 1191/1192 were issued in se-tenant pairs within the sheet.
The fluorescence was applied all over the stamps and appears red under a UV lamp.

> A prestige booklet containing an example of each pair of stamps (six stamps in pairs on three panes) issued jointly by People's Republic of China, Macau and Hong Kong was available at $12.80 (Price, £18 unused).

248 Drum

249 Potala Palace, Lhasa

(Des B. Lau. Photo Enschedé)

2003 (6 Nov). Traditional Instruments. T **248** and similar vert designs. Multicoloured. Two phosphor bands ($1.40) or one phosphor band (others). Granite paper. Perf 13½ (with one elliptical hole on each vert side).

1193	$1.40 Type **248**	80	65
1194	$2.40 Clappers	1·25	1·00
1195	$3 Cymbals	1·60	1·25
1196	$5 Gongs	2·50	2·10
1193/1196 Set of 4		5·50	4·50
MS1197 130×75 mm. $13 Bell (35×45 mm)		6·50	6·25

(Des B. Kwan. Litho Cartor)

2003 (25 Nov). UNESCO World Heritage Sites in China. T **249** and similar multicoloured designs. Two phosphor bands ($1.40, $1.80) or one phosphor band (others). Granite paper. Perf 13 (with two elliptical holes ($1.40) or one elliptical hole (others) on each vert side).

1198	$1.40 Type **249**	80	65
	a. Block of 6. Nos. 1198/1203	8·75	
1199	$1.80 Imperial Palace, Beijing (47×39 mm)	1·00	85
1200	$2.40 First Qin Emperor's Mausoleum, Shaanxi Province (47×39 mm)	1·25	1·00
1201	$2.50 Mount Huangshan, Anhui Province (39×47 mm)	1·40	1·10
1202	$3 Old Town, Lijang (39×47 mm)	1·60	1·25
1203	$5 Jiuzhaigou valley, Sichuan Province (77×30 mm)	2·50	2·10
1198/1203 Set of 6		7·75	6·25

250 Building Development and People on Walkways

251 Monkey

(Des Rebessc Leung and T. Ho. Photo Enschedé)

2003 (11 Dec). Development of Public Housing. T **250** and similar five sided designs. Multicoloured. Two phosphor bands ($1.40) or one phosphor band (others). Granite paper. Perf 13 (with one elliptical hole on each vert side).

1204	$1.40 Type **250**	80	65
1205	$2.40 L-shaped development and women through window	1·25	1·00
1206	$3 High-rise development and man reading with children	1·60	1·25
1207	$5 High-rise development and family walking in park	2·50	2·10
1204/1207 Set of 4		5·50	4·50

Nos. 1204/1207 respectively were each issued tête-bêche in two rows of four stamps within sheets of 20.

(Des B. Kwan. Litho and embossed (No. 1212) or litho (others) Enschedé)

2004 (4 Jan). New Year. Year of the Monkey. T **251** and similar vert designs. Multicoloured. No phosphor (No. **MS**1212c), two phosphor bands ($1.40) or one phosphor band (others). Ordinary paper (No. **MS**1212c) or granite paper (others). Perf 13½ (No. **MS**1212c) or 13½ (with one elliptical hole on each vert side) (others).

1208	$1.40 Type **251**	80	65
1209	$2.40 Mother and baby	1·25	1·00
1210	$3 Walking	1·60	1·25
1211	$5 Holding branch	2·50	2·10
1208/1211 Set of 4		5·50	4·50
MS1212a 136×85 mm. Nos. 1208/1211		5·25	5·00
MS1212b 136×85 mm. As No. 1211. Imperf		3·00	2·75
MS1212c 135×90 mm. $50×2 As No. 1155 (38×52 mm); As No. 1211 (38×52 mm) Perf 13½		40·00	40·00

No. **MS**1212c has the Ram and Monkey embossed with gold and silver foil.

252 Round Pudding and Greeting

(Des J. Chum. Litho Cartor (No. 1213(b)) or Enschedé (others))

2004 (30Jan–2 Feb). Hong Kong 2004 International Stamp Exhibition (3rd issue). Tourism. Five sheets, each 135×86 mm containing T **252** and similar horiz designs. Multicoloured. One phosphor band. Granite paper. Perf 13½ (with one elliptical hole on each vert side).
MS1213 (a) $10 Type **252**; (b) $10×2 Type **252**; (c) $10
New Year parade (31.1); (d) $10 Jade pendant (1.2);
(e) $10 Fire Dragon (2.2)... 32·00 32·00
The stamps of No. **MS**1213(b) were printed so that a different greeting was seen when the sheet was tilted in different directions.

(Des C. Tillyer and F. Li. Litho Walsall)

2004 (3 Feb). Hong Kong 2004 International Stamp Exhibition (4th issue). Hong Kong Landmarks and Tourist Attractions. Vert designs as T **201**. Multicoloured. Two phosphor bands. Granite paper. Perf 13×13½ (with one elliptical hole on each vert side).

1214	$1.40 As Type **201**	65	50
	a. Sheetlet of 21. Nos. 1214/1234	16·00	
1215	$1.40 As No. 974	65	50
1216	$1.40 As No. 975	65	50
1217	$1.40 As No. 976	65	50
1218	$1.40 As No. 977	65	50
1219	$1.40 As No. 978	65	50
1220	$1.40 As No. 979	65	50
1221	$1.40 As No. 980	65	50
1222	$1.40 As No. 980a	65	50
1223	$1.40 As No. 980b	65	50
1224	$1.40 As No. 981	65	50
1225	$1.40 As No. 982	65	50
1226	$1.40 As No. 982a	65	50
1227	$1.40 As No. 983	65	50
1228	$1.40 As No. 983b	65	50
1229	$1.40 As No. 984	65	50
1230	$1.40 As No. 985	65	50
1231	$1.40 As No. 986	65	50
1232	$1.40 As No. 986a	65	50
1233	$1.40 As No. 987	65	50
1234	$1.40 As No. 988	65	50
1214/1234 Set of 21		12·50	9·50

Nos. 1214/1234 were issued in se-tenant sheetlets of 21 stamps with an enlarged illustrated margin.

253 Hong Kong Team

(Des CommArts Design. Litho Enschedé)

2004 (25 Feb). Rugby Sevens. T **253** and similar horiz designs. Multicoloured. Two phosphor bands ($1.40) or one phosphor band (others). Granite paper. Perf 13½×14 (with one elliptical hole on each vert side).

1235	$1.40 Type **253**	80	65
	a. Block of 4. Nos. 1235/1238	5·50	
1236	$2.40 New Zealand team	1·25	1·00
1237	$3 Hong Kong Stadium	1·60	1·25
1238	$5 Westpac Stadium, Wellington	2·50	2·10
1235/1238 Set of 4		5·50	4·50

Stamps of the same design were issued by New Zealand.

254 Scissors, Paper, Stone (Ka-lai Tsoi)

(Litho Enschedé)

2004 (7 Apr). Winning Entries in Children's Stamp Design Competition. Games. T **254** and similar horiz designs. Multicoloured. Two phosphor bands ($1.40) or one phosphor band (others). Granite paper. Perf 13½×14 (with one elliptical hole on each vert side).

1239	$1.40 Type **254**	80	65
	a. Block of 4. Nos. 1239/1242	6·50	
1240	$2.40 Chinese chess (Belinda Hoi-yan Chan)	1·25	1·00
1241	$3 Bubble blowing (April Nga-pui Yuen)	1·60	1·25
1242	$5 Hopscotch (Chap-yin Lui)	2·50	2·10
1239/1242 Set of 4		5·50	4·50

Nos. 1239/1242, respectively, were each issued individually in sheets of 25 stamps and together in se-tenant blocks of four stamps in sheets of 16.

 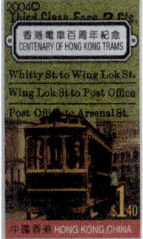

255 The Chen Clan Academy, Guangzhou **256** First Tram (1904)

(Des M. Fung. Litho Enschedé)

2004 (6 May). Mainland Scenery (2nd issue). Sheet 140×90 mm. One phosphor band. Granite paper. Perf 13½ (with one elliptical hole on each vert side).
MS1243 **255** $10 multicoloured............................ 6·00 7·00

(Des R. Solley. Litho Enschedé)

2004 (27 May). Centenary of Hong Kong Tramway. T **256** and similar vert design. Two phosphor bands ($1.40) or one phosphor band (others). Perf 13½ (with one elliptical hole on each vert side).

1244	$1.40 Type **256**	80	65
1245	$2.40 Open-topped tram	1·25	1·00
1246	$3 Canvas-topped tram	1·60	1·25
1247	$5 Modern tram	2·50	2·10
1244/1247 Set of 4		5·50	4·50
MS1248 Two sheets, each 136×85 mm. (a) Nos.			
1244/1247; (b) $5 Millennium New Tram		9·25	9·00

257 Soldiers, Sailors and Airmen

(Des T. Ho and P. Wong. Litho Enschedé)

2004 (30 June). Armed Forces. T **257** and similar horiz designs. Multicoloured. Two phosphor bands ($1.40, $1.80) or one phosphor band (others). Perf 13½×14½ (with one elliptical hole on each vert side).

1249	$1.40 Type **257**	80	65
1250	$1.80 Serviceman giving blood	1·00	85
1251	$2.40 Servicemen and children	1·25	1·00
1252	$2.50 Soldiers	1·40	1·10
1253	$3 Sailors	1·60	1·25
1254	$5 Airmen and Kawasaki OH-1 helicopters	2·50	2·10
1249/1254 Set of 6		7·75	6·25

A prestige booklet sold at ($85) was also issued on 30 June 2004. This consisted of 18 panes, six of which contained four examples each of Nos. 1249/1254, respectively and showed Armed Forces.

258 Preparing to Dive **259** Flags and Deng Xiaoping

(Des B. Kwan and P. Wong. Litho Banknote Corporation of America Inc, Browns Summit, North Carolina (Nos. 1255/1274) or Enschedé (No. 1275))

2004 (20 July–13 Aug). Olympic Games, Athens. Sports. T **258** and similar vert designs. Multicoloured. One phosphor band (No. **MS**1275) or two phosphor bands (others). Perf 13½ (with one elliptical hole on each vert side).

1255	$1.40 Type **258**	70	60
	a. Strip of 4. Nos. 1255/1258	4·00	
	b. Sheetlet of 20. Nos. 1255/1274	20·00	

1256	$1.40 Diver twisting forward	70	60
1257	$1.40 Descending with arms extended	70	60
1258	$1.40 Entering water	70	60
1259	$1.40 Volleyball player with bent knees	70	60
	a. Strip of 4. Nos. 1259/1262	3·00	
1260	$1.40 Jumping to hit ball	70	60
1261	$1.40 Hitting ball	70	60
1262	$1.40 Opponent trying to save	70	60
1263	$1.40 Two cyclists	70	60
	a. Strip of 4. Nos. 1263/1266	3·00	
1264	$1.40 Cyclist	70	60
1265	$1.40 Cyclists at speed	70	60
1266	$1.40 Victory salute	70	60
1267	$1.40 Badminton player preparing to hit shuttlecock	70	60
	a. Strip of 4. Nos. 1267/1270	3·00	
1268	$1.40 Player with arm extended	70	60
1269	$1.40 Player leaning backwards	70	60
1270	$1.40 Player leaning to right	70	60
1271	$1.40 Start of relay race	70	60
	a. Strip of 4. Nos. 1271/1274	3·00	
1272	$1.40 Runners	70	60
1273	$1.40 Baton exchange	70	60
1274	$1.40 Runner with baton raised	70	60
1255/1274 Set of 20		12·50	11·00

MS1275 130×75 mm. $5×2, Classical Olympic runner;
Modern runner (13 August) .... 5·25 5·00

Nos. 1255/1258, 1259/1262, 1263/1266, 1267/1270 and 1271/1274, respectively, were issued in horizontal *se-tenant* strips of four stamps within the sheet, each strip illustrating a particular discipline, diving (Nos. 1255/1258), volleyball (Nos. 1259/1262), cycling (Nos. 1263/1266), badminton (Nos. 1267/1270) and relay race (Nos. 1271/1274).

(Des M. Fung. Litho)

2004 (22 Aug). Birth Centenary of Deng Xiaoping (leader of China, 1978–1989). Two sheets containing T **259** and similar horiz designs. Multicoloured. One phosphor band (No. **MS**1276(b)) or two phosphor bands (others). Perf 13×13½.

MS1276 (a) 175×130 mm. ($1.40) Type **259**; ($1.40)
Wearing blue suit, each×4. (b) 130×75 mm. ($10)
As young man.. 10·50 10·00

260 First Bronze Coin, 1863

(Des B. Lau. Litho Enschedé)

2004 (2 Sept). Currency. T **260** and similar horiz designs. Multicoloured. One phosphor band (No. **MS**1281(b)) or two phosphor bands (others). Perf 13½×14½ (with one elliptical hole on each vert side).

1277	$1.40 Type **260**	80	65
1278	$2.40 First silver coin, 1866	1·25	1·00
1279	$3 First paper currency, 1935	1·60	1·25
1280	$5 Gold coin to commemorate Hong Kong Special Administrative Region, 1997	2·50	2·10
1277/1280 Set of 4		5·50	4·50

MS1281 (a) 130×80 mm. Nos. 1277/1280. (b) 130×75
mm. $5 Reverse of $10 dollar coin, 1997................. 12·00 12·00

261 Building and Bridge

262 Straw Mushrooms

(Des A. Lam. Litho Enschedé)

2004 (19 Oct). Development of Pearl River Delta Region. T **261** and similar horiz designs. Multicoloured. Two phosphor bands ($1.40) or one phosphor band (others). Perf 13½×14½ (with one elliptical hole on each vert side).

1282	$1.40 Type **261**	80	65
	a. Block or strip of 4	6·50	
1283	$2.40 Container and crane	1·25	1·00
1284	$3 Views of Hong Kong, Guangdong and Macau	1·60	1·25
1285	$5 Harbour views and men shaking hands	2·50	2·10
1282/1285 Set of 4		5·50	4·50

Nos. 1282/1285 were issued in sheets of individual values or in a sheetlet of 16, providing *se-tenant* blocks or strips.

(Des S. Li. Litho Enschedé)

2004 (23 Nov). Fungi. T **262** and similar vert designs. Multicoloured. Two phosphor bands ($1.40) or one phosphor band (others). Perf 13½ (with one elliptical hole on each vert side).

1286	$1.40 Type **262**	80	65
1287	$2.40 Red-orange mushroom	1·25	1·00
1288	$3 Violet Marasmius	1·60	1·25
1289	$5 Lingzhi	2·50	2·10
1286/1289 Set of 4		5·50	4·50

MS1290 (a) 130×85 mm. Nos. 1286/1289. (b) 130×75
mm. $5 Hexagon fungus.. 9·25 9·00

263 Clothes Peg (A)　　**264** Rooster

(Des B. Lau. Litho Enschedé)

2005 (4 Jan). Greetings Stamps. Alphabet. Sheet 230×162 mm containing T **263** and similar vert designs showing household objects as letters of the alphabet. Multicoloured. Two phosphor bands. Perf 13½×14 (with one elliptical hole on each vert side).

(a) Ordinary gum. Perf 13½×14 (with one elliptical hole on each vert side).

MS1291 $1.40×30, Type **263**×2; Scissors handle (B);
Lamp (C); Plastic lid (D); Rack (E)×2; Gauge (F);
Clamp (G); Bamboo (H); Torch (I)×2; Cleaning
mop (J); Stapler (K); Sock (L); Maths equipment
(M); Swiss Army knife (N); Elastic band (O)×2;
Sieve (P); Stainless steel ring (Q); Sunglasses (R);
Coat hanger (S); Brush (T); Flip flops (U); Drawing
compass (V); Corkscrew (W); Tap (X); Meat skewer
(Y); Paint roller (Z).. 22·00 24·00

The stamps and margin of No. **MS**1291 form a composite design.

(b) Self-adhesive gum. Die-cut perf 13 (with one elliptical hole on each vert side).

MS1291*a* $1.40×30, Type **263**×2; Scissors handle (B);
Lamp (C); Plastic lid (D); Rack (E)×2; Gauge (F);
Clamp (G); Bamboo (H); Torch (I)×2; Cleaning
mop (J); Stapler (K); Sock (L); Maths equipment
(M); Swiss Army knife (N); Elastic band (O)×2;
Sieve (P); Stainless steel ring (Q); Sunglasses (R);
Coat hanger (S); Brush (T); Flip flops (U); Drawing
compass (V); Corkscrew (W); Tap (X); Meat skewer
(Y); Paint roller (Z).. 22·00 24·00

(Des B. Kwan. Litho and embossed Southern Colour (No. 1296), Cartor (No. 1296) or litho Australia Post Sprintpak (others))

2005 (30 Jan). New Year. Year of the Rooster. T **264** and similar vert designs. Multicoloured. No phosphor (No. **MS**1296*b*), two phosphor bands ($1.40) or one phosphor band (others). Ordinary paper (No. **MS**1296*b*) or granite paper (others). Perf 13½ (No. **MS**1296*b*) or 13½ (with one elliptical hole on each vert side) (others).

1292	$1.40 Type **264**	80	65
1293	$2.40 With black neck feathers	1·25	1·00
1294	$3 With leg raised	1·60	1·25
1295	$5 Crowing	2·50	2·10
1292/1295 Set of 4		5·50	4·50

MS1296 136×85 mm. Nos. 1292/1295. Imperf........ 6·50 6·25
MS1296*a* 136×85 mm. As No. 1295. Imperf........... 3·25 3·00
MS1296*b* 135×90 mm. $50×2 As No. 1209 (38×52 mm);
As No. 1292 (38×52 mm) Perf 13½....................... 42·00 42·00

No. **MS**1296*b* has the Rooster and Monkey embossed with gold and silver foil.

265 The Ugly Duckling   **266** Opera House, Sydney

(Des M. Fung. Litho Enschedé)

2005 (22 Mar). Birth Bicentenary of Hans Christian Andersen (writer). T **265** and similar square designs. Two phosphor bands ($1.40) or one band (others). Perf 14 (with one elliptical hole on each vert side).

1297	$1.40 bright turquoise blue	80	65
1298	$2.40 bright green	1·25	1·00
1299	$3 bright orange	1·60	1·25
1300	$5 magenta	2·50	2·10
1297/1300 Set of 4		5·50	4·50

Designs: $1.40 T **265**; $2.40 The Little Mermaid; $3 The Little Match Girl; $5 The Emperor's New Clothes.

(Des C. Tillyer and Arion Wong. Litho Banknote Corporation of America Inc, Browns Summit, North Carolina)

2005 (21 Apr). Pacific Explorer 2005 International Stamp Exhibition, Australia. Sheet 130×75 mm. One phosphor band. Perf 14 (with one elliptical hole on each vert side).

MS1301 **266** $10 multicoloured		6·00	6·50

267 Variegated Pearl-scale

(Des Arde Lam. Litho Enschedé)

2005 (12 May). Goldfish. T **267** and similar horiz designs. Multicoloured. Two phosphor bands ($1.40) or one phosphor band (others). Granite paper. Perf 13½×14½ (with one elliptical hole on each vert side).

1302	$1.40 Type **267**	80	65
1303	$2.40 Red and White Swallowtail	1·25	1·00
1304	$3 Pale Bronze Egg Phoenix	1·60	1·25
1305	$5 Blue Wenyu	2·50	2·10
1302/1305 Set of 5		5·50	4·50
MS1306 Two sheets, each 130×75 mm. (a) Nos. 1302/1305. (b) $5 Red and White Dragon-Eye (45×35 mm)		8·75	8·50

268 Zheng He   **269** Coloured Shapes

2005 (28 June). 600th Anniversary of the Voyages of Zheng He (Ma Sanbao). T **268** and similar multicoloured designs. One phosphor band (No. MS1310). Perf 13×13½.

1307	$1.40 Type **268**	1·00	65
	a. Horiz strip of 3. Nos. 1307/1309	3·00	
	b. Sheetlet of 6. Nos. 1307/1309, each×2	6·00	
1308	$1.40 Giraffe, jars and ship	1·00	65
1309	$1.40 Ships and compass	1·50	65
1307/1309 Set of 3		3·00	1·75
MS1310 139×80 mm. $10 Nine-masted Treasure ship (50×30 mm)		6·00	6·50

Nos. 1307/1309, each×2, were issued in se-tenant sheetlets of six stamps with an enlarged illustrated margin.

Stamps of a similar design were issued by China, Macau and Singapore.

(Des Arde Lam. Litho Cartor)

2005 (21 July). Creative Industries. T **269** and similar horiz designs. Multicoloured. Two phosphor bands ($1.40), one phosphor band and surface phosphor ($5) or one phosphor band (others). Granite paper. Perf 14 (with one elliptical hole on each vert side).

1311	$1.40 multicoloured	80	65
	a. Booklet pane. Nos. 1311/1314, each×4	26·00	
1312	$2.40 apple green and black	1·25	1·00
1313	$3 scarlet, black and bronze	1·60	1·25
1314	$5 multicoloured	2·50	2·10
1311/1114 Set of 4		5·50	4·50

Designs: $1.40 T **269** (advertising, architecture and design); $2.40 Digital symbols (digital entertainment, publishing and computers); $3 Coloured grids (media); $5 Streamers (arts, antiques, crafts and performing arts).

The stamps of booklet pane No. 1311a were arranged in two blocks of eight stamps each with an inscribed selvage.

270 Early Compass   **271** Mickey and Minnie (Main Street, USA)

(Des Wang Huming. Litho Enschedé)

2005 (18 Aug). Chinese Inventions. T **270** and similar horiz designs. Multicoloured. Two phosphor bands ($1.40) or one phosphor band (others). Granite paper. Perf 13½×14½ (with one elliptical hole on each vert side).

1315	$1.40 Type **270**	80	65
	a. Block or strip of 4. Nos. 1315/1318	6·50	
1316	$2.40 Printing	1·25	1·00
1317	$3 Gunpowder	1·60	1·25
1318	$5 Paper making	2·50	2·10
1315/1318 Set of 4		5·50	4·50

Nos. 1315/1318 were each issued in sheets of 25, and together in horizontal or vertical se-tenant strips of four stamps within sheetlets of 16.

(Litho and embossed (No. 1324(c)) or litho (others) Cartor)

2005 (12 Sept). Disneyland Hong Kong. Grand Opening. T **271** and similar square designs. Multicoloured. Ordinary paper ($50) or granite paper (others). No phosphor bands ($50), two phosphor bands ($1.40) or one phosphor band (others). Perf 14 (with one elliptical hole on each vert side).

1319	$1.40 Type **271**	80	65
1320	$2.40 Dumbo (Fantasyland)	1·25	1·00
1321	$3 Simba and Nala (Adventureland)	1·60	1·25
1322	$5 Pluto (Tomorrowland)	2·50	2·10
1319/1322 Set of 4		5·50	4·50
MS1323 Three sheets, each 135×85 mm. (a) Nos. 1319/1322. (b) $5 Mickey. (c) $50 As No.			
MS1323(b)		40·00	40·00

No. MS1323(c) has Mickey embossed with gold foil.

272 Qiantang Bore

(Des Kan Tai-keung. Litho Enschedé)

2005 (16 Sept). Mainland Scenery (3rd issue). Sheet 141×90 mm. Perf 13½×13 (with one elliptical hole on each vert side).

MS1324 **272** $10 multicoloured		5·50	5·25

273 Boat, Tai O, Hong Kong   **274** Wong ka Kui

(Des Sofia Martins. Litho)

2005 (18 Oct). Fishing Villages. T **273** and similar horiz designs. Multicoloured. Granite paper. Perf 14½ (with one elliptical hole on each vert side).

1325	$1.40 Type **273**	80	65
	a. Horiz pair. Nos. 1325 and 1327	2·50	2·10
	b. Block or strip of 4. Nos. 1325/1328	6·50	
1326	$2.40 Fisherman and boats, Aldeia da Carrasqueira	1·25	1·00
	a. Horiz pair. Nos. 1326 and 1328	4·00	3·25
1327	$3 Wrapped fish, Tai O	1·60	1·25
1328	$5 Moorings and pier, Aldeia da Carrasqueira	2·50	2·10
1325/1328 Set of 4		5·50	4·50

Nos. 1325 and 1327, and 1326 and 1328, respectively were issued in horizontal *se-tenant* pairs within the sheet, each pair forming a composite design.

Stamps of the same design were issued by Portugal.

2005 (8 Nov). Pop Singers. T **274** and similar vert designs. Multicoloured. Granite paper. Two phosphor bands (Nos. 1329/1330) or one phosphor band (others). Perf 14½ (with one elliptical hole on each vert side).

1329	$1.40 Type **274**	80	65
1330	$1.80 Danny Chan	1·00	85
1331	$2.40 Roman Tam	1·25	1·00
1332	$3 Leslie Cheung	2·00	1·25
1333	$5 Anita Mui	3·00	2·10
1329/1333 Set of 5		7·50	5·25

Nos. 1329/1333 were issued in sheets of 25 or individual sheetlets of four with decorative borders.

275 Dog

276 Lantern enclosing Woman

(Des B. Kwan. Litho and embossed Cartor (No. 1339) or litho Enschedé (others))

2006 (15 Jan). Chinese New Year. Year of the Dog. T **275** and similar vert designs. Multicoloured. No phosphor (No. **MS**1339), two phosphor bands ($1.40) or one phosphor band (others). Ordinary paper (No. **MS**1339) or granite paper (others). Perf 13½ (No. **MS**1339) or 13½ (with one elliptical hole on each vert side) (others).

1334	$1.40 Type **275**	80	65
1335	$2.40 Pekinese	1·25	1·00
1336	$3 German Shepherd	1·60	1·25
1337	$5 Beagle	2·50	2·10
1334/1337 Set of 4		3·50	2·75
MS1338 Two sheets, each 136×85 mm. (a) No. 1334/1337. (b) As No. 1337. Imperf		9·50	9·50
MS1339 135×90 mm Size 38×52 mm. $50×2, As No. 1292; As No. 1335		45·00	45·00

No. **MS**1339 has the Rooster and Dog embossed with gold and silver foil.

(Des J. Chum. Litho China State Ptg Wks, Beijing)

2006 (12 Feb). Chinese Lanterns. T **276** and similar vert designs. Multicoloured. Two phosphor bands ($1.40 and $1.80) or one phosphor band (others). Ordinary paper. Perf 13½ (with one elliptical hole on each vert side).

MS1340 108×131 mm. $1.40×2, Type **276**×2; $1.80×2, Lantern enclosing flowers×2; $2.40×2, Lantern enclosing birds×2		6·75	6·50
MS1341 130×75 mm $5 Children holding Dragon lantern (38×49 mm)		4·00	4·00

277 Bear wearing Hakka Costume (Yuen-ching Lee)

278 Mount Taishan

(Litho Cartor)

2006 (30 Mar). Dress up Bear. Winning Entries in Children's Design a Stamp Competition. T **277** and similar square designs. Multicoloured. Two phosphor bands ($1.40 and $1.80) or one phosphor band (others). Granite paper. Perf 13½ (with one elliptical hole on each vert side).

1342	$1.40 Type **277**	65	65
1343	$1.80 Wearing wedding costume (Sean Sheung-nam Lam)	85	85
1344	$2.40 Wearing pleated skirt (Chun-hin Chow)	1·00	1·00
1345	$2.50 Wearing embroidered apron and shoes (Hong-wan Lau)	1·10	1·10
1346	$3 Wearing striped top and hat (Man-lok Chiu)	1·25	1·25
1347	$5 Wearing leaf skirt (Michelle Hiu-tung Lau)	2·10	2·10
1342/1347 Set of 6		6·25	6·25
MS1348 115×115 mm. Nos. 1342/1347		6·25	6·25

A premium board cover booklet containing Nos. 1342/1347 and stickers was on sale for $30.

(Des Li Shik Kwong. Litho Enschedé)

2006 (4 May). Mainland Scenery (4th issue). Sheet 140×90 mm. Perf 14½ (with one elliptical hole on each vert side).

MS1349 **278** $10 multicoloured		4·50	3·00

279 Rainbow

(Des B. Lau. Litho Cartor)

2006 (27 May). Washington 2006 Philatelic Exhibition. Sheet 130×75 mm. Perf 13½×14 (with one elliptical hole on each vert side).

MS1350 **279** $10 multicoloured		4·50	5·00

280 'Respect makes a Successful Marriage'

281 Central and Western District

(Des M. Fung. Litho Cartor)

2006 (15 June). Chinese Idioms. T **280** and similar square designs. Multicoloured. Two phosphor bands ($1.40) or one phosphor band (others). Granite paper. Perf 14 (with one elliptical hole on each vert side).

1351	$1.40 Type **280**	65	50
1352	$2.40 'Reading is always rewarding'	1·00	85
1353	$3 'Prepare for success'	1·25	1·00
1354	$5 'All in the same boat'	2·10	1·75
1351/1354 Set of 4		4·50	3·75
MS1355 135×85 mm. Nos. 1351/1354		5·50	5·25

(Des Shirman Lai. Litho Cartor)

2006 (18 July). Hong Kong Districts. T **281** and similar square designs. Multicoloured. Two phosphor bands. Granite paper. Perf 14 (with one elliptical hole on each vert side).

1356	$1.40 Type **281**	55	50
	a. Sheetlet of 18. Nos. 1356/1373	10·00	
1357	$1.40 Eastern	55	50
1358	$1.40 Southern	55	50
1359	$1.40 Wan Chai	55	50
1360	$1.40 Yau Tsim Mong	55	50
1361	$1.40 Wong Tai Sin	55	50
1362	$1.40 Kwun Tong	55	50
1363	$1.40 Sham Shui Po	55	50
1364	$1.40 Kowloon City	55	50
1365	$1.40 Sai Kung	55	50
1366	$1.40 Kwai Tsing	55	50
1367	$1.40 Tai Po	55	50
1368	$1.40 North	55	50
1369	$1.40 Tsuen Wan	55	50

1370	$1.40 Sha Tin	55	50
1371	$1.40 Tuen Mun	55	50
1372	$1.40 Yuen Long	55	50
1373	$1.40 Islands district	55	50
1356/1373	Set of 18	10·00	10·00

282 Fireworks over Victoria Harbour   **283** Love

(Des A. Tuma. Photo)

2006 (22 Aug). Fireworks. T **282** and similar horiz designs. Multicoloured. One phosphor band ($5). Granite paper. Perf 14×14½.

1374	$5 Type **282**	2·10	1·75
1375	$5 Fireworks over Giant Ferris Wheel, Vienna, Austria	2·10	1·75
MS1376	146×85 mm. $50×2, As Type **282**; As No. 1375	40·00	42·00
MS1376a	146×85 mm. $50 of Hong Kong (As Type **282**) and 375c. stamp of Austria	45·00	48·00

No. **MS**1376 has crystals applied to the surface of the stamps and was sold in a folder.

Stamps of a similar design were issued by Austria.

No. **MS**1376a was also issued by Austria.

The stamps were only valid for postage in the country of origin.

(Des Wong Chun-hong. Litho Enschedé)

2006 (21 Sept). International Day of Peace. T **283** and similar vert designs. Multicoloured. Two phosphor bands ($1.40 and $1.80) or one phosphor band (others). Granite paper. Perf 14×13½ (with one elliptical hole on each vert side).

1377	$1.40 Type **283**	65	50
1378	$1.80 Peace	85	70
1379	$2.40 Hope	1·00	85
1380	$3 Caring	1·25	1·00
1381	$5 Harmony	2·10	1·75
1377/1381	Set of 5	5·25	4·25
MS1382	150×85 mm. Nos. 1377/1381	6·00	6·50

284 Security Bus

(Des Wong Chun-hong. Litho Enschedé)

2006 (19 Oct). Government Transport. T **284** and similar vert designs. Multicoloured. Two phosphor bands ($1.40 and $1.80) or one phosphor band (others). Granite paper. Perf 14×13½ (with one elliptical hole on each vert side).

1383	$1.40 Type **284**	65	50
	a. Block or vertical strip of 6. Nos. 1383/1388	7·00	
1384	$1.80 Mobile X-ray unit	85	70
1385	$2.40 Hydraulic lift fire appliance	1·00	85
1386	$2.50 Aerospatiale AS 332 Super Puma helicopter	1·10	90
1387	$3 Traffic Control motorcycle	1·25	1·00
1388	$5 Immigration Dept launch	2·10	1·75
1383/1388	Set of 6	7·00	5·00

Nos. 1383/1388 were issued in sheets of 25 or a sheetlet of 18 giving three se-tenant blocks or strips.

285 Sun Yat-Sen

(Des Alan Chan. Litho Cartor)

2006 (12 Nov). 140th Birth Anniversary of Sun Yat-Sen (revolutionary). T **285** and similar horiz designs. Multicoloured. Two phosphor bands ($1.40) or one phosphor band (others). Granite paper. Perf 13½×14 (with one elliptical hole on each vert side).

1389	$1.40 Type **285**	65	50
1390	$2.40 Seated wearing suit	1·00	85
1391	$3 Standing wearing suit	1·25	1·00
1392	$5 As older man	2·10	1·75
1389/1392	Set of 4	4·50	3·75
MS1393	130×75 mm. $5 Seated wearing traditional dress	2·75	2·50

A premium booklet of five pages was on sale for $25.

286 Bottles   **287** White-bellied Sea Eagle

2006 (28 Nov). Greetings Stamps. T **286** and similar vert designs. Multicoloured. Two phosphor bands ($1.40) or one phosphor band (others). Granite paper. Perf 13½ (with one elliptical hole on each vert side).

(a) Inscribed 'Local Mail Postage'.

1394	($1.40) Type **286**	65	50
1395	($1.40) Hearts	65	50

(b) AIR. Inscr 'Air Mail Postage'.

1396	($3) Glasses	1·25	1·00
1397	($3) Flowers	1·25	1·00
1394/1397	Set of 4	3·50	2·75

No. 1397 is impregnated with a rose scent.

Two Types of 10c.:

Type I. As illustrated with imprint date in lower left corner.

Type II. Imprint date raised level with base of value and 'White-bellied Sea Eagle' repositioned.

2006 (31 Dec)–**10**. Birds. T **287** and similar vert designs. Multicoloured. Granite paper.

(a) Two phosphor bands (Nos. 1398/1403) or one phosphor band (others). Perf 13×14 (one elliptical hole on each vert side).

1398	10c. Type **287**	15	15
	a. Booklet pane. No. 1398/1409	9·75	
	b. Type II	15	15
1399	20c. Collared Scops Owl	25	20
1400	50c. Scarlet Minivet	25	25
1401	$1 Kingfisher	40	40
1402	$1.40 Fork-tailed Sunbird	65	65
	a. Booklet pane. No. 1402×10	6·50	
1403	$1.80 Roseate Tern	85	85
	a. Booklet pane. No. 1403×10	8·50	
1404	$1.90 Black-faced Spoonbill	90	90
1405	$2 Little Egret	95	1·00
1406	$2.40 Greater Painted Snipe	1·00	1·00
	a. Booklet pane. No. 1406×10	10·50	
1407	$2.50 Swallow	1·10	1·10
1408	$3 Red-whiskered Bulbul	1·25	1·25
	a. Booklet pane. No. 1408×10	14·00	
1409	$5 Long-tailed Shrike	2·10	2·10

(b) Size 28×33 mm. One phosphor band. Perf 13½ (one elliptical hole on each vert side).

1410	$10 White Wagtail	3·75	4·00
1411	$13 Northern Shoveler	4·75	5·00
1412	$20 Magpie	7·50	7·50
1413	$50 Dalmatian Pelican	18·00	18·00
1398/1413	Set of 16	42·00	45·00
MS1414	220×160 mm. Nos. 1398/1409	8·00	9·75
MS1415	150×90 mm. Nos. 1410/1413. Perf 13½×13 (with one elliptical hole on each vert side)	32·00	38·00
MS1416	130×75 mm. Size 28×33 mm. $10 As No. 1410 (White Wagtail) (21.9.10)	3·75	4·50

(c) Coil stamps, 17×21 mm. Perf 14½×13½.

1417	$1.40 Fork-tailed Sunbird	90	75
1418	$180 Roseate Tern	1·10	90
1419	$2.40 Greater Painted Snipe	1·60	1·25
1420	$3 Red-whiskered Bulbul	1·90	1·50
1417/1420	Set of 4	5·00	4·25

The booklet panes No. 1402a, 1403a, 1406a and 1408a have upper, lower and outer straight edges, giving stamps with one or two sides imperf depending on position.

Nos. 1410/1413 are also perforated around the face value of each stamp.

Nos. 1421/1424 are vacant.

288 Pig and Piglet   **289** Robert Baden-Powell (founder)

(Des B. Kwan)

2007 (4 Feb). Chinese New Year. Year of the Pig. T **288** and similar vert designs. Multicoloured.

*(a) Two phosphor bands ($1.40) or one phosphor band (others). Granite paper. Imperf (No. **MS**1429(b)) or perf 14×13½ (with one elliptical hole on each vert side) (others). Litho Enschedé.*

1425	$1.40 Type **288**	65	50
1426	$2.40 Pot-bellied Pig	1·00	85
1427	$3 Spotted Pig	1·25	1·00
1428	$5 Piglet	2·10	1·75
1425/1428	*Set of 4*	4·50	3·75
MS1429	Two sheets, each 135×85 mm. (a) Nos. 1425/1428; (b) $5 No. 1428	7·00	6·75

(b) One phosphor band. Flocked paper. Perf 13. Litho Cartor.

1430	$10 As No. 1210 Year of the Monkey	3·50	3·00
	a. Block of 4. Nos. 1430/1433	14·50	14·50
1431	$10 As No. 1292 Year of the Rooster	3·50	3·00
1432	$10 As No. 1335 Year of the Dog	3·50	3·00
1433	$10 As No. 1427 Year of the Pig	3·50	3·00
1430/1433	*Set of 4*	12·00	11·00

(c) Size 38×51 mm. Ordinary paper. Perf 13½. Litho embossed and foil stamped Cartor.

MS1434	136×90 mm. $50 As No. 1337 Year of the Dog; $50 As No. 1425	50·00	50·00

Nos. 1430/1433 were issued in *se-tenant* blocks of four stamps within sheets of 16.

No. **MS**1434 has the animals embossed with gold and silver foil.

(Des C. Yick. Litho Enschedé)

2007 (1 Mar). Centenary of World Scouting. T **289** and similar horiz designs. Multicoloured. Two phosphor bands ($1.40) or one phosphor band (others). Perf 13½×14½ (with one elliptical hole on each vert side).

1435	$1.40 Type **289**	65	50
1436	$2.40 Emblem and compass	1·00	85
1437	$3 Rucksack and reef knot	1·25	1·00
1438	$5 Scouts	2·10	1·75
1435/1439	*Set of 4*	4·50	3·75
MS1439	130×75 mm. Nos. 1435/1438	5·50	5·25

290 Two Rabbits (Spot   **291** Shilin, Kunming
the differences)

(Des Michael Fung. Litho Cartor)

2007 (22 Mar). Children's Stamps. Bunny Fun and Games. T **290** and similar square designs. Multicoloured. Two phosphor bands ($1.40 and $1.80) or one phosphor band (others). Granite paper. Perf 14 (with one elliptical hole on each vert side).

1440	$1.40 Type **290**	65	50
1441	$1.80 Outline (colour in dotted areas)	85	70
1442	$2.40 Maize (trace your way out)	1·00	85
1443	$2.50 Rabbit and Easter eggs (hunt for Easter eggs)	1·10	90
1444	$3 Tree containing Rabbits (spot ten Rabbits)	1·25	1·00
1445	$5 Rabbit in egg (look for a star)	2·10	1·75
1440/1445	*Set of 6*	6·25	5·25
MS1446	140×90 mm. Nos. 1440/1445	7·00	6·75

A premium board cover booklet containing Nos. 1440/1445 was on sale for $36.

(Des Jason Chum. Litho Enschedé)

2007 (4 May). Mainland Scenery (5th issue). Sheet 140×90 mm. Perf 14½ (with one elliptical hole on each vert side).

MS1447	**291** $10 multicoloured	4·25	4·25

292 Southern Lion Dance   **293** *Faunis eumeus*

2007 (22 May). Lion Dance and Martial Arts. T **293** and similar horiz designs. Multicoloured. Two phosphor bands ($1.40) or one phosphor band (others). Granite paper. Perf 14 (with one elliptical hole on each vert side).

1448	$1.40 Type **292**	65	50
1449	$2.40 Nanquan	1·00	85
1450	$3 Northern Lion Dance	1·25	1·00
1451	$5 Beitui	2·10	1·75
1448/1451	*Set of 4*	4·50	3·75
MS1452	130×90 mm. Nos. 1448/1451	5·25	5·00

Nos. 1448/1451 each has a small gold symbol signifying the design in lower left ($1.40 and $5) or right ($2.40 and $3) corners.

(Des Benny Lau. Litho Enschedé)

2007 (14 June). Butterflies. T **293** and similar horiz designs. Multicoloured. Two phosphor bands ($1.40, $1.80) or one phosphor band (others). Granite paper. Perf 14×13½ (with one elliptical hole on each vert side).

1453	$1.40 Type **293**	65	50
1454	$1.80 *Prioneris philpnome*	85	70
1455	$2.40 *Polyura nepenthes*	1·00	85
1456	$3 *Tajura maculata*	1·25	1·00
1457	$5 *Acraea issoria*	2·10	1·75
1453/1457	*Set of 5*	5·25	4·25

A limited edition premium booklet containing four panes of text interleaved with one pane containing Nos. 1453/1455 and another containing Nos. 1456/1457 was for sale at $38.

294 Children

(Des Benny Lau. Litho Enschedé)

2007 (1 July). Tenth Anniversary of Reunification of Hong Kong. T **294** and similar multicoloured designs. Two phosphor bands ($1.40, $1.80) or one phosphor band (others). Granite paper. Perf 13½×14½ (with one elliptical hole on each vert side) (single stamps) or 13½ (No. **MS**1465).

1458	$1.40 Type **294**	65	50
1459	$1.40 *Forever Blooming Bauhinia* (sculpture) (symbol of Hong Kong) (44×33 mm)	65	50
1460	$1.80 Heritage Museum	85	70
1461	$2.40 Tsing Ma bridge	1·00	85
1462	$2.50 International Wetland Park	1·10	90
1463	$3 Two IFC building	1·25	1·00
1464	$5 Fireworks over city	2·10	1·75
1458/1464	*Set of 7*	7·00	5·75
MS1465	130×91 mm. Size 30×60 mm. $10×3, Victoria Harbour waterfront	12·00	12·00
MS1465*a*	110×150 mm. No. 1459 and Nos. 5189/5191 of China	16·00	16·00

The stamps and margins of No. **MS**1465 form a composite view of Victoria Harbour waterfront from the sea.

A stamp of a similar design to No. 1459 was issued by China.

No. 1459 was issued in sheetlets of ten stamps with enlarged inscribed margins.

Nos. 1458/**MS**1465 were also on sale enclosed in a large decorative folder.

295 Symbols of Transport and Guardian God

(Des Leung Kam-hung. Litho Enschedé)

2007 (3 Aug). Bangkok 2007, International Philatelic Exhibition. Sheet 130×75 mm. One phosphor band. Granite paper. Perf 13½×14½ (with one elliptical hole on each vert side).
MS1466 **295** $10 multicoloured... 5·00 5·00

296 Scales and People of Many Nations (Human Rights)

297 Tin Hau Temple, Causeway Bay

(Des Lam Man-yin and Benny Lau. Litho Cartor)

2007 (23 Aug). Civil Responsibility. T **296** and similar hexagonal designs. Multicoloured. Two phosphor bands ($1.40) or one phosphor band (others). Granite paper. Perf 13 (with one elliptical hole on each lower left and upper right oblique sides).
1467	$1.40 Type **296**	65	50
1468	$2.40 Buildings with faces (Rule of Law)	1·00	85
1469	$3 Clasped hands (Social Participation)	1·25	1·00
1470	$5 Rainbow and hands enclosing fruit (Corporate Citizenship)	2·10	1·75
1467/1470 Set of 4		4·50	3·75

(Recess and litho)

2007 (20 Sept). Official Monuments. T **297** and similar horiz designs. Multicoloured. Two phosphor bands ($1.40, $1.80) or one phosphor band (others). Granite paper. Perf 13.
1471	$1.40 Type **297**	70	55
1472	$1.80 Old Post Office, Wan Chai	90	75
1473	$2.40 Former Central Police Station Compound	1·10	90
1474	$2.50 Former Yamen building, Kowloon Walled City	1·10	95
1475	$3 Kun Lung Gate Tower, Lung Yeuk Tau	1·40	1·10
1476	$5 Tang Lung Chai lighthouse	2·40	1·90
1471/1476 Set of 6		6·75	5·50
MS1477 145×78 mm. Nos. 1471/1476		7·50	7·25

298 Stocking

299 Qing Dynasty Carved Chair

(Litho and varnish)

2007 (11 Oct). Christmas. T **298** and similar vert designs. Multicoloured. Two phosphor bands ($1.40) or one phosphor band (others). Granite paper. Perf 13.
1478	$1.40 Type **298**	70	55
1479	$2.40 Gingerbread man	1·10	90
1480	$3 Inscribed bell	1·40	1·10
1481	$5 Snowman	2·40	1·90
1478/1481 Set of 4		5·00	4·00

(Des Ken Li (No. 1480) or Markku Kosonen (No. 1481). Litho Enschedé)

2007 (2 Nov). Woodcraft. T **299** and similar horiz designs. Multicoloured. One phosphor band. Granite paper. Perf 13½×14½ (with one elliptical hole on each vert side).
1482	$5 Type **299**	2·40	1·90
1483	$5 Wooden bowls	2·40	1·90
MS1484 106×70 mm. Nos. 1482/1483		5·50	5·50

Stamps of a similar design were issued by Finland.

300 Firework

301 Rat

(Des A. Lam. Litho Enschedé)

2007 (28 Dec). Greetings Stamps. With service indicator. T **300** and similar square designs. Two phosphor bands ($1.40) or one phosphor band ($3). Multicoloured. Granite paper. Perf 13½ (with one elliptical hole on each vert side).
(a) Inscribed 'Local Mail Postage'.
1485	($1.40) Type **300**	70	55
1486	($1.40) Two birds	70	55

(b) AIR. Inscribed 'Air Mail Postage'.
1487	($3) Parcels and balloons	1·40	1·10
1488	($3) Slippers	1·40	1·10
1485/1488 Set of 4		3·75	3·00

No. 1485/1486 were for use on letters up to 30 grams within Hong Kong and Nos. 1487/1488 were for use on airmail letters up to 20 grams to addresses outside Hong Kong.

Nos. 1485/1488, respectively, were each issued individually and together in vertical se-tenant pairs, each stamp with a label attached at right, within sheets of 20 stamps. The stamps were arranged with two horizontal rows of four stamps and labels at top, two rows at bottom and a pair at either side of a central label.

The stamps could be personalised by the addition of a photograph.

(Des Bon Kwan)

2008 (26 Jan). Chinese New Year. Year of the Rat. T **301** and similar vert designs. Multicoloured.
(a) Two phosphor bands ($1.40) or one phosphor band (others). Granite paper. Imperf (No. MS1493(b)) or Perf 14×13½ (with one elliptical hole on each vert side) (others). Litho Enschedé.
1489	$1.40 Type **301**	70	55
1490	$2.40 Rat seated	1·10	90
1491	$3 Rat facing left	1·40	1·10
1492	$5 Rat facing right	2·40	1·90
1489/1492 Set of 4		5·00	4·00
MS1493 Two sheets, each 135×85 mm. (a) Nos. 1489/1492 (b) $5 As No. 1492		7·75	7·50

(b) Size 38×51 mm. Ordinary paper. Perf 13½. Litho embossed and foil stamped Cartor.
MS1494 136×90 mm. $50 As No. 1425 Year of the Pig; $50 As No. 1492		42·00	42·00

Nos. 1489/1492 were issued in se-tenant blocks of four stamps within sheets of 16.

No. MS1494 has the animals embossed with gold and silver foil.

302 Huanglong

(Litho Enschedé)

2008 (28 Feb). Mainland Scenery (6th issue). Sheet 140×90 mm. One phosphor band. Perf 14½ (with one elliptical hole on each vert side).
MS1495 **302** $10 multicoloured.. 5·00 5·00

303 Hibiscus

(Des George Tang)

2008 (14 Mar). Flowers. T **303** and similar horiz designs. Multicoloured. Two phosphor bands ($1.40 and $1.80) or one phosphor band (others). Granite paper. Perf 13½×13 (with one elliptical hole on each vert side).

1496	$1.40 Type **303**	70	55
1497	$1.80 Cotton Tree Blooms	90	75
1498	$2.40 Allamanda	1·10	90
1499	$2.50 Azalea	1·10	95
1500	$3 Lotus blossom	1·40	1·10
1501	$5 Morning Glory	2·40	1·90
1496/1501 *Set of 6*		7·00	5·50
MS1502 220×123 mm. Nos. 1496/1501		7·75	9·00

304 Bauhinia (Yu-tong Chua)   **305** Flower Hat Jellyfish

(Des Shirman Lai. Litho Austrian State Ptg Wks, Vienna)

2008 (22 May). Paper Folding. T **304** and similar multicoloured designs. Two phosphor bands ($1.40 and $1.80) or one phosphor band (others). Granite paper. Perf 14½×13½ (vert) or 13½×14½ (horiz) (each with one elliptical hole on each vert side).

1503	$1.40 Type **304**	70	55
1504	$1.80 Bear (Shing-him (Bernard) Yeung) (*horiz*)	90	75
1505	$2.40 New Year decorations (Wing-tung Lau; Ka-wing Cheung)	1·10	90
1506	$2.50 Rainbow and Lotus blossom (Hiu-yu Chau; Hiu-ling Wong) (*horiz*)	1·10	95
1507	$3 Koala Bears and Monkey holding Banana (Wing-tung Lo; Ka-wing Cheung)	1·40	1·10
1508	$5 Christmas scene and Santa Claus (Po-chu Yeung and Lesley Chu; Hon-keung and Hazel Li Hin) (*horiz*)	2·40	1·90
1503/1508 *Set of 6*		7·00	5·50
MS1509 218×122 mm. Nos. 1503/1508		7·75	9·00

(Des Kam-hung Leung and Ken Wong. Litho and luminous varnish Sprintpak, Austalia)

2008 (12 June). Jellyfish. T **305** and similar multicoloured designs. Two phosphor bands ($1.40 and $1.80) or one phosphor band (others). Granite paper. Perf 14½×13½ (vert) or 13½×14½ (horiz) (each with one elliptical hole on each vert side).

1510	$1.40 Type **305**	70	55
1511	$1.80 Octopus Jellyfish (*horiz*)	90	75
1512	$2.40 Brown Sea Nettle	1·10	90
1513	$2.50 Moon Jellyfish (*horiz*)	1·10	95
1514	$3 Lion's Mane Jellyfish	1·40	1·10
1515	$5 Pacific Sea Nettle	2·40	1·90
1510/1515 *Set of 6*		7·00	5·50
MS1516 135×85 mm. Nos. 1510/1515		7·75	9·00

Nos. 1510/**MS**1516 have the jellyfish highlighted by varnish which glows in the dark.

A premium booklet containing five pages of text and three panes containing Nos. 1510/1511, 1512/1513 and 1515/1516 respectively, was also available.

306 Ying Ying and Le Le   **307** Show Jumping

(Des Arde Lam. Litho Cartor)

2008 (1 July). Pandas. T **306** and similar square designs. Two phosphor bands ($1.40) or one phosphor band (others). Granite paper. Perf 14 (each with one elliptical hole on each vert side).

1517	$1.40 Type **306**	70	55
1518	$2.40 Ying Ying	1·10	90

1519	$3 Le Le	1·40	1·10
1520	$5 Ying Ying and Le Le in tree	2·40	1·90
1517/1520 *Set of 4*		5·00	4·00
MS1521 176×210 mm. Nos. 1517/1520, each×2		10·50	10·00

(Des Eddy Yu and Roxy Lau. Litho Enschedé)

2008 (9 Aug). Olympic Games, Beijing. Equestrian Events in Hong Kong. T **307** and similar horiz designs. Two phosphor bands ($1.40) or one phosphor band (others). Granite paper. Perf 14 (each with one elliptical hole on each vert side).

1522	$1.40 Type **307**	70	55
1523	$2.40 Dressage	1·10	90
1524	$3 Eventing	1·40	1·10
1525	$5 Stylised winning horse and rider	2·40	1·90
1522/1525 *Set of 4*		5·00	4·00
MS1526 135×85 mm. Nos. 1522/1525		5·75	5·50

308 Cityscape

(Des Ken Wong and Leung Kam-hung. Litho Enschedé)

2008 (12 Sept). Praga 2008 International Stamp Exhibition, Prague, Czech Republic. Sheet 130×75 mm. Granite paper. Perf 14 (with one elliptical hole on each vert side).

MS1527 **308** $10 multicoloured	4·75	4·50

309 Chwibari (Bongsan Mask Dance)   **310** Justice

2008 (6 Nov). Masks. T **309** and similar vert design. Multicoloured. One phosphor band. Granite paper. Perf 13½×14 (each with one elliptical hole on each vert side).

1528	$5 Type **309**	2·40	1·90
1529	$5 Big Head Buddha (Chinese Lion Dance)	2·40	1·90
MS1530 106×70 mm. Nos. $5×2, Nos. 1528/1529		4·75	4·50

Stamps of a similar design were issued by South Korea.

2008 (27 Nov). The Judiciary. T **310** and similar vert designs. Multicoloured. Two phosphor bands ($1.40) or one phosphor band (others). Granite paper. Perf 14 (each with one elliptical hole on each vert side).

1531	$1.40 Type **310**	1·25	55
1532	$2.40 Court building	2·10	90
1533	$3 Barristers and judges	2·50	1·10
1534	$5 Gavel	4·00	1·90
1531/1534 *Set of 4*		9·00	4·50
MS1535 136×85 mm. Nos. 1531/1534		9·00	5·50

311 Ox   **312** Mount Tianshan

(Des Bon Kwan)

2009 (17 Jan). Chinese New Year. Year of the Ox. T **311** and similar vert designs. Multicoloured.

(a) Two phosphor bands ($1.40) or one phosphor band (others). Granite paper. Imperf (No. MS1541) or Perf 14 (with one elliptical hole on each vert side) (others). Litho Enschedé.

1536	$1.40 Type **311**	70	55
1537	$2.40 Friesian Cow	1·10	90
1538	$3 Yak	1·40	1·10
1539	$5 Water Buffalo	2·40	1·90
1536/1539 Set of 4		5·00	4·00
MS1540 135×85 mm. Nos. 1536/1538.		5·75	5·50
MS1541 135×85 mm. $5 No. 1539.		2·50	2·40

(b) Size 38×51 mm. Ordinary paper. Perf 13½. Litho embossed and foil stamped Cartor.

MS1542 136×90 mm. $50 As No. 1489 Year of the Rat;		
$50 As No. 1536.	50·00	48·00

No. **MS**1542 has the Rat and Ox embossed with gold and silver foil.

(Litho Enschedé)

2009 (24 Feb). Mainland Scenery (7th issue). Sheet 140×90 mm. One phosphor band. Perf 14½ (with one elliptical hole on each vert side).

MS1543 312 $10 multicoloured	4·75	4·50

313 Peony and *Bauhinia blakeana* (flowers of Hong Kong and Luoyang)

(Des Michael Fung. Litho Cartor)

2009 (7 Apr). China 2009 International Stamp Exhibition, Luoyang. Sheet 130×75 mm. One phosphor band. Perf 14½ (with one elliptical hole on each vert side).

MS1544 313 $5 multicoloured	2·50	2·40

314 Tangram Pieces as Figure   **315** Calligraphy (Wang Duo)

(Des Colin Tillyer. Litho)

2009 (14 May). Hong Kong 2009, 23rd Asian International Stamp Exhibition. Sheet 135×85 mm. One phosphor band. Perf 13½.

MS1545 314 $50 multicoloured.	23·00	22·00

No. **MS**1545 was issued with a plastic screen which, when held against the sheet and tilted, showed hidden inscriptions.

2009 (16 May). Hong Kong Museums Collections. T **315** and similar multicoloured designs. Two phosphor bands ($1.40) or one phosphor band (others). Granite paper. Perf 13½×14 (vert) or 14×13½ (horiz) (all with one elliptical hole on each vert side).

1546	$1.40 Type **315**	70	55
1547	$1.80 Mountains (Wang Yuanqi)	90	75
1548	$2.40 Calligraphy (Wang Xizhi)	1·10	90
1549	$2.50 Moon and bird on blossom branch	1·10	95
1550	$3 Fan (Ju Lian) (*horiz*)	1·40	1·10
1551	$5 Calligrapher and assistants (Gu Huai)		
	(*horiz*)	2·40	1·90
1546/1551 Set of 6		7·00	5·50
MS1552 140×90 mm. Nos. 1546/1551.		7·75	7·50

316 Flowers

317 Sniffer Dog

(Des Jason Chum. Litho)

2009 (25 June). Greetings Stamps. With service indicator. T **316** and similar square designs showing felt appliqué. Two phosphor bands ($1.40) or one phosphor band ($3). Multicoloured. Granite paper. Perf 13½ (with one elliptical hole on each vert side).

(a) Inscribed 'Local Mail Postage'.

1553	($1.40) Type **316**	70	55
	a. Strip of 4. Nos. 1553/1556.	3·75	
1554	($1.40) Lion costume	70	55

(b) AIR. Inscribed 'Air Mail Postage'.

1555	($3) Conical hats and musical notes	1·40	1·10
1556	($3) Butterflies	1·40	1·10
1553/1556 Set of 4		3·75	3·00

No. 1553/1554 were for use on letters up to 30 grams within Hong Kong and Nos. 1555/1556 were for use on airmail letters up to 20 grams to addresses outside Hong Kong.

Nos. 1553/1556, were issued both in large sheets and in vertical *se-tenant* strips of four stamps, each with a label attached at right, within sheets of 20 stamps and 20 labels. The labels could be personalised by the addition of a photograph.

2009 (17 Sept). Centenary of Customs and Excise Service. T **317** and similar horiz designs. Two phosphor bands ($1.40) or one phosphor band (others). Multicoloured. Granite paper. Perf 13½ (with one elliptical hole on each vert side).

1557	$1.40 Type **317**	70	55
1558	$2.40 Custom and Excise vehicle	1·10	90
1559	$3 Coastguard vessel	1·40	1·10
1560	$5 Service men	2·40	1·90
1557/1560 Set of 4		5·00	4·00
MS1561 135×85 mm. Nos. 1557/1560.		5·75	5·50

318 Victoria Harbour and Tiananmen Square   **319** Hong Kong Player

(Des Ka-ching Tsoi and Chi-ming Cheng)

2009 (1 Oct). 60th Anniversary of People's Republic of China. T **318** and similar vert (No. **MS**1569) or fan shaped (others) designs. Multicoloured. Two phosphor bands ($1.40 and $1.80) or one phosphor band (others). Granite paper. Perf 13½ (with one elliptical hole on each vert side (No. **MS**1569) or horiz side (others)).

1562	$1.40 Type **318**	70	55
1563	$1.80 National Flag and *Forever Blooming Bauhinia* (symbol of Hong Kong)	90	75
1564	$2.40 National Stadium	1·10	90
1565	$2.50 CZ-2F rocket	1·10	95
1566	$3 Temple of Heaven, Beijing	1·40	1·10
1567	$5 Dragon and Great Wall of China	2·40	1·90
1562/1567 Set of 6		7·00	5·50
MS1568 140×90 mm. Nos. 1562/1567.		7·75	7·50
MS1569 140×90 mm. $5×2, Forbidden City; Hong Kong skyline.		5·25	5·00

Nos. 1562/1567 were perforated in the shape of a fan enclosed in an outer white perforated (13½) rectangle.

The phosphor extends beyond the stamp into the outer rectangle.

(Des Chung-hong Wong)

2009 (5 Nov). Hong Kong–Brazil Diplomatic Relations. Football. T **319** and similar horiz designs. Multicoloured. Two phosphor bands ($1.40) or one phosphor band (others). Granite paper. Perf 13½ (with one elliptical hole on each vert side).

1570	$1.40 Type **319**	70	55
1571	$2.40 Hong Kong goalkeeper	1·10	90
1572	$3 Brazilian player	1·40	1·10
1573	$5 Brazilian player (*different*)	2·40	1·90
1570/1573 Set of 4		5·00	4·00
MS1574 135×85 mm. Nos. 1570/1573.		5·75	5·50

Similar stamps were issued by Brazil.

320 Judo, Football and Kayaking **321** Tower and Suspension Cables

(Des Clement Yick. Litho and foil die-stamped)

2009 (5 Dec). East Asian Games, Hong Kong. T **320** and similar horiz designs showing athletes, colours of athletes given. Multicoloured. Two phosphor bands ($1.40) or one phosphor band (others). Granite paper. Perf 13½ (with one elliptical hole on each vert side).

1575	$1.40 Type **320**	70	55
1576	$1.40 Badminton, athletics, martial arts and rifle shooting (gold)	70	55
1577	$2.40 Cycling, weightlifting and tennis (silver)	1·10	90
1578	$2.40 Men's volleyball, hockey, women's table tennis and diving (silver)	1·10	90
1579	$3 Men's table tennis, women's volleyball, dance and snooker (bronze)	1·40	1·10
1580	$3 Wind surfing, football, basketball and taekwando (bronze)	1·40	1·10
1575/1580 *Set of 6*		5·75	4·50
MS1581 150×90 mm. Nos. 1575/1581		6·50	6·25

(Des Shik-kwong Li)

2009 (17 Dec). Opening of Stonecutters Bridge. T **321** and similar multicoloured designs. Two phosphor bands ($1.40) or one phosphor band (others). Granite paper. Perf 13½ (with one elliptical hole on each vert side).

1582	$1.40 Type **321**	70	55
1583	$2.40 Aerial view of bridge	1·10	90
1584	$3 Bridge from river	1·40	1·10
1585	$5 Aerial view of tower and suspension cables	2·40	1·90
1582/1585 *Set of 4*		5·00	4·00
MS1586 150×90 mm. Nos. 1582/1585		5·75	5·50

323 Fujian Tolou

(Des Arde Lam)

2010 (18 Mar). Mainland Scenery (8th issue). Sheet 140×90 mm. Granite paper. One phosphor band. Perf 14½ (with one elliptical hole on each vert side).

MS1594 **323** $10 multicoloured		5·50	5·50

324 Skyline with Dragon's Head

(Des Wong Chun-hong. Litho)

2010 (27 Apr). Expo 2010, Shanghai. T **324** and similar horiz designs. Multicoloured. Granite paper. Two phosphor bands ($1.40) or one phosphor band (others). Perf 14 (with one elliptical hole on each vert side).

1595	$1.40 Type **324**	70	55
1596	$2.40 Skyline on leaf	1·10	90
1597	$3 Skyline on bridge	1·40	1·10
1598	$5 Skyline on profiled head	2·40	1·90
1595/1598 *Set of 4*		5·00	4·00
MS1599 135×85 mm. Nos. 1595/1598		5·75	5·50

322 Tiger

(Des Bon Kwan)

2010 (6 Feb). Chinese New Year. Year of the Tiger. T **322** and similar vert designs. Multicoloured. Perf 14 (with one elliptical hole on each vert side).

*(a) Two phosphor bands ($1.40) or one phosphor band (others). Granite paper. Imperf (**MS**1592) or Perf 14 (with one elliptical hole on each vert side) (others).*

1587	$1.40 Type **322**	70	55
1588	$2.40 Facing left	1·10	90
1589	$3 Seated	1·40	1·10
1590	$5 White Tiger	2·40	1·90
1587/1590 *Set of 4*		5·00	4·00
MS1591 135×85 mm. Nos. 1587/1590		5·75	5·50
MS1592 135×85 mm. $5 No. 1590		2·50	2·40

(b) Size 38×51 mm. Ordinary paper. Perf 13½.

MS1593 136×90 mm. $50 As No. 1537 Year of the Ox; $50 As No. 1588		45·00	45·00

No. **MS**1593 has the Ox and Tiger embossed with gold and silver foil.

325 Symbols of Hong Kong and London **326** Pottinger Street

(Des Colin Tillyer)

2010 (8 May). London 2010 Festival of Stamps. London 2010 International Stamp Exhibition. Sheet 130×75 mm. One phosphor band. Perf 14 (with one elliptical hole on each vert side).

MS1600 **325** $10 bright scarlet and deep ultramarine		5·50	5·50

(Des Gideon Lai)

2010 (24 June). Streets of Hong Kong. T **326** and similar vert designs. Multicoloured. Granite paper. Two phosphor bands ($1.40) or one phosphor band (others). Perf 14 (with one elliptical hole on each vert side).

1601	$1.40 Type **326**	70	55
1602	$1.40 Nathan Road	70	55
1603	$2.40 Temple Street	1·10	90
1604	$2.40 Hollywood Road	1·10	90
1605	$3 Des Voeux Road West	1·40	1·10
1606	$3 Stanley Market	1·40	1·10
1601/1606 *Set of 6*		5·75	4·50
MS1607 140×90 mm. Nos. 1601/1606		6·50	6·25

327 Paradise Fish (only freshwater fish named after the territory)

328 Steam Locomotive and Hong Kong Railway Museum.

(Des Leung Kam Hung and Ken Wong)

2010 (15 July). Biodiversity. T **327** and similar horiz designs. Multicoloured. Granite paper. Two phosphor bands ($1.40) or one phosphor band (others). Perf 13½×14½ (with one elliptical hole on each vert side).

1608	$1.40 Type **327**	70	55
1609	$2.40 Romer's Tree Frog (smallest Frog species found in Hong Kong)	1·10	90
1610	$3 *Sinopora hongkongensis* (plant first discovered in Tai Mo Shan and new to science)	1·40	1·10
1611	$5 *Fukienogomphus choifongae* (Dragonfly first discovered in Wu Kau Tang and new to science)	2·40	1·90
1608/1611 *Set of 4*		5·00	4·00
MS1612 135×85 mm. Nos. 1608/1611.		5·75	5·50

(Des Clement Yick. Litho and holography (No. 1620) or litho (others) Enschedé)

2010 (28 Sept). Centenary of Hong Kong Railway. T **328** and similar vert designs. Multicooured. Granite paper. Two phosphor bands ($1.40) or one phosphor band (others). Perf 14×13½ (with one elliptical hole on each vert side).

1613	$1.40 Type **328**	70	55
1614	$1.80 Diesel locomotive and Clock Tower of old Kowloon–Canton Railway terminus, Tsim Sha Tsui	90	75
1615	$2.40 Electric locomotive and old Hung Hom terminus	1·10	90
1616	$2.50 MTR Passenger train and International Finance Centre, above MTR Hong Kong Station	1·25	95
1617	$3 Kowloon–Guangzhou through train and MTR Hung Hom Station	1·40	1·10
1618	$5 Airport Express train and Hong Kong International Airport	2·40	1·90
1613/1618 *Set of 6*		7·00	5·50
MS1619 135×85 mm. Nos. 1613/1618.		7·75	7·50
MS1620 135×85 mm. $20 As Type **328** (38×51 mm)		9·00	8·75

The lower part of the stamp of No. **MS**1620 is hologram of a locomotive which appears to move when tilted.

A limited edition premium booklet containing four panes of text interleaved with one pane containing Nos. 1453/1455 and another containing Nos. 1613/1618 was for sale at $36.

329 *Harbour of Hong Kong* (Hei-chun Man)

330 Dwelling with Scaffolding

(Litho Cartor)

2010 (21 Oct). Hong Kong in My Eyes. Winning Designs in Children's Design a Stamp Competition. T **329** and similar horiz designs. Multicoloured. Granite paper. Two phosphor bands ($1.40) or one phosphor band (others). Perf 13½×14 (with one elliptical hole on each vert side).

1621	$1.40 Type **329**	70	55
1622	$2.40 *Beautiful Hong Kong* (Ying-jun Tan)	1·10	90
1623	$3 *Hong Kong is Fun* (Tsz-yu Soong)	1·40	1·10
1624	$5 *City Beat* (Yvette Chantal Yao)	2·40	1·90
1621/1624 *Set of 4*		5·00	4·00
MS1625 135×85 mm. Nos. 1621/1624.		5·75	5·50

(Des Benny Lau. Litho Cartor)

2010 (16 Nov). Redevelopment. T **330** and similar square designs. Multicoloured. Granite paper. Two phosphor bands ($1.40) or one phosphor bands (others). Perf 14 (with one elliptical hole on each vert side).

1626	$1.40 Type **330**	70	55
1627	$2.40 Work	1·10	90
1628	$3 Transport	1·40	1·10
1629	$5 Community	2·40	1·90
1626/1629 *Set of 4*		5·00	4·00
MS1630 150×85 mm. Nos. 1626/1629.		5·75	5·50

331 Cape D'Aguilar

332 Rabbit

(Des Jason Chum. Litho Enschedé)

2010 (29 Dec). Lighthouses. Multicoloured. Granite paper. Two phosphor bands ($1.40 and $1.80) or one phosphor band (others). Perf 13½ (with one elliptical hole on each vert side).

1631	$1.40 Type **331**	70	55
1632	$1.80 Old Green Island	90	75
1633	$2.40 New Green Island	1·10	90
1634	$3 Tang Lung Chau	1·40	1·10
1635	$5 Waglan	2·40	1·90
1631/1635 *Set of 5*		5·75	4·75
MS1636 150×85 mm. Nos. 1631/1635.		6·50	6·25

(Des Bon Kwan)

2011 (22 Jan). Chinese New Year. Year of the Rabbit. T **332** and similar vert designs. Multicoloured. Perf 14 (with one elliptical hole on each vert side).

(a) Two phosphor bands ($1.40) or one phosphor band (others). Granite paper. Perf 14 (with one elliptical hole on each vert side).

1637	$1.40 Type **332**	70	55
1638	$2.40 Wild Rabbit	1·10	90
1639	$3 Brown and white Rabbit	1·40	1·10
1640	$5 Long-haired dwarf Rabbit	2·40	1·90
1637/1640 *Set of 4*		5·00	4·00
MS1641 210×150 mm. $1.40×12, As Type **301**; As No. 1537; As Type **322**; As Type **332**; As Type **206**; As Type **288**; As Type **215**; As No. 1335; As Type **264**; As No. 1211; As No. 1157; As Type **226**.		8·50	8·00
MS1642 135×85 mm. As Nos. 1637/1640.		5·75	5·50
MS1643 135×85 mm. As No. 1640.		2·50	2·40

(b) One phosphor band. Flocked paper. Litho Cartor. Perf 13.

1644	$10 As No. 1492	3·50	3·00
1645	$10 As Type **311**	3·50	3·00
1646	$10 As Type **322**	3·50	3·00
1647	$10 As No. 1639	3·50	3·00
1644/1647 *Set of 4*		12·50	11·00

(c) Size 38×51 mm. Ordinary paper. Litho, embossed and foil stamped Cartor. Perf 13½.

MS1648 136×90 mm. $50×2, As No. 1589; As Type **332**.		42·00	42·00

Nos. 1644/1647 were printed, *se-tenant*, in blocks of four stamps within sheets of 16.

No. **MS**1648 has the Tiger and Rabbit embossed with gold and silver foil.

333 Farman Biplane Replica (on display at Hong Kong International Airport Passenger Terminal)

334 Note and Leaf on Diary Page (planting trees)

(Des Wong Chun-hong. Litho Cartor)

2011 (18 Mar). Centenary of Powered Flight. Sheet 135×85 mm containing T **333** and similar horiz design. Multicoloured. Granite paper. One phosphor band. Perf 14 (with one elliptical hole on each vert side).

MS1649	$3×2, Type **333**; Lift-off of Farman biplane (flown by Charles Van den Born), from tidal flats......	4·00	4·00

(Des Cheng Chi-ming (Carl). Litho Cartor)

2011 (29 Mar). Tenth Anniversary of International Year of Volunteers. T **334** and similar multicoloured designs. Multicoloured. Granite paper. Two phosphor bands ($1.40) or one phosphor band (others). Perf 13½ (No. **MS**1654) or 13½ (with one elliptical hole on each vert side) (others).

1650	$1.40 Type **334**	70	55
1651	$2.40 Internet recruitment leaflet to rally support for community charity event...	1·10	90
1652	$3 Email brings good news on school redevelopment...	1·40	1·10
1653	$5 Calendar reminder of upcoming home visit with elderly volunteer...	2·40	1·90
1650/1653	*Set of 4*	5·00	4·00
MS1654	135×90 mm. $5 'VOLUNTEERISM' (36×35 mm (heart-shaped))...	2·50	2·40

335 Tap and Globe as Droplet of Water ('Conserve Water')

336 'Founding, 1861'

(Des Jason Chum. Litho Cartor)

2011 (14 Apr). Green Living. T **335** and similar square designs. Multicoloured. Granite paper. Perf 14 (with one elliptical hole on each vert side).

1655	$1.40 Type **335**	70	55
1656	$2.40 Clouds, tree and globe as sun ('Clean Air')	1·10	90
1657	$3 Low energy light bulb and globe as lamp ('Save Energy')	1·40	1·10
1658	$5 Globe, recycle emblem, can, bottle and paper ('Recycle')	2·40	1·90
1655/1658	*Set of 4*	5·00	4·00
MS1659	122×78 mm. $5 Plantlet growing from globe ('Treasure the Earth')	2·50	2·40

No. **MS**1659 was cut around in the shape of a leaf.

(Des Shirman Lai)

2011 (26 May). 150th Anniversary of Hong Kong General Chamber of Commerce. Multicoloured. Granite paper. Two phosphor bands ($1.40) or one phosphor band (others). Perf 14×13½ (with one elliptical hole on each vert side).

1660	$1.40 Type **336**	70	55
1661	$2.40 Shipyard ('Issue of Certificates of Origin, 1923')	1·10	90
1662	$3 'Sponsorship for Good Citizen Award, 1973'	1·40	1·10
1663	$5 'Entry into China Market, 1978'	2·40	1·90
1660/1663	*Set of 4*	5·00	4·00
MS1664	135×85 mm. Nos. 1660/1663	5·75	5·50

337 'Mutual Help in Hard Times'

338 Dunhuang Grottoes

(Des Freeman Lau and Steve Yong. Litho Enschedé)

2011 (28 June). Children Stamps. Chinese Idioms and Their Stories. Multicoloured. Granite paper. Two phosphor bands ($1.40 and £1.80) or one phosphor band (others). Perf 13½×14½ (with one elliptical hole on each vert side).

1665	$1.40 Type **337**	70	55
1666	$1.80 'Water drops wear away rocks'	90	75
1667	$2.40 'Practise makes perfect'	1·10	90
1668	$3 'Save to give'	1·40	1·10
1669	$5 'As deft as a master butcher'	2·40	1·90
1665/1669	*Set of 5*	5·75	4·75
MS1670	150×85 mm. As Nos. 1665/1669, but with parts of the design printed without colour...	6·50	6·25

MS1670 was sold with a sheet of multicoloured self-adhesive stickers which could be placed over the uncoloured areas on the sheet.

(Des Gideon Lai. Litho Enschedé)

2011 (2 Aug). Mainland Scenery (9th issue). Dunhuang Grottoes (No. **MS**1671) or Complete Mainland Scenery Series (No. **MS**1672). Two sheets containing T **338** and similar multicoloured designs. Multicoloured. Granite paper. One phosphor band. Perf 13½ (with one elliptical hole on each vert side).

MS1671	140×90 mm. $10 Type **338**	4·75	4·50
MS1672	210×149 mm. $2.40×9, Qiangtang Bore (As Type **272**) (76×30 mm); Dunhuang Grottoes (As Type **338**); Mount Tianshan (As Type **312**) (45×28 mm); Huanglong (As Type **302**) (45×28 mm); Fujian Tulou (As Type **323**) (45×28 mm); Master of Nets' Garden (As Type **241**) (45×40 mm); Glen Clan Academy (As Type **255**); Shilin (As Type **291**) (45×28 mm); Mount Taishan (As Type **278**) (45×28 mm)	12·00	12·00

339 Early and Modern Post Boxes

340 Main Building and the Golden Trowel

(Des Bon Kwan. Litho, embossed and foil die-stamped. Enschedé)

2011 (25 Aug). 170th Anniversary of Hong Kong Postal Service. Sheet 130×75 mm. Granite paper. Perf 13 (with one star shaped hole on each vert side).

MS1673	**339** $10 multicoloured	5·50	5·50

(Des Arde Lam. Litho Cartor)

2011 (15 Sept). Centenary of University of Hong Kong. T **340** and similar multicoloured designs. Multicoloured. Granite paper. Two phosphor bands ($1.40, $1.80) or one phosphor band (others). Perf 13½ (single stamps) or 14×14½ (No. **MS**1680), each with one elliptical hole on each vert side.

1674	$1.40 Type **340**	70	55
1675	$1.80 Main Building in 1912 and Fête and Bazaar poster	90	75
1676	$2.40 Union Building in 1919, Main Building in the background and statue of Dr. Sun Yat-sen	1·10	90
1677	$2.50 Roofless Main Building in 1946 and Mace	1·10	95
1678	$3 Main Building and West Gate, 1940's, and inkstand	1·40	1·10
1679	$5 Main Building and courtyard, today, and Coat of Arms	2·40	1·90
1674/1679	*Set of 6*	7·00	5·50
MS1680	130×75 mm. $5 Letters Patent from College of Arms granting Full Coat of Arms (35×45 mm)	2·50	2·40

A premium booklet containing Nos. 1674/1679 and the stamp from No. **MS**1680 and ten pages of text celebrating the Anniversary was on sale for $45.

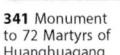

341 Monument to 72 Martyrs of Huanghuagang

342 Lion's Head Rice Flour Figurine (Hong Kong)

(Des Roxy Lau. Litho Cartor)

2011 (10 Oct). Centenary of Xinhai Revolution (Revolution of 1911). T **341** and similar designs highlighting key figures and events of Xinhai Revolution. Each black and carmine-vermilion. Each black and carmine-vermilion. Granite paper. Two phosphor bands ($1.40) or one phosphor band (others). Perf 13½ with one elliptical hole on each vert side.

1681	$1.40 Type **341**	70	55
1682	$2.40 Wuchang Uprising	1·10	90
1683	$3 'Cai Yuanpei and Zhang Taiyan, leaders of Guangfuhui (Restoration Society), Huang Xing and Song Jiaoren, (founders of Huaxinghui (Society for the Revival of China)) (forerunners of Xinhai Revolution)'	1·40	1·10
1684	$5 Sun Yat-sen assuming office of Provisional President	2·40	1·90
1681/1684	Set of 4	5·00	4·00
MS1685	130×75 mm. $5×2, Central School (present-day Queen's College), Hong Kong where Sun Yat-sen was educated (*horiz*); Sun Yat-sen's election as president of Tongmenghui and his proclamation in Min Bao (*horiz*)	4·75	4·50

Nos. 1681/MS1685 were a joint issue with People's Republic China and Macau. A presentation folder containing the three miniature sheets was prepared by Hong Kong Post in which the Hong Kong sheet was printed gravure, rather than litho.

(Des Mihai Vamasescu (Romania) or Colin Tillyer (Hong Kong). Litho Enschedé)

2011 (24 Nov). Handicrafts. T **342** and similar square design. Multicoloured. Granite paper. Perf 13½.

1686	$5 Type **342**	2·40	1·90
1687	$5 Painted egg (Romania)	2·40	1·90
MS1688	135×85 mm. Nos. 1686/1687	4·75	4·50

Stamps of a similar design were issued by Romania.

343 Headdress from Cantonese Opera

344 Chief Executive's Office, Central Government Offices and Legislative Council Complex

(Des Arde Lam. Litho and varnish Cartor)

2011 (22 Nov). Hong Kong Museums' Collections. T **343** and similar multicoloured designs showing museum exhibits. Multicoloured. Granite paper. Two phosphor bands ($1.40, $1.80) or one phosphor band (others). Perf 14.

1689	$1.40 Type **343**	70	55
1690	$1.80 Qipao (women's dress)	90	75
1691	$2.40 Silver footed bowl decorated in repousse (*horiz*)	1·10	90
1692	$2.50 Sequined reversible palace costume (*horiz*)	1·10	95

1693	$3 Green glazed barrel for herbal tea (*horiz*)	1·40	1·10
1694	$5 Baby-carrier with head support (*horiz*).	2·40	1·90
1689/1694	Set of 6	7·00	5·50
MS1695	145×95 mm. Nos. 1689/1694.	7·75	7·50

(Des Gideon Lai. Litho Cartor)

2011 (15 Dec). Tamar Development Project. Sheet 140×90 mm. Granite paper. One phosphor band. Perf 13½.

MS1696	**344** $10 multicoloured	4·75	4·50

345 Fire Dragon and Joss Sticks

(Des Clement Yick and Lulu Ngie (Nos. 1697/1704) or Bon Kwan (No. 1705))

2012 (14 Jan). Chinese New Year. Year of the Dragon. T **345** and similar multicoloured designs. Multicoloured.

(a) Two phosphor bands ($1.40) or one phosphor band (others). Granite paper. Perf 13½ (MS1701/MS1703) or 13½×14 (others) each with one elliptical hole on each vert side.

1697	$1.40 Type **345**	70	55
1698	$2.40 Golden Dragon	1·10	90
1699	$3 Dragon dance head	1·40	1·10
1700	$5 Long thin Dragon	2·40	1·90
1697/1700	Set of 4	5·00	4·00
MS1701	136×90 mm. $10 Flying Dragon	4·75	4·50
MS1702	210×150 mm. $1.40×12, As No. 1007 (Dragon); As No. 1041 (Snake); As Type **226** (Horse); As No. 1157 (Ram); As No. 1211 (Monkey); As No. 1294 (Cockerel); As No. 1335 (Dog); As Type **288** (Pig); As No. 1492 (Rat); As Type **311** (Ox); As No. 1588 (Tiger); As Type **332** (Rabbit)	8·50	8·00
MS1703	210×150 mm. $1.40×12, As Type **217** (Dragon); As Type **215** (Snake); As No. 1081 (Horse); As Type **238** (Ram); As No. 1209 (Monkey); As No. 1295 (Cockerel); As No. 1337 (Dog); As No. 1426 (Pig); As Type **301** (Rat); As No. 1537 (Ox); As No. 1589 (Tiger); As No. 1639 (Rabbit)	8·50	8·00

(b) Silk-faced paper. Granite paper. Miniature sheet. Perf 13½ (with one elliptical hole on each vert side).

MS1704	80×80 mm. $50 Flying Dragon (design as stamp of No. MS1701 but multicoloured) (45×45 mm)	23·00	22·00

(c) Size 38×51 mm. Ordinary paper. Miniature sheet. Perf 14.

MS1705	136×90 mm. $50×2, As Type **332**; Dragon	42·00	40·00

No. MS1702 has silver margins.
No. MS1703 has gold margins.

346 College Building

347 *Château Douglas* (painting)

(Des Tong Wai Pang. Litho (No. 1706) and glitter die-stamped, varnished, embossed and gold foil die-stamped (No. 1707))

2012 (27 Mar). 150th Anniversary of Queen's College. Two sheets containing T **346** and similar shield-shaped designs. Multicoloured. Granite paper. One phosphor bar. Perf 13½.

MS1706	130×75 mm. $10 Type **346**.	4·75	4·50
MS1707	120×130 mm. $10×4, As Type **346**, glitter applied to shield outline; As Type **346**, varnish applied to central design and bronze face value; As Type **346**, Arms and building embossed; As Type **346**, building and face value gold foil die-stamped.	18·00	18·00

(Des Jason Chum)

2012 (4 May). Art of France and Hong Kong. T **347** and similar square designs. Multicoloured. Granite paper. Two phosphor bands ($1.40) or one phosphor band (others). Perf 13½×13 (with one elliptical hole on each vert side).

1708	$1.40 Type **347**	70	55
1709	$2.40 *Crab #4* (Yee Cheung)	1·10	90
1710	$3 *The Racetrack* (painting) (Edgar Degas)	1·40	1·10
1711	$5 *Le Cheval* (sculpture) (Raymond Duchamp-Villon)	2·40	1·90
1708/1711 *Set of 4*		5·00	4·00
MS1712 140×90 mm. As No. 1708/1711		5·75	5·50

Stamps of a similar design were issued by France.

348 Tin Hau Festival   **349** Beagle (Ministry of Agriculture, Fisheries and Conservation)

(Des Arde Lam)

2012 (22 May). Hong Kong Festivals. T **348** and similar vert designs. Multicoloured. Granite paper. Two phosphor bands ($1.40) or one phosphor band (others). Perf 14 (with one elliptical hole on each vert side).

1713	$1.40 Type **348**	70	55
1714	$2.40 Kwun Yum Festival	1·10	90
1715	$3 Birthday of Buddha	1·40	1·10
1716	$5 Tuen Ng Festival	2·40	1·90
1713/1716 *Set of 4*		5·00	4·00
MS1717 135×85 mm. $5 Mid Autumn Festival		2·50	2·40

(Des Wong Chun-hong. Litho)

2012 (19 June). Working Dogs in Government Service. T **349** and similar horiz designs. Multicoloured. Granite paper. Two phosphor bands ($1.40 and $1.80) or one phosphor band (others). Perf 13½×14½ (with one elliptical hole on each vert side).

1718	$1.40 Type **349**	70	55
1719	$1.80 German Shepherd (Correctional Services)	90	75
1720	$2.40 Springer Spaniel (Custom and Excise)	1·10	90
1721	$2.50 Golden Labrador (Fire Services)	1·10	95
1722	$3 Black Labrador (Food and Environmental Hygiene)	1·40	1·10
1723	$5 Malinois (Hong Kong Police)	2·40	1·90
1718/1723 *Set of 6*		7·00	5·50
MS1724 135×85 mm. $5 As Nos. 1718/1723, head and shoulders only (*detail*) (100×40 mm)		2·50	2·40

A premium booklet containing 15 pages of text, describing the Dogs and their work, interleaved with panes containing Nos. 1718/1719, 1720/1721 and 1722/1723, respectively, was on sale for $45.

350 Statue of Justice   **351** Stylised Windsurfer and '2'

(Des Freeman Lau. Litho)

2012 (1 July). 15th Anniversary of Establishment of Hong Kong Special Administrative Region. Sheet 140×90 mm containing T **350** and similar horiz designs. Multicoloured. Granite paper. One phosphor band. Perf 13½×14 (with one elliptical hole on each vert side).

MS1725 $5×3, Type **350**; Skyscrapers; Chek Lap Kok Airport	7·50	7·50

(Des Bon Kwan)

2012 (27 July). Olympic Games, London. T **351** and similar square designs. Multicoloured. Granite paper. Two phosphor bands ($1.40) or one phosphor band (others). Perf 14 (with one elliptical hole on each vert side).

1726	$1.40 Type **351**	70	55
1727	$2.40 Handball player, archer and '0'	1·10	90
1728	$3 Tennis player, cyclist and '1'	1·40	1·10
1729	$5 Swimmer and '2'	2·40	1·90
1726/1729 *Set of 4*		5·00	4·00
MS1730 As Nos. 1726/1729		5·75	5·50

Nos. 1726/1729, when placed together in a block of four, form a composite design as No. **MS**1730.

352 Egg Tarts and Milk Tea

(Des Eddy Yu)

2012 (30 Aug). Hong Kong Delicacies. T **352** and similar horiz designs. Multicoloured. Granite paper. Two phosphor bands ($1.40) or one phosphor band (others). Perf 14 (with one elliptical hole on each vert side).

1731	$1.40 Type **352**	70	55
1732	$2.40 Wonton noodles	1·10	90
1733	$3 Roast goose	1·40	1·10
1734	$5 Seafood	2·40	1·90
1731/1734 *Set of 4*		5·00	4·00
MS1735 135×85 mm. As Nos. 1731/1734		5·75	5·50

353 The Great Wall of China   **354** Capricorn

(Des Li Shik-kwong Ken. Litho and silk screen printed Enschedé)

2012 (27 Sept). World Heritage Sites in China (1st series). The Great Wall. Sheet 140×90 mm. Granite paper. One phosphor band. Perf 13½×14 (with one elliptical hole on each vert side).

MS1736 **353** $10 multicoloured	4·75	4·50

See also Nos. **MS**1810, **MS**1922, **MS**1967, **MS**2014 and **MS**2075.

(Des Michael Fung. Litho Enschedé)

2012 (1 Nov). Signs of the Western Zodiac. T **354** and similar square designs. Multicoloured. Granite paper. Two phosphor bands.

(a) Ordinary gum. Perf 14.

1737	$1.40 Type **354**	70	55
1738	$1.40 Aquarius	70	55
1739	$1.40 Pisces	70	55
1740	$1.40 Aries	70	55
1741	$1.40 Taurus	70	55
1742	$1.40 Gemini	70	55
1743	$1.40 Cancer	70	55
1744	$1.40 Leo	70	55
1745	$1.40 Virgo	70	55
1746	$1.40 Libra	70	55
1747	$1.40 Scorpio	70	55
1748	$1.40 Sagittarius	70	55
1737/1748 *Set of 12*		7·50	6·00
MS1749 210×150 mm. As Nos. 1737/1748		8·50	8·00

(b) Booklet stamps. Self-adhesive. Die-cut perf 14 (with one elliptical hole on each vert side).

1750	$1.40 As Type **354**	70	55
	a. Booklet pane. Nos. 1750/1761	8·50	
1751	$1.40 As No. 1738	70	55
1752	$1.40 As No. 1739	70	55
1753	$1.40 As No. 1740	70	55
1754	$1.40 As No. 1741	70	55
1755	$1.40 As No. 1742	70	55
1756	$1.40 As No. 1743	70	55
1757	$1.40 As No. 1744	70	55
1758	$1.40 As No. 1745	70	55
1759	$1.40 As No. 1746	70	55
1760	$1.40 As No. 1747	70	55
1761	$1.40 As No. 1748	70	55
1750/1761 *Set of 12*		8·50	8·00

355 *Cosmoscarta bispecularis*

356 1862 2c. Stamp (As Type 1), Quill pen and Ink Well

(Des Tai-keung Kan. Litho Enschedé)

2012 (22 Nov). Insects. Multicoloured. Multicoloured. Granite paper. Two phosphor bands ($1.40) or one phosphor band (others). Perf 13½×14½ (with one elliptical hole on each vert side).

1762	$1.40 Type **355**	70	55
1763	$1.80 Flower Mantis (*Creobroter gemmatus*) (inscr 'Flower Mantid' *Creobroter gemmata*)	90	75
1764	$2.40 China-mark *Eristena* (inscr 'Mangrove china-mark')	1·10	90
1765	$2.50 White Dragontail (*Lamproptera curius*)	1·10	95
1766	$3 Four-spot Midget (*Mortonagrion hirosei*)	1·40	1·10
1767	$5 Bent-winged Firefly (*Pteroptyx maipo*)	2·40	1·90
1762/1767 Set of 6		7·00	5·50
MS1768 145×95 mm. Nos. 1762/1767		7·75	7·50

(Des Ken Wong (booklet) or Colin Tillyer (others))

2012 (8 Dec). 150th Anniversary of First Hong Kong Stamps. T **356** and similar multicoloured designs. Multicoloured. Granite paper. Two phosphor bands ($1.40) or one phosphor band (others). Perf 14 (with one elliptical hole on each vert side).

1769	$1.40 Type **356**	70	55
1770	$1.80 Fountain pen and 1862 8c. stamp	90	75
1771	$2.40 Ballpoint pen and 1862 12c. stamp	1·10	90
1772	$2.50 1862 18c. stamp and typewriter	1·10	95
1773	$3 1862 24c. stamp and keyboard	1·40	1·10
1774	$5 Quick response code and 1862 48c. stamp	2·40	1·90
1769/1774 Set of 6		7·00	5·50
MS1775 130×75 mm. $10 1862 96c. stamp and barcode (65×24 mm)		4·75	4·50

A booklet containing 15 panes of text and three panes of stamps. Pane 1 Nos. 1769/1771; Pane 2 Nos. 1772/1774 and Pane 3 the stamp of No. **MS**1775 was on sale for $50.

Stamp similar to Nos. 1769 and 1773, but in square formats were issued on the same date inscribed 'Local Mail Postage' and 'Air Mail Postage'. They were sold in sheets of 12 (face value $16.80) for $40 and eight (face value $24) for $55 respectively.

357 Stylised Snake

(Des Tai-keung Kan or Clement Yick (Dragon stamp of No. 1782))

2013 (26 Jan). Chinese New Year. Year of the Snake. T **357** and similar multicoloured designs. Multicoloured. Granite paper.

(a) Two phosphor bands ($1.40) or one phosphor band (others). Perf 13½ (**MS**1780) or 13½×14½ (others) each with one elliptical hole on each vert side.

1776	$1.40 Type **357**	70	55
1777	$2.40 Snake glyphs	1·10	90
1778	$3 Snake	1·40	1·10
1779	$5 Jade Snake	2·40	1·90
1776/1779 Set of 4		5·00	4·00
MS1780 135×85 mm. $10 Multicoloured Snake breathing fire (45×45 mm)		4·75	4·50

(b) Silk-faced paper. Miniature sheet. Perf 13½ (with one elliptical hole on each vert side).

MS1781 80×80 mm. $50 Snake (design as stamp of No. **MS**1780) (45×45 mm)		23·00	22·00

(c) Size 45×28 mm. Miniature sheet. Perf 13½ (with one elliptical hole on each vert side).

MS1782 136×90 mm. $50×2, As Type **357**; Dragon (As No. 1700)		42·00	40·00

Stamps similar to Nos. 1776 and 1778, but on square format were issued on 12 February 2013 inscribed 'Local Mail Postage' and 'Air Mail Postage'. They were sold with *se-tenant* labels attached in sheets of 12 (face value $16.80 and 36) for $40 and $66 respectively.

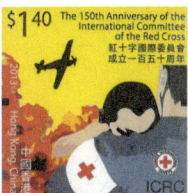

358 Carrying Child (Protection)

359 My Dog

(Des Pui-kay Mou and Pak-keung Leung. Litho Cartor)

2013 (28 Feb). 150th Anniversary of Red Cross. T **358** and similar square designs. Multicoloured. Multicoloured. Granite paper. Two phosphor bands ($1.40) or one phosphor band (others). Perf 14 (with one cross-shaped hole on each vert side).

1783	$1.40 Type **358**	70	55
1784	$2.40 Bandaging (Assistance)	1·10	90
1785	$3 Teaching (Prevention)	1·40	1·10
1786	$5 Carrying parcel (Co-operation)	2·40	1·90
1783/1786 Set of 4		5·00	4·00
MS1787 135×85 mm. $1.40 As No. 1783; $2.40 As No. 1784; $3 As No. 1785; $5 As No. 1786.		5·75	5·50

(Des Benny Lau. Litho Cartor)

2013 (28 Mar). Children's Stamps. My Pet and I. T **359** and similar square designs. Multicoloured. Granite paper. Two phosphor bands ($1.40 and £1.80) or one phosphor bands (others). Perf 14.

1788	$1.40 Type **359**	70	55
1789	$1.80 My Cat	90	75
1790	$2.40 My Tortoise	1·10	90
1791	$2.50 My Guinea Pig	1·10	95
1792	$3 My Rabbit	1·40	1·10
1792a	$5 My Hamster	2·40	1·90
1788/1792a Set of 6		6·75	5·50
MS1793 140×90 mm. $1.40 Type **359**; $1.80 My Cat; $2.40 My Tortoise; $2.50 My Guinea Pig; $3 My Rabbit; $5 My Hamster.		7·75	7·50

Stamp similar to the $1.40 and $3 values were issued on 12 February 2013 inscribed 'Local Mail Postage' and 'Air Mail Postage' and having postal values of $1.40 and $3 respectively. They were sold in sheets of eight with *se-tenant* labels depicting children with Dogs or Rabbits for $30 (face value $11.20) and $55 (face value $24) (*Price for 3 sheets, £25 unused*).

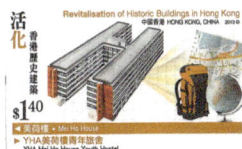

360 YHA Mei Ho House Youth Hostel

(Des Ying-chi Lee)

2013 (7 May). Revitalisation of Historic Buildings in Hong Kong. T **360** and similar multicoloured designs. Multicoloured. Granite paper. Two phosphor bands ($1.40 and $1.80) or one phosphor band (others). Perf 13½×14½ (with one elliptical hole on each vert side).

1794	$1.40 Type **360**	70	55
1795	$1.80 Fong Yuen Study Hall, Yuen Yuen Institute	90	75
1796	$2.40 Jao Tsung-I Academy	1·10	90
1797	$2.50 Hong Kong Baptist University School of Chinese Medicine–Lui Seng Chun	1·10	95
1798	$3 Tai O Heritage Hotel	1·40	1·10
1799	$5 SCAD Hong Kong	2·40	1·90
1794/1799 Set of 6		7·00	5·50
MS1800 180×75 mm. Nos. 1794/1799 (65×24 mm)		7·75	7·50

A booklet containing 15 panes of text and three panes of stamps. Pane 1 Nos. 1794/1795; Pane 2 Nos. 1796/1797 and Pane 3 1798/1799 was on sale for $45.

361 Kai Tak Cruise Terminal (*image scaled to 65% of original size*)

(Des Carl Chi-ming Cheng. Litho (No. 1801) or litho and silver hot foil effect (No. 1802) Enschedé)

2013 (11 June). Kai Tak Cruise Terminal. Two sheets, each 130×75 mm, containing T **361** and similar horiz design. Granite paper. One phosphor band (**MS**1801). Perf 13½×13 (with one elliptical hole on each vert side).

MS1801	**361** $10 multicoloured	4·75	4·50
MS1802	**361** $20 multicoloured	9·00	8·75

362 Chinese Newly Weds

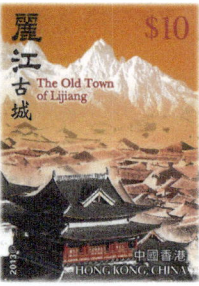

363 Jade Dragon Snow Mountain and Wanjuan Pavilion, Mu's Mansion

(Des Eric Chan. Litho Enschedé)

2013 (23 July). Chinese and Western Wedding Customs. T **362** and similar multicoloured designs. Multicoloured. Granite paper. Two phosphor bands ($1.40 and $1.80) or one phosphor band (others). Perf 13½×13 (with one elliptical hole on each vert side).

1803	$1.40 Type **362**	70	55
1804	$1.80 Western newly weds	90	75
1805	$2.40 Gift Presentation (traditional Chinese pre-wedding etiquette)	1·10	90
1806	$2.50 Western couple cutting the cake	1·10	95
1807	$3 Dragon and Phoenix (auspicious Chinese marriage symbols)	1·40	1·10
1808	$5 Western white wedding with bells and archway	2·40	1·90
1803/1808 *Set of 6*		7·00	5·50
MS1809	135×90 mm. $10 Chinese and western newly weds (100×40 mm)	4·75	4·50

Stamps similar to Nos. 1803 and 1808, but in square format were issued on the same date inscribed 'Local Mail Postage' and 'Air Mail Postage'. They were sold in sheets of eight with *se-tenant* labels attached (face value $11.20 and $40) for $30 and $55 respectively.

(Des Gideon Lai. Litho and embossed Enschedé)

2013 (22 Aug). World Heritage Sites in China (2nd series). Old Town of Lijiang. Sheet 140×90 mm. Granite paper. One phosphor band. Perf 14 (with one elliptical hole on each vert side).

MS1810	**363** $10 multicoloured	4·75	4·50

364 Tilling Stevens Bus (1947)

364a Figure with Arms Raised

(Des Clement Yick (booklet) or Kam-hung Leung (others). Litho and lenticular (No. 1818) or litho (others) Enschedé (No. 1818) or Cartor (others))

2013 (24 Sept). Hong Kong Buses. T **364** and similar multicoloured designs. Multicoloured. Granite paper. Two phosphor bands ($1.40 and $1.80) or one phosphor band (others). Perf 14 (No. **MS**1817), P 13 (No. **MS**1818) or P 13½ (others) (all with one elliptical hole on each vert side).

1811	$1.40 Type **364**	70	55
1812	$1.80 Daimler A (1949)	90	75
1813	$2.40 Single-decker Albion Coach (1975)	1·10	90
1814	$2.50 Leyland Olympian 11m (1988)	1·10	95

1815	$3 Volvo Olympian 11m (1995)	1·40	1·10
1816	$5 Dennis Trident (1997)	2·40	1·90
1811/1816 *Set of 6*		7·00	5·50
MS1817	140×90 mm. $5 Euro V Bus (100×40 mm)	2·50	2·40
MS1818	140×90 mm. $20 Euro V Bus (*different*) (100×40 mm)	9·00	8·75

A booklet containing 12 panes of text and three panes of stamps. Pane 1 Nos. 1811/1813; Pane 2 Nos. 1814/1816 and Pane 3 Stamp of No. **MS**1817 was on sale for $50.

(Des Arde Lam. Litho Enschedé ('Local Mail') or Cartor ('Air Mail'))

2013 (1 Oct). Greetings Stamps. With service indicator. T **364a** and similar square designs. Multicoloured. Perf 13½ (with one elliptical hole on each vert side).

(a) Inscr 'Local Mail Postage'. Perf 13½ (with one elliptical hole on each vert side).

1818*a*	($1.70) Type **364a**	85	70

(ai) Booklet Stamp. Inscr 'Local Mail Postage'.

1818*b*	($1.70) As Type **364a**	85	70
	ba. Booklet pane. No. 1818*b*×10	8·50	

(b) AIR. Inscr 'Air Mail Postage'.

1818*c*	($3.70) Figure and heart-shaped tree	2·00	1·75

(bi) Booklet Stamp. AIR. Inscr 'Air Mail Postage'.

1818*d*	($3.70) As No. 1818*c*	2·00	1·75
	a. Booklet pane. No. 1818*d*×10	20·00	

Nos. 1818*a*/1818*b* are as Nos. 1182 and 1184 but with the designs redrawn. The booklet panes have straight edges, giving stamps with two or three sides perforated depending on position.

Nos. 1818*a*/1818*b* were for use on letters up to 30 grams within Hong Kong and 1818*c*/1818*d* were for use on airmail letters up to 20 grams to addresses outside Hong Kong.

365 *Thanksgiving* (Chan Tung Mui)

(Des John Au)

2013 (15 Oct). Inclusive Arts. T **365** and similar horiz designs. Multicoloured. Granite paper. Two phosphor bands ($1.70) or one phosphor band (others). Perf 13½×14½ (with one elliptical hole on each vert side).

1819	$1.70 Type **365**	85	70
1820	$2.90 *Always by your Side* (Cheng Kai Man)	1·40	1·10
1821	$3.70 *The Vitality of Hong Kong* (Ko Nam)	1·90	1·75
1822	$5 *How are you?* (Liu Tung Mui)	2·40	2·25
1819/1822 *Set of 4*		6·00	5·25
MS1823	135×90 mm. Nos. 1819/1822	6·00	6·00

366 Symbols of Green Energy Generation

(Des Arde Lam)

2013 (19 Nov). Innovation and Technology. T **366** and similar horiz designs. Multicoloured. Granite paper. Two phosphor bands ($1.70 and $2.20) or one phosphor band (others). Perf 13½×13 (with one elliptical hole on each vert side).

1824	$1.70 Type **366** (Green technology)	85	70
1825	$2.20 Computer code (Information and communication technology)	1·10	90
1826	$2.90 ECG chart (Chinese medicine)	1·40	1·10
1827	$3.10 Stylised Sweetcorn (Biotechnology)	1·60	1·25
1828	$3.70 'NANO' (Nano and advanced materials)	1·90	1·75
1829	$5 Radio waves (Radio frequency identification)	2·40	2·25
1824/1829 *Set of 6*		8·25	7·25
MS1830	190×105 mm. Nos. 1824/1829	8·25	8·25

No. 1829 has 'RFID', printed in flourescent ink, included in the design. No. **MS**1830 has all corners removed, creating an elongated octagon shape.

367 Legislative Complex, 2011

368 Fabric Horse

(Des Shirman Lai. Litho Cartor)

2013 (5 Dec). Our Legislative Council. T **367** and similar vert designs. Multicoloured. Granite paper. Two phosphor bands ($1.70) or one phosphor band (others). Perf 13½×13 (with one elliptical hole on each vert side).

1831	$1.70 Type **367**	85	70
1832	$2.90 Old Supreme Court building, Central Hong Kong (1985 to November 2011)..	1·40	1·10
1833	$3.70 Council chamber in new Complex	1·90	1·75
1834	$5 President's chair in old legislative room	2·40	2·25
1831/1834 Set of 4		6·00	5·25
MS1835 135×85 mm. Nos. 1831/1834		6·00	6·00

(Des Tai-keung Kan)

2014 (11 Jan). Chinese New Year. Year of the Horse. T **368** and similar multicoloured designs. Multicoloured.

*(a) Two phosphor bands ($1.70) or one phosphor band (others). Granite paper. Perf 13½ (**MS**1840) or 13½×14½ (others) each with one elliptical hole on each vert side.*

1836	$1.70 Type **368**	85	70
1837	$2.90 Craved wooden Horse	1·40	1·10
1838	$3.70 Stylised Horse (gold-coloured steel sculpture)	1·90	1·75
1839	$5 Laquer Horse	2·40	2·25
1836/1839 Set of 4		6·00	5·25
MS1840 135×85 mm. $10 Decorated Horse puppet (45×45 mm)		4·25	4·25

(b) Silk-faced and granite paper. Miniature sheet. Perf 13½ (with one elliptical hole on each vert side).

MS1841 80×80 mm. $50 Decorated Horse puppet (as stamp of No. **MS**1840) (45×45 mm)	26·00	26·00

(c) Granite paper. Miniature sheet. Perf 13½×14 (with one elliptical hole on each vert side).

MS1842 136×90 mm. $50×2, Snake; Horse	42·00	42·00

369 Champagne Glass   **370** Daxiatitan binglingi

(Des Jason Chum. Litho and silver foil die-stamped Cartor)

2014 (23 Jan). Greetings Stamps. Multicoloured. Granite paper. Two phosphor bands ($1.70) or one phosphor band (others). Perf 13½ (with one elliptical perf on each vert side).

1843	($1.70) Type **369**	85	70
1844	($1.70) Giving flower	85	70
1845	($1.70) Cake with candle	85	70
1846	($3.70) Fireworks	1·90	1·75
1847	($3.70) Bunting, presents and cake	1·90	1·75
1848	($3.70) Heart-shaped balloons	1·90	1·75
1843/1848 Set of 6		7·50	6·75

Nos. 1843/1845 were inscribed 'Local Mail Postage' and Nos. 1846/1848 were inscribed 'Airmail Postage'.

(Des Wai-pang Tong and Keith Yip. Litho and luminosity Enschedé)

2014 (20 Feb). Chinese Dinosaurs. Multicoloured. Two phosphor bands ($1.70 and $2.20) or one phosphor band (others). Perf 13½ (with one elliptical hole on each vert side).

1849	$1.70 Type **370**	85	70
1850	$2.20 Microraptor gui	1·00	90
1851	$2.90 Lufengosaurus magnus	1·40	1·10

1852	$3.10 Tuojiangosaurus multispinus	1·60	1·25
1853	$3.70 Protoceratops andrewsi	1·90	1·75
1854	$5 Yangchuanosaurus shangyouensis	2·40	2·25
1849/1854 Set of 6		8·25	7·25
MS1855 170×100 mm. Nos. 1849/1854		8·25	8·25

Nos. 1849/**MS**1855 have the central design coated with a luminous substance which causes the image to glow in the dark.

371 Rainbow   **372** Postal Building

(Des Benny Lau. Litho and lenticular (No. 1863) or litho (others) Enschedé)

2014 (27 Mar). Weather Phenomena. Multicoloured. Two phosphor bands ($1.70 and $2.20) or one phosphor band (others). Perf 14 (with one elliptical hole on each vert side).

1856	$1.70 Type **371**	85	70
1857	$2.20 Frost on leaves	1·00	90
1858	$2.90 Clouds forming	1·40	1·10
1859	$3.10 Lightning	1·60	1·25
1860	$3.70 Fog	1·90	1·75
1861	$5 Rain over seaside	2·40	2·25
1856/1861 Set of 6		8·25	7·25
MS1862 135×85 mm. $5 Typhoon Vicente		2·40	2·40
MS1863 135×85 mm. $20 Typhoon Vicente (lenticular)		8·50	8·50

A premium booklet containing 12 pages of text, describing weather systems, interleaved with panes containing Nos. 1856/1858, 1859/1861 and **MS**1862, respectively, was on sale for $53.

(Des Arde Lam. Litho Cartor)

2014 (29 Apr). Postal History. Old General Post Office Building. Sheet 200×120 mm. Granite paper. One phosphor band. Perf 14 (with one elliptical hole on each vert side).

MS1864 **372** $20 multicoloured	8·50	8·50

373 'Filial Piety'

(Des Pui-kay Mou and Pak-keung Leung. Litho Enschedé)

2014 (15 May). International Day of Families. T **373** and similar vert designs. Multicoloured. Granite paper. Two phosphor bands ($1.70) or one phosphor band (others). Perf 13½ (with one elliptical hole on each vert side).

1865	$1.70 Type **373**	85	70
1866	$2.90 'Love'	1·40	1·10
1867	$3.70 'Harmony'	1·90	1·75
1868	$5 'Care'	2·40	2·25
1865/1868 Set of 4		6·00	5·25
MS1869 145×95 mm. Nos. 1865/1869		6·00	6·00

374 *Victoria Harbour*

(Des Chi-ming (Carl) Cheng. Litho Cartor)

2014 (17 June). Hong Kong Museums' Collections. Paintings by Wu Guanzhong. T **374** and similar multicoloured designs. Multicoloured. Granite paper. Two phosphor bands ($1.70 and $2.20) or one phosphor band (others). Perf 13½×13 (No. **MS**1876) or 13½ (others) (all with one elliptical hole on each vert side).

1870	$1.70 Type **374**	85	70
1871	$2.20 Memories of Home	1·00	90
1872	$2.90 Waterway (vert)	1·40	1·10
1873	$3.10 Faces Unchanged (vert)	1·60	1·25
1874	$3.70 Two Swallows	1·90	1·75
1875	$5 The Farthest Corner of the World (vert) …	2·40	2·25
1870/1875 Set of 6		8·25	7·25
MS1876 145×90 mm. $10 At Rest (129×66 mm)		4·25	4·25

375 North Ninepin Island **376** Female Great Han Costume

(Des Shirman Lai. Litho Enschedé)

2014 (24 July). Hong Kong Global Geopark of China. T **375** and similar vert designs. Multicoloured. Granite paper.

(a) Size 25×29 mm. Perf 13½×14 (with one elliptical hole on each vert side).

1877	10c. Type **375**	15	15
1878	20c. Basalt Island	20	20
1879	50c. Tai Long Wan	30	25
1880	$1 Po Pin Chau	40	30
1881	$1.70 High Island Reservoir East Dam	85	70
1882	$2 Port Island	95	85
1883	$2.20 Wong Chuk Kok Tsui	1·00	90
1884	$2.30 Bride's Pool	1·10	90
1885	$2.90 Lan Kwo Shui	1·40	1·10
1886	$3.10 Lung Lok Shui	1·60	1·25
1887	$3.70 Kang Lau Shek	1·90	1·75
1888	$5 Ap Chau	2·40	2·25
1877/1888 Set of 12		11·00	9·50
MS1889 220×160 mm. Nos. 1877/1888		11·00	11·00

(b) Size 17×21 mm. Coil stamps. Perf 14½ (with one elliptical hole on each vert side).

1890	$1.70 As No. 1881	85	70
1891	$2.20 As No. 1883	1·00	90
1892	$2.90 As No. 1885	1·40	1·10
1893	$3.70 As No. 1887	1·90	1·75
1890/1893 Set of 4		4·75	4·00

(c) Size 25×29 mm. Self-adhesive booklet stamps. Die-cut perf 13½×14 (with one elliptical hole on each vert side).

1894	$1.70 As No. 1881	85	70
1895	$2.20 As No. 1883	1·00	90
1896	$2.90 As No. 1885	1·40	1·10
1897	$3.70 As No. 1887	1·90	1·75
1894/1897 Set of 4		4·75	4·00

(d) Size 28×33 mm. Perf 13½ (with one elliptical hole on each vert side).

1898	$10 Sharp Island	4·25	3·50
1899	$15.50 High Island	6·50	5·75
1900	$20 Lai Chi Chong	8·50	7·50
1901	$50 Pak Sha Tau Tsui	22·00	18·00
1898/1901 Set of 4		38·00	32·00
MS1902 150×90 mm. Nos. 1898/1901		45·00	45·00

See also Nos. 2143/2145.

(Des Michael Fung. Litho Cartor)

2014 (21 Aug). Cantonese Opera Costumes. T **376** and similar multicoloured designs. Multicoloured. Granite paper. Two phosphor bands ($1.70 and $2.20) or one phosphor band (others). Perf 14 (No. **MS**1909) or 13½ (others) (all with one elliptical hole on each vert side).

1903	$1.70 Type **376**	85	70
	a. Block of 6. Nos. 1903/1908	8·25	
1904	$2.20 Gown with a sloping collar	1·00	90
1905	$2.90 Dress for young ladies	1·40	1·10
1906	$3.10 Military uniform for soldiers	1·60	1·25
1907	$3.70 Python ceremonial robe	1·90	1·75

1908	$5 Gown with a vertical collar	2·40	2·25
1903/1908 Set of 6		8·25	7·25
MS1909 145×90 mm. $10 The Joint Investiture (100×40 mm)		4·25	4·25

Nos. 1903/1908 were printed, se-tenant, in blocks of six stamps within sheets of 12, with enlarged illustrated margins.

377 Symbols of Shopping and Food

(Des Shirman Lai. Litho and foil die-stamping Enschedé)

2014 (18 Sept). Asian International Stamp Exhibition Hong Kong 2015. Sheet 135×34 mm. Granite paper. One phosphor band. Perf 13½ (with one elliptical hole on each vert side).

MS1910 **377** $20 multicoloured		8·50	8·50

See also Nos. **MS**1983/**MS**1984.

378 Egg Waffle **379** Santa Claus

(Des Tsoi Ka-ching and K. Y. Lim. Litho Cartor)

2014 (9 Oct). Local Food. T **378** and similar vert designs. Multicoloured. Granite paper. Two phosphor bands ($1.70) or one phosphor band (others). Perf 13½ (with one elliptical hole on each vert side).

1910a	$1.70 Type **378**	85	70
1910b	$2.90 Nasi Lemak	1·40	1·10
1910c	$3.70 Poon Choi	1·90	1·75
1910d	$5 Satay	2·40	2·25
1910a/1910d Set of 4		6·00	5·25
MS1911 135×85 mm. $1.70 As Type **378**; $2.90 As No. 1910b (Nasi Lemak); $3.70 As No, 1910c (Poon Choi); $5 As No. 1910d (Satay)		6·00	6·00

Stamps of a similar design were issued by Malaysia.

(Des Shirman Lai. Litho Cartor)

2014 (4 Nov). Christmas. T **379** and similar vert designs. Multicoloured. Granite paper (Nos. 1911/**MS**1915). Two phosphor bands ($1.70) or one phosphor band (others).

(a) Ordinary gum. Perf 13½ (with one elliptical hole on each vert side).

1912	$1.70 Type **379**	85	70
1913	$2.90 Rudolf	1·40	1·10
1914	$3.70 Snowman	1·90	1·75
1915	$5 Angel	2·40	2·25
1912/1915 Set of 4		6·00	5·25
MS1916 150×90 mm. Nos. 1912/1915		6·00	6·00

(b) Self-adhesive. Die-cut 13½ (with on elliptical hole on each vert side).

1917	$1.70 As Type **379**	85	70
1918	$2.90 As No. 1913	1·40	1·10
1919	$3.70 As No. 1914	1·90	1·75
1920	$5 As No. 1915	2·40	2·25
1917/1920 Set of 4		6·00	5·25
MS1921 150×90 mm. Nos. 1917/1920		6·00	6·00

Nos. 1917/1920, respectively, were printed in sheets of four stamps.

380 Danxia   **381** Ram

(Des Gideon Lai. Litho and silk screen printing Enschedé)

2014 (4 Dec). World Heritage Sites in China (3rd Series). Danxia. Sheet 140×90 mm. Granite paper. One phosphor band. Perf 14 (with one elliptical hole on each vert side).
MS1922 **380** $10 multicoloured.................................... 4·25   4·25

(Des Tai-keung Kan)

2015 (24 Jan). Chinese New Year. Year of the Ram. T **381** and similar multicoloured designs.

(a) Two phosphor bands ($1.70) or one phosphor band (others). Granite paper. Perf 13½ (with one elliptical hole on each vert side).
1923	$1.70 Type **381**	85	70
1924	$2.90 Ceramic Ram with large curled horns......	1·40	1·10
1925	$3.70 Ceramic Ram with curlique design	1·90	1·75
1926	$5 Jade Ram	2·40	2·25
1923/1926 *Set of 4*		6·00	5·25
MS1927 135×80 mm. $10 Blue decorated Ram with yellow horns......................................		4·25	4·25

(b) Litho and foil embossed Cartor. Granite paper. Perf 13½×13 (with one elliptical hole on each vert side).
1928	$10 As No. 1698 (Dragon)	4·25	3·75
	a. Block of 4. Nos. 1928/1931	16·00	
1929	$10 As No. 1777 (Snake)	4·25	3·75
1930	$10 As No. 1836 (Horse)	4·25	3·75
1931	$10 As No. 1926	4·25	3·75
1928/1931 *Set of 4*		16·00	13·50

(c) Size 45×45 mm. Miniature sheet. Silk-faced and granite paper. Perf 13½ (with one elliptical hole on each vert side).
MS1932 80×80 mm. $50 Blue decorated Ram with yellow horns......................................		18·00	16·00

(d) Miniature sheet. Granite paper. Perf 13½×14 (with one elliptical hole on each vert side).
MS1933 136×90 mm. $50×2, Horse; Ram........................		38·00	38·00

Nos. 1928/1931 were printed, *se-tenant*, in blocks of four stamps within sheets of 16.

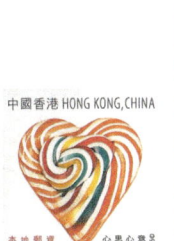

382 Candy Heart   **383** Eclipse

(Des Arde Lam. Litho and embossed Cartor)

2015 (12 Feb). Greetings Stamps. T **382** and similar square designs. Multicoloured. Granite paper. Two phosphor bands ($1.70) or one phosphor band (others). Perf 13½ (with one elliptical hole on each vert side).
1934	($1.70) Type **382**..................................	85	70
1935	($1.70) Heart-shaped tin............................	85	70
1936	($1.70) Heart-shaped egg on toast	85	70
1937	($3.70) Heart-shaped green plants	1·90	1·75
1938	($3.70) Heart-shape with flowers and bow........	1·90	1·75
1939	($3.70) Balloons making heart-shape	1·90	1·75
1934/1939 *Set of 6*		7·50	6·75

Nos. 1934/1936 were inscribed 'Local Mail Postage' and Nos. 1937/1939 were inscribed 'Airmail Postage'.

Nos. 1934/1939 were printed, both in sheets, and together, each×2, in blocks of six stamps and six labels in sheets of 12 stamps and 12 labels. The labels could be personalised by the addition of a photograph or logo.

(Des Ken Li Shik-kwong. Litho and 3 Litho and 3D printing (**MS**1947) or litho and varnish (others) Enschedé)

2015 (17 Mar). Astronomical Phenomena. T **383** and similar vert designs. Multicoloured. Granite paper. Two phosphor bands ($1.70) or one phosphor band (others). Perf 14 (Nos. **MS**1946/**MS**1947) or 14×14½ (others) (each with one elliptical hole on each vert side).
1940	$1.70 Type **383**..................................	85	70
	a. Strip of 6. Nos. 1940/1945.......................	8·25	
1941	$2.20 Meteor shower	1·10	90
1942	$2.90 Comet	1·40	1·10
1943	$3.10 Saturn's Ring tilt variation	1·60	1·25
1944	$3.70 Sunspot	1·90	1·75
1945	$5 Moon–planet conjunction	2·40	2·25
1940/1945 *Set of 6*		8·25	7·25
MS1946 135×85 mm. $10 Lunar eclipse (33×58 mm)......		4·25	4·25
MS1947 135×85 mm. $20 Moon (33×58 mm)..............		8·50	8·50

Nos. 1940/1945 were printed, *se-tenant*, in strips of six stamps within the sheet.

A premium booklet containing 11 pages of text, describing weather systems, interleaved with panes containing Nos. 1960/1961, 1943/1944 and **MS**1946 was also available.

384 Chief Executive's Office and Central Government   **385** Cycling

(Des Bianca Chiu and Bon Kwan. Litho Cartor)

2015 (2 Apr). 25th Anniversary of Promulgation of the Basic Law. T **384** and similar horiz designs. Multicoloured. Granite paper. Two phosphor bands ($1.70) or one phosphor band (others). Perf 13×13½ (with one elliptical hole on each vert side).
1948	$1.70 Type **384**..................................	85	70
1949	$2.90 Shenzhen Bay Bridge	1·10	90
1950	$3.70 Monument in Commemoration of the Return of Hong Kong to China and the *Forever Blooming Bauhinia* sculpture.....	1·90	1·75
1951	$5 Spiral Lookout Tower in Tai Po	2·40	2·25
1948/1951 *Set of 4*		5·75	5·00
MS1952 220×160 mm. $1.70 As No. 1948; $2.90 As No, 1949; $3.70 As No. 1950; $5 As No. 1951..............		5·75	5·75

(Des Kar-wai Cheng. Litho and thermochromatic ink Cartor)

2015 (9 Apr). Sports in Hong Kong. T **385** and similar vert designs. Multicoloured. Granite paper. Two phosphor bands ($1.70 and $2.20) or one phosphor band (others). Perf 13½ (with one elliptical hole on each vert side).
1953	$1.70 Type **385**..................................	85	70
1954	$2.20 Table tennis	1·10	90
1955	$2.90 Football	1·40	1·10
1956	$3.10 Athletics	1·60	1·25
1957	$3.70 Badminton	1·90	1·75
1958	$5 Swimming	2·40	2·25
1953/1958 *Set of 6*		8·25	7·25
MS1959 180×79 mm. $1.70 As No. 1953; $2.20 As No. 1954; $2.90 As No. 1955; $3.10 As No. 1956; $3.70 As No. 1957; $5 As No. 1958......................		8·25	8·25

The silhouettes of the athletes are printed in thermochromic ink and their colours vary with a change in temperature.

386 Sector Patrol Launch

(Des Chun-hong Wong. Litho Enschedé)

2015 (21 May). Government Vessels. T **386** and similar horiz designs. Multicoloured. Granite paper. Two phosphor bands ($1.70 and $2.20) or one phosphor band (others). Perf 13½ (with one elliptical hole on each vert side).
1960	$1.70 Type **386**..................................	85	70
	a. Block or strip of 6. Nos. 1960/1965........	8·25	

1961	$2.20 Port Quarantine Launch	1·10	90
1962	$2.90 Marine Monitoring Vessel	1·40	1·10
1963	$3.10 Fireboat	1·60	1·25
1964	$3.70 Training Launch	1·90	1·75
1965	$5 Hydrographic Survey launch	2·40	1·75
1960/1965 Set of 6		8·25	7·25
MS1966 145×110 mm. $10 All six ships (75×40 mm)		4·25	4·25

Nos. 1960/1965 were printed both in large sheets and, *se-tenant*, as a block or strip of six stamps in sheets on 18.

No. **MS**1966 is cut around in the shape of a boat along the top edge.

A premium booklet containing nine pages of text, interleaved with panes containing Nos. 1953/1954, 1955/1956 and 1957/1958 was on sale for $50.

387 Rice Terraces

(Des Tony Ho. Litho and embossed Enschedé)

2015 (18 June). World Heritage Sites in China (4th Series). Honghe Hani Rice Terraces. Sheet 140×90 mm. Granite paper. One phosphor band. Perf 13½ (with one elliptical hole on each vert side).

MS1967 **387** $10 multicoloured	4·25	4·25

388 'The Old Man Who Moved Mountains'

(Des Michael Fung. Litho Cartor)

2015 (16 July). Children Stamps. Chinese and Foreign Folklore. T **388** and similar square designs. Multicoloured. Granite paper. Two phosphor bands ($1.70 and $2.20) or one phosphor bands (others).

(a) Ordinary gum. Perf 14 (with one elliptical hole on each vert side).

1968	$1.70 Type **388**	85	80
1969	$2.20 'The tortoise and the Hare'	1·00	90
1970	$2.90 'The Little Engine that Could'	1·40	1·25
1971	$3.10 'The Wild Swans'	1·60	1·50
1972	$3.70 'The Three Little Pigs'	1·90	1·75
1973	$5 'The Parable of the Pipeline'	2·40	2·25
1968/1973 Set of 6		8·25	7·50
MS1974 140×90 mm. As Nos. 1968/1973		8·25	8·25

(b) Self-adhesive. Die-cut perf 14 (with one elliptical hole on each vert side).

MS1975 140×90 mm. As No. **MS**1974	8·25	8·25

389 70th Anniversary of Victory of the Chinese People's War of Resistance against Japanese Aggression

(Des Peter Ng Seung-ho. Litho Cartor)

2015 (2 Sept). 70th Anniversary of End of World War II. Sheet 135×85 mm. Granite paper. One phosphor band. Perf 14 (with one elliptical hole on each vert side).

MS1976 **389** $10 multicoloured	4·25	4·25

390 The Court of Final Appeal

(Des Wai-pang Tong. Litho Enschedé)

2015 (30 Sept). The Court of Final Appeal. Sheet 135×85 mm. Granite paper. One phosphor band. Perf 14 (with one elliptical hole on each vert side).

MS1977 **390** $10 multicoloured	4·25	4·25

391 Hands making Bird Shape

(Des Ying-chi Lee. Litho Enschedé)

2015 (9 Oct). World Post Day. T **391** and similar horiz designs. Multicoloured. Granite paper. Two phosphor bands ($1.70) or one phosphor band (others). Perf 13½×14½.

1978	$1.70 Type **391**	85	80
1979	$2.90 Hands, lower left	1·40	1·25
1980	$3.70 Hands, upper right	1·90	1·75
1981	$5 Hands, upper left	2·40	2·25
1978/1981 Set of 4		6·00	5·50
MS1982 140×90 mm. As Nos. 1978/1981		6·00	6·00

The stamps of No. **MS**1982 form a composite design.

392 Food and Shopping

(Des Shirman Lai. Litho and foil die-stamping Enschedé)

2015 (20 Nov). Asian International Stamp Exhibition. Hong Kong 2015 (2nd issue). Sheet 135×34 mm. Granite paper. One phosphor band. Perf 13½ (with one elliptical hole on each vert side).

MS1983 **392** $20 multicoloured	8·50	8·50

393 Shopping and Food

(Des Shirman Lai. Litho and foil die-stamping Enschedé)

2015 (23 Nov). Asian International Stamp Exhibition. Hong Kong 2015 (3rd issue). Sheet 135×34 mm. Granite paper. One phosphor band. Perf 13½ (with one elliptical hole on each vert side).

MS1984 **393** $20 multicoloured	8·50	8·50

394 Zhang Heng (Seismoscope)

(Des So-hing Chau. Litho Cartor)

2015 (8 Dec). Scientists in Ancient China. T **394** and similar horiz designs. Multicoloured. Granite paper. Two phosphor bands ($1.70) or one phosphor band (others). Perf 13½ (with one elliptical hole on each vert side).

1985	$1.70 Type **394**	85	80
1986	$2.90 Zu Chongzhi (value of pi)	1·40	1·25
1987	$3.70 Guo Shoujing (equatorial torquetum) (inscr 'simplified armila')	1·90	1·75
1988	$5 Li Shizhen (compendium of *Materia Medica*)	2·40	2·25
1985/1988 *Set of 4*		6·00	5·50
MS1989 135×85 mm. As Nos. 1985/1988		6·00	6·00

395 Monkey

(Des Kan Tai-keung)

2016 (16 Jan). Chinese New Year. Year of the Monkey. T **395** and similar multicoloured designs. Multicoloured.

(a) Two phosphor bands ($1.70) or one phosphor band (others). Granite paper. Perf 13½×14 (with one elliptical hole on each vert side).

1990	$1.70 Type **395**	85	80
1991	$2.90 Monkey with brown fur	1·40	1·25
1992	$3.70 Silver Monkey	1·90	1·75
1993	$5 Stylised Monkey	2·40	2·25
1990/1993 *Set of 4*		6·00	5·50

(b) Miniature sheet. Size 45×45 mm. Litho and foil die-stamped Enschedé. Granite paper. One phosphor band. Perf 13½ (with one elliptical hole on each vert side).

MS1994 135×85 mm. $10 Monkey holding Peach	4·25	4·25

(c) Miniature sheet. Size 45×45 mm. Silk-faced and granite paper. Perf 13½ (with one elliptical hole on each vert side).

MS1995 80×80 mm. $50 Monkey holding Peach (As No. **MS**1994)	20·00	20·00

(d) Miniature sheet. Litho and foil embossed. Granite paper. Perf 13½ (with one elliptical hole on each vert side).

MS1996 135×90 mm. $50 Ram with silver horns; $50 Golden Monkey	38·00	38·00

396 Girl Guide (current uniform) and First Aid and Community Health Badges

(Des Arde Lam. Litho Cartor)

2016 (22 Feb). Centenary of Hong Kong Girl Guides. T **396** and similar horiz designs showing Guide uniforms and achievement badges. Multicoloured. Granite paper. Two phosphor bands ($1.70) or one phosphor band (others). Perf 13½×14 (with one cross-shaped hole on each vert side) (No. **MS**2001) or 13½ (with one elliptical hole on each vert side) (others).

1997	$1.70 Type **396**	85	80
1998	$2.90 Brownie uniform, 1970s and Against corruption, Book lover, Friendship and Thrift badges	1·40	1·25
1999	$3.70 Sea Rangers uniform, 1940s and Orienteering, Country walking, Basic survival and Star gazing badges	1·90	1·75

2000	$5 Chinese style Brownie uniform, 1930s and Artist, Signaller, Craft and Knotting badges	2·40	2·25
1997/2000 *Set of 4*		6·00	5·50
MS2001 35×85 mm. As Nos. 1997/2000		6·00	6·00

A premium booklet containing five pages of text, interleaving with panes containing Nos. 1997/1998 and 1999/2000, was on sale for $45.

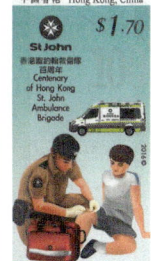

397 Hong Kong Museum of Coastal Defence

398 Ambulance Service

(Des Colin Tillyer. Litho Cartor)

2016 (31 Mar). Public Architecture in Hong Kong. T **397** and similar horiz designs. Multicoloured. Two phosphor bands ($1.70 and $2.20) or one phosphor band (others). Perf 13½ (with one elliptical hole on each vert side).

2002	$1.70 Type **397**	85	80
2003	$2.20 Victoria Park Swimming Pool	1·00	90
2004	$2.90 Sai Kung Waterfront Park	1·40	1·25
2005	$3.10 Ping Shan Tin Shui Wai Leisure and Cultural Building	1·60	1·50
2006	$3.70 Hong Kong Wetland Park	1·90	1·75
2007	$5 Electrical and Mechanical Services Department Headquarters	2·40	2·25
2002/2007 *Set of 6*		8·25	7·50
MS2008 158×87 mm. As Nos. 2002/2007		8·25	8·25

(Des Ka-ching Tsoi. Litho Cartor)

2016 (14 Apr). Centenary of Hong Kong St John Ambulance Brigade. T **398** and similar vert designs. Multicoloured. Granite paper. Two phosphor bands ($1.70) or one phosphor band (others). Perf 13½ (with one elliptical hole on each vert side).

2009	$1.70 Type **398**	85	80
2010	$2.90 First Aid	1·40	1·25
2011	$3.70 Dental Care for the disabled and those with special needs	1·90	1·75
2012	$5 Youth Service	2·40	2·25
2009/2012 *Set of 4*		6·00	5·50
MS2013 135×85 mm. As Nos. 2009/2012		6·00	6·00

A premium booklet containing six pages of text, interleaving with panes containing Nos. 2009/2010 and 2011/2012, was also available.

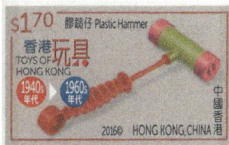

399 Boats on the Canal

400 Toy Hammer

(Des Michael Miller Yu. Litho and embossed Enschedé)

2016 (10 May). World Heritage Sites in China (5th Series). Grand Canal. Sheet 140×90 mm. Granite paper. One phosphor band. Perf 13½ (with one elliptical hole on each vert side).

MS2014 **399** $10 multicoloured	4·25	4·25

(Des Clement Yick and Siu-Kin Wong. Litho and varnish Enschedé)

2016 (8 June). Toys of Hong Kong, 1940s–1960s. T **400** and similar horiz designs. Multicoloured. Granite paper. Two phosphor bands ($1.70 and $2.20) or one phosphor band (others). Perf 13½×14½ (with one elliptical hole on each vert side).

2015	$1.70 Type **400**	85	80
	a. Vert strip of 6. Nos. 2015/2020	8·25	8·25
	b. Sheet of 18. No. 2015a×3	24·00	
2016	$2.20 Paper cut-out dolls	1·00	90

2017	$2.90 Water pistol	1·40	1·25
2018	$3.10 Mini plastic swords	1·60	1·50
2019	$3.70 Yellow plastic roll-along Ducks	1·90	1·75
2020	$5 Tin Frog	2·40	2·25
2015/2020 Set of 6		8·25	7·50

Nos. 2015/2020 were printed, se-tenant, in vertical strips of six stamps within sheets of 18.

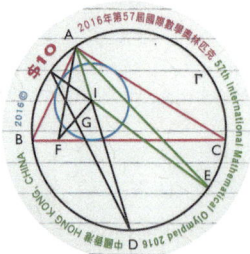

401 Ceva's Theorem

(Des Carl Chi-ming Cheng)

2016 (6 July). 57th International Mathematical Olympiad 2016. Sheet 135×85 mm. Granite paper. Perf 13.

MS2021 **401** $10 multicoloured		4·25	4·25

402 Cycling

403 Open Book and Love (Nurture and Growth)

(Des Jason Chum. Litho and hot foil)

2016 (5 Aug). Olympic Games, Rio 2016. T **402** and similar square designs. Multicoloured. Granite paper. Two phosphor bands ($1.70) or one phosphor band (others). Perf 14 (with one elliptical hole on each vert side).

2022	$1.70 Type **402**	85	80
2023	$2.90 Table Tennis and Badminton	1·40	1·25
2024	$3.70 Windsurfing and Swimming	1·90	1·75
2025	$5 Rugby and Golf	2·40	2·25
2022/2025 Set of 4		6·00	5·50
MS2026 135×85 mm. As Nos. 2022/2025		6·00	6·00

(Des Andrew Lo. Litho Enschedé)

2016 (8 Sept). A Tribute to Teachers. T **403** and similar vert designs. Multicoloured. Granite paper. Two phosphor bands ($1.70) or one phosphor band (others). Perf 13½ (with one elliptical hole on each vert side).

2027	$1.70 Type **403**	85	80
2028	$2.90 Children with arms around teacher (Mentoring and Care)	1·40	1·25
2029	$3.70 Trophy (Potential and Confidence)	1·90	1·75
2030	$5 Teacher awarding diploma (Dedication and Support)	2·40	2·25
2027/2030 Set of 4		6·00	5·50
MS2030a 135×85 mm. $10 Books and mortarboard (Knowledge and Learning)		4·25	4·25

404 Mui Wo to Nam Shan

(Des Eric Chan. Litho Cartor)

2016 (13 Oct). Hong Kong Hiking Trails. Lantau Trail. T **404** and similar horiz designs. Multicoloured. Granite paper. Two phosphor bands.

(a) Sheet stamps. Ordinary gum. Perf 13½ (one elliptical hole on each vert side).

2031	$1.70 Type **404**	85	80
	a. Sheet of 12. Nos. 2031/2042	9·00	
2032	$1.70 Nam Shan to Pak Kung Au	85	80
2033	$1.70 Pak Kung Au to Ngong Ping	85	80
2034	$1.70 Ngong Ping to Sham Wat Road	85	80
2035	$1.70 Sham Wat Road to Man Cheung Po	85	80
2036	$1.70 Man Cheung Po to Tai O	85	80
2037	$1.70 Tai O to Kau Ling Chung	85	80
2038	$1.70 Kau Ling Chung to Shek Pik	85	80
2039	$1.70 Shek Pik to Shui Hau	85	80
2040	$1.70 Shui Hau to Tung Chung Road	85	80
2041	$1.70 Tung Chung Road to Pui O	85	80
2042	$1.70 Pui O to Mui Wo	85	80
2031/2042 Set of 12		9·00	8·75

(b) Booklet stamps. Self-adhesive. Die-cut perf 13½ (one elliptical hole on each vert side).

2043	$1.70 As Type **404**	85	80
2044	$1.70 As No. 2032	85	80
2045	$1.70 As No. 2033	85	80
2046	$1.70 As No. 2034	85	80
2047	$1.70 As No. 2035	85	80
2048	$1.70 As No. 2036	85	80
2049	$1.70 As No. 2037	85	80
2050	$1.70 As No. 2038	85	80
2051	$1.70 As No. 2039	85	80
2052	$1.70 As No. 2040	85	80
2053	$1.70 As No. 2041	85	80
2054	$1.70 As No. 2042	85	80
2043/2054 Set of 12		9·00	8·75

Nos. 2031/2042 were printed both in sheets, and together, in sheets of 12 stamps.

405 Sun Yat-sen

(Des Michael Fung. Litho Cartor)

2016 (12 Nov). 150th Birth Anniversary of Sun Yat-sen. T **405** and similar multicoloured designs. Two phosphor bands ($1.70) or one phosphor band (others). Perf 13½×14 (with one elliptical hole on each vert side).

2055	$1.70 Type **405**	85	80
2056	$2.90 Seated wearing white (vert)	1·40	1·25
2057	$3.70 Wearing blue (vert)	1·90	1·75
2058	$5 Seated wearing green	2·40	2·25
2055/2058 Set of 4		6·00	5·50
MS2059 135×85 mm. As Nos. 2055/2058		6·00	6·00

Booklet containing nine panes of text and two panes of stamps. Pane 1 Nos. 2055/2056; Pane 2 Nos. 2057/2058 was on sale for $45.

406 Aberdeen (1991)

(Des Gideon Lai. Recess and litho Enschedé)

2016 (6 Dec). Hong Kong Museums Collection. Pencil Drawings by Mr. Kong Kai-ming. T **406** and similar horiz designs. Multicoloured. Granite paper. Two phosphor bands ($1.70 and $2.20) or one phosphor band (others). Perf 13½×14 (No. **MS**2067) or 13½ (others) (all with one elliptical hole on each vert side).

2060	$1.70 Airport Tunnel, Hung Hom (1989) (50×36 mm)	85	80
2061	$2.20 Argyle Street, Mong Kok (1990) (50×36 mm)	1·00	90
2062	$2.90 Kwun Tong MTR Station (1989) (50×36 mm)	1·40	1·25

2063	$3.10 *Wan Chai Tram Depot (1989)* (50×36 mm)	1·60	1·50
2064	$3.70 *Canton Road (1991)* (50×36 mm)	1·90	1·75
2065	$5 *Zoroastrian Church, Causeway Bay (1986)* (50×36 mm)	2·40	2·25
2060/2065 *Set of 6*		8·25	7·50
MS2066 135×85 mm. $10 Type **406** (50×36 mm)		4·25	4·25

No. 2067 is vacant.

407 Rooster

(Des Tai-keung Kan)

2016 (6 Dec). Chinese New Year. Year of the Rooster. T **407** and similar multicoloured designs. Multicoloured.

(a) Two phosphor bands ($1.70) or one phosphor band (others). Litho. Enschedé. Granite paper. Perf 13½×14 (with one elliptical hole on each vert side).

2068	$1.70 Type **407**	85	80
2069	$2.90 Tin Rooster	1·40	1·25
2070	$3.70 Rooster made from shells	1·90	1·75
2071	$5 Gold-plated silver Rooster	2·40	2·25
2068/2071 *Set of 4*		6·00	5·50

(b) Miniature sheet. Size 45×45 mm. Litho and foil die-stamped. Enschedé. Granite paper. One phosphor band. Perf 13½ (with one elliptical hole on each vert side).

MS2072 135×85 mm. $10 Monkey holding peach		4·25	4·25

(c) Miniature sheet. Size 45×45 mm. Litho. Cartor. Silk-faced and granite paper. Perf 13½ (with one elliptical hole on each vert side).

MS2073 80×80 mm. $50 Rooster (As No. MS2072)		18·00	18·00

(d) Miniature sheet. Litho and silver foil (Monkey), litho and 22-carat gold-plated metal lace (Rooster). Cartor. Granite paper. One phosphor band. Perf 13½ (with one elliptical hole on each vert side).

MS2074 135×90 mm. $50 Monkey with silver-tipped fur; $50 Golden Rooster		35·00	35·00

408 Diaolou Towers on Farmland, Zili Village

409 Viva Blue House, Wanchai

(Des Ying-chi Lee. Litho and embossed Cartor)

2017 (16 Feb). World Heritage Sites in China (6th Series). Kaiping Diaolou and Villages. Sheet 140×90 mm. Granite paper. One phosphor band. Perf 13×13½ (with one elliptical hole on each vert side).

MS2075 **408** $10 multicoloured		4·25	4·25

(Des Eric Chan. Litho and foil Enschedé)

2017 (25 Apr). Revitalisation of Historic Buildings in Hong Kong. T **409** and similar horiz designs. Multicoloured. Granite paper. Two phosphor bands ($1.70 and $2.20) or one phosphor band (others). Perf 13½×14½ (with one elliptical hole on each vert side).

2076	$1.70 Type **409**	85	80
2077	$2.20 Oil (former clubhouse of the Royal Hong Kong Yacht Club) Oil Street, North Point	1·00	90
2078	$2.90 Green Hub in Tai Po	1·40	1·25
2079	$3.10 Stone Houses Family Garden	1·60	1·50
2080	$3.70 Former Police Married Quarters (PMG) on Hollywood Road	1·90	1·75
2081	$5 Mallory Street Revitalisation Project, Wanchai	2·40	2·25
2076/2081 *Set of 6*		8·25	7·50
MS2082 180×75 mm. As Nos. 2076/2081		8·25	8·25

Booklet containing 15 panes of text and three panes of stamps. Pane 1 Nos. 2076/2077; Pane 2 Nos. 2078/2079 and Pane 3 Nos. 2080/2081 was on sale for $50.

410 Picnic and Barbecue

411 Stand By

(Des Simon Chung. Litho Enschedé)

2017 (16 May). Outdoor Fun. T **410** and similar vert designs. Multicoloured. Granite paper. Two phosphor bands ($1.70 and $2.20) or one phosphor band (others). Perf 13½ (with one elliptical hole on each vert side).

2083	$1.70 Type **410**	85	80
2084	$2.20 Cycling	1·00	90
2085	$2.90 Visiting Heritage Sites	1·40	1·25
2086	$3.10 Bech fun	1·60	1·50
2087	$3.70 Hiking	1·90	1·75
2088	$5 Outdoor photography	2·40	2·25
2083/2088 *Set of 6*		8·25	7·50
MS2089 135×102 mm. As Nos. 2083/2088		8·25	8·25

(Des Kallen Yan. Litho and braille ink Cartor)

2017 (13 June). Centenary of Numbered Typhoon Signals. T **411** and similar black and gold designs. Granite paper. Two phosphor bands (€1.70 and $2.20) or one phosphor band (others). Perf 14½ (No. MS2095) or 13½ (others) (all with one elliptical hole on each vert side).

2090	$1.70 Type **411**	85	80
2091	$2.20 Strong Wind	1·00	90
2092	$2.90 Gale or Storm	1·40	1·25
2093	$3.70 Increasing Gale or Storm	1·90	1·75
2094	$5 Hurricane	2·40	2·25
2090/2094 *Set of 5*		6·75	6·25
MS2095 140×90 mm. $10 Hurricane (*different*) (63×34 mm)		4·25	4·25

Booklet containing ten panes of text and two panes of stamps. Pane 1 Nos. 2090/2092; Pane 2 Nos. 2093/2094 was on sale for $45.

412 Parade

(Des Jason Chum. Litho Cartor)

2017 (20 June). 20th Anniversary of Chinese People's Liberation Army in Hong Kong. Sheet 135×85 mm. Granite paper. One phosphor band. Perf 14 (with one elliptical hole on each vert side).

MS2096 **412** $10 multicoloured		5·00	5·00

413 Central Government Complex

(Des Shirman Lai. Litho and foil Enschedé)

2017 (1 July). 20th Anniversary of Establishment of Hong Kong Special Administrative Region. T **413** and similar horiz designs. Multicoloured. Granite paper. Two phosphor bands ($1.70) or one phosphor band (others). Perf 14×13½ (with one elliptical hole on each vert side).

2097	$1.70 Type **413**	85	80
2098	$2.90 Activities in Hong Kong	1·40	1·25
2099	$3.70 Finacial District	1·90	1·75
2100	$5 Children and balloons	2·40	2·25
2097/2100 *Set of 4*		6·00	5·50
MS2101 135×85 mm. As Nos. 2097/2100		6·00	6·00

414 Symbols of Celebration

415 Hearing

(Des Bing-wah Hon. Gravure Beijing Postage Stamp Printing House. Gravure Beijing Postage Stamp Printing House)

2017 (1 July). 20th Anniversary of the Return of Hong Kong to China. Two phosphor bands. Perf 13 (with one elliptical hole on each vert side).

2102	**414**	$1.70 multicoloured	85	80

A stamp of a similar design was issued by China.

(Des Seung-ho Ng. Litho and thermography ($1.70); Litho and heat inflating ink ($5) or litho (others) Cartor)

2017 (18 July). Children's Stamps. The Five Senses. T **415** and similar horiz designs. Multicoloured. Granite paper. Two phosphor bands ($1.70 and £2.20) or one phosphor band (others). Perf 14½×14 (with one elliptical hole on each vert side) or 14 (others) (all with one elliptical hole on each vert side).

2103	$1.70 Type **415**	85	80
2104	$2.20 Sight	1·00	90
2105	$2.90 Smell	1·40	1·25
2106	$3.70 Taste	1·90	1·75
2107	$5 Touch	2·40	2·25
2103/2107 Set of 5		6·75	6·25
MS2108 145×90 mm. $10 Composite design as Nos. 2103/2107 (105×60 mm)		4·25	4·25

No. 2103 has sand applied to the surface which makes a sound when rubbed, No. 2104 has a central die-cut hole where the camera lense should be, No. 2105 is impregnated with a Peach scent which is released when rubbed, No. 2106 has Vanilla-flavoured gum and No. 2107 has heat inflating ink applied to the ball to give the texture of a basketball.

416 Ilex graciliflora

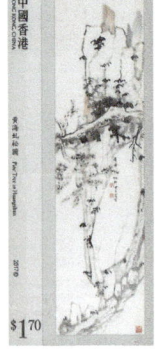

417 Pine Tree in Huangshan (1984)

(Des Bon Kwan. Litho Enschedé)

2017 (17 Aug). Rare and Precious Plants in Hong Kong. T **416** and similar square designs. Multicoloured. Granite paper. Two phosphor bands ($1.70) or one phosphor band (others). Perf 14.

2109	$1.70 Type **416**	85	80
2110	$2.90 Bulbophyllum bicoloris	1·40	1·25
2111	$3.70 Begonia hongkongensis	1·90	1·75
2112	$5 Illicium angustisepalum	2·40	2·25
2109/2112 Set of 4		6·00	5·50
MS2113 135×85 mm. As Nos. 2109/2112		6·00	6·00

The stamps and margins of **MS**2113 form a composite design.

(Des Chi-ming Carl Cheng. Litho Cartor)

2017 (5 Sept). Paintings and Calligraphy of Jao Tsung-I. T **417** and similar multicoloured designs. Granite paper. Two phosphor bands ($1.70 and $2.20) or one phosphor band (others). Perf 14×14½ (No. **MS**2120) or 14½ (others) (all with one elliptical hole on each vert side).

2114	$1.70 Type **417**	85	80
2115	$2.20 Pine Trees and Arhat (1993)	1·00	90
2116	$2.90 Five-character Couplet in Official Script (1998)	1·40	1·25
2117	$3.10 Victoria Peak after the Rain (2010)	1·60	1·50
2118	$3.70 Avalokitesvara after the style of Tang Dynasty (1998)	1·90	1·75
2119	$5 Calligraphy in Bronze Script (Undated)	2·40	2·25
2114/2119 Set of 6		8·25	7·50
MS2120 135×185 mm. $10 Four-screen Lotus Set (2011) (74×65 mm)		4·25	4·25

418 Goldfish Market

(Des Clement Yick. Litho Enschedé)

2017 (19 Sept). Hong Kong Shopping Streets. T **418** and similar horiz designs. Multicoloured. Granite paper. Two phosphor bands ($1.70 and $2.20) or one phosphor band (others). Perf 13½×13.

2121	$1.70 Type **418**	85	80
2122	$2.20 Chinese Medicine Street	1·00	90
2123	$2.90 Jade Market	1·40	1·25
2124	$3.10 Kitchenware Street	1·60	1·50
2125	$3.70 Flower Market	1·90	1·75
2126	$5 Yau Ma Tei Wholesale Fruit Market	2·40	2·25
2121/2126 Set of 6		8·25	7·50
MS2127 135×85 mm. As Nos. 2121/2126		8·25	8·25

419 Qipao in 1920s

420 Cricket Cage carved in Liuqing Low Relief with Flowers and Insects

(Des Tony Ho. Litho Enschedé)

2017 (17 Oct). Qipao, Traditional Chinese Dress for Women. T **419** and similar vert designs. Multicoloured. Silk-faced and granite paper (**MS**2135) or granite paper (others). Two phosphor bands ($1.70 and $2.20) or one phosphor band (others). Perf 13 (Nos. **MS**2134/**MS**2135) or 13½ (with one elliptical hole on each vert side) (others).

2128	$1.70 Type **419**	85	80
2129	$2.20 In 1930s	1·00	90
2130	$2.90 In 1940s	1·40	1·25
2131	$3.10 In 1950s	1·60	1·50
2132	$3.70 In 1960s	1·90	1·75
2133	$5 In 1970s	2·40	2·25
2128/2133 Set of 6		8·25	7·50
MS2134 135×185 mm. $10 Contemporay Qipao (35×77 mm)		4·25	4·25
MS2135 135×185 mm. $20 As No. **MS**2134 (35×77 mm)		8·50	8·50

Booklet containing 12 panes of text and two panes of stamps. Pane 1 Nos. 2128/2130; Pane 2 Nos. 2131/2133 was on sale for $60.

The stamps of Nos. **MS**2134/**MS**2135 are perforated around the design.

(Des Shirman Lai. Litho and embossed Cartor)

2017 (14 Nov). Hong Kong Museums Collection. Bamboo Carvings. T **420** and similar multicoloured designs. Multicoloured. Granite paper. Two phosphor bands ($1.70 and $2.20) or one phosphor band (others). Perf 13½×14 (No. **MS**2067) or 13½ (others) (all with one elliptical hole on each vert side).

2136	$1.70 Type **420**	85	80
2137	$2.20 Lingzhi Fungi and Narcissus carved in the round (50×30 mm)	1·00	90
2138	$2.90 Brushpot carved in high relief with scene from Night Visit to the Red Cliff (50×30 mm)	1·40	1·25
2139	$3.10 Incense holder carved in openwork with woman reading a letter in secret	1·60	1·50
2140	$3.70 Water container carved in the round with plum branches (50×30 mm)	1·90	1·75
2141	$5 Jar carved in low relief with Kui-dragon and animal masks (50×30 mm)	2·40	2·25
2136/2141 Set of 6		8·25	7·50
MS2142 175×85 mm. As Nos. 2136/2141		8·25	8·25

421 Ma Shi Chau   **422** Dog

(Des Shirman Lai. Litho Enschedé)

2018. Hong Kong Global Geopark of China. T **421** and similar vert designs. Multicoloured. Granite paper. One phosphor band. Perf 13×14 (one elliptical hole on each vert side).

2143	$2.60 Type **421**	1·25	1·10
2144	$3.40 Yan Chau	1·75	1·60
2145	$4.90 Fa Shan	2·40	2·25
2143/2145 Set of 3		4·75	4·50

(Des Tai-keung Kan. Litho and varnish (No. 2146) or litho and embossed (No. 2147) Southern Colour Print, New Zealand)

2018 (27 Jan). Greetings Stamps. Year of the Dog. With service indicator. T **422** and similar square design. Multicoloured. Granite paper. Two phosphor bands ($1.90) or one phosphor band (others). Perf 13½×13.

(a) Inscr 'Local Mail Postage'.

2146	($1.90) Type **422**	90

(b) AIR. Inscr 'Air Mail Postage'.

2147	($4.90) Cloth Dog	2·40	2·25

No. 2147 was for use on airmail letters up to 20g. to addresses outside Hong Kong.

No. 2146 was for use on letters up to 30g. within Hong Kong.

Nos. 2146/2147, respectively, were issued in sheets of 12 stamps and 12 labels, which could be personalised by the addition of a photograph.

423 Dog

(Des Tai-keung Kan)

2018 (27 Jan). Chinese New Year. Year of the Dog. T **423** and similar multicoloured designs. Multicoloured.

(a) Two phosphor bands ($2) or one phosphor band (others). Granite paper. Perf 13½×14 (with one elliptical hole on each vert side).

2148	$2 Type **423**	95	90
2149	$3.70 Wooden Dog	1·90	1·75
2150	$4.90 Cloth Dog	2·40	2·25
2151	$5 Dog made from shells	2·40	2·25
2148/2151 Set of 4		7·00	6·50

(b) Miniature sheet. Granite paper. Perf 13½ (with one elliptical hole on each vert side).

MS2152 135×85 mm. $10 Ceramic Dog wearing collar with bell (45×45 mm).......................		4·25	4·25

(c) Miniature sheet. Silk-faced and granite paper. Perf 13½ (with one elliptical hole on each vert side).

MS2153 80×80 mm. $50 Dog (As No. **MS**2152) (45×45 mm).......................		17·00	17·00

(d) Miniature sheet. Granite paper. Perf 13½ (with one elliptical hole on each vert side).

MS2154 135×90 mm. $50 Multicoloured Rooster; $50 Golden Dog.......................		35·00	35·00

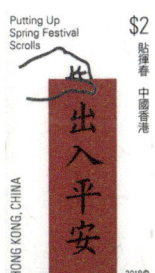 

424 Putting up   **425** Apliu and Kweilin Streets, Sham Shui
Spring Festival Scrolls   Po District

(Des Kar-wai Cheng. Litho and foil Cartor)

2018 (27 Feb). Festive Customs. T **424** and similar vert designs. Multicoloured. Granite paper. Two phosphor bands ($2) or one phosphor band (others). Perf 13½×14 (with one elliptical hole on each vert side).

2155	$2 Type **424**..........................	95	90
2156	$2.60 Throwing Wishing Placards......	1·25	1·10
2157	$3.40 Offering First Incense in Chinese New Year	1·75	1·60
2158	$3.70 Spinning Wheels of Fortune	1·90	1·75
2159	$4.90 Drawing Chinese Fortune Sticks ...	2·40	2·25
2160	$5 Unicorn Dance	2·40	2·25
2155/2160 Set of 6		9·50	5·75
MS2161 180×80 mm. $21.60 As Nos. 2155/2160...........		9·50	9·50

(Des Carl Chi-ming Cheng. Litho Southern Colour Print, New Zealand)

2018 (22 Mar). Hong Kong By Night. T **425** and similar horiz designs. Multicoloured. Granite paper. Two phosphor bands ($2) or one phosphor band (others). Perf 14½×15 (with one elliptical hole on each vert side).

2162	$2 Type **425**..........................	95	90
2163	$3.70 Central Hong Kong with light trails	1·90	1·75
2164	$4.90 Looking up at 'Monster Building', a housing complex in Quarry Bay comprised of five conjoined old buildings	2·40	2·25
2165	$5 Tian Tan Buddha......................	2·40	2·25
2162/2165 Set of 4		7·00	6·50
MS2166 135×85 mm. $15.60 As Nos. 2162/2165...........		7·00	7·00

426 Pump Escape, 1950s

(Des Kam-shing Yuen. Litho Cartor)

2018 (8 May). 150th Anniversary of the Hong Kong Fire Services Department. T **426** and similar horiz designs. Multicoloured. Two phosphor bands ($2) or one phosphor band (others). Perf 14×14½ (with one elliptical hole on each vert side).

2167	$2 Type **426**..........................	95	90
2168	$2.60 First generation Mobile Command Unit	1·25	1·10
2169	$3.40 Ambulance, 1980s.................	1·75	1·60
2170	$3.70 Major Pump	1·90	1·75
2171	$4.90 Current model of Mobile Command Unit	2·40	2·25
2172	$5 Currently used ambulance	2·40	2·25
2167/2172 Set of 6		9·50	8·75
MS2173 150×80 mm. $10 Service personnel (130×30 mm).......................		4·25	4·25

427 'Friend'

(Des Ching-tsui Chan. Litho, braille ink and lenticular ($20) or litho and braille ink (others) Cartor)

2018 (7 June). Inclusive Communication. T **427** and similar multicoloured designs illustrating greetings in English, Chinese, Braile and Sign Language. Granite paper. Two phosphor bands ($2) or one phosphor band (others). Perf 13½ (with one elliptical hole on each vert side).

2174	$2 Type **427**..........................	95	90
2175	$2.60 'Good Morning' (75×33 mm)......	1·25	1·10
2176	$3.40 'Hello'.............................	1·75	1·60
2177	$3.70 'Keep it Up '(75×33 mm)	1·90	1·75
2178	$4.90 'Love'	2·40	2·25
2179	$5 'Thank You' (75×33 mm).............	2·40	2·25
2174/2179 Set of 6			
MS2180 100×140 mm. $20 'Inclusive communication' in sign language (28×45 mm)...................		9·50	9·50

The stamp of No. **MS**2180 is lenticular and when tilted allows the sign language for 'Inclusive Communication' to be read.

428 'O'

(Des Ho-pan Tang. Litho Enschedé)

2018 (17 July). Children Stamps. Fun with Numbers and Symbols. T **428** and similar square designs. Multicoloured. Granite paper. Two phosphor bands. Perf 13 (with one elliptical hole on each vert side).

2181	$2 Type **428**	95	90
2182	$2 '1'	95	90
2183	$2 '2'	95	90
2184	$2 '3'	95	90
2185	$2 '4'	95	90
2186	$2 '5'	95	90
2187	$2 '6'	95	90
2188	$2 '7'	95	90
2189	$2 '8'	95	90
2190	$2 '9'	95	90
2191	$2 '+'	95	90
2192	$2 '-'	95	90
2193	$2 '×'	95	90
2194	$2 '÷'	95	90
2195	$2 '%'	95	90
2196	$2 '='	95	90
2181/2196 *Set of 16*			
MS2197 135×130 mm. $32 As Nos. 2181/2196		15·00	15·00

429 Pagoda

(Des Tony Ho. Litho and embossed Cartor)

2018 (10 Aug). World Heritage Sites in China (7th Series). Temple of Heaven. Sheet 140×90 mm. Granite paper. One phosphor band. Perf 13½×13 (with one elliptical hole on each vert side).

MS2198 **429** $10 multicoloured		5·50	5·50

430 Lantern, Pagoda, Teapot and Tower

(Des Ling Wong. Litho Southern Colour Print, New Zealand)

2018 (17 Sept). The Hong Kong Section of the Guangzhou–Shenzhen–Hong Kong Express Rail Link. T **430** and similar horiz designs. Multicoloured. One phosphor band. Perf 14 (with one elliptical hole on each vert side).

2199	$2 Type **430**	95	90
2200	$3.70 Symbols of Chinese life and activities...	1·90	1·75
2201	$4.90 Symbols of photography, shopping, and dining	2·30	2·20
2202	$5 Towers, ship, lipstick and Dolphin	2·45	2·30
2199/2202 *Set of 4*			
MS2203 200×80 mm. $15.60 As Nos. 2199/2202		7·75	7·75

431 Lotus and Bahinia Blossoms

(Des Ching-Tsui Chan. Litho Cartor Security Printing, France)

2018 (21 Sept). Macau 2018, Asian international Stamp Exhibition. Sheet 130×75 mm. One phosphor band. Perf 13½ (with one elliptical hole on each vert side).

MS2204 **431** $10 multicoloured		4·25	4·25

432 *The Princess Changping*   **434** 'H' (Hong Kong)

(Des Arde Lam and Martin Lau. Litho Enschedé)

2018 (9 Oct). Cantonese Opera Repertory. T **432** and similar horiz designs. Multicoloured. Two phosphor bands (No. 2205) or one phosphor bands (others). Perf 14×13½ (with one elliptical hole on each vert side).

2205	$2 Type **432**	95	90
2206	$2.60 *The Moon Pavilion*	1·20	1·10
2207	$3.40 *Lord Guan Gong releasing Lady Diao Chan*	1·75	1·60
2208	$3.70 *The Princess in Distress*	1·90	1·75
2209	$4.90 *Butterfly Lovers*	2·30	2·20
2210	$5 *Lady Zhaojun departing for the Frontier.*	2·45	2·30
2205/2210 *Set of 6*			
MS2211 200×225 mm. $41.20 As Nos. 2205/2210, each×2		15·00	15·00

T **433** is unavailable.

(Des Sun Chan and Hikoko Chan. Litho Enschedé)

2018 (30 Oct). Hong Kong–Zhuhai–Macau Bridge. T **434** and similar square designs. Multicoloured. Two phosphor bands (No. 2212) or one phosphor band (others). Perf 14 (with one elliptical hole on each vert side).

2212	$2 Type **434**	95	90
2213	$3.70 'Z' (Zhuhai)	1·90	1·75
2214	$4.90 'M' (Macau)	2·30	2·20
2215	$5 'B' (Bridge)	2·45	2·30
2212/2215 *Set of 4*			
MS2216 135×85 mm. $10 Stylised bridge (100×40 mm)		4·50	4·50

No. 2217 is left for combined miniature sheet issued 31 October 2018

435 Robert Morrison and Students

(Des Freeman Lau. Litho Cartor Security Printing, France)

2018 (9 Nov). Bicentenary of Ying Wa College. Sheet 135×85 mm. One phosphor band. Perf 14.

MS2217 **435** $10 multicoloured		4·50	4·50

(Des Gideon Lei and Chi-Ching Lee. Litho Enschedé)

2018 (6 Dec). Characters from Jin Yong's Novels. Multicoloured. Two phosphor bands (No. 2218) or one phosphor band (others). Perf 14×13½ (with one elliptical hole on each vert side).

2218	$2 Guo Jing and Huang Rong (*The Eagle shooting Heroes*)	95	90
2219	$2.60 Chen Jialuo (*The Book and the Sword*) ...	1·20	1·10
2220	$3.40 Linghu Chong and Ren Yingying (*The Smiling Proud Wanderer*)	1·75	1·60
2221	$3.40 Zhang Wuji (*The Heaven Sword and Dragon Sabre*)	1·75	1·60
2222	$4.90 Yang Guo and Xiaolongnu (*The Giant Eagle and its Companion*)	2·30	2·20
2223	$5 Wei Xiaobao and Kangxi (*The Deer and the Cauldron*)	2·45	2·30
2218/2223 *Set of 6*			
MS2224	135×85 mm. $10 Qiao Feng, Xu Zhu and Duan Yu (*The Demi-Gods and Semi-Devils*)	4·50	4·50

T **436** is unavailable.

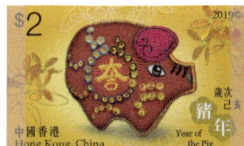

437 Red Embroidered Pig

(Des Chun-Hong Wong)

2019 (12 Jan). Chinese New Year. Year of the Pig. T **437** and similar multicoloured designs showing Pigs and other zodiac animals. Multicoloured. Perf 13½.

(a) Two phosphor bands ($2) or one phosphor band (others). Granite paper. Perf 13½×14 (with one elliptical hole on each vert side).

2225	$2 Type **437**	95	90
2226	$3.70 Two wooden Pigs	1·90	1·75
2227	$4.90 Pink porcelain Pig	2·30	2·20
2228	$5 Green jade Pig	2·45	2·30
2225/2228 *Set of 4*			

(b) Miniature sheet. Granite paper. Perf 13½×14½ (with one elliptical hole on each vert side).

MS2229	135×85 mm $10 Golden Pig with six suspended Piglets (45×45 mm)	4·50	4·50

(c) Miniature sheet. Silk-faced and granite paper. Perf 13½ (with one elliptical hole on each vert side).

MS2230	80×80 mm. $50 Golden Pig with six suspended Piglets (As No. MS2229) (45×45 mm)	24·00	24·00

(d) Miniature sheet. Granite paper. Perf 13½×14½ (with one elliptical hole on each vert side).

MS2231	135×90 mm. $50 Cloth Dog (As No. 2150); $50 Golden Pig	48·00	48·00

(Des Chun-Hong Wong. Litho and varnish (No. 2231) or litho and embossed (No. 2232) Southern Colour Print, New Zealand)

2019 (12 Jan). Greetings Stamps. Year of the Pig. As Nos. 2225 and 2227 with Service Indicator. Size 30×30 mm. Multicoloured. Granite paper. Two phosphor bands ($2) or one phosphor band ($4.90). Perf 13½ (with one elliptical hole on each vert side).

(a) Inscr 'Local Mail Postage'.

2232	($2) Embroidered Pig (As No. 2225)	95	90

(b) AIR. Inscr 'Air Mail Postage'.

2233	($4.90) Porcelain Pig (As No. 2227)	2·30	2·20

T **438** is unavailable.
Nos. 2232/2233 were printed in sheets of 12 with 12 stamp size labels which could be personalised by the addition of a photograph or logo.

(Des Wong Chun-hong. Litho and foil embossed Cartor)

2019 (12 Jan). Chinese New Year. Multicoloured. Granite paper. Phosphor markings. Perf 13½×13 (with one elliptical hole on each vert side).

2233a	$10 Monkey (As Type **395**)	5·00	
	b. Block of 4. Nos. 2233a/2233d	20·00	
2233b	$10 Rooster (As No. 2070)	5·00	
2233c	$10 Dog (As No. 2151)	5·00	
2233d	$10 Pig (As No. 2227)	5·00	

Nos. 2233a/2233d were printed, *se-tenant*, in blocks of four within sheets of 16 stamps. Designs printed chequerboard, allowing various, *se-tenant*, combinations.

439 Air Ambulance (EC I55 B1 Helicopter)

(Des Ying-Chi Lee. Litho Enschedé)

2019 (28 Feb). Government Flying Service. Operations. T **439** and similar horiz designs. Multicoloured. Granite paper. Two phosphor bands ($2) or one phosphor band (others). Perf 13½×14 (with one elliptical hole on each vert side).

2234	$2 Type **439**	95	90
2235	$2.60 Inshore Search and Rescue (AS332L2 Super Puma helicopter)	1·20	1·10
2236	$3.40 Offshore Search and Rescue (AS332L2 Super Puma helicopter and Bombardier Challenger 605 aircraft)	1·75	1·60
2237	$3.70 Firefighting (AS332L2 Super Puma helicopter)	1·90	1·75
2238	$4.90 Aerial survey (Bombardier Challenger 605 aircraft)	2·30	2·20
2239	$5 Internal Security (Airbus H175 Cheetah helicopter)	2·45	2·30
2234/2239 *Set of 6*			
MS2240	150×90 mm. $10 *Semper Paratus* (Always Ready) (108×38 mm)	4·50	4·50
MS2241	162×230 mm. $21.60 As Nos. 2234/2239, each×2	10·50	10·50

440 Xiqu Centre

(Des Michael Miller Yu. Litho (No. **MS**2242) or litho, silver foil die-stamped and embossed (No. **MS**2243) Cartor)

2019 (19 Mar). West Kowloon Cultural District. Two sheets each 140×90 mm containing T **440** and similar horiz design. Multicoloured. Granite paper. One phosphor band. Perf 14×13½ (with one elliptical hole on each vert side).

MS2242	$10 Type **440**	4·50	4·50
MS2243	$20 As No. MS2242	8·50	8·50

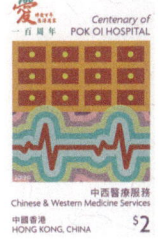

441 Chinese and Western Medicine Services

442 Boundary Security

(Des Colin Tillyer. Litho Enschedé)

2019 (2 Apr). Centenary of Pok Oi Hospital. T **441** and similar vert designs. Multicoloured. Granite paper. Two phosphor bands ($2) or one phosphor band (others). Perf 13½ (with one elliptical hole on each vert side).

2244	$2 Type **441**	95	90
2245	$3.70 Education Services	1·90	1·75
2246	$4.90 Elderly Services	2·30	2·20
2247	$5 Youth and Family Services	2·45	2·30
2244/2247 *Set of 4*			
MS2248	120×70 mm. $15.60 As Nos. 2244/2247	7·75	7·75

(Des Jason Chum and Chow Lee. Litho Enschedé)

2019 (30 Apr). Our Police Force. T **442** and similar horiz designs. Multicoloured. Granite paper. Two phosphor bands ($2) or one phosphor band (others). Perf 13½x14½ (with one elliptical hole on each vert side).

2249	$2 Type **442**	95	90
2250	$2.60 Crime Investigation and Detection	1·20	1·10
2251	$3.40 Cultural Diversity and Equal Opportunity	1·75	1·60
2252	$3.70 Police Training	1·90	1·75
2253	$4.90 International Collaboration	2·30	2·20
2254	$5 Traffic Management	2·45	2·30
2249/2254 *Set of 6*			
MS2255 135x85 mm. $10 Team leaving Police van (60x40 mm)		4·50	4·50

443 Jar of
Lucky Stars

(Des Ka-ching Tsoi. Litho silver foil die-stamped (Nos. 2260/2261) or litho (others) Enschedé)

2019 (11 June). Greetings Stamps. T **443** and similar vert designs. Multicoloured. Granite paper. One phosphor band (Nos. 2260/2261) or two phosphor bands (others). Perf 12 (with one elliptical hole on each vert side).

(a) Inscr 'Local Mail Postage'.

2256	($2.80) Type **443**	1·30	1·20
2257	($2.80) Fireworks	1·30	1·20
2258	($2.80) Rose in heart (Love)	1·30	1·20
2259	($2.80) Envelope emptying hearts (Blessings)	1·30	1·20
2256/2259 *Set of 4*			

(b) Air. Inscr 'Air Mail Postage'.

2260	($3.40) Mirror balls (Party)	1·75	1·60
2261	($3.40) Diamond (Eternal Appreciation)	1·75	1·60

Nos. 2256/2259 were inscribed 'Local'.
Nos 2260/2261 were inscribed 'Airmail'.
Nos. 2256/2261 were printed with a *se-tenant* at right which could be personalised by the addition of photograph or logo.

444 Landmarks of Wuhan and
Hong Kong

(Des Margaret Chu. Litho Cartor)

2019 (11 June). CHINA 2019 International Stamp Exhibition, Wuhan. Sheet 130x75 mm. Granite paper. One phosphor band. Perf 13½ (with one elliptical hole on each vert side).

MS2262 **444** $10 multicoloured		4·50	4·50

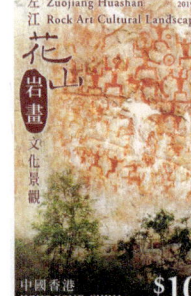

445 Threadfin Butterflyfish,
Brownbanded Butterflyfish and
Yellow Boxfish

446 Paintings on Rock Cliffs

(Des Shirman Lai. Litho Cartor)

2019 (16 July). Underwater World of Hong Kong. T **445** and similar horiz designs. Multicoloured. Granite paper. Two phosphor bands (No. 2263) or one phosphor band (others). Perf 13½ (with one elliptical hole on each vert side).

2263	$2 Type **445**	95	90
2264	$2.60 Papuan Jellyfish, Indo-Pacific Sergeant and Hong Kong Pufferfish	1·20	1·10
2265	$3.40 Chinese White Dolphin and Green Turtle	1·75	1·60
2266	$3.70 Yellowtail Clownfish and Many-lined Chromodoris	1·90	1·75
2267	$4.90 Spotted Seahorse and Blotched Fantail Ray	2·30	2·20
2268	$5 Chicken Grunt and Blue Dorid	2·45	2·30
2263/2268 *Set of 6*			
MS2269 200x115 mm. $21.60 As Nos.2263/2268		10·50	10·50

No. **MS**2269 was cut around in the shape of a fish.

(Des Ka-man Wong. Litho and embossed Cartor)

2019 (13 Aug). World Heritage Sites in China (8th issue). Zuojiang Huashan Rock Art Cultural Landscape. Sheet 140x90 mm. Granite paper. One phosphor band. Perf 13½.

MS2270 **446** $10 multicoloured		4·50	4·50

447 Map of Area with Landmarks Highlighted

(Des Gideon Lai. Litho Cartor)

2019 (26 Sept). Guangdong–Hong Kong–Macau Greater Bay Area. Sheet 140x90 mm. Granite paper. One phosphor band. Perf 14x13½ (with one elliptical hole on each vert side).

MS2271 **447** $10 multicoloured		5·00	5·00

448 Golden Dragon

(Des Bon Kwan. Litho (Nos. 2272/2275) or gravure (No. **MS**2276/ **MS**2277) Cartor (Nos. 2272/2275) or Beijing Stamp Printing House (No. **MS**2276/**MS**2277))

2019 (1 Oct). 70th Anniversary of People's Republic of China. T **448** and similar triangular designs. Multicoloured. Granite paper (Nos. 2272/ **MS**2276). Two phosphor bands (No. 2272) or one phosphor band (others). Perf 14 (with one elliptical hole on each short side).

2272	$2 Type **448**	95	90
2273	$3.70 Green leaves (Environment. Emphasis on Going Green)	1·90	1·75
2274	$4.90 Fibre optic cable (Technology. Development of the Internet)	2·30	2·20
2275	$5 Red ribbon (Economy and International Affairs. Forging ahead with Belt and Road Initiative)	2·45	2·30
2272/2275 *Set of 4*			
MS2276 140x90 mm. $15.60 As Nos. 2272/2275		7·75	7·75
MS2277 140x90 mm. $10 Ruyi knot (46x46 mm, diamond)		4·50	4·50

Nos. 2272/2275 when placed together form a traditional ruyi knot.

449 Pak Tam Chung to Long Ke, Maclehose Trail

(Des So-hing Chau. Litho Enschedé)

2019 (24 Oct). Hong Kong Hiking Trails. Maclehose Trail. T **449** and similar horiz designs. Multicoloured. Granite paper. Two phosphor bands.

(a) Sheet stamps. Ordinary gum. Perf 13½ (one elliptical hole on each vert side).

2278	$2 Type **449**	95	90
2279	$2 Long Ke to Pak Tam Au	95	90
2280	$2 Pak Tam Au to Kei Ling Ha	95	90
2281	$2 Kei Ling Ha to Tate's Cairn	95	90
2282	$2 Tate's Cairn to Tai Po Road	95	90
2283	$2 Tai Po Road to Shing Mun	95	90
2284	$2 Shing Mun to Lead Mine Pass	95	90
2285	$2 Lead Mine Pass to Route Twisk	95	90
2286	$2 Route Twisk to Tin Fu Tsai	95	90
2287	$2 Tin Fu Tsai to Tuen Mun	95	90
2278/2287 *Set of 10*			

(b) Miniature sheet. Perf 13½ (one elliptical hole on each vert side).

MS2288 210×150 mm. $20 As Nos. 2278/2287		8·50	8·50

(c) Booklet stamps. Self-adhesive. Die-cut perf 13½ (one elliptical hole on each vert side).

2289	$2 As Type **449**	95	90
2290	$2 As No. 2279	95	90
2291	$2 As No. 2280	95	90
2292	$2 As No. 2281	95	90
2293	$2 As No. 2282	95	90
2294	$2 As No. 2283	95	90
2295	$2 As No. 2284	95	90
2296	$2 As No. 2285	95	90
2297	$2 As No. 2286	95	90
2298	$2 As No. 2287	95	90
2289/2298 *Set of 10*			

450 Mr Q **451** Clay Rat

(Des Arde Lam. Litho, varnished and embossed (No. **MS**2308) or litho (others) Enschedé (Nos. 2299/2306) or Cartor (Nos. **MS**2307/**MS**2308))

2019 (5 Dec). *Old Master Q* (comic). T **450** and similar multicoloured designs. Granite paper. One phosphor band (Nos. **MS**2307/**MS**2308) or two phosphor bands (others). Perf 13½.

2299	$2 Type **450**	95	90
2300	$2 Let's go on a date	95	90
2301	$2 Fortune telling stall	95	90
2302	$2 Old Master Q as Superman	95	90
2303	$2 Eating buns with tea	95	90
2304	$2 Eating hot pot	95	90
2305	$2 Sheltering under umbrella	95	90
2306	$2 Cooked meat stall	95	90
2299/2306 *Set of 8*			
MS2307 130×85 mm. $10 Characters sitting on top of tram (65×53 mm)		4·50	4·50
MS2308 130×85 mm. $20 As No. **MS**2307 but characters embossed and varnished		8·50	8·50

Nos. 2299/2306 are additionally printed with various motifs from the comic on the reverse of the stamps.

(Des Simon Chung. Litho (Nos. 2309/2312, **MS**2314) or litho and red foil die-stamped (No. **MS**2313) or litho and silver foil (Pig), litho and 22-carat gold-plated metal lace (Rat) (No. **MS**2315) Cartor)

2020 (11 Jan). Chinese New Year. Year of the Rat. T **451** and similar horiz and square designs. Multicoloured. Granite paper.

(a) Two phosphor bands ($2) or one phosphor band (others). Perf 13½×13 (with one elliptical hole on each vert side).

2309	$2 Type **451**	95	95
2310	$3.70 Embroidered Rat	1·90	1·75

2311	$4.90 Ceramic Rat	2·25	2·25
2312	$5 Glass Rat	2·50	2·50
2309/2312 *Set of 4*		5·00	5·00

(b) Miniature sheet. One phosphor band. Perf 13½ (with one elliptical hole on each vert side).

MS2313 135×85 mm $10 Metal Rat (square) (45×45 mm)		5·00	5·00

(c) Miniature sheet. Silk-faced and granite paper. Perf 13½ (with one elliptical hole on each vert side).

MS2314 80×80 mm. $50 Metal Rat (As No. **MS**2213) (square) (45×45 mm)		40·00	40·00

(d) Miniature sheet. One phosphor band. Perf 13½×13 (with one elliptical hole on each vert side).

MS2315 135×90 mm. $50 Pink porcelain Pig (As No. 2227); $50 Golden Rat (As No. 2309)		40·00	40·00

452 Clay Rat

(Des Simon Chung. Litho (No. 2316) or litho and embossed (No. 2317) Southern Colour Print, New Zealand)

2020 (11 Jan). Greetings Stamps. Year of the Rat. With service indicator. T **452** and similar square design. Multicoloured. Granite paper. Two phosphor bands ($2) or one phosphor band ($4.90). Perf 13½ (with one elliptical hole on each vert side).

(a) Inscr 'Local Mail Postage'.

2316	($2) Type **452**	1·00	75

(b) Air. Inscr 'Air Mail Postage'.

2317	($4.90) Ceramic Rat	1·90	1·90

Nos. 2316/2317 were printed in sheets of 12 with 12 stamp-size labels which could be personalised by the addition of a photograph or logo.

453 Spring Showers **454** Baby (Women and Family Services)

(Des Shirman Lai. Litho Cartor)

2020 (4 Feb). Solar Terms, Spring. T **453** and similar vert designs. Multicoloured. Granite paper. Two phosphor bands. Perf 13×13½ (with one elliptical hole on each vert side).

2318	$2 Type **453**	95	95
	a. Pair, tête-bêche. No. 2318	1·90	
2319	$2 Spring commences	95	95
	a. Pair, tête-bêche. No. 2319	1·90	
2320	$2 Vernal equinox	95	95
	a. Pair, tête-bêche. No. 2320	1·90	
2321	$2 Insects waken	95	95
	a. Pair, tête-bêche. No. 2321	1·90	
2322	$2 Corn rain	95	95
	a. Pair, tête-bêche. No. 2322	1·90	
2323	$2 Bright and clear	95	95
	a. Pair, tête-bêche. No. 2323	1·90	
2318/2323 *Set of 6*		11·00	11·00
MS2324 140×115 mm. $2×6 As Nos. 2318/2323		5·50	5·50

Nos. 2318/2323 were printed, *se-tenant*, in, *tête-bêche*, pairs within sheets of 24 stamps. Nos. 2318a/2323a were perforated in a circle around the design enclosed in an outer perforated square.

(Des Michael Miller Yu. Litho Enschedé)

2020 (10 Mar). Centenary of Hong Kong Young Women's Christian Association. T **454** and similar vert designs. Multicoloured. Granite paper. Two phosphor bands ($2) or one phosphor band (others). Perf 14 (with one elliptical hole on each vert side).

2325	$2 Type **454**	95	95
2326	$3.70 Girl (Youth and community services)	1·90	1·90
2327	$4.90 Woman (Education and employment services)	2·25	2·25

2328	$5 Older woman (Elderly services)	2·50	2·50
2325/2328 Set of 4		5·50	5·50
MS2329 140×90 mm. $15.60 As Nos. 2325/2328		5·50	5·50

455 Chinese Chess

(Des Alex NG. Litho Enschedé)

2020 (21 Apr). Children's Stamps. Chess Games. T **455** and similar square designs. Multicoloured. Granite paper. Two phosphor bands ($2) or one phosphor band (others). Perf 14 (with one elliptical hole on each vert side) (Nos. 2330/2335) or 13½ (with one different shaped hole on each vert side) (No. **MS**2336).

2330	$2 Type **455**	1·50	1·50
2331	$2.60 Jungle	1·90	1·90
2332	$3.40 Aeroplane chess games	2·25	2·25
2333	$3.70 Chess	2·50	2·50
2334	$4.90 Chinese checkers	2·50	2·50
2335	$5 Go	2·50	2·50
2330/2335 Set of 6		12·00	12·00
MS2336 200×120 mm. $21.60 As Nos. 2330/2335		12·00	12·00

456 Landscapes Depicting Poems of Huang Yanlü by Shitao

(Des Arde Lam. Litho Cartor)

2020 (21 May). Hong Kong Museums Collection. Selection from the Chih Lo Lou Collection. T **456** and similar horiz and vert designs. Multicoloured. Granite paper (No. 2337/**MS**2343) or silk-faced and granite paper (No. **MS**2344). Two phosphor bands (No. 2337) or one phosphor band (Nos. 2338/**MS**2343). Perf 14 (with one elliptical hole on each vert side) (Nos. 2337/2342) or 13½×13 (with one elliptical hole on each vert side) (Nos. **MS**2343/**MS**2344).

2337	$2 Type **456**	1·50	1·50
2338	$2.60 Gathering Fungus by Lu Zhi (vert) (41×44 mm)	1·90	1·90
2339	$3.40 Miscellaneous Subjects by Chen Zi	2·25	2·25
2340	$3.70 Peach Blossom Retreat by Tang Yin (Part 1) (vert) (41×44 mm)	2·50	2·50
2341	$4.90 Peach Blossom Retreat by Tang Yin (Part 2) (vert) (41×44 mm)	2·50	2·50
2342	$5 Peach Blossom Retreat by Tang Yin (Part 3) (vert) (41×44 mm)	2·50	2·50
2337/2342 Set of 6		12·00	12·00
MS2343 78×145 mm. $10 Splashed-colour Landscape by Zhang Daqian (vert) (60×85 mm)		6·50	6·50
MS2344 $20 As No. **MS**2344		13·00	13·00

Nos. 2340/2342 were printed separately in sheets of 25 stamps, but forming a composite design.

457 Qinghai-Tibet Plateau and Herd of Wild Yak

(Des Eric Shum. Litho Enschedé)

2020 (23 June). World Heritage Sites in China (9th Series). Qinghai Hoh Xil. Sheet 140×90 mm. Granite paper. One phosphor band. Perf 13 (with one elliptical hole on each vert side).

MS2345 **457** $10 multicoloured	6·50

458 Indo-Pacific Bottlenose Dolphin

(Des Wong Fun Fun. Litho Enschedé)

2020 (18 Aug). Hong Kong Theme Park Ocean Park Hong Kong. T **458** and similar horiz designs. Multicoloured. Granite paper. Two phosphor bands ($2) or one phosphor band (others). Perf 13½×14½ (with one elliptical hole on each vert side) (Nos. 2346/2351) or 14 (with one elliptical hole on each vert side) (No. **MS**2352).

2346	$2 Type **458**	1·50	1·50
2347	$2.60 Toco Toucan	1·90	1·90
2348	$3.40 Sichuan Golden Snub-nosed Monkey	2·25	2·25
2349	$3.70 Meerkat	2·50	2·50
2350	$4.90 Giant Panda	2·50	2·50
2351	$5 King Penguin	2·50	2·50
2346/2351 Set of 6		12·00	12·00
MS2352 135×85 mm. $10 Map of Ocean Park (91×29 mm)		7·00	7·00

459 Office Buildings

(Des Clement Yick. Litho Cartor)

2020 (17 Sept). International Legal Hub. Sheet 140×90 mm. Granite paper. One phosphor band. Perf 14 (with one elliptical hole on each vert side).

MS2353 **459** $10 multicoloured	7·00	7·00

460 View of Victoria Harbour in 1962 and 2020 (Part 1)

461 Artwork At Peace with the World of Wind (1995), Cover Art for Vol. 186 of the Tin Ha Pictorial

(Des Colin Tillyer. Litho Enschedé)

2020 (29 Sept). Hong Kong Past and Present. Victoria Harbour. T **460** and similar vert designs. Multicoloured. Granite paper. Two phosphor bands ($2) or one phosphor band (others). Perf 13½×14 (with one elliptical hole on each vert side).

2354	$2 Type **460**	1·90	
	a. Strip of 4. Nos. 2354/2357	8·50	8·50
2355	$3.70 View of Victoria Harbour in 1962 and 2020 (Part 2)	2·25	2·25

2356	$4.90 View of Victoria Harbour in 1962 and 2020 (Part 3)	2·50	2·50
2357	$5 View of Victoria Harbour in 1962 and 2020 (Part 4)	2·50	2·50
2354/2357 Set of 4		12·00	12·00
MS2358 135×101 mm. $15.60 As Nos. 2354/2357		8·50	8·50

Nos. 2354/2357 were printed, *se-tenant*, in horizontal strips of four within sheets of 12 stamps, each strip forming a composite design.

(Des GrowthRing & Co. Litho (No. 2359/**MS**2365) or litho and gold foil die-stamped (No. **MS**2366) Cartor)

2020 (29 Oct). *Storm Riders*. T **461** and similar vert and horiz designs. Multicoloured. Granite paper. Two phosphor bands ($2) or one phosphor band (others). Perf 14½×13½ (with one elliptical hole on each vert side) or 14½ (with one elliptical hole on each vert side).

2359	$2 Type **461**	1·90	1·90
2360	$2.60 Artwork *Lament over the Loss* of Cloud (1997), cover art for Vol. 237 of the *Tin Ha Pictorial*	2·25	2·25
2361	$3.40 Artwork *Tranquility* of Cloud (1996), cover art for Vol. 223 of the *Tin Ha Pictorial*	3·00	3·00
2362	$3.70 Artwork of *Nameless* (1990), cover art for Vol. 62 of the *Tin Ha Pictorial*	3·00	3·00
2363	$4.90 Artwork *Rising Storm* of Wind (1989), cover art for Vol. 13 of the *Tin Ha Pictorial*	3·50	3·50
2364	$5 Artwork *Death at the Door* of Cloud (2002), cover art for Vol. 52 of the *Storm Riders Joint Edition*	3·50	3·50
2359/2364 Set of 6		14·00	14·00
MS2365 150×80 mm. $10 Artwork *Braving the Wind Alone* of Wind (1989), cover art for Vol. 2 of the *Storm Riders Joint Edition* (horiz) (72×48 mm)		7·00	7·00
MS2366 150×80 mm. $20 Artwork *The Winner Takes It All* (1993), cover art for Vol. 9 of the *Storm Riders Joint Edition* (horiz) (72×48 mm)		14·00	14·00

462 Jeet Kune Do

463 Santa Eating Dim Sum

(Des Gideon Lai. Litho (No. 2367/**MS**2373) or litho and gold foil embossed (No. **MS**2374) Southern Colour Print, New Zealand)

2020 (27 Nov). Bruce Lee's Legacy in the World of Martial Arts. T **462** and similar vert designs. Multicoloured. Granite paper. Two phosphor bands ($2) or one phosphor band (others). Perf 14 (with one elliptical hole on each vert side) (Nos. 2367/2372) or 14½ (with one elliptical hole on each vert side) (No. **MS**2373/**MS**2374).

2367	$2 Type **462**	1·90	1·90
2368	$2.60 Film *The Big Boss*	2·25	2·25
2369	$3.40 Film *Fist of Fury*	2·50	2·50
2370	$3.70 Film *The Way of the Dragon*	2·50	2·50
2371	$4.90 Film *Game of Death*	3·00	3·00
2372	$5 Philosophy	3·00	3·00
2367/2372 Set of 6		14·00	14·00
MS2373 135×85 mm. $10 Bruce Lee's legacy (38×62 mm)		7·00	7·00
MS2374 $20 As No. **MS**2373		14·00	14·00

(Des Wong Chun-hong. Litho and gold foil Enschedé)

2020 (4 Dec). Christmas. T **463** and similar horiz designs. Multicoloured. Granite paper. Two phosphor bands ($2) or one phosphor band (others).

(a) Ordinary gum. Perf 14 (with one elliptical hole on each vert side).

2375	$2 Type **463**	1·90	1·90
2376	$3.70 Santa and Rudolph on swing	2·25	2·25
2377	$4.90 Santa performing tai chi	2·50	2·50
2378	$5 Santa on double-decker bus	2·50	2·50
2375/2378 Set of 4		6·00	6·00
MS2379 195×95 mm. $15.60 As Nos. 2375/2378		12·00	12·00

(b) Self-adhesive. Die-cut perf 13½ (with one elliptical hole on each vert side).

2380	$2 As Type **463**	1·90	1·90
2381	$3.70 As No. 2376	2·25	2·25
2382	$4.90 As No. 2377	2·50	2·50
2383	$5 As No. 2378	2·50	2·50
2380/2383 Set of 4		8·50	8·50
MS2384 195×90 mm. $15.60 As Nos. 2380/2383		12·00	12·00

No. **MS**2384 was cut around the upper margin.

464 Emergency Workers

(Des Arde Lam. Litho and varnish Enschedé)

2020 (29 Dec). Combat Corona Campaign. Together, We Fight the Virus. Sheet 150×90 mm. T **464** and similar vert design. Multicoloured. Granite paper. One phosphor band. Perf 14 (with one elliptical hole on each vert side).

MS2385 $10 Type **464**	7·00	7·00
MS2386 $10 Testing using the Huo-Yan air lab	7·00	7·00

465 Boxwood Carved Ox

(Des Kan Tai-keung. Litho (Nos. 2387/2390, **MS**2392) or litho and red foil die-stamped (No. **MS**2391) or litho and silver foil die-stamped (Rat), litho and 22-carat gold-plated metal lace (Ox) (No. **MS**2393) Cartor)

2021 (28 Jan). Chinese New Year. Year of the Ox. T **465** and similar horiz and square designs. Multicoloured. Granite paper.

(a) Two phosphor bands ($2) or one phosphor band (others). Perf 14½ (with one elliptical hole on each vert side).

2387	$2 Type **465**	1·90	1·90
2388	$3.70 Zisha bisque fired Calf	2·25	2·25
2389	$4.90 Bronze Ox	2·50	2·50
2390	$5 Ceramic Ox	2·50	2·50
2387/2390 Set of 4		8·50	8·50

(b) Miniature sheet. One phosphor band. Perf 13½ (with one elliptical hole on each vert side).

MS2391 135×85 mm $10 Lacquered illuminated carved from wood Ox (*square*) (45×45 mm)	7·00	7·00

(c) Miniature sheet. Silk-faced and granite paper. Perf 13½ (with one elliptical hole on each vert side).

MS2392 80×80 mm. $50 Lacquered illuminated carved from wood Ox (As No. **MS**2391) (*square*) (45×45 mm)	35·00	35·00

(d) Miniature sheet. One phosphor band. Perf 13½×13 (with one elliptical hole on each vert side).

MS2393 135×90 mm. $50 Embroidered Rat (As No. 2310); $50 Golden Ox (As No. 2387)	35·00	35·00

466 Boxwood Carved
Ox

(Des Kan Tai-keung. Litho Southern Colour Print, New Zealand)

2021 (28 Jan). Greetings Stamps. Year of the Ox. With service indicator.
T **466** and similar square design. Multicoloured. Granite paper. Two
phosphor bands ($2) or one phosphor band ($4.90). Perf 13½ (with
one elliptical hole on each vert side).

(a) Inscr 'Local Mail Postage'.
2394	($2) Type **466**	1·90	1·90

(b) Air. Inscr 'Air Mail Postage'.
2395	($4.90) Bronze Ox	2·50	2·50

Nos. 2394/2395 were printed in sheets of 12 with 12 stamp-size labels
which could be personalised by the addition of a photograph or logo.

467 Lion Dance   **468** Scene 'The Oath of
the Peach Garden'

(Des Eric Chan. Litho (Nos. 2396/**MS**2400) or litho and gold foil die-
stamped (No. **MS**2401) Cartor)

2021 (23 Feb). Intangible Cultural Heritage. Dragon and Lion Dance. T
467 and similar vert and horiz designs. Multicoloured. Granite paper.
Two phosphor bands ($2) or one phosphor band (others). Perf 13½
(with one elliptical hole on each vert side) (Nos. 2396/2399) or 14½
(with one elliptical hole on each vert side) (Nos. **MS**2400/**MS**2401).

2396	$2 Type **467**	1·90	1·90
2397	$3.70 Pixiu Dance	2·25	2·25
2398	$4.90 Unicorn Dance	2·50	2·50
2399	$5 Dragon Dance	2·50	2·50
2396/2399 *Set of 4*		8·50	8·50

MS2400 135×85 mm. $10 Fire Dragon Dance, purple
background (*horiz*) (112×48 mm).................. 7·00   7·00

MS2401 135×85 mm. $20 Fire Dragon Dance, olive-
bistre background (*horiz*) (112×48 mm),.......... 14·00   14·00

(Des Shirman Lai. Litho (Nos. 2402/**MS**2408) or litho and embossed
(No. **MS**2409) Cartor)

2021 (16 Mar). Classical Novels of Chinese Literature. *Romance of the Three
Kingdoms* by Luo Guanzhong. T **468** and similar vert and triangular
designs. Multicoloured. Granite paper. Two phosphor bands ($2) or
one phosphor band (others). Perf 14×13½ (with one elliptical hole on
each vert side) (Nos. 2402/2407) or 14½×14½×14 (with one elliptical
hole on each vert side) (No. **MS**2408) or 14½×14×14½ (with one
elliptical hole on each vert side) (No. **MS**2409).

2402	$2 Type **468**	1·90	1·90
2403	$2.60 Scene 'A Notion of Heroes over Warm Wine'................................	2·25	2·25
2404	$3.40 Scene 'Escorting Sisters-in-law over a Thousand Miles'	2·50	2·50
2405	$3.70 Scene 'Three Visits to the Thatched Cottage'........................	2·50	2·50
2406	$4.90 Scene 'Zhao Yun Saving the Young Lord'........................	2·50	2·50
2407	$5 Scene 'Empty Fort Stratagem'................	2·50	2·50
2402/2407 *Set of 6*		12·00	12·00

MS2408 135×85 mm. $10 Scene 'The Arrow through
the Halberd' (*triangular*) (85×116×78 mm).......... 7·00   7·00

MS2409 135×85 mm. $20 Scene 'Borrowing Arrows
with Straw Boats' (*triangular*) (116×78×85 mm).......... 14·00   14·00

469 Fishballs   **470** *Queen's Road looking east from
Canton Bazaar*

(Des Colin Tillyer. Litho and embossed Enschedé)

2021 (22 Apr). Local Snacks in Hong Kong. T **469** and similar vert designs.
Multicoloured. Granite paper. Two phosphor bands ($2) or one
phosphor band (others). Perf 13½ (with one elliptical hole on each
vert side) (Nos. 2410/2415) or 14½×14 (with one elliptical hole on
each vert side) (No. **MS**2416).

2410	$2 Type **469**	1·90	1·90
2411	$2.60 Candy and coconut wrap	2·25	2·25
2412	$3.40 Stuffed three treasures	2·25	2·25
2413	$3.70 Buttered pineapple bun................	2·25	2·25
2414	$4.90 Stewed skewers	2·50	2·50
2415	$5 Peanut candy	2·50	2·50
2410/2415 *Set of 6*		12·00	12·00

MS2416 135×85 mm. $10 Steamed rice rolls (42×70
mm).. 7·00   7·00

(Des Shirman Lai. Litho (Nos. 2417/**MS**2423) or litho and embossed
(No. **MS**2424) Cartor)

2021 (25 May). Hong Kong Museums Collection. 19th Century China Trade
Paintings. T **470** and similar horiz and vert designs. Multicoloured.
Granite paper. Two phosphor bands ($2) or one phosphor band
(others). Perf 14×13½ (with one elliptical hole on each vert side)
(Nos. 2417/2422) or 14½×14 (with one elliptical hole on each vert
side) (Nos. **MS**2423/**MS**2424).

2417	$2 Type **470**	1·90	1·90
2418	$2.60 *Cake Shop, Canton* (*vert*)	2·25	2·25
2419	$3.40 *Porcelain Shop, Canton* (*vert*)................	2·25	2·25
2420	$3.70 *Production of Ceramics: Packing in Barrels*........................	2·25	2·25
2421	$4.90 *New China Street*	2·50	2·50
2422	$5 *Production of Silk: Spinning Silk Threads*	2·50	2·50
2417/2422 *Set of 6*		12·00	12·00

MS2423 138×80 mm. $10 *The Studio of Tingqua* (72×51
mm).. 7·00   7·00

MS2424 138×80 mm. $20 *Packing of Tea* (*vert*) (47×66
mm).. 14·00   14·00

471 Dog

(Des Hikoko Ito. Litho Enschedé)

2021 (22 June). Centenary of the Society for the Prevention of Cruelty
to Animals. T **471** and similar horiz designs. Multicoloured. Granite
paper. Two phosphor bands ($2) or one phosphor band (others). Perf
13½×14½ (with one elliptical hole on each vert side).

2425	$2 Type **471**	1·90	1·90
2426	$2.60 Hamster........................	2·25	2·25
2427	$3.40 Red-eared Slider (Terrapin)	2·25	2·25
2428	$3.70 Rabbit........................	2·50	2·50
2429	$4.90 Domestic Shorthair........................	2·50	2·50
2430	$5 Cockatiel	2·50	2·50
2425/2430 *Set of 6*		12·00	12·00

MS2431 150×80 mm. $21.60 As Nos. 2425/2430............. 16·00   16·00

472 Memorial of the First National
Congress of the Communist Party
of China

(Des Tony Ho. Litho Beijing Stamp Printing House Company Limited)

2021 (1 July). Centenary of the Founding of the Communist Party of China. T **472** and similar horiz and vert designs. Multicoloured. Two phosphor bands ($2) or one phosphor band (others). Perf 13½×12½ (with one elliptical hole on each vert side) (Nos. 2432/2435) or 13 (with one elliptical hole on each vert side) (No. **MS**2436).

2432	$2 Type **472**	1·90	1·90
2433	$3.70 Tiananmen Square, Beijing	2·25	2·25
2434	$4.90 City skyline	2·50	2·50
2435	$5 High-speed train	2·50	2·50
2432/2435 *Set of 4*		8·50	8·50
MS2436 140×90 mm. $10 Anniversary emblem (*vert*) (46×72 mm)		7·00	7·00

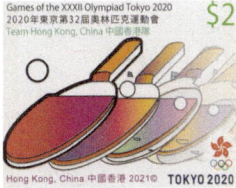

473 Table Tennis　　**474** Old General Post Office Building and Postman on Bicycle

(Des Hikoko Ito. Litho and foil die-stamped Cartor)

2021 (23 July). 2020 Summer Olympics, Tokyo. T **473** and similar horiz designs. Multicoloured. Granite paper. Two phosphor bands ($2) or one phosphor band (others). Perf 13½ (with one elliptical hole on each vert side).

2437	$2 Type **473**	1·90	1·90
2438	$3.70 Windsurfing	2·25	2·25
2439	$4.90 Cycling	2·50	2·50
2440	$5 Swimming	2·50	2·50
2437/2440 *Set of 4*		8·50	8·50
MS2441 195×95 mm. $15.60 As Nos. 2437/2440		16·00	16·00

(Des Bon Kwan. Litho Cartor)

2021 (25 Aug). 180th Anniversary of Hong Kong Postal Service. T **474** and similar square designs. Multicoloured. Granite paper. Two phosphor bands ($2) or one phosphor band (others). Perf 14 (with one elliptical hole on each vert side).

2442	$2 Type **474**	1·90	1·90
2443	$2.60 Postman delivering post for tenement building	2·25	2·25
2444	$3.40 Two postal workers sorting post	2·25	2·25
2445	$3.70 Postal worker pushing handcart with parcels	2·50	2·50
2446	$4.90 Women with letter and men with parcel	2·50	2·50
2447	$5 Postal worker and sorting machine	2·50	2·50
2442/2447 *Set of 6*		13·00	13·00
MS2448 218×122 mm. $21.60 As Nos. 2442/2447		15·00	15·00

475 Lok　　**476** Karst Landscape

(Des Andrew Lo. Litho (Nos. 2449/**MS**2455) or litho and varnish (No. **MS**2456) Enschedé)

2021 (16 Sept). *Feel 100%* Comic Book by Lau Wan-kit. T **475** and similar vert and horiz designs. Multicoloured. Granite paper. Two phosphor bands ($2) or one phosphor band (others). Perf 13½ (with one elliptical hole on each vert side).

2449	$2 Type **475**	1·90	1·90
2450	$2.60 Jerry	2·25	2·25
2451	$3.40 Cherie	2·25	2·25
2452	$3.70 Jackie	2·25	2·25
2453	$4.90 Jerry and Jenny	2·50	2·50
2454	$5 Jerry and Cherie	2·50	2·50
2449/2454 *Set of 6*			

MS2455 135×85 mm. $10 Hui Lok, Jerry and Cherie (*horiz*) (55×44 mm)		7·00	7·00
MS2456 135×85 mm. $20 Hui Lok and Cherie (*horiz*) (55×44 mm)		14·00	14·00

(Des Cheng Kar-wai. Litho and embossed Enschedé)

2021 (12 Oct). World Heritage Sites in China (10th issue). South China Karst. Sheet 140×90 mm. Granite paper. One phosphor band. Perf 14½×14 (with one elliptical hole on each vert side).

MS2457 **476** $10 multicoloured		7·00	7·00

(Des Cheng Kar-wai. Litho Enschedé)

2021 (12 Oct). World Heritage Sites in China. Sheet 220×160 mm. As T **353**. Multicoloured. Granite paper. One phosphor band. Perf 13½×14 (with one elliptical hole on each vert side) (As Type **353**) or 13½×13 (with one elliptical hole on each vert side) (As Type **387, 476**) or 13×13½ (with one elliptical hole on each vert side) (As Type **363, 399, 408, 446**) or 13½ (with one elliptical hole on each vert side) (As Type **380, 429, 457**).

MS2458 $2.60×10, As Type **353**; As Type **363**; As Type **380**; As Type **387**; As Type **399**; As Type **408**; As Type **429**; As Type **446**; As Type **457**; As Type **476**...		19·00	19·00

No. **MS**2458 comprising all the ten issues *World Heritage Sites in China* but with new year date '2021' and new face value.

477 Fencing　　**478** *Camellia hongkongensis*

(Des Hikoko Ito. Litho Beijing Stamp Printing House Company Limited)

2021 (28 Oct). Outstanding Achievements of the Hong Kong, China Team at the Tokyo 2020 Olympic Games. Sheet 219×160 mm. T **477** and similar horiz designs. Multicoloured. One phosphor band. Perf 13½×13 (with one elliptical hole on each vert side).

MS2459 $10×5, Type **477**; Swimming; Table tennis; Karate; Cycling		30·00	30·00

(Des Chau So-hing. Litho Cartor)

2021 (16 Nov). Hong Kong Special Flora. T **478** and similar horiz and vert designs. Multicoloured. Granite paper. Two phosphor bands ($2) or one phosphor band (others). Perf 13½ (with one elliptical hole on each vert side).

2460	$2 Type **478**	1·90	1·90
2461	$2.60 *Rhododendron hongkongense*	2·25	2·25
2462	$3.40 *Lysimachia alpestris*	2·25	2·25
2463	$3.70 *Thismia hongkongensis* (*vert*)	2·50	2·50
2464	$4.90 *Carpinus insularis* (*vert*)	2·50	2·50
2465	$5 *Impatiens hongkongensis*	2·50	2·50
2460/2465 *Set of 6*		12·50	12·50
MS2466 165×120 mm. $21.60 As Nos. 2460/2465		12·00	12·00

479 Santa Claus and Gingerbread Man in Kau U Fong

(Des Young Hoi-chun. Litho Cartor)

2021 (2 Dec). Movie Scenic Locations in Hong Kong. T **479** and similar horiz designs. Multicoloured. Granite paper. Two phosphor bands ($2) or one phosphor band (others). Perf 14 (with one elliptical hole on each vert side).

2467	$2 Type **479**	1·90	1·90
2468	$3.70 Santa Claus and Monster Building	2·25	2·25
2469	$4.90 Santa Claus and gingerbread fly through magic in the sky over Two International Finance Centre	2·50	2·50
2470	$5 Santa Claus near Jumbo Floating Restaurant	2·50	2·50
2467/2470 *Set of 4*		8·50	8·50
MS2471 150×90 mm. $15.60 As Nos. 2467/2470		12·00	12·00

480 Table Tennis

481 Tiger Soft Toy

(Des T **480** and similar horiz designs. Litho Beijing Stamp Printing House Company Limited)

2021 (9 Dec). Outstanding Achievements of the Hong Kong, China Team at the Tokyo 2020 Paralympic Games. Sheet 194×95 mm. T **480** and similar horiz designs. Multicoloured. One phosphor band. Perf 13½×13 (with one elliptical hole on each vert side).
MS2472 $10×3, Type **480**; Bocce; Badminton.................. 19·00   19·00

(Des Kan Tai-keung. Litho (Nos. 2473/2476, **MS**2478) or litho and gold foil die-stamped (No. **MS**2477) or litho and silver foil die-stamped (Ox), litho and 22-carat gold-plated metal lace (Tiger) (No. **MS**2479) Cartor)

2022 (18 Jan). Chinese New Year. Year of the Tiger. T **481** and similar horiz and square designs. Multicoloured. Granite paper.

(a) Two phosphor bands ($2) or one phosphor band (others). Perf 13½×13 (with one elliptical hole on each vert side).

2473	$2 Type **481**	1·90	1·90
2474	$3.70 Porcelain Tiger	2·25	2·25
2475	$4.90 Ceramic Tiger	2·50	2·50
2476	$5 Paper art Tiger	2·50	2·50
2473/2476 Set of 4		8·00	8·00

(b) Miniature sheet. One phosphor band. Perf 13½ (with one elliptical hole on each vert side).
MS2477 135×85 mm. $10 Porcelain Tiger wearing an embroidered hat (square) (45×45 mm)................... 7·00   7·00

(c) Miniature sheet. Silk-faced and granite paper. Perf 13½ (with one elliptical hole on each vert side).
MS2478 80×80 mm. $50 Porcelain Tiger wearing an embroidered hat (As No. **MS**2477) (square) (45×45 mm)... 30·00   30·00

(d) Miniature sheet. One phosphor band. Perf 13½×13 (with one elliptical hole on each vert side).
MS2479 135×90 mm. $50 Ceramic Ox (As No. 2390); $50 Golden Tiger (As No. 2476)................................. 55·00   55·00

482 Tiger Soft Toy

(Des Kan Tai-keung. Litho Southern Colour Print, New Zealand)

2022 (18 Jan). Greetings Stamps. Year of the Tiger. With service indicator. T **482** and similar square design. Multicoloured. Granite paper. Two phosphor bands ($2) or one phosphor band ($4.90). Perf 13½ (with one elliptical hole on each vert side).

(a) Inscr 'Local Mail Postage'.
2480   ($2) Type **482**.. 1·90   1·90

(b) Air. Inscr 'Air Mail Postage'.
2481   ($4.90) Ceramic Tiger .... 4·00   4·00
Nos. 2480/2481 were printed in sheets of 12 with 12 stamp-size labels which could be personalised by the addition of a photograph or logo.

483 Skiing

484 Central Commercial District, Hong Kong

(Des Eric Chan. Litho Cartor)

2022 (4 Feb). Winter Olympic Games, Beijing. Sheet 160×85 mm. T **483** and similar horiz designs. Multicoloured. Granite paper. Two phosphor bands ($2) or one phosphor band (others). Perf 13½×14 (with one elliptical hole on each vert side).
MS2482 $2 Type **483**; $3.70 Ice hockey; $4.90 Figure skating; $5 Speed skating.. 7·00   7·00

(Des Tong Wai-pang. Litho Cartor)

2022 (18 Feb). Guangdong-Hong Kong-Macao Greater Bay Area Development. T **484** and similar square designs. Multicoloured. Granite paper. Two phosphor bands. Perf 14 (with one elliptical hole on each vert side).

2483	$2 Type **484**	1·90	1·90
2484	$2 Archway of St Paul, Macau	1·90	1·90
2485	$2 Fair Pavillion, Guangzhou	1·90	1·90
2486	$2 Civic Centre, Shenzhen	1·90	1·90
2487	$2 Grand Theatre, Zhuhai	1·90	1·90
2488	$2 New Town Cultural Centre, Foshan	1·90	1·90
2489	$2 Sizhou Pagoda, Huizhou	1·90	1·90
2490	$2 Huawei, Dongguan	1·90	1·90
2491	$2 Sun Yat Sen House, Zhongshan	1·90	1·90
2492	$2 Kaiping Watch Towers, Jiangmen	1·90	1·90
2493	$2 Dinghu Mountain, Zhaoqing	1·90	1·90
Set of 12		18·00	18·00
MS2494 220×160 mm. $2×11 As Nos. 2483/2493		18·00	18·00

485 Tiangong Space Station, 2021

(Des Arde Lam. Litho and holography Cartor)

2022 (21 Apr). China's Aerospace Development. Sheet 178×120 mm. T **485** and similar round design. Multicoloured. Granite paper. One phosphor band. Perf 14½ (with one elliptical hole on each vert side).
MS2495 $10 Type **485**; $10 Dong Fang Hong 1 Satellite, 1970.. 14·00   14·00
No. **MS**2495 was cut in the shape of ellipse.

486 Egg Tart and Coconut Tart

(Des Shirman Lai. Litho and embossed Cartor)

2022 (26 May). Local Snacks in Hong Kong. T **486** and similar horiz designs. Multicoloured. Granite paper. Two phosphor bands ($2) or one phosphor band (others). Perf 14×14½ (with one elliptical hole on each vert side) (Nos. 2496/2501) or 14 (with one elliptical hole on each vert side and with HK shaped hole on top horiz side) (No. **MS**2502).

2496	$2 Type **486**	1·90	1·90
2497	$2.60 Faux shark fin soup and fish and lettuce soup	2·25	2·25
2498	$3.40 French toast and Hong Kong waffle	2·25	2·25
2499	$3.70 Ding ding candy and dragon's beard candy	2·50	2·50
2500	$4.90 Iced gem biscuit and sachima	2·50	2·50
2501	$5 Banana roll and black sesame roll	2·50	2·50
2496/2501 Set of 6		7·00	7·00
MS2502 135×85 mm. $10 Aeroplane olive, siu mai and stinky tofu (112×71 mm, with curved corners)		12·00	12·00

487 *Ta Kung Pao* Building in Tianjin in Past and Cityscape of Hong Kong in Present

(Des Chan Ching-tsui. Litho Beijing Stamp Printing House Company Limited)

2022 (17 June). 120th Anniversary of the *Ta Kung Pao* Newspaper. Sheet 135×90 mm. One phosphor band. Perf 13 (with one elliptical hole on each vert side).

MS2503 **487** $10 multicoloured.. 7·00   7·00

488 Two Ladies by a Moon Gate, Qing Dynasty

(Des Bon Kwan. Litho Enschedé)

2022 (30 June). Hong Kong Palace Museum. T **488** and similar horiz, trapezium and square designs. Multicoloured. Granite paper. Two phosphor bands ($2) or one phosphor band (others). Perf 13½ (with one elliptical hole on each vert side) (Nos. 2504, 2509) or 13½×13 (with one elliptical hole on each lateral side) (Nos. 2505/2508) or 14½ (with one elliptical hole on each vert side) (Nos. **MS**2510/**MS**2511).

2504	$2 Type **488**	1·90	1·90
2505	$2.60 Dish with Narcissus, Yuan Dynasty (*inverted trapezium*) (104×24 mm)	2·25	2·25
2506	$3.40 Cup in the shape of raft with seated figure, Yuan Dynasty (*rotated left trapezium*) (24×104 mm)	2·25	2·25
2507	$3.70 Mirror with polo players, Tang Dynasty (*trapezium*) (104×24 mm)	2·50	2·50
2508	$4.90 Zhao Mengfu, Yuan Dynasty (*rotated right trapezium*) (24×104 mm)	2·50	2·50
2509	$5 Headrest in the shape of reclining boy, Northern Song Dynasty	2·50	2·50
2504/2509	*Set of 6*	12·00	12·00

MS2510 135×85 mm. $10 Cup and tray with flowers, Qing Dynasty (*square*) (62×62 mm)........ 7·00   7·00
MS2511 135×85 mm. $20 Jar with fish and aquatic plants, Ming Dynasty (*square*) (62×62 mm).............. 14·00   14·00

Nos. 2504/2509 form a square.

489 Soldiers at Flag Ceremony

(Des Jason Chum. Litho and red foil die-stamped Cartor)

2022 (1 July). 25th Anniversary of the Establishment of the Hong Kong Special Administrative Region. T **489** and similar horiz designs. Multicoloured. Granite paper. Two phosphor bands ($2) or one phosphor band (others). Perf 13½×14½ (with one elliptical hole on each vert side).

2512	$2 Type **489**	1·90	1·90
2513	$3.70 Legislative Council chamber	2·25	2·25
2514	$4.90 Qianhai Shenzhen-Hong Kong Youth Innovation and Entrepreneur Hub	2·50	2·50
2515	$5 Children at flag ceremony	2·50	2·50
2512/2515	*Set of 4*	8·00	8·00

MS2516 140×90 mm. $15.60 As Nos. 2512/2515............. 10·00   10·00

490 Chinese People's Liberation Army Hong Kong Garrison Exhibition Centre and Military Parade

(Des Lee Ying-chi. Litho and gold foil die-stamped Cartor)

2022 (1 July). 25th Anniversary of the Stationing of the Chinese People's Liberation Army in Hong Kong. Sheet 133×99 mm. Granite paper. One phosphor band. Perf 14½×13½ (with one elliptical hole on each horiz side).

MS2517 **490** $20 multicoloured.. 14·00   14·00

491 Orange

(Des Peter Ng Seung-Ho. Litho and embossed Cartor)

2022 (18 Aug). Fruits. T **491** and similar horiz designs. Multicoloured. Granite paper. Two phosphor bands ($2) or one phosphor band (others). Perf 13½×13 (with one elliptical hole on each vert side) (Nos. 2518/2523) or 13½×14 (with one elliptical hole on each vert side) (No. **MS**2524).

2518	$2 Type **491**	1·90	1·90
2519	$2.60 Watermelon	2·25	2·25
2520	$3.40 Guava	2·25	2·25
2521	$3.70 Lychee	2·50	2·50
2522	$4.90 Banana	2·50	2·50
2523	$5 Papaya	2·50	2·50
2518/2523	*Set of 6*	12·00	12·00

MS2524 135×85 mm. $10 Orange, Guava, Watermelon, Papaya, Banana, Lychee.. 7·00   7·00

492 Measuring Procedure

(Des Hikoko Ito. Litho Cartor)

2022 (22 Sept). Intangible Cultural Heritage. Cheongsam Making Technique. T **492** and similar horiz designs. Multicoloured. Granite paper. Two phosphor bands ($2) or one phosphor band (others). Perf 13½×14 (with one elliptical hole on each vert side).

2525	$2 Type **492**	2·00	2·00
2526	$3.70 Cutting procedure	2·25	2·25
2527	$4.90 Ironing and pressing procedure	2·50	2·50
2528	$5 Stitching procedure	2·50	2·50
2525/2528	*Set of 4*	8·50	8·50

MS2529 128×82 mm. $10 Sewing using sewing machine.. 7·00   7·00
MS2530 128×82 mm. $20 Flower button-making technique.. 14·00   14·00

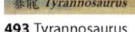

493 Tyrannosaurus

494 Miss 13 Dots in Lilac Hat and Dress

(Des Carl Cheng Chi-ming. Litho and embossed Cartor)

2022 (15 Nov). Dinosaurs. T **493** and similar horiz designs. Multicoloured. Granite paper. Two phosphor bands ($2.20) or one phosphor band (others). Perf 13½ (with one elliptical hole on each vert side).

2531	$2.20 Type **493**	1·90	1·90
2532	$2.80 Spinosaurus	2·25	2·25
2533	$3.70 Triceratops	2·25	2·25
2534	$4 Diplodocus	2·50	2·50
2535	$5.40 Brachiosaurus	2·50	2·50
2536	$5.50 Allosaurus and Hesperosaurus	2·50	2·50
2531/2536 *Set of 6*		12·00	12·00
MS2537 220×115 mm. $23.60 As Nos. 2531/2536		16·00	16·00

(Des Arde Lam. Litho (Nos. 2538/**MS**2544) or litho and holography (No. **MS**2545) Cartor)

2022 (6 Dec). *Miss 13 Dots Comics* by Li Huizhen. T **494** and similar vert, stadium and round designs. Multicoloured. Granite paper. Two phosphor bands ($2.20) or one phosphor band (others). Perf 14×14½ (with one elliptical hole on each vert side) (Nos. 2538/2543) or 14 (with one elliptical hole on each vert side) (Nos. **MS**2544/2545).

2538	$2.20 Type **494**	1·90	1·90
2539	$2.80 Miss 13 Dots in blue with carmine dress	2·25	2·25
2540	$3.70 Miss 13 Dots in green hat and skirt	2·25	2·25
2541	$4 Miss 13 Dots in red hair scarf and skirt	2·50	2·50
2542	$5.40 Miss 13 Dots in red striped hat and jumpsuit	2·50	2·50
2543	$5.50 Miss 13 Dots in deep mauve hat and deep mauve with green dress	2·50	2·50
2538/2543 *Set of 6*		12·00	12·00
MS2544 148×85 mm. $10 Miss 13 Dots among girls (*stadium*) (49×75 mm)		7·00	7·00
MS2545 148×85 mm. $20 Miss 13 Dots wearing turquoise-green hat (*round*) (64 mm)		14·00	14·00

Nos. **MS**2544/**MS**2545 were cut around the margins.

495 Porcelain Rabbit with Floral Pattern, orange and pink background

(Des Kan Tai-keung. Litho (Nos. 2546/2549, **MS**2551) or litho and red foil die-stamped (No. **MS**2550) or litho and silver foil die-stamped (Tiger), litho and 22-carat gold-plated metal lace (Rabbit) (No. **MS**2552) Cartor)

2023 (10 Jan). Chinese New Year. Year of the Rabbit. T **495** and similar horiz and square designs. Multicoloured. Granite paper.

(a) Two phosphor bands ($2.20) or one phosphor band (others). Perf 13½×13 (with one elliptical hole on each vert side).

2546	$2.20 Type **495**	2·00	2·00
2547	$4 Porcelain Rabbit with floral pattern, yellow-green and green background	3·00	3·00
2548	$5.40 Porcelain Rabbit with floral pattern, light blue and purple background	4·00	4·00
2549	$5.50 Porcelain Rabbit with floral pattern, yellow and orange background	4·00	4·00
2546/2549 *Set of 4*		12·00	12·00

(b) Miniature sheet. One phosphor band. Perf 13½ (with one elliptical hole on each vert side).

MS2550 135×85 mm $10 Porcelain Rabbit with gold pattern (*square*) (45×45 mm)	7·00	7·00

(c) Miniature sheet. Silk-faced and granite paper. Perf 13½ (with one elliptical hole on each vert side).

MS2551 80×80 mm. $50 Porcelain Rabbit with gold pattern (As No. **MS**2550) (*square*) (45×45 mm)	35·00	35·00

(d) Miniature sheet. One phosphor band. Perf 13½×13 (with one elliptical hole on each vert side).

MS2552 135×90 mm. $50 Ceramic Tiger (As No. 2475); $50 Golden Rabbit (As No. 2547)	35·00	35·00

496 Porcelain Rabbit with Floral Pattern, orange and pink background

(Des Kan Tai-keung. Litho Southern Colour Print, New Zealand)

2023 (10 Jan). Greetings Stamps. Year of the Rabbit. With service indicator. T **496** and similar square design. Multicoloured. Granite paper. Two phosphor bands ($2.20) or one phosphor band ($5.40). Perf 13½ (with one elliptical hole on each vert side).

(a) Inscr 'Local Mail Postage'.

2553	($2.20) Type **496**	2·00	2·00

(b) Air. Inscr 'Air Mail Postage'.

2554	($5.40) Porcelain Rabbit with floral pattern, light blue and purple background	4·00	4·00

Nos. 2553/2554 were printed in sheets of 12 with 12 stamp-size labels which could be personalised by the addition of a photograph or logo.

497 Rat

(Des Kan Tai-keung. Litho and multicoloured foil embossed Cartor)

2023 (10 Jan). Chinese New Year. T **497** and similar horiz designs. Multicoloured. Granite paper. Phosphor markings. Perf 13½×13 (with one elliptical hole on each vert side).

2555	$10 Type **497** (As No. 2310)	7·00	7·00
	a. Block of 4. Nos. 2555/2558	28·00	28·00
2556	$10 Ox (As No. 2388)	7·00	7·00
2557	$10 Tiger (As No. 2473)	7·00	7·00
2558	$10 Rabbit (As No. 2548)	7·00	7·00
2555/2558 *Set of 4*		28·00	28·00

Nos. 2555/2558 were printed, *se-tenant*, in blocks of four within sheets of 16 stamps. Designs printed chequerboard, allowing various, *se-tenant*, combinations.

(Des Kan Tai-keung. Litho Enschedé)

2023 (10 Jan). Chinese New Year. Twelve Animals. Sheets 220×160 mm. As T **345**. Multicoloured. Granite paper. Two phosphor bands ($2.20) or one phosphor band (others). Perf 13½×13 (with one elliptical hole on each vert side).

MS2559 $2.20×12, As Type **345** (Dragon); As Type **357** (Snake); As Type **368** (Horse); As Type **381** (Ram); As Type **395** (Monkey); As Type **407** (Rooster); As Type **423** (Dog); As Type **437** (Pig); As Type **451** (Rat); As Type **465** (Ox); As Type **481** (Tiger); As Type **495** (Rabbit)		15·00	15·00
MS2560 $4×12, As No. 1698 (Dragon); As No. 1777 (Snake); As No. 1837 (Horse); As No. 1924 (Ram); As No. 1991 (Monkey); As No. 2069 (Rooster); As No. 2149 (Dog); As No. 2226 (Pig); As No. 2310 (Rat); As No. 2388 (Ox); As No. 2474 (Tiger); As No. 2547 (Rabbit)		29·00	29·00
MS2561 $5.40×12, As No. 1699 (Dragon); As No. 1778 (Snake); As No. 1838 (Horse); As No. 1925 (Ram); As No. 1992 (Monkey); As No. 2070 (Rooster); As No. 2150 (Dog); As No. 2227 (Pig); As No. 2311 (Rat); As No. 2389 (Ox); As No. 2475 (Tiger); As No. 2548 (Rabbit)		35·00	35·00
MS2562 $5.50×12, As No. 1700 (Dragon); As No. 1779 (Snake); As No. 1839 (Horse); As No. 1926 (Ram); As No. 1993 (Monkey); As No. 2071 (Rooster); As No. 2151 (Dog); As No. 2228 (Pig); As No. 2312 (Rat); As No. 2390 (Ox); As No. 2476 (Tiger); As No. 2549 (Rabbit)		42·00	42·00

Nos. **MS**2559/**MS**2562 comprising all twelve *Chinese New Year* issues from 2012-2023 but with new year date '2023' and new face values.

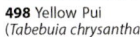

498 Yellow Pui (*Tabebuia chrysantha*)

499 *Mountain Ranges From the Front* by Zhu Qizhan

(Des Lau Yi. Litho Cartor)

2023 (14 Feb). Seasonal Trees in Hong Kong. T **498** and similar vert designs. Multicoloured. Granite paper. Two phosphor bands ($2·20) or one phosphor band (others). Perf 13½ (with one elliptical hole on each vert side).

2563	$2·20 Type **498**	1·90	1·90
2564	$4 Jacaranda (*Jacaranda mimosifolia*)	2·25	2·25
2565	$5·40 Bald Cypress (*Taxodium distichum*)	2·50	2·50
2566	$5·50 Bell-flower Cherry (*Prunus campanulata*)	2·50	2·50
2563/2566	*Set of 4*	8·00	8·00
MS2567	140×90 mm. $17.10 As Nos. 2563/2566	10·00	10·00

(Des Toby Ng. Litho Cartor)

2023 (23 Mar). Hong Kong Museums Collection. Jingguanlou. T **499** and similar vert and horiz designs. Multicoloured. Granite paper (Nos. 2568/MS2574) or silk-faced and granite paper (No. MS2575). Two phosphor bands ($2·20) or one phosphor band (Nos. 2568/MS2574). Perf 13½×14½ (with one elliptical hole on each vert side).

2568	$2·20 Type **499**	2·00	2·00
2569	$2·80 Towering Peaks by Xie Zhiliu	2·25	2·25
2570	$3·70 Wintry Mountains by Zhu Qizhan	2·25	2·25
2571	$4 Birds and Bamboo by Xie Zhiliu and Chen Peiqiu	2·50	2·50
2572	$5·40 Jiangnan in March by Zhu Qizhan	2·50	2·50
2573	$5·50 Landscape and Calligraphy by Chen Peiqiu	2·50	2·50
2568/2573	*Set of 6*	12·00	12·00
MS2574	150×70 mm. $10 Cicada Resting on a Red Leaf by Chen Peiqiu (*horiz*) (63×44 mm)	7·00	7·00
MS2575	150×70 mm. $20 Valleys in Mountains by Xie Zhiliu (*horiz*) (63×44 mm)	14·00	14·00

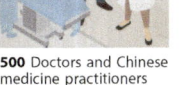

500 Doctors and Chinese medicine practitioners

501 Corn Forms

(Des Tong Wai-pang. Litho Cartor)

2023 (18 Apr). Tribute to Healthcare Workers. T **500** and similar vert and horiz designs. Multicoloured. Granite paper. Two phosphor bands ($2·20) or one phosphor band (others). Perf 13½ (with one elliptical hole on each vert side).

2576	$2·20 Type **500**	2·00	2·00
2577	$4 Nurses	3·00	3·00
2578	$5·40 Other healthcare professionals	3·50	3·50
2579	$5·50 Care-related support staff	4·00	4·00
2576/2579	*Set of 4*	11·00	11·00
MS2580	130×85 mm. $10 Health workers and nurse station (*horiz*) (80×59 mm)	7·00	7·00

(Des Shirman Lai. Litho Cartor)

2023 (4 May). Solar Terms, Summer. T **501** and similar vert designs. Multicoloured. Granite paper. Two phosphor bands. Perf 13×13½ (with one elliptical hole on each vert side).

2581	$2·20 Type **501**	2·00	2·00
	a. Pair, *tête-bêche*. No. 2581	4·00	
2582	$2·20 Summer commences	2·00	2·00
	a. Pair, *tête-bêche*. No. 2582	4·00	

2583	$2·20 Summer solstice	2·00	2·00
	a. Pair, *tête-bêche*. No. 2583	4·00	
2584	$2·20 Corn on ear	2·00	2·00
	a. Pair, *tête-bêche*. No. 2584	4·00	
2585	$2·20 Great heat	2·00	2·00
	a. Pair, *tête-bêche*. No. 2585	4·00	
2586	$2·20 Moderate heat	2·00	2·00
	a. Pair, *tête-bêche*. No. 2586	4·00	
2581/2586	*Set of 6*	11·00	11·00
MS2587	140×115 mm. $2.20×6 As Nos. 2581/2586	11·00	11·00

Nos. 2581/2586 were printed, *se-tenant*, in, *tête-bêche*, pairs within sheets of 24 stamps. Nos. 2581a/2586a were perforated in a circle around the design enclosed in an outer perforated square.

502 Recreation Chess

503 Pouring Tea into Strainer

(Des Bryan Wong. Litho and varnish Cartor)

2023 (13 June). Toys of Hong Kong from 1970s to 1980s. T **502** and similar horiz designs. Multicoloured. Granite paper. Two phosphor bands ($2·20) or one phosphor band (others). Perf 13½ (with one elliptical hole on each vert side).

2588	$2·20 Type **502**	2·00	2·00
2589	$2·80 Spinning top	2·25	2·25
2590	$3·70 Alloy toys	2·25	2·25
2591	$4 Rocket	2·50	2·50
2592	$5·40 Play kitchen	2·50	2·50
2593	$5·50 Robot	2·50	2·50
2588/2593	*Set of 6*	12·00	12·00

(Des Lai Wai-ying. Litho (Nos. 2594/MS2598) or litho and embossed (No. MS2599) Cartor)

2023 (25 July). Intangible Cultural Heritage. Hong Kong-style Milk Tea Making Technique. T **503** and similar vert and horiz designs. Multicoloured. Granite paper. Two phosphor bands ($2·20) or one phosphor band (others). Perf 13½×14½ (with one elliptical hole on each vert side) (Nos. 2594/2597) or 14½ (with one elliptical hole on each vert side) (Nos. MS2598/MS2599).

2594	$2·20 Type **503**	2·00	2·00
2595	$4 Tea brewing in teapot on stove	3·00	3·00
2596	$5·40 Pouring brewed tea into strainer	3·50	3·50
2597	$5·50 Pouring tea into cup	3·50	3·50
2594/2597	*Set of 4*	11·00	11·00
MS2598	135×85 mm. $10 Cups, teapots, strainer, milk cans and sugar (*horiz*) (112×48 mm)	7·00	7·00
MS2599	135×85 mm. $20 Cup of tea, teapot on stove, pouring brewed tea into strainer (*horiz*) (112×48 mm)	14·00	14·00

504 Hong Kong Cultural Centre

(Des Peter Ng Seung-ho. Litho and gold foil die-stamped (Nos. 2600/2605) or litho (No. MS2606) Enschedé)

2023 (22 Aug). Cultural Landmarks in Hong Kong. T **504** and similar horiz and round designs. Multicoloured. Granite paper. Two phosphor bands ($2·20) or one phosphor band (others). Perf 13½×14½ (with one elliptical hole on each vert side) (Nos. 2600/2605) or 14½ (with one elliptical hole on each vert side) (No. MS2606).

2600	$2·20 Type **504**	2·25	2·25
2601	$2·80 Hong Kong Museum of Art	2·25	2·25
2602	$3·70 M+ Complex	2·50	2·50
2603	$4 Hong Kong Palace Museum	2·50	2·50
2604	$5·40 Xiqu Centre	3·00	3·00
2605	$5·50 Hong Kong City Hall	3·00	3·00
2600/2605	*Set of 6*	14·00	14·00
MS2606	135×85 mm. $10 Tai Kwun (*round*) (48 mm)	7·00	7·00

505 Different Types of Transportation and Anniversary Emblem

(Des Gideon Lai. Litho Henan Post and Telecommunications Technology Company Limited)

2023 (7 Sept). Tenth Anniversary of the Belt and Road Initiative. Sheet 140×90 mm. One phosphor band. Perf 13 (with one elliptical hole on each vert side).

MS2607 **505** $10 multicoloured.. 7·00   7·00

506 Carrots

507 Lion Rock

(Des Benny Lau. Litho Enschedé)

2023 (21 Sept). Hong Kong Vegetables. T **506** and similar square designs. Multicoloured. Granite paper. Two phosphor bands ($2.20) or one phosphor band (others). Perf 14 (with one elliptical hole on each vert side) (Nos. 2608/2613) or 13½ (with one elliptical hole on each vert side) (No. MS2614).

2608	$2.20 Type **506**	2·00	2·00
2609	$2.80 Corns	2·25	2·25
2610	$3.70 Daikon Radishes..	2·25	2·25
2611	$4 Flowering Chinese Cabbages........................	2·50	2·50
2612	$5.40 Sweet Potatoes...	2·50	2·50
2613	$5.50 Chinese White Cabbages	2·50	2·50
2608/2613 Set of 6		12·50	12·50

MS2614 135×85 mm. $10 Basket of vegetables (square) (60×60 mm)... 7·00   7·00

(Des Ella Wong. Litho (Nos. 2615/MS2621) or litho and matte varnish (No. MS2622) Cartor)

2023 (26 Oct). Hong Kong Landscapes. Mountains. T **507** and similar horiz designs. Multicoloured. Granite paper. Two phosphor bands ($2.20) or one phosphor band (others). Perf 13½ (with one elliptical hole on each vert side) (Nos. 2615/2620) or 13½×14 (with one mountain-shaped hole on each vert side) (Nos. MS2621/MS2622).

2615	$2.20 Type **507**	2·00	2·00
2616	$2.80 Sharp Peak...	2·25	2·25
2617	$3.70 High Junk Peak..	2·25	2·25
2618	$4 Dragon's Back	2·50	2·50
2619	$5.40 Hi Tung Shan	2·50	2·50
2620	$5.50 Lantau Peak	2·50	2·50
2615/2620 Set of 6		12·30	12·50

MS2621 135×85 mm. $10 Lion Rock (124×36 mm)........... 7·00   7·00
MS2622 135×85 mm. $20 Pyramid Hill and Wan Kuk Shan (124×36 mm).................................... 14·00   14·00

508 East Rail Line

(Des Ken Li. Litho (Nos. 2623/MS2629) or litho, embossed and varnish (No. MS2630) Enschedé)

2023 (23 Nov). Development of Railway Services in Hong Kong. T **508** and similar parallelogram designs. Multicoloured. Granite paper. Two phosphor bands ($2.20) or one phosphor band (others). Perf 13½×13 (with one elliptical hole on each vert side) (Nos. 2623/2628) or 13½ (with one elliptical hole on each vert side) (Nos. MS2629/MS2630).

2623	$2.20 Type **508**	2·00	2·00
2624	$2.80 Tuen Ma Line	2·25	2·25
2625	$3.70 South Island Line	2·25	2·25
2626	$4 Kwun Tong Line..	2·50	2·50
2627	$5.40 Tseung Kwan O Line	2·50	2·50
2628	$5.50 Tung Chung Line	2·50	2·50
2623/2628 Set of 6		12·50	12·50

MS2629 135×85 mm. $10 Airport Express (68×45 mm).. 7·00   7·00
MS2630 135×85 mm. $20 High Speed Rail (68×45 mm).. 14·00   14·00

509 General Post Office 1841-1845

(Des Chau So-hing. Litho Cartor)

2023 (19 Dec). Hong Kong Past and Present. Post Office Headquarters. T **509** and similar horiz designs. Granite paper. Two phosphor bands ($2.20) or one phosphor band (others). Perf 13½ (with one elliptical hole on each vert side).

2631	$2.20 Type **509** (black, stone and brown-olive)	2·00	2·00
2632	$4 General Post Office 1846-1911 (olive-green, black and dull blue-green)	2·25	2·25
2633	$5.40 General Post Office 1911-1976 (multicoloured)	2·50	2·50
2634	$5.50 General Post Office 1976-2023 (multicoloured)...	2·50	2·50
2631/2634 Set of 4		8·50	8·50

MS2635 130×75 mm. $10 General Post Office since 2023 (multicoloured)............................... 7·00   7·00

510 Dragon, stone background

(Des Wong Chun-hong. Litho (Nos. 2636/2639) or litho and red foil die-stamped (No. MS2640) or litho, red foil die-stamped and laser cut (No. MS2641) or litho and silver foil die-stamped (Rabbit), litho and 22-carat gold-plated metal lace (Dragon) (No. MS2642) Cartor)

2024 (5 Jan). Chinese New Year. Year of the Dragon. T **510** and similar horiz and square designs. Multicoloured. Granite paper.

(a) Two phosphor bands ($2.20) or one phosphor band (others). Perf 13½ (with one elliptical hole on each vert side).

2636	$2.20 Type **510**	2·00	2·00
2637	$4 Dragon, flesh background...........................	2·25	2·25
2638	$5.40 Two dragons, pink background..............	2·50	2·50
2639	$5.50 Dragon, lilac background.......................	2·50	2·50
2636/2639 Set of 4..		8·50	8·50

(b) Miniature sheet. One phosphor band. Perf 13½ (with one elliptical hole on each vert side).

MS2640 135×85 mm $10 Traditional paper cut of Dragon (square) (47×47 mm).......................... 7·00   7·00

(c) Miniature sheet. One phosphor band. Perf 13½ (with one elliptical hole on each vert side).

MS2641 135×85 mm $50 Traditional paper cut of Dragon (As No. MS2640) (square) (47×47 mm)......... 32·00   32·00

(d) Miniature sheet. One phosphor band. Perf 13½×13 (with one elliptical hole on each vert side).

MS2642 135×90 mm. $50 Porcelain Rabbit with floral pattern, yellow and orange background (As No. 2549); $50 Golden Dragon (As No. 1699)................. 35·00   35·00

No. MS2641 is laser cut through the backing paper.

511 Dragon, stone background

(Des Wong Chun-hong. Litho and varnish (No. 2643) or litho, varnish and embossed (No. 2644) Blue Star Group, New Zealand)

2024 (5 Jan). Greetings Stamps. Year of the Dragon. With service indicator. T **511** and similar square design. Multicoloured. Granite paper. Two phosphor bands ($2.20) or one phosphor band (others). Perf 13½ (with one elliptical hole on each vert side).

(a) Inscr 'Local Mail Postage'.

2643	($2.20) Type **511**	2·00	2·00

(b) Air. Inscr 'Air Mail Postage'.

2644	($4) Dragon, lilac background	4·00	4·00

Nos. 2643/2644 were printed in sheets of 12 with 12 stamp-size labels which could be personalised by the addition of a photograph or logo.

(Des Wong Chun-hong. Litho Cartor)

2024 (5 Jan). Chinese New Year. Twelve Animals, Gold and Silver Sheet. Sheet 210×150 mm. Multicoloured. Granite paper. Two phosphor bands. Perf 13½×13 (with one elliptical hole on each vert side).

MS2645	$2.20×12, Dragon (As No. MS1782); Snake (As No. MS1842); Horse (As No. MS1933); Ram (As No. MS1996); Monkey (As No. MS2074); Rooster (As No. MS2154); Dog (As No. MS2231); Pig (As No. MS2315); Rat (As No. MS2393); Ox (As No. MS2479); Tiger (As No. MS2552); Rabbit (As No. MS2642)	20·00	22·00
MS2646	$2.20×12, Dragon (As No. MS2642); Snake (As No. MS1782); Horse (As No. MS1842); Ram (As No. MS1933); Monkey (As No. MS1996); Rooster (As No. MS2074); Dog (As No. MS2154); Pig (As No. MS2231); Rat (As No. MS2315); Ox (As No. MS2393); Tiger (As No. MS2479); Rabbit (As No. MS2552)	20·00	22·00

Nos. MS2645/MS2646 comprising all twelve silver foil and 22-carat gold-plated metal lace *Chinese New Year* Miniature Sheets from 2013-2024 but with new year date '2024', new face values and imitation of silver foil and 22-carat gold-plated metal lace.

512 ICAC Headquarters Building

513 Guo Jing (*The Eagle shooting Heroes*)

(Des Ito Hikoko. Litho Cartor)

2024 (15 Feb). Anti-corruption in Hong Kong. T **512** and similar vert and horiz designs. Multicoloured. Granite paper. Two phosphor bands ($2.20) or one phosphor band (others). Perf 14×14½ (with one elliptical hole on each vert side) (Nos. 2647/2652) or 13½×14 (with one elliptical hole on each vert side) (No. 2653).

2647	$2.20 Type **512**	1·90	1·90
2648	$2.80 People sitting around table	2·25	2·25
2649	$3.70 Smiling young people	2·25	2·25
2650	$4 Technological innovations to fight corruption	2·50	2·50
2651	$5.40 Handshake	2·50	2·50
2652	$5.50 Cup of coffee	2·50	2·50
2647/2652 Set of 6		12·50	12·50
MS2653	150×85 mm. $10 Victoria Harbour view (*horiz*) (59×40 mm)	7·00	7·00

(Des Wong Ka-man. Litho (Nos. 2654/MS2661) or litho, embossed and gold foil die-stamped (No. MS2662) Cartor)

2024 (14 Mar). Characters from Jin Yong's Novels. T **513** and similar vert, horiz and stadium designs. Multicoloured. Granite paper. Two phosphor bands ($2.20) or one phosphor band (others). Perf 14½×14 (with one elliptical hole on each vert side) (Nos. 2654, 2656, 2658) or 14×13½ (with one elliptical hole on each vert side) (Nos. 2655, 2657, 2659) or 13½×14 (with one elliptical hole on each vert side) (Nos. MS2660/MS2661) or 13 (with one elliptical hole on each vert side) (No. MS2662).

2654	$2.20 Type **513**	2·00	2·00
2655	$2.80 Linghu Chong (*The Smiling Proud Wanderer*) (*horiz*)	2·25	2·25
2656	$3.70 Ren Woxing (*The Smiling Proud Wanderer*)	2·25	2·25
2657	$4 Ouyang Feng (*The Eagle shooting Heroes*) (*horiz*)	2·50	2·50
2658	$5.40 Qiao Feng (*The Demi-Gods and Semi-Devils*)	2·50	2·50

2659	$5.50 Huang Rong (*The Eagle shooting Heroes*) (*horiz*)	2·50	2·50
2654/2659 Set of 6		12·00	12·00
MS2660	150×80 mm. $10 Xiaolongnü (*The Giant Eagle and its Companion*) (*horiz*) (74×42 mm)	7·00	7·00
MS2661	150×80 mm. $10 Yang Guo (*The Giant Eagle and its Companion*) (*horiz*) (74×42 mm)	7·00	7·00
MS2662	150×80 mm. $20 Jim Yong (*stadium*) (36×64 mm)	14·00	14·00

514 Teapot with Landscape Painting

(Des Gary Tong. Litho (Nos. 2663/MS2669) or litho and varnish (No. MS2670) Enschedé)

2024 (18 Apr). Hong Kong Museums Collection. Selected Tea Ware from China and the World. T **514** and similar horiz and vert designs. Multicoloured. Two phosphor bands ($2.20) or one phosphor band (others). Perf 13½ (with one elliptical hole on each vert side) (Nos. 2663/2668) or 13½×14 (with one elliptical hole on each vert side) (Nos. MS2669/MS2670).

2663	$2.20 Type **514**	2·00	2·00
2664	$2.80 Teapot with religious motifs painting (*vert*)	2·25	2·25
2665	$3.70 Red clay teapot with flowers and birds painting (*vert*)	2·25	2·25
2666	$4 Teapot with people and harbour view painting	2·50	2·50
2667	$5.40 Teapot with rose pattern painting	2·50	2·50
2668	$5.50 Red clay teapot	2·50	2·50
2663/2668 Set of 6		12·00	12·00
MS2669	135×80 mm. $10 Teapot with blue painting (partial) (79×39 mm)	7·00	7·00
MS2670	135×80 mm. $10 Teapot with floral, animal and people painting (partial) (79×39 mm)	7·00	7·00

Nos. MS2669/MS2670 were cut in the shape of a teapot on the left side.

515 Gods and Deities for Worshipping

(Des Carl Cheng Chi-ming. Litho (Nos. 2671/MS2675) or litho and embossed (No. MS2676) Enschedé)

2024 (9 May). Intangible Cultural Heritage. Cheung Chau Jiao Festival. T **515** and similar horiz and vert designs. Multicoloured. Granite paper. Two phosphor bands ($2.20) or one phosphor band (others). Perf 13½×14½ (with one elliptical hole on each vert side) (Nos. 2671/2674) or 14½×14 (with one elliptical hole on each vert side) (Nos. MS2675/MS2676).

2671	$2.20 Type **515**	2·00	2·00
2672	$4 Traditional dragon dances	2·25	2·25
2673	$5.40 Musician procession	2·50	2·50
2674	$5.50 Palanquin carrying competition	2·50	2·50
2671/2674 Set of 4		8·00	8·00
MS2675	135×85 mm. $10 Child dressed in traditional clothes with spear suspending above the crowd (*vert*) (55×69 mm)	7·00	7·00
MS2676	135×85 mm. $20 Climbers race up a tower of buns (*vert*) (55×69 mm)	14·00	14·00

516 Bonham Road Government Primary School

(Des Eric Chan. Litho Enschedé)

2024 (20 June). Declared Monuments in Hong Kong. T **516** and similar horiz designs. Multicoloured. Granite paper. Two phosphor bands ($2.20) or one phosphor band (others). Perf 13½×14½ (with one elliptical hole on each vert side).

2677	$2.20 Type **516**	2·00	2·00
2678	$2.80 Bethany Seminary	2·25	2·25
2679	$3.70 Signal Tower at Blackhead Point	2·25	2·25
2680	$4 Kowloon Reservoir main dam	2·50	2·50
2681	$5.40 Kam Tong Hall	2·50	2·50
2682	$5.50 Block 10 of the Old Lei Yue Mun Barracks	2·50	2·50
2677/2682 *Set of 6*		12·00	12·00
MS2683 175×85 mm. $23.60 As Nos. 2677/2682		15·00	15·00

517 Fencing

(Des Chan Ching-tsui. Litho Enschedé)

2024 (26 July). Summer Olympic Games, Paris. T **517** and similar horiz designs. Multicoloured. Granite paper. Two phosphor bands ($2.20) or one phosphor band (others). Perf 13½ (with one elliptical hole on each vert side).

2684	$2.20 Type **517**	2·00	2·00
2685	$4 Swimming	2·25	2·25
2686	$5.40 Badminton	2·50	2·50
2687	$5.50 Cycling	2·50	2·50
2684/2687 *Set of 4*		8·00	8·00
MS2688 160×85 mm. $17.10 As Nos. 2684/2687		13·00	13·00

518 Mickey Mouse

(Des Ng Venus. Litho (Nos. 2689/**MS**2696, **MS**2699) or litho and embossed (No. **MS**2697) or litho, embossed and 22-carat gold-plated embossed (No. **MS**2698) Cartor)

2024 (12 Sept). Disney. T **518** and similar square, horiz and round designs. Multicoloured. Granite paper. Two phosphor bands ($2.20) or one phosphor band (others).

*(a) Ordinary gum. Perf 14×13½ (with one elliptical hole on each vert side) (Nos. 2689/**MS**2695) or 14½×14 (with one elliptical hole on each vert side) (No. **MS**2696) or 14½ (with one elliptical hole on each vert side) (Nos. **MS**2697/**MS**2698).*

2689	$2.20 Type **518**	2·00	2·00
2690	$2.80 Minnie Mouse	2·25	2·25
2691	$3.70 Pluto	2·25	2·25
2692	$4 Donald Duck	2·50	2·50
2693	$5.40 Chip	2·50	2·50
2694	$5.50 Dale	2·50	2·50
2689/2694 *Set of 6*		12·00	12·00
MS2695 165×120 mm. $23.60 As Nos. 2689/2694		16·00	16·00
MS2696 150×70 mm. $10 Mickey and friends (*horiz*) (117×59 mm)		7·00	7·00
MS2697 115×97 mm. $20 Mickey Mouse and Minnie Mouse (*round*) (55 mm)		14·00	14·00
MS2698 115×97 mm. $50 as No. **MS**2697 (*round*) (55 mm)		32·00	32·00

(b) Self-adhesive. Die-cut perf 14×13½ (with one elliptical hole on each vert side).

MS2699 180×100 mm. $23.60 As Nos. 2689/2694		15·00	15·00

Nos. **MS**2697/**MS**2698 were cut in the shape of Mickey Mouse's head.

519 Mother and Daughter

(Des Asrar Abdelkrim. Litho Brebner Print, New Zealand)

2024 (26 Sept). Children Stamps. Chinese Idioms and Their Stories. T **519** and similar square designs. Multicoloured. Granite paper. Two phosphor bands ($2.20) or one phosphor band (others). Perf 14 (with one elliptical hole on each vert side).

2700	$2.20 Type **519**	2·00	2·00
2701	$2.80 Grandmother and grandson	2·25	2·25
2702	$3.70 Woman writing her thoughts and ideas	2·50	2·50
2703	$4 Man cooking and reading	2·50	2·50
2704	$5.40 Man fighting through thorns and thistles	2·50	2·50
2705	$5.50 Two people and house	2·50	2·50
2700/2705 *Set of 6*		12·00	12·00
MS2706 170×100 mm. $23.60 As Nos. 2700/2705		13·00	13·00

520 Dove with Letter

(Des Lai Wai-ying. Litho Cartor)

2024 (9 Oct). 150th Anniversary of Universal Postal Union. Sheet 135×85 mm. Granite paper. One phosphor band. Perf 14 (with one elliptical hole on two sides).

MS2707 **520** $10 multicoloured		7·00	7·00

521 Tai Lam Chung Reservoir

(Des Wong Bryan. Litho (Nos. 2708/**MS**2716) or litho and embossed (No. **MS**2717) Enschedé)

2024 (19 Nov). Hong Kong Landscapes. Ten Natural Wonders. T **521** and similar horiz designs. Multicoloured. Granite paper. Two phosphor bands ($2.20) or one phosphor band (others). Perf 13½ (with one elliptical hole on each vert side).

2708	$2.20 Type **521**	2·00	2·00
2709	$2.20 Tai Mo Shan	2·00	2·00
2710	$2.20 Sharp Island	2·00	2·00
2711	$2.20 Shing Mun Reservoir	2·00	2·00
2712	$2.20 Ha Pak Nai	2·00	2·00
2713	$2.20 Tai Tong	2·00	2·00
2714	$2.20 Tung Ping Chau	2·00	2·00
2715	$2.20 Sunset Peak	2·00	2·00
2708/2715 *Set of 8*		11·00	11·00
MS2716 135×90 mm. $10 Tai O Waterways (122×65 mm)		7·00	7·00
MS2717 135×90 mm. $20 High Island Reservoir (122×65 mm)		14·00	14·00

522 Pandas

(Des Wong Fun-fun. Litho Cartor)

2024 (12 Dec). Welcome Giant Pandas. Sheet 135×85 mm. Granite paper. One phosphor band. Perf 13½×14 (with one elliptical hole on each vert side).

MS2718 **522** $10 multicoloured.. 7·00 7·00

523 Cloisonné Enamel Elephant with Vase

(Des Tong Wai-pang. Litho (Nos. 2719/**MS**2725) or litho, embossed and varnish (No. **MS**2726) Brebner Print, New Zealand)

2024 (17 Dec). Hong Kong Palace Museum. T **523** and similar vert and square designs. Multicoloured. Granite paper. Two phosphor bands ($2.20) or one phosphor band (others). Perf 14×13½ (with one elliptical hole on each vert side) (Nos. 2719/2724) or 14½ (with one elliptical hole on each vert side) (Nos. **MS**2725/**MS**2726).

2719	S2.20 Type **523**	2·00	2·00
2720	$2.80 Cloisonné enamel hotpot with flowers	2·25	2·25
2721	$3.70 Old stupa with inlays	2·25	2·25
2722	$4 Painted enamel ewer with flowers and figures in cartouches......................	2·50	2·50
2723	$5.40 Gold double-gourd-shaped hanging with auspicious characters......................	2·50	2·50
2724	$5.50 Jade incense burner in the form of Luduan......................................	2·50	2·50
2719/2724 *Set of 6*..		12·00	12·00

MS2725 135×85 mm. $10 Clock with gilding and painted enamels (*square*) (61×61 mm)..................... 7·00 7·00
MS2726 135×85 mm. $20 Gold 'Son of Heaven' seal with double-headed dragon (*square*) (61×61 mm).. 14·00 14·00

524 Vivian Kong, Fencing

(Des Chan Ching-tsui. Litho Cartor (No. **MS**2727) or Enschedé (No. **MS**2728))

2024 (30 Dec). Medallists of Olympic and Paralympic Summer Games, Paris. Sheet 220×160 mm. T **524** and similar horiz designs. Multicoloured. Granite paper. One phosphor band. Perf 13½ (with one elliptical hole on each vert side) (No. **MS**2727) or 14×13½ (with one elliptical hole on each vert side) (No. **MS**2728).

MS2727 $10×3, Type **524**; Cheung Ka Long, fencing; Siobhán Haughey, swimming................................ 20·00 20·00
MS2828 $10×3, Swimming; Boccia; Badminton,............... 20·00 20·00

MACHINE LABELS

A single machine operated at the GPO from 30 December 1986 issuing 10c., 50c., $1.30 and $1.70 labels showing a Carp. These are inscribed 'O1'. A second machine was installed at Tsim Sha Tsui post office from 18 August 1987 which issued labels coded 'O2'.

From 1987 a new design was introduced each year to reflect the Chinese calendar. Details of the various issues are as follows:

ML1		**ML2**

ML1	Year of the Rabbit 10c., 50c., $1.30, $1.70 (18.8.1987)................................
ML2	Year of the Dragon 10c., 50c., $1.30, $170 (23.3.1988)................................
ML3	Year of the Dragon 10c., 60c., $1.40, $1.80 (1.9.1988)................................
ML4	Year of the Snake 10c., 60c., $1.40, $1.80 (24.2.1989)................................
ML5	Year of the Horse 10c., 60c., $1.40, $1.80 (21.2.1990)................................
ML6	Year of the Ram 10c., 60c., $1.40, $1.80 (21.2.1991)................................
ML7	Year of the Ram 10c., 80c., $1.80, $2.30 (2.4.1991)................................
ML8	Year of the Monkey 10c., 80c., 90c., $1.70, $1.80, $2.30, $5 (12.3.1992)......
ML9	Year of the Cock 10c., 80c., 90c., $1.70, $1.80, $2.30, $5 (10.2.1993)......
ML10	Year of the Cock 10c., $1, $1.90, $2.40 (1.11.1993)................................
ML11	Year of the Dog 10c., 80c., $1, $1.20, $1.30, $1.90, $2, $2.40, $5 (1.3.1994) .....
ML12	Year of the Pig 10c., 80c., $1, $1.20, $1.30, $1.90, $2, $2.40, $5 (15.2.1995)...
ML13	Year of the Rat 10c., $1.20, $1.50, $2.10, $2.30, $2.60, $5 (28.2.1996)......
ML14	Year of the Ox 10c., $1.30, $1.60, $.50, $2.60, $3.10, $5 (12.3.1997)......
ML15	Year of the Tiger 10c., $1.30, $2.50, $3.10, $5 (11.2.1998)...................

From 8 November 1991 the 'O1' machine, in addition to the fixed face values, could be used to produce labels of any value in 10c. steps between 10c. and $5.

A new machine was installed at the GPO and Tsim Sha Tsui post office on 7 December 1998, initially dispensing labels in values from 10c. to $270. The first label design featured flowers.

POSTAGE DUE STAMPS

PRINTERS. Nos. D1/D19 were typographed by De La Rue & Co.

D1 Post office Scales

1923 (1 Dec)–**56**. Wmk Mult Script CA. Ordinary paper. Perf 14.

D1	**D1**	1c. brown..	3·50	75
		a. Wmk sideways (1931).................	1·75	2·50
		ab. Chalk-surfaced paper (21.3.56)......	30	1·00
D2		2c. green..	48·00	12·00
		a. Wmk sideways (1928).................	15·00	5·50
D3		4c. scarlet......................................	55·00	7·50
		a. Wmk sideways (1928).................	35·00	7·50
D4		6c. yellow.......................................	40·00	15·00
		a. Wmk sideways (1931).................	95·00	40·00
D5		10c. bright ultramarine....................	32·00	9·00
		a. Wmk sideways (1934).................	£130	10·00
D1/D5 *Set of 5*			£160	40·00
D1a/D5a *Set of 5*...			£250	55·00
D1s/D5s Optd 'SPECIMEN' *Set of 5*................			£425	

1938 (Feb)–**63**. Wmk Mult Script CA (sideways*). Ordinary paper. Perf 14.

D6	**D1**	2c. grey..	8·00	10·00
		a. Chalk-surfaced paper (21.3.56)......	2·00	12·00
D7		4c. orange	15·00	3·00
		a. Chalk-surfaced paper. *Orange-yellow* (23.5.61)..............	4·50	14·00

D8		6c. scarlet	5·00	5·50
D9		8c. chestnut (26.2.46)	6·50	38·00
D10		10c. violet	30·00	50
		a. Chalk-surfaced paper (17.9.63)	18·00	32·00
D11		20c. black (26.2.46)	7·50	1·75
D12		50c. blue (7.47)	75·00	20·00
D6a/D12 *Set of 7*			£100	70·00
D6s/D12s Perf 'SPECIMEN' *Set of 7*			£475	

* The sideways watermark shows Crown to left of CA, *as seen from the back of the stamps*.

1965 (15 Apr)–**72**. Chalk-surfaced paper. Perf 14.

*(a) W w **12** (sideways*).*

D13	**D1**	4c. yellow-orange	3·50	40·00
D14		5c. red (13.5.69)	2·50	5·00
		a. Glazed paper (17.11.72)	32·00	65·00
D15		10c. violet (27.6.67)	3·50	9·00
D16		20c. black (1965)	6·00	3·50
D17		50c. deep blue (1965)	38·00	8·00
		a. Blue (13.5.69)	28·00	2·00
D13/D17a *Set of 5*			35·00	45·00

* The sideways watermark shows Crown to right of CA (4c.) or to the left of CA (others), *as seen from the back of the stamps*.

*(b) W w **12** (upright).*

D18	**D1**	5c. red (20.7.67)	5·00	9·00
D19		50c. deep blue (26.8.70)	50·00	18·00

The 5c. is smaller, 21×18 mm.

1972 (17 Nov)–**74**. Glazed, ordinary paper. W w **12** (sideways).

(a) Perf 14×14½.

D20	**D1**	10c. bright reddish violet	6·50	4·50
D21		20c. grey-black	7·50	8·00
D22		50c. deep dull blue	4·50	13·00

(b) Perf 13½×14.

D23	**D1**	5c. brown-red (1.5.74)	2·50	7·00
D20/D23 *Set of 4*			19·00	30·00

(Typo Walsall)

1976 (19 Mar)–**78**. Smaller design (21×17 mm) with redrawn value-tablet. Glazed, ordinary paper. W w **14**. Perf 14.

D25	**D1**	10c. bright reddish violet	1·00	7·00
		a. Chalk-surfaced paper (15.12.78)	80	3·00
		aw. Wmk inverted		
D26		20c. grey-black	1·25	8·50
		a. Chalk-surfaced paper (15.12.78)	1·50	3·00
D27		50c. deep dull blue	1·25	5·00
		a. Chalk-surfaced paper (15.12.78)	1·50	3·00
		aw. Wmk inverted		
D28		$1 yellow (1.4.76)	12·00	15·00
		a. Chalk-surfaced paper (15.12.78)	1·40	4·00
D25/D28 *Set of 4*			14·00	32·00
D25a/D28a *Set of 4*			4·75	12·00

*This is the London release date. It is believed that the stamps were not released locally until 14 April.

(Typo Walsall)

1986 (11 Jan). As Nos. D27a/D28a, but without watermark. Perf 14.

D29	**D1**	50c. slate-blue	2·00	6·50
D30		$1 lemon	2·50	10·00

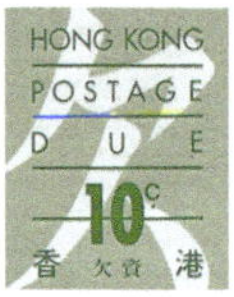

D2

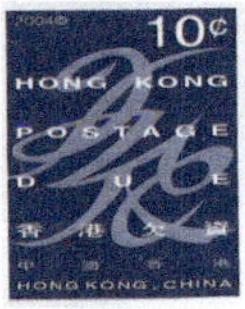

D3

(Des A. Chan. Litho B.D.T)

1987 (25 Mar). Postage Due. Perf 14×15.

D31	**D2**	10c. light green	10	70
D32		20c. red-brown	10	70
D33		50c. bright violet	10	20
D34		$1 yellow-orange	15	30
D35		$5 dull ultramarine	80	2·50
D36		$10 bright rose-red	1·60	4·50
D31/D36 *Set of 6*			2·50	8·00

(Litho Enschedé)

2004 (23 Sept). Postage Due. Perf 14×14½.

D37	**D3**	10c. deep ultramarine	15	20
D38		20c. deep new blue	15	20
D39		50c. bright orange	25	30
D40		$1 bright rose pink	40	50
D41		$5 yellow-green	2·10	2·25
D42		$10 bright magenta	3·75	4·00
D37/D42 *Set of 6*			6·00	6·75

POSTCARD STAMPS

Stamps specially surcharged for use on Postcards.

PRICES. Those in the left-hand column are for unused examples on complete postcards; those on the right for used examples off card. Examples used on postcards are worth much more.

3
CENTS.

(P1)

THREE

(P2)

1879 (1 Apr). Nos. 22 and 13 surch as T **P1** by Noronha & Sons.

P1	**3**	3c. on 16c yellow (No. 22)	£550	£450
P2		5c. on 18c lilac (No. 13)	£550	£500

1879 (Nov). No. P2 handstamped with T **P2**.

P3	**3**	3c. on 5c. on 18c. lilac	£9000	£9000

POSTAL FISCAL STAMPS

I. Stamps inscribed 'STAMP DUTY'

NOTE. The dated circular 'HONG KONG' cancellation with 'PAID ALL' in lower segment was used for fiscal purposes, in black, from 1877. Previously it appears in red on mail to the USA, but is usually not used as a cancellation.

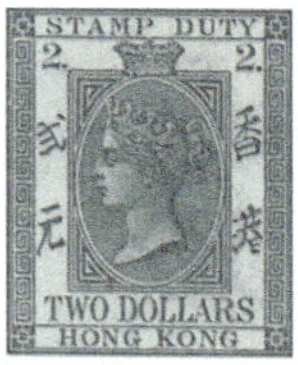

F1

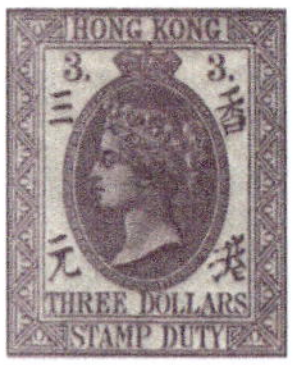

F2

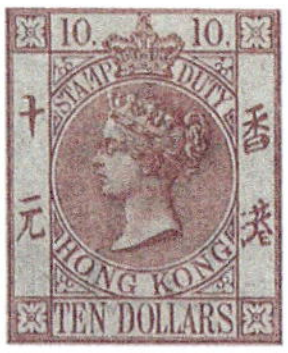

F3

1874–1902. Wmk Crown CC.

(a) Perf 15½×15. Perf 15½×15.

F1	**F1**	$2 olive-green	£425	75·00
F2	**F2**	$3 dull violet	£425	60·00
		b. Bluish paper		
F3	**F3**	$10 rose-carmine	£8500	£850

(b) Perf 14. Perf 14.

F4	**F1**	$2 dull bluish green (10.97)	£475	£300
F5	**F2**	$3 dull mauve (3.02)	£750	£600
		a. Bluish paper	£2500	
F6	**F3**	$10 grey-green	£12000	£11000
F4s/F5s Optd 'SPECIMEN' *Set of 2*			£450	

Nos. F1/F3 and F7 exist on various papers, ranging from thin to thick.

All three of the values perforated 15½×15 were authorised for postal use in 1874. The $10 rose-carmine was withdrawn from such use in 1880, the $2 in September 1897 and the $3 in 1902.

The $2 and $3 perforated 14 were available for postal purposes until July 1903.

The $10 in grey-green was issued for fiscal purposes in 1884 and is known with postal cancellations.

12
CENTS.

(F4)

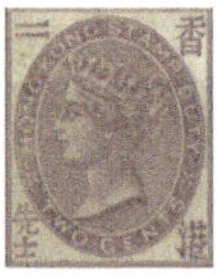

(F5)

1880. No. F3 surch with T **F4** by Noronha and Sons, Hong Kong.

F7	**F3**	12c. on $10 rose-carmine	£1000	£400

1890 (24 Dec). Wmk Crown CA. Perf 14.

F8	**F5**	2c. dull purple	£200	50·00
		w. Wmk inverted	£2500	

No. F8 was authorised for postal use between 24 and 31 December 1890.

5 DOLLARS
(F6)

ONE DOLLAR
(F7)

(F8)

1891 (1 Jan). Surch with T **F6** by D.L.R. Wmk Crown CA. Perf 14.
F9 **F3** $5 on $10 purple/*red*.................. £450 £130
s. Optd 'SPECIMEN' £350
No. F9 was in use for postal purposes until June 1903.

1897 (Sept). Surch with T **F7** by Noronha and Sons, Hong Kong, and with the value in Chinese characters subsequently applied twice by handstamp as T **15**.
F10 **F1** $1 on $2 olive-green (No. F1) £250 £140
a. Both Chinese handstamps omitted £4250 £3000
b. Diagonal Chinese handstamp omitted £22000
F11 $1 on $2 dull bluish green (No. F4) £300 £160
a. Both Chinese handstamps omitted £2000 £1700
b. Diagonal Chinese handstamp omitted £40000
c. Vertical Chinese handstamp omitted ....
s. Handstamped 'SPECIMEN' £150

1938 (11 Jan). Wmk Mult Script CA. Perf 14.
F12 **F8** 5c. green .... £100 17·00
No. F12 was authorised for postal use between 11 and 20 January 1938 due to a shortage of 5c., No 121.
Forged cancellations are known on this stamp inscribed 'VICTORIA 9.AM 11 JA 38 HONG KONG' without side bars between the rings.

II. Stamps overprinted 'S.O.' (Stamp Office) or 'S.D.' (Stamp Duty)

(S1)   (S2)

1891 (1 Jan). Optd with T **S1** or T **S2**.
S1 **S1** 2c. carmine (No. 33) £1000 £400
S2 **S2** 2c. carmine (No. 33) £650 £225
a. Opt inverted .... † £9000
S3 **S1** 10c. purple/*red* (No. 38) £2250 £475
Examples of No. S1 exist with the 'O' amended to 'D' in manuscript.

Other fiscal stamps are found apparently postally used, but there is no evidence that this use was authorised.

STAMP BOOKLETS

BOOKLET CONTENTS. In Nos. SB1/SB4 and SB6/SB7 the 1c. and 2c. were each in blocks of 12 and the 4c. in blocks of 12 and 4, all having been taken from normal sheets. No. SB5 had both the 2c. and 4c. in blocks of 12 and 4 or as two blocks of 8. Other content formats exist.

The 'metal fastener' used for Nos. SB2/SB2b, SB3 and SB7ca was a Hotch-kiss 'Herringbone' stapler.

1904 (1 Jan). Black on cream cover showing contents and postage rates with 'K & W LD' imprint on front. Stapled.
SB1 $1 booklet containing 12×1c. (No. 62), 12×2c. (No. 56) and 16×4c. (No. 57) ....
a. 4c. No. 64 (King Edward VII) instead of No. 57 (Q.V.) £9000

1905 (May)–**07**. Black on cream cover showing contents and postage rates with 'Hongkong Printing Press' imprint on front. Metal fastener.
SB2 $1 booklet containing 12×1c., 12×2c. and 16×4c. (Nos. 62/64) £7000
a. 2c. and 4c. (Nos. 77/78) (MCA ordinary paper) instead of Nos. 63/64 (CA) (3.06)................................. £9000
b. 2c. and 4c. (Nos. 77a/78a) (MCA chalk-surfaced paper) instead of Nos. 77/78 (MCA ordinary paper) (1.07) £10000

Some examples of No. SB2 show the reference to Australia on the front cover officially deleted in manuscript.
No. SB2a has the rate information reset to omit 'EXCEPT AUSTRALIA'.

1907 (Nov)–**10**. Black on cream cover showing contents and postage rates for both Hong Kong and Agencies in China with 'Hongkong Printing Press' imprint. Metal fastener.
SB3 $1 booklet containing 12×1c. (No. 62), 12×2c. (No. 92) and 16×4c. (No. 93) ....
a. Stapled (6.10) £5500

1911 (Jan)–**12**. Black on cream cover showing contents, but no postage rates, with 'Hongkong Printing Press' imprint on front. Stapled.
SB4 $1 booklet containing 12×1c. (No. 62), 12×2c. (No. 92) and 16×4c. (No. 93) ....
a. 1c. No. 91 (MCA) instead of No. 62 (CA) (7.12) (off-white cover) £5500

1912 (July). Black on cream cover showing contents, but no postage rates, with 'Hongkong Printing Press' imprint on front. Stapled.
SB5 $1 booklet containing 4×1c., 16×2c. and 16×4c. (Nos. 91/93) £700

1913 (Mar). Black on cream cover showing contents, but no postage rates, with 'Hongkong Printing Press' imprint on front. Stapled.
SB6 $1 booklet containing 12×1c., 12×2c. and 16×4c. (Nos. 100/102) (MCA wmk) £4500

1922 (June). Black on cream cover showing contents, but no postage rates, with 'Hongkong Printing Press' imprint on front. Inscribed 'Price $1'. Stapled.
SB7 $1 booklet containing 12×1c., 12×2c. and 16×4c. (Nos. 117/118, 120) (Script wmk)............................. £5000

1923 (Jan)–**25**. Black on grey cover showing contents but no postage rates, with 'Ye Olde Printerie' imprint on front. Inscribed 'Price $1'. Stapled.
SB7a $1 With 'Ye Olde Printerie' imprint (1.23).... £6000
b. Imprint revised to 'Ye Older Printerie Ltd' (5.23) ....
c. Inscribed 'Price $' (9.24) £6000
ca. Bound with Metal fastener (2.25) ....

1965 (10 May). Orange-brown (No. SB8) or yellow-green (No. SB9) covers. Stitched.
SB8 $2 booklet containing 8×5c. and 16×10c. (Nos. 196/197) in blocks of 4 .... 35·00
SB9 $5 booklet containing 12×5c., 8×10c., 8×20c. and 4×50c. (Nos. 196/197, 199, 203) in blocks of 4.......................... £120

1973 (12 June). Buff (No. SB10) or green (No. SB11) covers. Stitched.
SB10 $2 booklet containing 20×10c. (No. 283) in blocks of 4 .... 45·00
SB11 $5 booklet containing 8×10c., 4×15c., 8×20c. and 4×50c. (Nos. 283, 284/285, 289) each in blocks of 4 .... 90·00

1975 (27 Jan). Covers as Nos. SB10/SB11. Stitched.
SB12 $2 booklet containing 20×10c. (No. 311) in blocks of 4 .... 45·00
SB13 $5 booklet containing 8×10c., 4×15c., 8×20c. and 4×50c. (Nos. 311/313, 317) in blocks of 4 .... 90·00

1976 (1 July). Orange (No. SB14) or green (No. SB15) covers. Stitched.
SB14 $2 booklet containing 4×10c. and 8×20c. (Nos. 311, 313) in blocks of 4 .... 16·00
SB15 $5 booklet containing 8×10c., 4×15c., 8×20c. and 4×50c. (Nos. 311, 284, 313, 289) in blocks of 4........................ 75·00

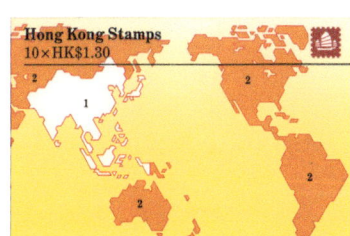

B1 World Map

1985 (1 Apr). Multicoloured cover as T **B1**. Stamps attached by selvedge.
SB16 $13 booklet containing $1.30 (No. 464) in block of 10........................... 42·00
a. Containing No. 469 in block of 10 .... 22·00

b. Containing No. 490 in block of 10
(June) .... 55·00
c. Containing No. 500 in block of 10
(Sept) .... 65·00
d. Containing No. 504 in block of 10
(Nov) .... 55·00

Supplies of a similar $13 booklet, but containing ten examples of No.
495, were produced for sale by the Crown Agents Stamp Bureau. Such
booklets are reported not to have been available from post offices in
Hong Kong.

1985 (2 Sept)–**87**. Multicoloured cover as T **B1**. Stamps attached by
selvedge.
SB18 $17 booklet containing $1.70 (No. 482) in
block of 10... 45·00
a. Containing No. 547A in block of 10
(1987) .... 29·00

1985 (28 Oct)–**87**. Multicoloured cover as T **B1**, showing map of Hong
Kong. Stamps attached by selvedge.
SB19 $5 booklet containing 50c. (No. 475) in
block of 10... 7·50
a. Containing No. 540 in block of 10
(1987) .... 7·00

B2 Hong Kong Bank Headquarters and Lion's Head
(*Illustration further reduced. Actual size 159×86 mm*)

1986 (7 Apr). New Hong Kong Bank Headquarters. Multicoloured cover
as T **B2**. Booklet contains text and illustrations on interleaving pages.
Stitched.
SB20 $29 booklet containing 50c. in block of 24
(sideways) and $1 in block of 10 (Nos.
475, 505)... 40·00

B3 Early and Modern Views of the Peak Tramway
(*Illustration further reduced. Actual size 161×91 mm*)

1988 (26 Aug). Centenary of The Peak Tramway. Multicoloured cover as
T **B3**. Booklet contains text and illustrations on interleaving pages.
Stitched.
SB21 $26 booklet containing No. **MS**581×3 .... 24·00

B4 (*Illustration futher reduced. Actual size 145×55
mm*)

1989 (18 Jan). Year of the Snake. Multicoloured cover as T **B4**. Pane
attached by selvedge.
SB22 $12 booklet containing *se-tenant* pane of
10 (No. 587a)... 8·50

B5 (*Illustration further reduced. Actual size 140×65
mm*)

1990 (23 Jan). Year of the Horse. Multicoloured cover as T **B5** Pane
attached by selvedge.
SB23 $14.50 booklet containing two *se-tenant*
panes of 6 (No. 631a).................................... 13·00
Face value of stamps $14.40.

1990 (3 May). Stamp World London 90 International Stamp Exhibition. As
No. SB23, but Stamp World London 90 emblem printed on cover and
top selvedge of each pane.
SB24 $14.50 booklet. Contents as No. SB23 .... 19·00
No. SB24 additionally includes an imperforate black print on gummed
paper of the 60c. and $1.80 values of the New Year issue.

B6 Hong Kong Skyline at Night (*Illustration further
reduced. Actual size 168×86 mm*)

1990 (29 Nov). Centenary of Electricity Supply. Multicoloured cover as
T **B6**. Booklet contains text and illustrations on interleaving pages.
Stitched.
SB25 $26 booklet containing No. **MS**651×4 .... 25·00

1991 (24 Jan). Year of the Ram. Multicoloured cover as T **B5**. Pane attached
by selvedge.
SB26 $14.40 booklet containing two *se-tenant*
panes of 6 (No. 658a).................................... 9·00

1992 (22 Jan). Year of the Monkey. Multicoloured cover as T **B5**. Panes
attached by selvedge.
SB27 $18.60 booklet conaining two *se-tenant*
panes of 6 (No. 686a).................................... 11·00

B7 'Greetings' (*Illustration further reduced. Actual size
153×67 mm*)

1992 (19 Nov). Greetings Stamps. Multicoloured cover as T **B7**. Panes
attached by selvedge.
SB28 $24 booklet containing two *se-tenant*
panes of 6 (No. 728a) and 24 half
stamp-size labels .... 9·00

1993 (7 Jan). Year of the Cock. Multicoloured cover as T **B5**. Panes attached
by selvedge.
SB29 $18.60 booklet containing two *se-tenant*
panes of 6 (No. 732a).................................... 8·00

B8 Skyscrapers

1993 (14-28 Dec). Multicoloured cover as T **B8** Panes attached to selvedge.

SB30	$10 booklet containing pane of 10×$1 (No. 757a)	9·00
SB31	$19 booklet containing pane of 10×$1.90 (No. 758a) (cover showing Exhibition Centre) (28.12)	13·00
SB32	$24 booklet containing pane of 10×$2.40 (No. 759a) (cover showing historical buildings) (28.12)	14·00

B10 Waterfront

1997 (26 Jan). Multicoloured covers as T **B10**, each incorporating the design from the stamps included. Panes attached by selvedge.

SB43	$13 booklet containing pane of 10×$1.30 (No. 853a)	3·25
SB44	$25 booklet containing pane of 10×$2.50 (No. 858a)	4·75
SB45	$31 booklet containing pane of 10×$3.10 (No. 859a)	5·00

B9 (*Illustration further reduced. Actual size* 160×85 mm)

1994 (12 Jan). 'A History of Hong Kong definitive stamps 1862–1992'. Multicoloured cover T **B9**. Booklet contains text and illustrations on pane and interleaving pages. Stapled.

SB33	booklet containing three different se-tenant panes of 6 (No. 760a/762a)	16·00
	a. With all panes inverted	

No. SB33a shows all panes in the booklet inverted so that they are stapled at the right of the panes and show untrimmed binding margins at left. Face value of stamps $30.80.

1994 (27 Jan). Year of the Dog. Multicoloured cover as T **B5**. Panes attached by selvedge.

SB34	$20.40 booklet containing two se-tenant panes of 6 (No 766a)	11·00

1995 (17 Jan). Year of the Pig. Multicoloured cover as T **B5**. Panes attached by selvedge.

SB35	$20.40 booklet containing two se-tenant panes of 6 (No 793a)	8·00

1995 (1 June). Multicoloured covers as Nos. SB30/SB32. Panes attached by selvedge.

SB36	$12 booklet containing pane of 10×$1.20 (No. 757ba) (Type **B8** cover)	6·50
SB37	$21 booklet containing pane of 10×$2.10 (No. 758ba) (cover as SB31)	8·50
SB38	$26 booklet containing pane of 10×$2.60 (No. 759ca) (cover as SB32)	8·50

On the initial supply of No. SB36 the inside of the card covers were matt. A printing later in 1995 showed both sides of the cover card glossy.

1996 (31 Jan). Year of the Rat. Multicoloured cover as T **B5**. Panes attached by selvedge.

SB39	$22.80 booklet containing two se-tenant panes of 6 (No. 816a)	5·00

1996 (2 Sept). Multicoloured covers as No. SB30/SB32. Panes attached by selvedge.

SB40	$13 booklet containing pane of 10×$1.30 (No. 757ca) (Type **B8** cover)	4·50
SB41	$25 booklet containing pane of 10×$2.50 (No. 759ba) (cover as No. SB31)	5·50
SB42	$31 booklet containing pane of 10×$3.10 (No. 759da) (cover as No. SB32)	5·50

B11 Hong Kong Waterfront (*Illustration further reduced. Actual size* 183×130 mm)

1997 (14 Feb). Hong Kong Past and Present. Multicoloured cover as T **B11**. Booklet containing text and illustrations on interleaving pages. Stitched.

SB46	$55 booklet containing three different se-tenant panes of 6 (Nos. 757cc, 757db and 758bd)	20·00
	Face value of stamps $45.	

1997 (27 Feb). Year of the Ox. Multicoloured cover as T **B5**. Panes attached by selvedge.

SB47	$26.40 booklet containing two panes of 6 (No. 879a)	6·00

1998 (4 Jan). Year of the Tiger. Multicoloured cover as T **B5** of British Crown Colony, but 150×65 mm. Pane attached by selvedge.

SB48	$26.40 booklet containing one pane of 12 (915ab)	14·50

B12 Waterfront (*Illustration further reduced. Actual size* 100×64 mm)

1999 (18 Oct). Multicoloured covers as T **B12**. Panes attached by selvedge.

SB49	$13 booklet containing pane of 10×$1.30 (No. 978a)	5·00
SB50	$25 booklet containing pane of 10×$2.50 (No. 983a)	11·50
SB51	$31 booklet containing pane of 10×$3.10 (No. 984a)	15·00

B13 (*Illustration further reduced. Actual size 100×64 mm*)

2002 (1 Apr). Covers as T **B13**. Stamps affixed by selvedge.
SB52 $14 booklet containing pane of 10×$1.40
      (No. 979a) (cover bright mauve and
      violet) .... 5·00
SB53 $24 booklet containing pane of 10×$2.40
      (No. 982ab) (cover bright greenish
      blue and violet) .... 11·50
SB54 $30 booklet containing pane of 10×$3
      (No. 983bc) (cover yellow-orange and
      violet) .... 15·00

B15a Waterbirds (*Illustration further reduced. Actual size 104×69 mm*)

2003 (4 Oct). Multicoloured cover as T **B15a**. Stamps affixed by selvedge.
SB58*a* $23.60 booklet containing 2 panes of 4 (No.
      1186a) .... 10·00

B14 Bakery Goods (Illustration further reduced. Actual size 100×76 mm)

2002 (14 Oct). Multicoloured covers as T **B14**. Stamps affixed by selvedge.
SB55 $14 booklet containing pane of 10×$1.40
      (No. 1123a) .... 5·50
SB56 $24 booklet containing pane of 10×$2.40
      (No. 1127a) .... 9·00
SB57 $30 booklet containing pane of 10×$3 (No.
      1129a) .... 11·50

B16 Shapes and Binary Code (*Illustration reduced. Actual size 100×78 mm*)

2005 (21 July). Covers as T **B16**. Stamps affixed by selvedge.
SB59 $47.20 booklet containing 2 panes of 8 (No.
      1311a) .... 21·00

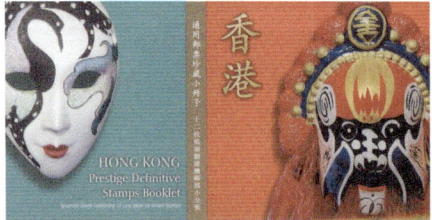

B15 Masks (*Illustration further reduced. Actual size 182×88 mm*)

2002 (14 Oct). Covers as T **B15**. Stamps affixed by selvedge.
SB58 $21.80 booklet containing pane of 12 (No.
      1119a) .... 8·75

B16a Pelican (*Illustration reduced. Actual size 145×113 mm*)

2006 (31 Dec). Covers as T **B16a**. Stamps affixed by selvedge.
SB59*a* $21.80 booklet containing pane of 12 (No.
      1398a) .... 9·75

B17 Forked-tailed Sunbird (*Illustration reduced. Actual size 101×65 mm*)

2006 (31 Dec). Covers as T **B17**. Stamps affixed by selvedge.
SB60 $14 booklet containing pane of 10 (No.
        1402a) ....   6·50

B18 Roseate Tern (*Illustration reduced. Actual size 101×65 mm*)

2006 (31 Dec). Covers as T **B18**. Stamps affixed by selvedge.
SB61 $18 booklet containing pane of 10 (No.
        1403a) ....   8·50

B19 Greater Painted Snipe (*Illustration reduced. Actual size 101×65 mm*)

2006 (31 Dec). Covers as T **B19**. Stamps affixed by selvedge.
SB62 $24 booklet containing pane of 10 (No.
        1406a) ....   10·50

B20 Red-whiskered Bulbul (*Illustration reduced. Actual size 101×165 mm*)

2006 (31 Dec). Covers as T **B20**. Stamps affixed by selvedge.
SB63 $30 booklet containing pane of 10 (No.
        1408a) ....   14·00

2013 (1 Oct). Greetings Stamps. Covers as T **B19**. Stamps affixed by selvage.
SB64 $17 booklet containing pane of 10 (No.
      1818ba) ....   8·50
SB65 $37 booklet containing pane of 10 (No.
      1818da) ....   20·00

2016 (13 Oct). Hong Kong Hiking Trails. Covers as T **B20**. Self-adhesive.
SB66 $20.40 booklet containing pane of 12 (Nos.
      2043/2054) ....   8·50

PREMIUM BOOKLETS

The following booklets were sold at a premium over the face value of the stamps contained. All booklets are stitched, have multicoloured covers, and have text and illustrations on panes and interleaving pages. All stamps are inscribed 'HONG KONG, CHINA' (except the designs as No. 859 from the second pane of No. SP6) and the panes have margins all round.

1999 (25 Mar). Hong Kong Maritime Heritage.
SP1 $25 booklet containing two panes of Nos.
      920/923 ....   45·00
   No. SP1 contains stamps with a face value of $11.90 and commemorates Australia 99 International Stamp Exhibition, Melbourne.

1999 (18 Oct). Hong Kong Landmarks and Tourist Attractions.
SP2 $35 booklet containing Nos. 973/985 in 13
           single-stamp panes ....   18·00
   Face value of stamps $22.

2000 (17 June). Nature.
SP3 $35 booklet containing three panes of
           single $5 stamps in re-drawn designs
           as Nos. 501, 840 and 998, all with one
           phosphor band and one elliptical hole
           on each vert side..........................   18·00
   No. SP3 contains stamps with a face value of $15. The pane containing No. 840 is perforated 14 and the others 14½×14.

2000 (30 Sept). Wetland Birds' Paradise.
SP4 $25 booklet containing two panes each
           of one *se-tenant* pair as Nos. 884/887
           in re-drawn designs, perforated 14½
           with one elliptical hole on each vert
           side..........................   14·50
   No. SP4 was issued to commemorate the opening of Phase One of the International Wetland Park, Tin Shui Wai, New Territories, Hong Kong.
   Face value of stamps $11.90.

2001 (21 July). Centenary of CLP Power.
SP5 $30 booklet containing two panes each
           containing two values as Nos. 572/575
           in re-drawn designs, with new values
           and printed by Questa ($1.30 As No.
           573, $2.50 Type **132**; $3.10 As No. 574,
           $5 As No. 575) ....   16·00
   Face value of stamps $11.90.

2001 (25 Aug). 160th Anniversary of Hong Kong Post Office.
SP6 $65 booklet containing three panes: Pane
           1: As No. 719×4 but re-drawn, with
           two phosphor bands and perforated
           with one elliptical hole on each vert
           side: Pane 2: Two pairs, as No. 984×2
           but perforated 13½×14 and No. 859×2,
           all with one phosphor band: Pane 3: As
           No. 927×4 but perforated 14×14½.........   30·00
   Face value of stamps $30.

2002 (14 Apr). Cyber Industry in Hong Kong.
SP7 $30 booklet containing two panes each of
           two stamps, Nos. 1091 and 1093, and
           Nos. 1092 and 1094 ....   16·00
   Face value of stamps $11.80.

2003 (10 May). Hong Kong Hoi Ha Wan Marine Park.
SP8 $25 booklet containing two panes each of
           one *se-tenant* pair as Nos. 1097/1098
           and 1099/1100 but all perforated
           13½×13 and $2.40 value with only one
           phosphor band. Each pair is presented
           within a panel perforated 14½............   14·50
   Face value of stamps $11.80.

2003 (16 Oct). First Chinese Manned Space Flight.
SP9 $12.80 booklet containing two panes of text
           and three panes each containing a
           se-tenant pair: Pane 1: Nos. 4851/4852
           of China: Pane 2: Nos. 1191/1192 and
           Pane 3: Nos 1376/1377 of Macau...........   14·50
   Face value of stamps 2y.80; $2.40 and $2.50.

2004 (30 June). Armed Forces.
SP10 $85 booklet containing 12 panes of text
          and six panes each containing a *se-
          tenant* block of four examples of Nos.
          1249/1254, respectively .... 45·00
    Face value of stamps $64.40.

2006 (30 Mar). Dress up Bear.
SP11 $30 booklet containing Nos. 1342/1347
          and a pane of stickers .... 14·00
    Face value of stamps $16.10.

2006 (12 Nov). 140th Birth Anniversary of Sun Yat-Sen.
SP12 $25 booklet containing three panes of
          text and two panes each containing a
          se-tenant pair: Pane 1: Nos. 1389/1390
          and Pane 2: Nos. 1391/1392 .... 13·00
    Face value of stamps $11.80.

2007 (22 Mar). Bunny Fun.
SP13 $36 booklet containing Nos. 1440/1445 ...... 17·00
    Face value of stamps $16.10.

2007 (14 June). Butterflies.
SP14 $38 booklet containing four panes of
          text and two panes of stamps: Pane
          1: containing a *se-tenant* strip of
          three stamps, Nos. 1453/1455: Pane
          2: containing a *se-tenant* pair, Nos.
          1456/1457 .... 24·00
    Face value of stamps $16.10.

2008 (12 June). Jellyfish.
SP15 $36 booklet containing five panes of text
          and two panes of stamps. Pane 1 Nos.
          1510/1511; Pane 2 Nos. 1512/1513
          and Pane 3 Nos. 1514/1515 .... 24·00
    Face value of stamps $16.10.

2012 (19 June). Working Dogs in Government Service.
SP16 $45 booklet containing 15 panes of text
          and three panes of stamps: Pane
          1: Nos. 1718/1719: Pane 2: Nos.
          1720/1721 and Pane 3: Nos. 1722/1723   18·00

2012 (8 Dec). 150th Anniversary of Stamp Issuance in Hong Kong.
SP17 $50 booklet containing 15 panes of
          text and three panes of stamps.
          Pane 1 Nos. 1769/1771; Pane 2 Nos.
          1772/1774 and Pane 3 the stamp of
          No. **MS**1775 .... 18·00
    Face value of stamps $26.10.

2013 (7 May). Revitalisation of Historic Buildings in Hong Kong.
SP18 $45 booklet containing 15 panes of
          text and three panes of stamps.
          Pane 1 Nos. 1794/1795; Pane 2 Nos.
          1796/1797 and Pane 3 Nos. 1798/1799   16·00
    Face value of stamps $16.10.

2013 (24 Sept). Hong Kong Buses.
SP19 $50 booklet containing 12 panes of text
          and three panes of stamps. Pane 1: Nos.
          1811/1813; Pane 2: Nos. 1814/1816 and
          Pane 3: Stamp of No. **MS**1817................... 17·00
    Face value of stamps $21.10.

2014 (27 Mar). Weather Phenomena.
SP20 $53 booklet containing 12 pages
          of text and three panes of stamps.
          Pane 1: Nos. 1856/1858; Pane 2: Nos.
          1859/1861 and Pane 3: No. **MS**1862...... 24·00
    Face value of stamps $23.60.

2015 (17 Mar). Astronomical Phenomena.
SP21 $60 booklet containing 11 pages
          of text and two panes of stamps.
          Pane 1: Nos. 1940/1942; Pane 2: Nos.
          1943/1945 and Pane 3: the stamp of
          No. **MS**1946 .... 18·00
    Face value of stamps $28.60.

2015 (21 May). Government Vessels.
SP22 $50 booklet containing nine panes of
          text and three panes of stamps.
          Pane 1: Nos. 1960/1961; Pane 2: Nos.
          1962/1963 and Pane 3: Nos. 1964/1965   20·00
    Face value of stamps $18.60.

2016 (22 Feb). Centenary of Hong Kong Girl Guides.
SP23 $45 booklet containing five panes of text
          and two panes of stamps. Pane 1 Nos.
          1997/1998 and Pane 2 Nos. 1999/2000   20·00
    Face value of stamps $13.30.

2016 (14 Apr). Centenary of Hong Kong St John Ambulance Brigade.
SP24 $45 booklet containing six panes of text
          and two panes of stamps. Pane 1: Nos.
          2009/2010 and Pane 2: Nos. 2011/2012   20·00
    Face value of stamps $13.30.

2016 (12 Nov). 150th Birth Anniversary of Sun Yat-sen.
SP25 $45 booklet containing nine panes of text
          and two panes of stamps. Pane 1: Nos.
          2055/2056 and Pane 2: Nos. 2057/2058   20·00
    Face value of stamps $13.30.

2017 (25 Apr). Revitalisation of Historic Buildings in Hong Kong.
SP26 $50 booklet containing 15 panes of
          text and three panes of stamps.
          Pane 1: Nos. 2076/2077; Pane 2:
          Nos. 2078/2079 and Pane 3: Nos.
          2080/2081. .... 24·00
    Face value of stamps $18.60.

2017 (13 June). Centenary of Typhoon Signals.
SP27 $45 booklet containing ten panes of text
          and two panes of stamps. Pane 1: Nos.
          2090/2092; Pane 2: Nos. 2093/2094....... 18·00
    Face value of stamps $15.50.

2017 (17 Oct). Qipao.
SP28 $60 booklet containing 12 panes of text
          and two panes of stamps. Pane 1: Nos.
          2128/2130; Pane 2: Nos. 2131/2133....... 35·00
    Face value of stamps $18.60.

2018 (9 Oct). Catonese Opera Repertory.
SP29 $35 booklet containing 12 panes
          of text and two panes of stamps.
          Pane 1 Nos. 2205/2206; Pane 2 Nos.
          2207/2208, all with one phosphor
          band .... 22·00
    No. SP29 contains stamps with a face value of $11.70

2019 (28 Feb). Government Flying Service. Operations.
SP30 $63 booklet containing 12 panes
          of text and four panes of stamps.
          Pane 1 Nos. 2234/2235; Pane 2 Nos.
          2236/2237, Pane 3 Nos. 2238/2239;
          Pane 4 No. **MS**2240 .... 35·00
    No. SP30 contains stamps with a face value of $31.60

2019 (2 Apr). Centenary of Pok Oi Hospital.
SP31 $48 booklet containing eight panes
          of text and two panes of stamps.
          Pane 1 Nos. 2244/2245; Pane 2 Nos.
          2246/2247 .... 22·00
    No. SP31 contains stamps with a face value of $15.60

2019 (30 Apr). Our Police Force.
SP32 $53 booklet containing seven panes
          of text and three panes of stamps.
          Pane 1 Nos. 2249/2250; Pane 2 Nos.
          2251/2252; Pane 3 Nos. 2253/2254........ 28·00
    No. SP32 contains stamps with a face value of $21.60

Where the same design, or subject, appears more than once in a set only the first number is given.

JAPANESE OCCUPATION OF HONG KONG

Hong Kong surrendered to the Japanese on 25 December 1941. The postal service was not resumed until 22 January 1942 when the GPO and Kowloon Central Office re-opened.

Japanese postmarks used in Hong Kong can be identified by the unique combination of horizontal lines in the central circle and three stars in the lower segment of the outer circle.

Dates shown on such postmarks are in the sequence Year/Month/Day with the first shown as a Japanese regnal year number so that Showa 17 = 1942 and so on.

Initially six current definitives, 1s., 2s., 3s., 4s., 10s. and 30s. (Nos. 297, 315/317, 322 and 327) were on sale, but the range gradually expanded to cover all values between ½s. and 10y. with

Nos. 313/314, 318, 325, 328/331, 391, 395/396, 398/399 and 405 of Japan also available from Hong Kong post offices during the occupation.

Philatelic covers exist showing other Japanese stamps, but these were not available from the local post offices. Supply of these Japanese stamps was often interrupted and, during the period between 28 July 1942 and 21 April 1943, circular 'Postage Paid' handstamps were sometimes used. A substantial increase in postage rates on 16 April 1945 led to the issue of the local surcharges, Nos. J1/J3.

PRICES FOR STAMPS ON COVER	
Nos. J1/J3	from × 7

(1)   (2)

1945 (16 Apr). Stamps of Japan surch with T **1** (No. J1) or as T **2**.
J1	1.50yen on 1s. brown	42·00	35·00
J2	3yen on 2s. scarlet	16·00	28·00
J3	5yen on 5s. claret	£950	£170

Designs: (18½×22 mm)—1s. Girl Worker; 2s. General Nogi; 5s. Admiral Togo.

No. J3 has four characters of value similarly arranged but differing from T **2**.

BRITISH POST OFFICES IN CHINA

Under the terms of the 1842 Treaty of Nanking, China granted Great Britain and its citizens commercial privileges in five Treaty Ports, Amoy, Canton, Foochow, Ningpo and Shanghai. British Consuls were appointed to each Port and their offices, as was usual during this period, collected and distributed mail for the British community. This system was formally recognised by a Hong Kong Government notice published on 16 April 1844. Mail from the consular offices was postmarked when it passed through Hong Kong.

The number of Chinese Treaty Ports was increased to 16 by the ratification of the Treaty of Peking in 1860 with British postal facilities being eventually extended to the Port of Chefoo, Hankow, Kiungchow (Hoihow), Swatow, Tainan (Anping) and Tientsin.

As postal businesses expanded the consular agencies were converted into packet agencies or post offices which passed under the direct control of the Hong Kong postal authorities on 1 May 1868.

In May 1898 the British Government leased the territory of Wei Hai Wei from China for use as a naval station to counter the Russian presence at Port Arthur.

The opening of the Trans-Siberian Railway and the extension of Imperial Penny Postage to the Treaty Port agencies resulted in them becoming a financial burden on the colonial post office. Control of the agencies reverted to the GPO, London, on 1 January 1911.

The pre-adhesive postal markings of the various agencies are a fascinating, but complex, subject. Full details can be found in Hong Kong & the Treaty Ports of China & Japan by F. W. Webb (reprinted edition J. Bendon, Limassol, 1992) and in various publications of the Hong Kong Study Circle.

From 15 October 1864 the use of Hong Kong stamps on mail from the Treaty Ports became compulsory, although such stamps were, initially, not cancelled (with the exception of Amoy) until they reached Hong Kong where the 'B62' killer was applied. Cancellation of mail at the actual Ports commenced during 1866 at Shanghai and Ningpo, spreading to all the agencies during the next ten years. Shanghai had previously used a c.d.s. on adhesives during 1863 and again in 1865–1866.

The main types of cancellation used between 1866 and 1930 are illustrated below. The illustrations show the style of each postmark and no attempt has been made to cover differences in type letters of figures, arrangements, diameter or colour.

Until 1885 the vertical and horizontal killers were used to obliterate the actual stamps with an impression of one of the circular date stamps shown elsewhere on the cover. Many of the early postmarks were also used as backstamps or transit marks and, in the notes which follow, references to use are for the first appearance of the mark, not necessarily its first use as an obliterator.

Illustrations in this section are taken from Hong Kong & the Treaty Ports of China & Japan by F. W. Webb and are reproduced with the permission of the Royal Philatelic Society, London.

Details of the stamps known used from each post office are taken, with permission, from British Post Offices in the Far East by Edward B. Proud, published by Proud-Bailey Co. Ltd.

Postmark Types

Type **A** Vertical Killer   Type **B** Horizontal killer

Type **C** Name horizontal   Type **D** Name curved

Type **E** Double circle Name at top   Type **F** Double circle Name at foot

Type **G** Single circle Name at top

PRICES. The prices quoted in this section are for fine used stamps which show a clear impression of a substantial part of the cancellation.

AMOY

One of the five original Treaty Ports, opened to British trade by the Treaty of Nanking in 1842. A consular postal agency was established in 1844 which expanded in 1876 into two separate offices, one on the off-shore island of Ku Lang Seu and the other in Amoy itself.

Amoy 'PAID' (supplied 1858) used 1859–1867

Type **A** ('A1') (supplied 1866) used at Ku Lang Seu 1869–1882

Type **D** (supplied 1866) used 1867–1922

Type **B** ('D.27') (supplied 1876) used at Amoy 1876–1884

Type **C** used 1876–1894

Type **F** (supplied 1913) used 1916–1922

Stamps of HONG KONG cancelled at Amoy between 1864 and 1916 with postmarks detailed above.

1862. No wmk (Nos. 1/7).
Z1	2c. brown	£300
Z2	8c. yellow-buff	£275
Z3	12c. pale greenish blue	£250
Z4	18c. lilac	£200
Z5	24c. green	£300
Z6	48c. rose	£1500
Z7	96c. brownish grey	£1200

1863–71. Wmk Crown CC (Nos. 8/19).
Z8	2c. brown	40·00
Z9	4c. grey	45·00
	a. Perf 12½	
Z10	6c. lilac	75·00
Z11	8c. orange	55·00
Z12	12c. blue	25·00
Z13	18c. lilac	£1100
Z14	24c. green	70·00
Z15	30c. vermilion	£170
Z16	30c. mauve	22·00
Z17	48c. rose	90·00
Z18	96c. olive-bistre	£3500
Z19	96c. brownish grey	£400

1876–77. (Nos. 20/21).
Z20	16c. on 18c. lilac	£375
Z21	28c. on 30c. mauve	£170

1877. Wmk Crown CC (No. 22).
Z22	16c. yellow	£150

1880. (Nos. 23/27).
Z23	5c. on 8c. orange	£160
Z24	5c. on 18c. lilac	£110
Z25	10c. on 12c. blue	£110
Z26	10c. on 16c. yellow	£250
Z27	10c. on 24c. green	£180

1880. Wmk Crown CC (Nos. 28/31).
Z28	2c. rose	75·00
Z29	5c. blue	£110
Z30	10c. mauve	95·00
Z31	48c. brown	£375

1882–96. Wmk Crown CA (Nos. 32/39).
Z31a	2c. rose-lake	85·00
Z32	2c. carmine	6·00
Z33	4c. slate-grey	20·00
Z34	5c. blue	5·50
Z35	10c. dull mauve	60·00
Z36	10c. green	7·50
Z37	10c. purple/red	7·50
Z38	30c. green	55·00

1885. (Nos. 40/42).
Z39	20c. on 30c. orange-red	22·00
Z40	50c. on 48c. yellowish brown	90·00
Z41	$1 on 96c. grey-olive	£200

1891. (Nos. 43/50).
Z42	7c. on 10c. green	28·00
Z43	14c. on 30c. mauve	£180
Z44	20c. on 30c. green (No. 48)	20·00
Z45	50c. on 48c. dull purple (No. 49)	20·00
Z46	$1 on 96c. purple/red (No. 50)	75·00

1891. 50th Anniversary of Colony (No. 51).
Z47	2c. carmine	£1400

1898. (No. 52).
Z48	$1 on 96c. black	75·00

1898. (No. 55).
Z49	10c. on 30c. green	£300

1900–01. Wmk Crown CA (Nos. 56/61).
Z50	2c. dull green	5·00
Z51	4c. carmine	4·00
Z52	5c. yellow	25·00
Z53	10c. ultramarine	6·50
Z54	12c. blue	£225
Z55	30c. brown	90·00

1903. Wmk Crown CA (Nos. 62/76).
Z56	1c. dull purple and brown	5·50
Z57	2c. dull green	5·00
Z58	4c. purple/red	3·25
Z59	5c. dull green and brown-orange	30·00
Z60	8c. slate and violet	8·50
Z61	10c. purple and blue/blue	4·50
Z62	12c. green and purple/yellow	21·00
Z63	20c. slate and chestnut	14·00
Z64	30c. dull green and black	75·00
Z65	50c. dull green and magenta	£120
Z66	$1 purple and sage-green	£200
Z67	$2 slate and scarlet	£650
Z68	$3 slate and dull blue	£900

1904–06. Wmk Mult Crown CA (Nos. 77/90).
Z71	2c. dull green	5·00
Z72	4c. purple/red	3·25
Z73	5c. dull green and brown-orange	21·00
Z74	8c. slate and violet	12·00
Z75	10c. purple and blue/blue	4·75
Z76	12c. green and purple/yellow	24·00
Z77	20c. slate and chestnut	13·00
Z78	30c. dull green and black	45·00
Z79	50c. green and magenta	45·00
Z80	$1 purple and sage-green	£120
Z81	$2 slate and scarlet	£400
Z83	$5 purple and blue-green	£700

1907–11. Wmk Mult Crown CA (Nos. 91/99).
Z85	1c. brown	5·50
Z86	2c. green	4·75
Z87	4c. carmine-red	3·25
Z88	6c. orange-vermilion and purple	21·00
Z89	10c. bright ultramarine	4·25
Z90	20c. purple and sage-green	90·00
Z91	30c. purple and orange-yellow	95·00
Z92	50c. black/green	80·00

1912–15. Wmk Crown CA (Nos. 100/116).
Z93	1c. brown	6·50
Z94	2c. green	6·00
Z95	4c. red	3·50
Z96	6c. orange	8·00
Z97	8c. grey	30·00
Z98	10c. ultramarine	4·50
Z99	12c. purple/yellow	38·00
Z100	20c. purple and sage-green	8·00
Z101	25c. purple and magenta (Type A)	£100
Z102	30c. purple and orange-yellow	30·00
Z103	50c. black/green	18·00
Z104	$1 purple and blue/blue	32·00
Z105	$3 green and purple	£275

POSTCARD STAMPS

1879. (Nos. P1/P2).
ZP106	3c. on 16c. yellow	£1000
ZP107	5c. on 18c. lilac	£1200

POSTAL FISCAL STAMPS

1874–1902. Wmk Crown CC. Perf 15½×15 (Nos. F1/F3)
ZF109	$2 olive-green	£225
ZF110	$3 dull violet	£225

1891. (No. F9).
ZF116	$5 on $10 purple/red	£350

1897. (Nos. F10/F11).
ZF118	$1 on $2 olive-green	
ZF119	$1 on $2 dull bluish green	£475

ANPING

Anping is the port for Tainan, on the island of Formosa, opened to British trade in 1860. A British Vice-consulate operated in the port and mail is known postmarked there between 1889 and 1895. Formosa passed under Japanese control in 1895 and British Treaty Port rights then lapsed.

Type **D** *used* 1889–1895

Stamps of HONG KONG cancelled at Anping between 1889 and 1895 with postmark detailed above.

1882–91. Wmk Crown CA (Nos. 32/39).

Z120	2c. carmine	£1200
Z121	5c. blue	£1000
Z123	10c. green	£1100
Z124	10c. purple/*red*	£1300

1885. (Nos. 40/42).

Z126	20c. on 30c. orange-red	£2000
Z127	50c. on 48c. yellowish brown	£3250

CANTON

A British postal service was organised in Canton from 1834, but was closed when the foreign communities were evacuated in August 1839. The city was one of the original Treaty Ports and a consular agency was opened there in 1844. The consulate closed during the riots of December 1856, being replaced by a temporary postal agency at Whampoa, further down the river. When British forces reached Canton a further temporary agency was set up on 23 March 1859, but both closed in July 1863 when the consulate was re-established.

Type **A** ('C1') *(supplied* 1866) *used* 1875–1884

Type **C** *(supplied* 1866) *used* 1870–1901

Type **D** *used* 1890–1922

Stamps of HONG KONG cancelled at Canton between 1870 and 1916 with postmarks detailed above.

1862. No wmk (Nos. 1/7).

Z135	18c. lilac	£225

1863–71. Wmk Crown CC (Nos. 8/19).

Z136	2c. brown	42·00
Z137	4c. grey	45·00
Z138	6c. lilac	75·00
Z139	8c. orange	55·00
Z140	12c. blue	25·00
Z142	24c. green	80·00
Z143	30c. vermilion	
Z144	30c. mauve	26·00
Z145	48c. rose	£150
Z147	96c. brownish grey	£450

1876–77. (Nos. 20/21).

Z148	16c. on 18c. lilac	£325
Z149	28c. on 30c. mauve	£140

1877. Wmk Crown CC (No. 22).

Z150	16c. yellow	£180

1880. (Nos. 23/27).

Z151	5c. on 8c. orange	£200
Z152	5c. on 18c. lilac	£150
Z153	10c. on 12c. blue	£120
Z154	10c. on 16c. yellow	£300
Z155	10c. on 24c. green	£225

1880. Wmk Crown CC (Nos. 28/31).

Z156	2c. rose	65·00
Z157	5c. blue	£110
Z158	10c. mauve	75·00

1882–96. Wmk Crown CA (Nos. 32/39).

Z159	2c. rose-lake	55·00
Z160	2c. carmine	4·50
Z161	4c. slate-grey	20·00
Z162	5c. blue	6·00
Z163	10c. dull mauve	50·00
Z164	10c. green	15·00
Z165	10c. purple/*red*	6·50
Z166	30c. green	55·00

1885. (Nos. 40/42).

Z167	20c. on 30c. orange-red	19·00
Z168	50c. on 48c. yellowish brown	90·00
Z169	$1 on 96c. grey-olive	£180

1891. (Nos. 43/50).

Z170	7c. on 10c. green	28·00
Z171	14c. on 30c. mauve	£180
Z171a	20c. on 30c. green (No. 45)	£350
Z172	20c. on 30c. green (No. 48)	25·00
Z173	50c. on 48c. dull purple (No. 49)	25·00
Z174	$1 on 96c. purple/*red* (No. 50)	75·00

1891. 50th Anniversary of Colony (No. 51).

Z175	2c. carmine	£1400

1898. (No. 52).

Z176	$1 on 96c. black	£180

1898. (No. 55).

Z177	10c. on 30c. grey-green	£225

1900–01. Wmk Crown CA (Nos. 56/61)

Z178	2c. dull green	4·50
Z179	4c. carmine	4·25
Z180	5c. yellow	40·00
Z181	10c. ultramarine	4·75
Z182	12c. blue	£160
Z183	30c. brown	80·00

1903. Wmk Crown CA (Nos. 62/76).

Z184	1c. dull purple and brown	4·75
Z185	2c. dull green	5·00
Z186	4c. purple/*red*	3·50
Z187	5c. dull green and brown-orange	28·00
Z188	8c. slate and violet	10·00
Z189	10c. purple and blue/*blue*	4·75
Z190	12c. green and purple/*yellow*	22·00
Z191	20c. slate and chestnut	12·00
Z192	30c. dull green and black	75·00
Z193	50c. dull green and magenta	£120
Z194	$1 purple and sage-green	£150

1904–06. Wmk Mult Crown CA (Nos. 77/90).

Z199	2c. dull green	4·75
Z200	4c. purple/*red*	3·50
Z201	5c. dull green and brown-orange	23·00
Z202	8c. slate and violet	15·00
Z203	10c. purple and blue/*blue*	4·50
Z204	12c. green and purple/*yellow*	28·00
Z205	20c. slate and chestnut	14·00
Z206	30c. dull green and black	45·00
Z207	50c. green and magenta	55·00
Z208	$1 purple and sage-green	95·00
Z209	$2 slate and scarlet	£500
Z210	$3 slate and dull blue	£650
Z212	$10 slate and orange/*blue*	£1800

1907–11. Wmk Mult Crown CA (Nos. 91/99).

Z213	1c. brown	4·75
Z214	2c. green	4·75
Z215	4c. carmine-red	3·50
Z216	6c. orange-vermilion and purple	24·00
Z217	10c. bright ultramarine	4·25
Z218	20c. purple and sage-green	90·00
Z219	30c. purple and orange-yellow	95·00
Z220	50c. black/*green*	55·00
Z221	$2 carmine-red and black	£600

1912–15. Wmk Mult Crown CA (Nos. 100/116).

Z222	1c. brown	4·75
Z223	2c. green	4·00
Z224	4c. red	3·25
Z225	6c. orange	8·00
Z226	8c. grey	25·00
Z227	10c. ultramarine	4·50
Z228	12c. purple/*yellow*	30·00
Z229	20c. purple and sage-green	7·00
Z230	25c. purple and magenta (Type A)	£120
Z231	30c. purple and orange-yellow	28·00
Z232	50c. black/*green*	10·00
Z233	$1 purple and blue/*blue*	42·00
Z234	$2 carmine red and grey-black	£150
Z235	$3 green and purple	£300
Z235b	$10 purple and black/*red*	£450

POSTCARD STAMPS

1879. (Nos. P1/P2).

ZP236	3c. on 16c. yellow	£850
ZP237	5c. on 18c. lilac	£1000

POSTAL FISCAL STAMPS

1874–1902. Wmk Crown CC. Nos. F1/F5.

(a) Perf 15½×15. Perf 15½×15.

ZF238	$2 olive-green	£225

(b) Perf 14. Perf 14.

ZF242	$3 dull mauve	£650

1891. (No. F9).

ZF246	$5 on $10 purple/*red*	£550

1897. (No. F10).

ZF247	$1 on $2 olive-green	

CHEFOO

Chefoo was opened to British trade in 1860. Although a consulate was established in 1863 no organised postal agency was provided until 1 January 1903 when one was opened at the premises of Curtis Brothers, a commercial firm.

Type **E** (*supplied* 1902) *used* 1903–1920

Type **D** (*supplied* 1907) *used* 1907–1913

Type **F** *used* 1916–1922

Stamps of HONG KONG cancelled at Chefoo between 1903 and 1916 with postmarks detailed above.

1882–96. Wmk Crown CA (Nos. 32/39).
Z249	5c. blue	45·00

1891. (Nos. 43/50).
Z250	20c. on 30c. grey-green (No. 48*a*)	85·00

1898. (No. 52).
Z251	$1 on 96c. black	£180

1900–01. Wmk Crown CA (Nos. 56/61).
Z252	2c. dull green	32·00
Z253	4c. carmine	30·00
Z254	5c. yellow	90·00
Z255	10c. ultramarine	32·00
Z257	30c. brown	£180

1903. Wmk Crown CA (Nos. 62/76).
Z258	1c. dull purple and brown	13·00
Z259	2c. dull green	11·00
Z260	4c. purple/*red*	10·00
Z261	5c. dull green and brown-orange	35·00
Z262	8c. slate and violet	22·00
Z263	10c. purple and blue/*blue*	14·00
Z264	12c. green and purple/*yellow*	45·00
Z265	20c. slate and chestnut	50·00
Z267	50c. dull green and magenta	£160
Z268	$1 purple and sage-green	£180

1904–06. Wmk Mult Crown CA (Nos. 77/90).
Z273	2c. dull green	11·00
Z274	4c. purple/*red*	9·00
Z275	5c. dull green and brown-orange	24·00
Z276	8c. slate and violet	20·00
Z277	10c. purple and blue/*blue*	11·00
Z278	12c. green and purple/*yellow*	40·00
Z279	20c. slate and chestnut	25·00
Z280	30c. dull green and black	80·00
Z281	50c. green and magenta	80·00
Z282	$1 purple and sage-green	£130
Z283	$2 slate and scarlet	£375
Z284	$3 slate and dull blue	£650
Z285	$5 green and blue-green	£950

1907–11. Wmk Mult Crown CA (Nos. 91/99).
Z287	1c. brown	13·00
Z288	2c. green	12·00
Z289	4c. carmine-red	10·00
Z290	6c. orange-vermilion and purple	45·00
Z291	10c. bright ultramarine	11·00
Z292	20c. purple and sage-green	£140
Z293	30c. purple and orange-yellow	£100
Z294	50c. black/*green*	80·00
Z295	$2 carmine-red and black	£750

1912–15. Wmk Mult Crown CA (Nos. 100/116).
Z296	1c. brown	10·00
Z297	2c. green	9·50
Z298	4c. red	7·50
Z299	6c. orange	21·00
Z300	8c. grey	45·00
Z301	10c. ultramarine	9·00
Z302	12c. purple/*yellow*	48·00
Z303	20c. purple and sage-green	15·00
Z304	30c. purple and orange-yellow	30·00
Z305	30c. purple and orange-yellow	30·00
Z306	50c. black/*green*	15·00
Z307	$1 purple and blue/*blue*	24·00
Z308	$2 carmine-red and grey-black	£120
Z309	$3 green and purple	£300
Z310	$5 green and red/*green*	£650
Z311	$10 purple and black/*red*	£450

FOOCHOW

Foochow, originally known as Foochowfoo, was one of the original Treaty Ports opened to British trade in 1842. A British consulate and postal agency was established in June 1844.

Type **A** ('F1') (*supplied* 1866) *used* 1873–1884

Type **D** (inscr 'FOOCHOWFOO') (*supplied* 1866) *used* 1867–1905

Type **D** (inscr 'FOOCHOW') (*supplied* 1894) *used* 1894–1917

Type **E** (inscr 'B.P.O.') *used* 1906–1910

Type **F** *used* 1915–1922

Stamps of HONG KONG cancelled at Foochow between 1867 and 1916 with postmarks detailed above.

1862. No wmk (Nos. 1/7).
Z312	18c. lilac	£225

1863–71. Wmk Crown CC (Nos. 8/19).
Z313	2c. brown	38·00
Z314	4c. grey	38·00
Z315	6c. lilac	60·00
Z316	8c. orange	55·00
Z317	12c. blue	22·00
Z318	18c. lilac	£1000
Z319	24c. green	80·00
Z320	30c. vermilion	£250
Z321	30c. mauve	22·00
Z322	48c. rose	£150
Z324	96c. brownish grey	£475

1876–77. (Nos. 20/21).
Z325	16c. on 18c. lilac	£350
Z326	28c. on 30c. mauve	£170

1877. Wmk Crown CC (No. 22).
Z327	16c. yellow	£160

1880. (Nos. 23/27).
Z328	5c. on 8c. orange	£400
Z329	5c. on 18c. lilac	£150
Z330	10c. on 12c. blue	£150
Z331	10c. on 16c. yellow	
Z332	10c. on 24c. green	£225

1880. Wmk Crown CC (Nos. 28/31).
Z333	2c. rose	55·00
Z334	5c. blue	£110
Z335	10c. mauve	55·00
Z336	48c. brown	£375

1882–96. Wmk Crown CA (Nos. 32/39).
Z336*a*	2c. rose-lake	50·00
Z337	2c. carmine	4·50
Z338	4c. slate-grey	14·00
Z339	5c. blue	6·00
Z340	10c. dull mauve	55·00
Z341	10c. green	20·00
Z342	10c. purple/*red*	5·50
Z343	30c. green	60·00

1885. (Nos. 40/42).
Z344	20c. on 30c. orange-red	25·00
Z345	50c. on 48c. yellowish brown	90·00
Z346	$1 on 96c. grey-olive	£190

1891. (Nos. 43/50).
Z347	7c. on 10c. green	70·00
Z348	14c. on 30c. mauve	£150
Z348*a*	20c. on 30c. green (No. 45)	£300
Z349	20c. on 30c. green (No. 48)	28·00
Z350	50c. on 48c. dull purple	30·00
Z351	$1 on 96c. purple/*red*	75·00

1898. (No. 52).
Z353	$1 on 96c. black	£150

1898. (No. 55).
Z354	10c. on 30c. green	£300

1900–01. Wmk Crown CA (Nos. 56/61).
Z355	2c. dull green	4·75
Z356	4c. carmine	5·50
Z357	5c. yellow	35·00
Z358	10c. ultramarine	5·00
Z360	30c. brown	£100

1903. Wmk Crown CA (Nos. 62/76).
Z361	1c. dull purple and brown	5·50
Z362	2c. dull green	4·75
Z363	4c. purple/*red*	3·25
Z364	5c. dull green and brown-orange	28·00
Z365	8c. slate and violet	14·00
Z366	10c. purple and blue/*blue*	4·75
Z367	12c. green and purple/*yellow*	26·00
Z368	20c. slate and chestnut	15·00
Z369	30c. dull green and black	65·00
Z370	50c. dull green and magenta	£110
Z371	$1 purple and sage-green	90·00

1904–06. Wmk Mult Crown CA (Nos. 77/90).
Z376	2c. dull green	4·75
Z377	4c. purple/*red*	3·25
Z378	5c. dull green and brown-orange	20·00
Z379	8c. slate and violet	12·00
Z380	10c. purple and blue/*blue*	4·75
Z381	12c. green and purple/*yellow*	28·00
Z382	20c. slate and chestnut	14·00
Z383	30c. dull green and black	55·00

Z384	50c. green and magenta	48·00
Z385	$1 purple and sage-green	95·00

1907–11. Wmk Mult Crown CA (Nos. 91/99).
Z390	1c. brown	4·25
Z391	2c. green	4·25
Z392	4c. carmine-red	3·25
Z393	6c. orange-vermilion and purple	23·00
Z394	10c. bright ultramarine	4·00
Z395	20c. purple and sage-green	95·00
Z396	30c. purple and orange-yellow	85·00
Z397	50c. black/green	60·00
Z398	$2 carmine-red and black	

1912–15. Wmk Mult Crown CA (Nos. 100/116).
Z399	1c. brown	6·00
Z400	2c. green	4·50
Z401	4c. red	3·50
Z402	6c. orange	15·00
Z403	8c. grey	30·00
Z404	10c. ultramarine	4·50
Z405	12c. purple/yellow	40·00
Z406	20c. purple and sage-green	8·00
Z407	25c. purple and magenta (Type A)	£120
Z408	30c. purple and orange-yellow	28·00
Z409	50c. black/green	25·00

POSTCARD STAMPS

1874–1902. (Nos. P1/P2).
ZP413	3c. on 16c. yellow	£1100

POSTAL FISCAL STAMPS

1874–1902. Wmk Crown CC. P 15½×15 (Nos. F1/F3).
ZF415	$2 olive-green	£225
ZF416	$3 dull violet	£180

HANKOW

Hankow, on the Yangtse River 600 miles from the sea, became a Treaty Port in 1860. A British consulate opened the following year, but no organised British postal agency was established until 1872

Type **D** (supplied 1874) used 1874–1916

Type **B** ('D.29') (supplied 1876) used 1878–1883

Type **F** used 1916–1922

Stamps of HONG KONG cancelled at Hankow between 1874 and 1916 with postmarks detailed above.

1862. No wmk (Nos. 1/7).
Z426	18c. lilac	£450

1863–71. Wmk Crown CC (Nos. 8/19).
Z427	2c. brown	£140
Z428	4c. grey	£140
Z429	6c. lilac	£180
Z430	8c. orange	£170
Z431	12c. blue	55·00
Z432	18c. lilac	£1400
Z433	24c. green	£275
Z435	30c. mauve	£150
Z436	48c. rose	£400
Z438	96c. brownish grey	

1876–77. (Nos. 20/21).
Z439	16c. on 18c. lilac	£550
Z440	28c. on 30c. mauve	£350

1877. Wmk Crown CC (No. 22).
Z441	16c. yellow	£800

1880. (Nos. 23/27).
Z442	5c. on 8c. orange	£450
Z443	5c. on 18c. lilac	£250
Z444	10c. on 12c. blue	£275
Z445	10c. on 16c. yellow	£500
Z446	10c. on 24c. green	£350

1880. Wmk Crown CC (Nos. 28/31).
Z447	2c. rose	£120
Z448	5c. blue	£150
Z449	10c. mauve	£160
Z450	48c. brown	£475

1882–96. Wmk Crown CA (Nos. 32/39).
Z450a	2c. rose-lake	£110
Z451	2c. carmine	10·00
Z452	4c. slate-grey	30·00
Z453	5c. blue	11·00
Z454	10c. dull mauve	£130
Z455	10c. green	16·00
Z456	10c. purple/red	12·00
Z457	30c. green	£100

1885. (Nos. 40/42).
Z458	20c. on 30c. orange-red	45·00
Z459	50c. on 48c. yellowish brown	£120
Z460	$1 on 96c. grey-olive	£250

1891. (Nos. 43/50).
Z461	7c. on 10c. green	45·00
Z462	14c. on 30c. mauve	£225
Z463	20c. on 30c. green	45·00
Z464	50c. on 48c. dull purple	50·00
Z465	$1 on 96c. purple/red	£110

1898. (No. 52).
Z467	$1 on 96c. black	£150

1898. (No. 55).
Z468	10c. on 30c. green	£350

1900–01. Wmk Crown CA (Nos. 56/61).
Z469	2c. dull green	7·00
Z470	4c. carmine	7·50
Z471	5c. yellow	45·00
Z472	10c. ultramarine	9·00
Z473	12c. blue	£190
Z474	30c. brown	£110

1903. Wmk Crown CA (Nos. 62/76).
Z475	1c. dull purple and brown	7·50
Z476	2c. dull green	7·00
Z477	4c. purple/red	6·00
Z478	5c. dull green and brown-orange	32·00
Z479	8c. slate and violet	22·00
Z480	10c. purple and blue/blue	6·50
Z481	12c. green and purple/yellow	30·00
Z482	20c. green and chestnut	20·00
Z483	30c. dull green and black	75·00
Z484	50c. dull green and magenta	£130
Z485	$1 purple and sage-green	£100

1904–06. Wmk Mult Crown CA (Nos. 77/90).
Z490	2c. dull green	6·50
Z491	4c. purple/red	5·50
Z492	5c. dull green and brown-orange	27·00
Z493	8c. slate and violet	13·00
Z494	10c. purple and blue/blue	6·50
Z495	12c. green and purple/yellow	32·00
Z496	20c. green and chestnut	20·00
Z497	30c. dull green and black	60·00
Z498	50c. green and magenta	45·00
Z499	$1 purple and sage-green	95·00
Z500	$2 slate and scarlet	£450
Z502	$5 purple and blue-green	£850
Z503	$10 slate and orange/blue	£2000

1907–11. Wmk Mult Crown CA (Nos. 91/99).
Z504	1c. brown	7·00
Z505	2c. green	6·00
Z506	4c. carmine-red	5·00
Z507	6c. orange-vermilion and purple	30·00
Z508	10c. bright ultramarine	6·50
Z509	20c. purple and sage-green	£120
Z510	30c. purple and orange-yellow	£140
Z512	$2 carmine-red and black	£950

1912–15. Wmk Mult Crown CA (Nos. 100/116).
Z513	1c. brown	8·00
Z514	2c. green	7·00
Z515	4c. red	5·50
Z516	6c. orange	17·00
Z517	8c. grey	38·00
Z518	10c. ultramarine	6·50
Z519	12c. purple/yellow	35·00
Z520	20c. purple and sage-green	16·00
Z522	30c. purple and orange-yellow	40·00
Z523	50c. black/green	21·00
Z524	$1 purple and blue/blue	80·00
Z525	$2 carmine-red and grey-black	
Z526	$3 green and purple	£300
Z527	$5 green and red/green	£750

POSTCARD STAMPS

1879. (Nos. P1/P2).
ZP528	3c. on 16c. yellow	£1600

POSTAL FISCAL STAMPS

1874–1902. Wmk Crown CC.
(a) Perf 15½×15 (Nos. F1/F3). Perf 15½×15 (Nos. F1/F3).
ZF529	$2 olive-green	£350

(b) Perf 14 (Nos. F4/F6). Perf 14 (Nos. F4/F6).
ZF532	$2 dull bluish green	£650

1897. (No. F11).
ZF533	$1 on $2 dull bluish green	£800

KIUNGCHOW (HOIHOW)

Kiungchow, a city on the island of Hainan, and its port of Hoihow was added to the Treaty Port system in 1860. A consular postal agency was opened at Kiungchow in 1876, being transferred to Hoihow in 1878. A second agency was opened at Kiungchow in 1879.

Type **B** ('D.28') (supplied 1876) used 1879–1883

Type **D** (inscr 'KIUNG-CHOW') (supplied 1878) used 1879–1881

'REGISTERED KIUNG-CHOW' with 'REGISTERED' removed (originally supplied 1876) used 1883–1885

Type **D** (inscr 'HOIHOW') used 1885–1922

Stamps of HONG KONG cancelled at Kiungchow (Hoihow) between 1879 and 1916 with postmarks detailed above.

1863–71. Wmk Crown CC (Nos. 8/19).
Z540	2c. brown	£1000
Z541	4c. grey	£800
Z542	6c. lilac	£1700
Z543	8c. orange	£1700
Z544	12c. blue	£550
Z546	24c. green	£1700
Z547	30c. vermilion	
Z548	30c. mauve	£300
Z549	48c. rose	£2750
Z551	96c. brownish grey	£2750

1876–77. (Nos. 20/21).
Z552	16c. on 18c. lilac	£1800
Z553	28c. on 30c. mauve	£1400

1877. (No. 22).
Z554	16c. yellow	£2750

1880. (Nos. 23/27).
Z555	5c. on 8c. orange	£1200
Z556	5c. on 18c. lilac	£1000
Z557	10c. on 12c. blue	£1000
Z558	10c. on 16c. yellow	£2000
Z559	10c. on 24c. green	

1880. Wmk Crown CC (Nos. 28/31).
Z561	5c. blue	£800
Z562	10c. mauve	£1000

1882–96. Wmk Crown CA (Nos. 32/39).
Z564	2c. carmine	75·00
Z565	4c. slate-grey	£140
Z566	5c. blue	75·00
Z567	10c. dull mauve	£850
Z568	10c. green	£120
Z569	10c. purple/red	75·00
Z570	30c. green	£170

1885. (Nos. 40/42).
Z571	20c. on 30c. orange-red	£170
Z572	50c. on 48c. yellowish brown	£190
Z573	$1 on 96c. grey-olive	£400

1891. (Nos. 43/50).
Z574	7c. on 10c. green	£200
Z576	20c. on 30c. green	85·00
Z577	50c. on 48c. dull purple	£110
Z578	$1 on 96c. purple/red	£250

1891. 50th Anniversary of Colony (No. 51).
Z579	2c. carmine	£3000

1898. (No. 52).
Z580	$1 on 96c. black	£375

1898. (No. 55).
Z581	10c. on 30c. green	£550

1900–01. Wmk Crown CA (Nos. 56/61).
Z582	2c. dull green	80·00
Z583	4c. carmine	45·00
Z584	5c. yellow	£130
Z585	10c. ultramarine	50·00
Z587	30c. brown	£225

1903. Wmk Crown CA (Nos. 62/76).
Z588	1c. dull purple and brown	32·00
Z589	2c. dull green	32·00
Z590	4c. purple/red	22·00
Z591	5c. dull green and brown-orange	75·00
Z592	8c. slate and violet	55·00
Z593	10c. purple and blue/blue	26·00
Z594	12c. green and purple/yellow	80·00
Z595	20c. slate and chestnut	80·00
Z596	30c. dull green and black	£150
Z597	50c. dull green and magenta	£250
Z598	$1 purple and sage-green	£300
Z599	$2 slate and scarlet	£900

1904. Wmk Mult Crown CA (Nos. 77/90).
Z603	2c. dull green	28·00
Z604	4c. purple/red	22·00
Z605	5c. dull green and brown-orange	75·00
Z606	8c. slate and violet	38·00
Z607	10c. purple and blue/blue	25·00
Z608	12c. green and purple/yellow	80·00
Z609	20c. slate and chestnut	85·00
Z610	30c. dull green and black	£110
Z612	$1 purple and sage-green	£450

1907–11. Wmk Mult Crown CA (Nos. 91/99).
Z617	1c. brown	28·00
Z618	2c. green	27·00
Z619	4c. carmine-red	22·00
Z620	6c. orange-vermilion and purple	75·00
Z621	10c. bright ultramarine	25·00
Z622	20c. purple and sage-green	£140
Z623	30c. purple and orange-yellow	£130

1912–15. Wmk Mult Crown CA (Nos. 100/116).
Z625	1c. brown	26·00
Z626	2c. green	25·00
Z627	4c. red	22·00
Z628	6c. orange	42·00
Z629	8c. grey	£100
Z630	10c. ultramarine	22·00
Z631	12c. purple/yellow	80·00
Z632	20c. purple and sage-green	50·00
Z633	25c. purple and magenta (Type A)	£160
Z634	30c. purple and orange-yellow	£110
Z635	50c. black/green	90·00
Z636	$1 purple and blue/blue	£110

POSTCARD STAMPS

1879. (Nos. P1/P2).
ZP640	3c. on 16c. yellow	£1800

POSTAL FISCAL STAMPS

1874–1902. Wmk Crown CC.
	(a) Perf 15½×15 (Nos. F1/F3). Perf 15½×15.	
ZF641	$2 olive-green	£550
	(b) Perf 14 (Nos. F4/F6). Perf 14.	
ZF644	$2 dull bluish green	£950

1897. (Nos. F10/F11).
ZF650	$1 on $2 olive-green	£700

NINGPO

Ningpo was one of the 1842 Treaty Ports and a consular postal agency was established there in 1844.

Type **A** ('N1') (supplied 1866) used 1870–1882

Type **C** (supplied 1866) used 1870–1899

Type **D** used 1899–1922

Stamps of HONG KONG cancelled at Ningpo between 1866 and 1916 with postmarks detailed above.

1862. No wmk (Nos. 1/7).
Z652	18c. lilac	£1200

1863–71. Wmk Crown CC (Nos. 8/19).
Z653	2c. brown	£450
Z654	4c. grey	£450
	a. Perf 12½	£2750
Z655	6c. lilac	£500
Z656	8c. orange	£450
Z657	12c. blue	£170
Z658	18c. lilac	
Z659	24c. green	£475
Z660	30c. vermilion	£600
Z661	30c. mauve	£160
Z662	48c. rose	£850
Z663	96c. olive-bistre	
Z664	96c. brownish grey	£1200

1876–77. (Nos. 20/21).
Z665	16c. on 18c. lilac	£700
Z666	28c. on 30c. mauve	£400

1877. Wmk Crown CC (No. 22).
Z667	16c. yellow	£550

1880. (Nos. 23/27).
Z668	5c. on 8c. orange	£500
Z669	5c. on 18c. lilac	£425
Z670	10c. on 12c. blue	£450
Z672	10c. on 24c. green	£550

1880. Wmk Crown CC (Nos. 28/31).
Z673	2c. dull rose	£300
Z674	5c. blue	£275
Z675	10c. mauve	£250
Z676	48c. brown	£1000

1882–96. Wmk Crown CA (Nos. 32/39).
Z677	2c. carmine	60·00
Z678	4c. slate-grey	£130
Z679	5c. blue	60·00
Z680	10c. dull mauve	£275
Z681	10c. green	£110
Z682	10c. purple/*red*	75·00
Z683	30c. green	£190

1885. (Nos. 40/42).
Z685	50c. on 48c. yellowish brown	£250

1891. (Nos. 43/50).
Z686	7c. on 10c. green	80·00
Z687	14c. on 30c. mauve	£350
Z688	20c. on 30c. green	60·00
Z689	50c. on 48c. dull purple	£100
Z690	$1 on 96c. purple/*red*	£190

1898. (No. 52).
Z692	$1 on 96c. black	£250

1898. (No. 55).
Z693	10c. on 30c. green	£425

1900–01. Wmk Crown CA (Nos. 56/61).
Z694	2c. dull green	38·00
Z695	4c. carmine	32·00
Z697	10c. ultramarine	40·00

1903. Wmk Crown CA (Nos. 62/76).
Z700	1c. dull purple and brown	32·00
Z701	2c. dull green	32·00
Z702	4c. purple/*red*	24·00
Z703	5c. dull green and brown-orange	80·00
Z704	8c. slate and violet	42·00
Z705	10c. purple and blue/*blue*	26·00
Z706	12c. green and purple/*yellow*	90·00
Z709	50c. dull green and magenta	£160

1904–06. Wmk Mult Crown CA (Nos. 77/90).
Z715	2c. dull green	30·00
Z716	4c. purple/*red*	26·00
Z718	8c. slate and violet	65·00
Z719	10c. blue/*blue*	
Z720	12c. green and purple/*yellow*	90·00
Z721	20c. slate and chestnut	80·00
Z722	30c. dull green and black	£120
Z723	50c. green and magenta	£100
Z724	$1 purple and sage-green	£160

1907–11. Wmk Mult Crown CA (Nos. 91/99).
Z729	1c. brown	26·00
Z730	2c. green	26·00
Z731	4c. carmine-red	23·00
Z732	6c. orange-vermilion and purple	
Z733	10c. bright ultramarine	26·00
Z734	20c. purple and sage-green	£160
Z735	30c. purple and orange-yellow	£150

1912–15. Wmk Mult Crown CA (Nos. 100/116).
Z738	1c. brown	27·00
Z739	2c. green	26·00
Z740	4c. red	24·00
Z742	8c. grey	£100
Z743	10c. ultramarine	26·00
Z745	20c. purple and sage-green	75·00
Z747	30c. purple and orange-yellow	£110
Z749	$1 purple and blue/*blue*	95·00

POSTCARD STAMPS

1879. (Nos. P1/P2).
ZP751	3c. on 16c. yellow	£1800

POSTAL FISCAL STAMPS

1874–1902. Wmk Crown CC. Perf 15½x15 (Nos. F1/F3).
ZF754	$2 olive-green	£500

1880. (No. F7).
ZF760	12c. on $10 rose-carmine	

1897. (No. F10).
ZF763	$1 on $2 olive-green	

SHANGHAI

Shanghai was one of the original Treaty Ports of 1842 and a packet agency was opened at the British consulate in April 1844. It moved to a separate premise in 1861 and was upgraded to a Post Office in September 1867.

British military post offices operated in Shanghai from 1927 until 1940

Type **D** (inscr 'SHANGHAE') (*supplied* 1861) *used* 1861–1899

Sunburst *used* 1864–1865

Type **A** ('S1') (*supplied* 1866) *used* 1866–1885

Type **D** (inscr 'SHANGHAI') (*supplied* 1885) *used* 1886–1906

Type **G** (inscr 'B.P.O.' at foot) (*supplied* 1904) *used* 1904–1921

Type **G** (inscr 'Br.P.O.' at foot) (*supplied* 1907) *used* 1907–1922

Type **E** (figures 'I' to 'VIII' at foot) *used* 1912–1922

Stamps of HONG KONG cancelled at Shanghai between 1863 and 1916 with postmarks detailed above.

1862. No wmk (Nos. 1/7).
Z765	2c. brown	£180
Z766	8c. yellow-buff	£250
Z767	12c. pale greenish blue	£170
Z768	18c. lilac	£140
Z769	24c. green	£275
Z770	48c. rose	£650
Z771	96c. brownish grey	£750

1863–71. Wmk Crown CC (Nos. 8/19).
Z772	2c. brown	12·00
Z773	4c. grey	11·00
	a. Perf 12½	£275
Z774	6c. lilac	25·00
Z775	8c. orange	19·00
Z776	12c. blue	11·00
Z777	18c. lilac	£400
Z778	24c. green	18·00
Z779	30c. vermilion	27·00
Z780	30c. mauve	9·00
Z781	48c. rose	45·00
Z782	96c. olive-bistre	£2500
Z783	96c. brownish grey	85·00

1876–77. (Nos. 20/21).
Z784	16c. on 18c. lilac	£180
Z785	28c. on 30c. mauve	65·00

1877. Wmk Crown CC (No. 22).
Z786	16c. yellow	80·00

1880. (Nos. 23/27).
Z787	5c. on 8c. orange	£120
Z788	5c. on 18c. lilac	75·00
Z789	10c. on 12c. blue	60·00
Z790	10c. on 16c. yellow	£200
Z791	10c. on 24c. green	£130

1880. Wmk Crown CC (Nos. 28/31).
Z792	2c. rose	48·00
Z793	5c. blue	80·00
Z794	10c. mauve	25·00
Z795	48c. brown	£170

1882–96. Wmk Crown CA (Nos. 32/39).
Z795*a*	2c. rose-lake	45·00
Z796	2c. carmine	3·50
Z797	4c. slate-grey	5·00
Z798	5c. blue	1·60
Z799	10c. dull mauve	30·00
Z800	10c. green	2·50
Z801	10c. purple/*red*	2·00
Z802	30c. green	45·00

1885. (Nos. 40/42).
Z803	20c. on 30c. orange-red	10·00
Z804	50c. on 48c. yellowish brown	60·00
Z805	$1 on 96c. grey-olive	£130

1891. (Nos. 43/50).

Z806	7c. on 10c. green	17·00
Z807	14c. on 30c. mauve	£120
Z807a	20c. on 30c. green (No. 45)	£225
Z807b	50c. on 48c. dull purple (No. 46)	£400
Z807c	$1 on 96c. purple/*red* (No. 47)	£450
Z808	20c. on 30c. green (No. 48)	18·00
Z809	50c. on 48c. dull purple (No. 49)	9·00
Z810	$1 on 96c. purple/*red* (No. 50)	32·00

1891. 50th Anniversary of the Colony (No. 51)

Z811	2c. carmine	£1500

1898. (No. 52).

Z812	$1 on 96c. black	45·00

1898. (No. 55).

Z813	10c. on 30c. green	£140

1900–01. Wmk Crown CA (Nos. 56/61).

Z814	2c. dull green	1·40
Z815	4c. carmine	1·40
Z816	5c. yellow	13·00
Z817	10c. ultramarine	2·75
Z818	12c. blue	£120
Z819	30c. brown	45·00

1903. Wmk Crown CA (Nos. 62/76).

Z820	1c. dull purple and brown	1·00
Z821	2c. dull green	3·25
Z822	4c. purple/*red*	85
Z823	5c. dull green and brown-orange	18·00
Z824	8c. slate and violet	3·25
Z825	10c. purple and blue/*blue*	2·00
Z826	12c. green and purple/*yellow*	12·00
Z827	20c. slate and chestnut	6·50
Z828	30c. dull green and black	45·00
Z829	50c. dull green and magenta	90·00
Z830	$1 purple and sage-green	45·00
Z831	$2 slate and scarlet	£450
Z832	$3 slate and dull blue	£650
Z833	$5 purple and blue-green	£750
Z834	$10 slate and orange/*blue*	£750

1904–06. Wmk Mult Crown CA (Nos. 77/90).

Z835	2c. dull green	3·25
Z836	4c. purple/*red*	85
Z837	5c. dull green and brown-orange	11·00
Z838	8c. slate and violet	3·50
Z839	10c. purple and blue/*blue*	1·75
Z840	12c. green and purple/*yellow*	14·00
Z841	20c. slate and chestnut	5·00
Z842	30c. dull green and black	32·00
Z843	50c. green and magenta	24·00
Z844	$1 purple and sage-green	55·00
Z845	$2 slate and scarlet	£200
Z846	$3 slate and dull blue	£500
Z847	$5 purple and blue-green	£650
Z848	$10 slate and orange/*blue*	£1800

1907–11. Wmk Mult Crown CA (Nos. 91/99).

Z849	1c. brown	2·00
Z850	2c. green	2·25
Z851	4c. carmine-red	85
Z852	6c. orange-vermilion and purple	12·00
Z853	10c. bright ultramarine	85
Z854	20c. purple and sage-green	75·00
Z855	30c. purple and orange-yellow	65·00
Z856	50c. black/*green*	30·00
Z857	$2 carmine-red and black	£550

1912–15. Wmk Mult Crown CA (Nos. 100/116).

Z858	1c. brown	1·40
Z859	2c. green	85
Z860	4c. red	70
Z861	6c. orange	4·00
Z862	8c. grey	15·00
Z863	10c. ultramarine	75
Z864	12c. purple/*yellow*	20·00
Z865	20c. purple and sage-green	2·25
Z866	25c. purple and magenta (Type A)	
Z867	30c. purple and orange-yellow	17·00
Z868	50c. black/*green*	7·00
Z869	$1 purple and blue/*blue*	11·00
Z870	$3 green and purple	£180

POSTCARD STAMPS

1879. (Nos. P1/P2).

ZP871	3c. on 16c. yellow	£550
ZP872	5c. on 18c. lilac	£650

POSTAL FISCAL STAMPS

1874–1902. Wmk Crown CC.

(a) Perf 15½×15 (Nos. F1/F5). Perf 15½×15.

ZF874	$2 olive-green	80·00
ZF875	$3 dull violet	60·00
ZF876	$10 rose-carmine	£950

(b) Perf 14. Perf 14.

ZF877	$2 dull bluish green	£350
ZF878	$3 dull mauve	£650

1880. (No. F7).

ZF880	12c. on $10 rose-carmine	£400

1891. (No. F9).

ZF882	$5 on $10 purple/*red*	£170

1897. (No. F10/F11).

ZF883	$1 on $2 olive-green	£200
ZF884	$1 on $2 dull bluish green	£275

SWATOW

Swatow became a Treaty Port in 1860 and a consular packet agency was opened in the area made available for foreign firms during the following year. In 1867 the original agency was transferred to the Chinese city on the other side of the Han River, but a second agency was subsequently opened in the foreign concession during 1883.

Type **A** ('S2') (*supplied* 1866) *used* 1875–1885

Type **C** (*supplied* 1866) *used* 1866–1890

Type **D** (*supplied* 1883) *used* 1884–1922

Type **F** *used* 1916–1922

Stamps of HONG KONG cancelled at Swatow between 1866 and 1916 with postmarks detailed above.

1862. No wmk (Nos. 1/7).

Z885	18c. lilac	£450

1863–71. Wmk Crown CC (Nos. 8/19).

Z886	2c. brown	£170
Z887	4c. grey	£160
	a. Perf 12½	
Z888	6c. lilac	£600
Z889	8c. orange	£160
Z890	12c. blue	65·00
Z891	18c. lilac	£1300
Z892	24c. green	£200
Z893	30c. vermilion	
Z894	30c. mauve	75·00
Z895	48c. rose	£350
Z897	96c. brownish grey	£1200

1876–77. (Nos. 20/21).

Z898	16c. on 18c. lilac	£500
Z899	28c. on 30c. mauve	£300

1877. Wmk Crown CC (No. 22).

Z900	16c. yellow	£600

1880. (Nos. 23/27).

Z901	5c. on 8c. orange	£350
Z902	5c. on 18c. lilac	£275
Z903	10c. on 12c. blue	£325
Z904	10c. on 16c. yellow	£550
Z905	10c. on 24c. green	£425

1880. Wmk Crown CC (Nos. 28/31).

Z906	2c. rose	£160
Z907	5c. blue	£190
Z908	10c. mauve	£225

1882–96. Wmk Crown CA (Nos. 32/39).

Z910	2c. carmine	9·00
Z911	4c. slate-grey	40·00
Z912	5c. blue	10·00
Z913	10c. dull mauve	£150
Z914	10c. green	15·00
Z915	10c. purple/*red*	8·50
Z916	30c. green	90·00

1885. (Nos. 40/42).

Z917	20c. on 30c. orange-red	25·00
Z917a	50c. on 48c. yellowish brown	£190
Z918	$1 on 96c. grey-olive	£225

1891. (Nos. 43/50).

Z919	7c. on 10c. green	45·00
Z920	14c. on 30c. mauve	£180
Z920a	50c. on 48c. dull purple (No. 46)	£450
Z921	$1 on 96c. purple/*red* (No. 47)	£650
Z922	20c. on 30c. green	35·00
Z923	50c. on 48c. dull purple (No. 49)	35·00
Z924	$1 on 96c. purple/*red* (No. 50)	85·00

1891. 50th Anniversary of Colony (No. 51).

Z925	2c. carmine	£1300

1898. (No. 52).

Z926	$1 on 96c. black	£120

1898. (No. 55).
Z927   10c. on 30c. green £325

1900–01. Wmk Crown CA (Nos. 56/61).
Z928   2c. dull green .... 9·00
Z929   4c. carmine .... 7·50
Z930   5c. yellow .... 35·00
Z931   10c. ultramarine .... 7·50
Z932   12c. blue £225
Z933   30c. brown .... 90·00

1903. Wmk Crown CA (Nos. 62/76).
Z934   1c. dull purple and brown .... 8·50
Z935   2c. dull green .... 8·00
Z936   4c. purple/*red*.................................... 6·50
Z937   5c. dull green and brown-orange........ 28·00
Z938   8c. slate and violet .... 18·00
Z939   10c. purple and blue/*blue* .... 8·00
Z940   12c. green and purple/*yellow* ...... 26·00
Z941   20c. slate and chestnut .... 13·00
Z942   30c. dull green and black .... 75·00
Z943   50c. dull green and magenta £130
Z944 $1 purple and sage-green £110

1904–06. Wmk Mult Crown CA (Nos. 77/90).
Z949   2c. dull green .... 8·50
Z950   4c. purple/*red*.................................... 6·50
Z951   5c. dull green and brown-orange........ 26·00
Z952   8c. slate and violet .... 16·00
Z953   10c. purple and blue/*blue* .... 7·50
Z954   12c. green and purple/*yellow* ...... 27·00
Z955   20c. slate and chestnut .... 16·00
Z956   30c. dull green and black .... 65·00
Z957   50c. green and magenta .... 45·00
Z958 $1 purple and sage-green £100
Z959 $2 slate and scarlet £400
Z962 $10 slate and orange/*blue* £2250

1907–11. Wmk Mult Crown CA (Nos. 91/99).
Z963   1c. brown .... 9·50
Z964   2c. green .... 9·00
Z965   4c. carmine-red .... 6·50
Z966   6c. orange-vermilion and purple...... 22·00
Z967   10c. bright ultramarine .... 7·00
Z968   20c. purple and sage-green £130
Z969   30c. purple and orange-yellow £110
Z970   50c. black/*green* .... 65·00

1912–15. Wmk Mult Crown CA (Nos. 100/116).
Z972   1c. brown .... 7·50
Z973   2c. green .... 6·50
Z974   4c. red .... 5·50
Z975   6c. orange .... 12·00
Z976   8c. grey .... 35·00
Z977   10c. ultramarine .... 5·50
Z978   12c. purple/*yellow*.......................... 32·00
Z979   20c. purple and sage-green .... 8·00
Z980   25c. purple and magenta (Type A) ...... 95·00
Z981   30c. purple and orange-yellow ...... 35·00
Z982   50c. black/*green* .... 20·00
Z983 $1 purple and blue/*blue* .... 35·00

POSTCARD STAMP

1879. (Nos. P1/P2).
ZP986   3c. on 16c. yellow £1400

POSTAL FISCAL STAMPS

1874–1902. Wmk Crown CC.
    (a) Perf 15½×15 (Nos. F1/F3). Perf 15½×15.
ZF988 $2 olive-green £225
ZF989 $3 dull violet £190
    (b) Perf 14. Perf 14.
ZF991 $2 dull bluish green £650

TIENTSIN

Tientsin became a Treaty Port in 1860. A British consulate was established in 1861, but no formal postal agency was organised there until 1882. It was not, however, very successful and was closed during 1890. The British Post Office reopened on 1 October 1906 under the management of the Chinese Engineering and Mining Company.
    British military post offices operated in Tientsin from 1927 until 1940.

Type **E** *used* 1906–1913

Type **G** (*supplied* 1907) *used* 1907–1922

Stamps of HONG KONG cancelled at Tientsin between 1906 and 1916 with postmarks detailed above.
1903. Wmk Crown CA (Nos. 62/76).
Z998   1c. dull purple and brown .... 20·00
Z998*b*   4c. purple/*red*.................................. 25·00

Z999   5c. dull green and brown-orange........ 50·00
Z1000   8c. slate and violet .... 22·00
Z1000*a*   12c. green and purple/*yellow* ...... 75·00

1904–06. Wmk Mult Crown CA (Nos. 77/90).
Z1001   2c. dull green .... 8·00
Z1002   4c. purple/*red*.................................... 5·00
Z1003   5c. dull green and brown-orange........ 24·00
Z1004   8c. slate and violet .... 18·00
Z1005   10c. purple and blue/*blue*.......... 6·50
Z1006   12c. green and purple/*yellow* ...... 30·00
Z1007   20c. slate and chestnut .... 17·00
Z1008   30c. dull green and black .... 60·00
Z1009   50c. green and magenta .... 45·00
Z1010 $1 purple and sage-green .... 85·00
Z1011 $2 slate and scarlet £325
Z1012 $3 dull green and dull mauve £800
Z1013 $5 purple and blue-green £950
Z1014 $10 slate and orange/*blue* £2250

1907–11. Wmk Mult Crown CA (Nos. 91/99).
Z1015   1c. brown .... 8·50
Z1016   2c. green .... 6·00
Z1017   4c. carmine-red .... 4·50
Z1018   6c. orange-vermilion and purple...... 26·00
Z1019   10c. bright ultramarine .... 5·50
Z1020   20c. purple and sage-green £130
Z1021   30c. purple and orange-yellow £110
Z1022   50c. black/*green* .... 75·00
Z1023 $2 carmine-red and black £850

1912–15. Wmk Mult Crown CA (Nos. 100/116).
Z1024   1c. brown .... 7·50
Z1025   2c. green .... 6·50
Z1026   4c. red .... 4·25
Z1027   6c. orange .... 11·00
Z1028   8c. grey .... 45·00
Z1029   10c. ultramarine .... 6·50
Z1030   12c. purple/*yellow*.......................... 48·00
Z1031   20c. purple and sage-green .... 12·00
Z1033   30c. purple and orange-yellow ...... 28·00
Z1034   50c. black/*green* .... 15·00
Z1035 $1 purple and blue/*blue*............. 21·00
Z1037 $3 green and purple £250
Z1038 $5 green and red/*green* £700

WEI HAI WEI

The territory of Wei Hai Wei was leased from the Chinese by the British Government from 24 May 1898 having been previously occupied by the Japanese. At that time there were no organised postal services from the area, although a private local post did operate between the port and Chefoo from 8 December 1898 until 15 March 1899. A Chinese Imperial post office opened in March 1899 to be followed by a British postal agency on the offshore island of Liu Kung Tau on 1 September 1899. A second British agency opened at Port Edward on 1 April 1904.

Liu Kung Tau oval *used* 1899–1901

Type **D** (inscr 'LIU KUNG TAU') (*supplied* 1899) *used* 1901–1930

Stamps of HONG KONG cancelled at Liu Kung Tau between 1899 and 1916 with postmarks detailed above.
1863–71. Wmk Crown CC (Nos. 8/19).
Z1039   12c. pale blue ....

1882–96. Wmk Crown CA (Nos. 32/39).
Z1040   2c. carmine .... 90·00
Z1041   4c. slate-grey £120
Z1042   5c. blue .... 90·00
Z1043   10c. purple/*red*................................. 60·00
Z1044   30c. green £130

1891. (Nos. 48/50).
Z1045   20c. on 30c. green .... 70·00
Z1046   50c. on 48c. dull purple .... 75·00

1898. (No. 52).
Z1047 $1 on 96c. black £160

1900–01. Wmk Crown CA (Nos. 56/61).

Z1049	2c. dull green	14·00
Z1050	4c. carmine	14·00
Z1051	5c. yellow	45·00
Z1052	10c. ultramarine	15·00
Z1053	12c. blue	£200
Z1054	30c. brown	£150

1903. Wmk Crown CA (Nos. 62/76).

Z1055	1c. dull purple and brown	9·50
Z1056	2c. dull green	9·00
Z1057	4c. purple/red	8·00
Z1058	5c. dull green and brown-orange	30·00
Z1059	8c. slate and violet	20·00
Z1060	10c. purple and blue/blue	13·00
Z1061	12c. green and purple/yellow	45·00
Z1062	20c. slate and chestnut	21·00
Z1063	30c. dull green and black	90·00
Z1064	50c. dull green and magenta	£150
Z1065	$1 purple and sage-green	£120

1904–06. Wmk Mult Crown CA (Nos. 77/90).

Z1070	2c. dull green	9·50
Z1071	4c. purple/red	9·00
Z1073	8c. slate and violet	18·00
Z1075	12c. green and purple/yellow	
Z1076	20c. slate and chestnut	38·00
Z1077	30c. dull green and black	£120
Z1078	50c. green and magenta	90·00
Z1079	$1 purple and sage-green	£160

1907–11. Wmk Mult Crown CA (Nos. 91/99).

Z1084	1c. brown	10·00
Z1085	2c. green	10·00
Z1086	4c. carmine-red	7·50
Z1087	6c. orange-vermilion and purple	
Z1088	10c. bright ultramarine	9·00
Z1089	20c. purple and sage-green	£130
Z1090	30c. purple and orange-yellow	£100
Z1091	50c. black/green	85·00

1912–15. Wmk Mult Crown CA (Nos. 100/116).

Z1093	1c. brown	13·00
Z1094	2c. green	9·50
Z1095	4c. red	7·50
Z1096	6c. orange	20·00
Z1097	8c. grey	45·00
Z1098	10c. ultramarine	8·50
Z1099	12c. purple/yellow	
Z1100	20c. purple and sage-green	
Z1103	50c. black/green	
Z1104	$1 purple and blue/blue	45·00

POSTAL FISCAL STAMP

1874–1902. Wmk Crown CC. Perf 14 (Nos. F4/F6).

Z1106	$2 dull bluish green	£1200

```
┌─────────────────────────┐
│   PORT EDWARD           │
│                         │
│   1 3 JUL 1904          │
│                         │
│   WEI-HAI-WEI           │
└─────────────────────────┘
```

Port Edward rectangle *used* 1904–1908
Type **D** (inscr 'WEI-HAI-WEI' at top and 'PORT EDWARD' at foot) (*supplied* 1907) *used* 1907–1930

Stamps of HONG KONG cancelled at Port Edward between 1904 and 1916 with postmarks detailed above.

1900–01. Wmk Crown CA (Nos. 56/61).

Z1109	2c. dull green	£100
Z1110	10c. ultramarine	£130

1903. Wmk Crown CA (Nos. 62/76).

Z1111	1c. dull purple and brown	38·00
Z1112	2c. dull green	38·00
Z1113	4c. purple/red	32·00
Z1114	5c. dull green and brown-orange	60·00
Z1115	8c. slate and violet	50·00
Z1116	10c. purple and blue/blue	40·00
Z1117	12c. green and purple/yellow	75·00
Z1118	20c. slate and chestnut	£110
Z1119	30c. dull green and black	£120
Z1120	50c. dull green and magenta	£150
Z1121	$1 purple and sage-green	£120

1904–06. Wmk Mult Crown CA (Nos. 77/90).

Z1126	2c. dull green	21·00
Z1127	4c. purple/red	19·00
Z1128	5c. dull green and brown-orange	35·00
Z1129	8c. slate and violet	25·00

Z1132	20c. slate and chestnut	£100
Z1133	30c. dull green and black	95·00
Z1134	50c. green and magenta	£100
Z1135	$1 purple and sage-green	£130

1907–11. Wmk Mult Crown CA (Nos. 91/99).

Z1140	1c. brown	21·00
Z1141	2c. green	21·00
Z1142	4c. carmine-red	15·00
Z1143	6c. orange-vermilion and purple	48·00
Z1144	10c. bright ultramarine	17·00
Z1145	20c. purple and sage-green	£150
Z1146	30c. purple and orange-yellow	£150
Z1148	50c. black/green	80·00

1912–15. Wmk Mult Crown CA (Nos. 100/116).

Z1151	1c. brown	19·00
Z1152	2c. green	14·00
Z1153	4c. red	8·50
Z1155	8c. grey	42·00
Z1156	10c. ultramarine	9·50
Z1157	12c. purple/yellow	50·00
Z1158	20c. purple and sage-green	25·00
Z1160	30c. purple and orange-yellow	45·00
Z1161	50c. black/green	35·00
Z1162	$1 purple and blue/blue	38·00

BRITISH POST OFFICES IN CHINA

PRICES FOR STAMPS ON COVER		
Nos.	1/4	*from* × 50
Nos.	15/17	—
Nos.	18/28	*from* × 30

The overprinted stamps Nos. 1/17 were introduced on 1 January 1917 to prevent currency speculation in the Treaty Ports. They were used in the then existing agencies of Amoy, Canton, Chefoo, Foochow, Hankow, Hoihow, Ningpo, Shanghai, Swatow, Tientsin and were also supplied to the British naval base of Wei Hai Wei.

CHINA
(1)

1917 (1 Jan)–**21**. Stamps of Hong Kong, 1912–1921 (wmk Mult Crown CA), optd with T **1**, at Somerset House.

1	1c. brown	16·00	1·75
	a. Black-brown	10·00	2·50
	b. Crown broken at right	£550	£400
	c. Wmk sideways	†	£3000
	w. Wmk inverted	†	£1800
2	2c. green	20·00	30
	w. Wmk inverted	†	£2000
	x. Wmk reversed	†	£2250
	y. Wmk inverted and reversed	†	£2000
3	4c. carmine-red	13·00	30
	a. Substituted crown in wmk	†	£1800
	w. Wmk inverted	†	£2500
4	6c. orange	10·00	1·75
	w. Wmk inverted	†	£1700
5	8c. slate	15·00	1·50
6	10c. ultramarine	21·00	40
	w. Wmk inverted	†	£2000
	y. Wmk inverted and reversed	†	£1200
7	12c. purple/yellow	18·00	11·00
8	20c. purple and sage-green	26·00	1·50
9	25c. purple and magenta (Type A)	15·00	18·00
11	30c. purple and orange-yellow	50·00	12·00
12	50c. black/blue-green (*olive back*)	75·00	1·50
	a. Emerald surface (1917?)	70·00	11·00
	b. On emerald back (1919)	55·00	7·00
	c. On white back (1920)	£1400	£225
13	$1 reddish purple and bright blue/blue	85·00	4·00
	a. Grey-purple and blue/blue (1921)	90·00	12·00
14	$2 carmine-red and grey-black	£225	£400
15	$3 green and purple	£700	£325
16	$5 green and red/blue-green (*olive back*)	£350	£400
17	$10 purple and black/red	£700	£850
1/17 *Set of 16*		£2000	£1500
12s/17s H/S 'SPECIMEN' (50c.) or *'SPECIMEN' Set of 6*	£2250		

1922 (Mar)–**27**. As last, but wmk Mult Script CA.

18	1c. brown	3·50	7·50
19	2c. green	9·00	2·25
	w. Wmk inverted	£475	
20	4c. carmine-rose	22·00	3·50
	a. Lower Chinese character at right broken at top	£325	£350
21	6c. orange-yellow	7·50	7·00
22	8c. grey	15·00	18·00
23	10c. bright ultramarine	24·00	4·50
	w. Wmk inverted	£300	
24	20c. purple and sage-green	22·00	5·00

25	25c. purple and magenta (Type B)	27·00	75·00
	a. Broken flower	£950	
26	50c. black/*emerald* (1927)	60·00	£350
	s. Handstamped '*SPECIMEN*'	£275	
27	$1 purple and blue/*blue*	85·00	80·00
28	$2 carmine-red and grey-black	£225	£300
18/28 *Set of 11*		£450	£750

STAMP BOOKLETS

1917. Black on red cover inscribed 'BRITISH POST OFFICE AGENCIES IN CHINA'. Stapled.

SB1	$1 booklet containing 8×2c., 6×4c. and 6×10c. (Nos. 2/3, 6)	£6500

Three settings of the front cover of No. SB1 are recognised.

1922. Cover as No. SB1. Stapled.

SB2	$1 booklet containing 8×2c., 6×4c., and 6×10c. (Nos. 19/20, 23)	£6000

The British PO's in the Treaty Ports closed by agreement with the Chinese on 30 November 1922, but the above overprinted issues continued in use at the Wei Hai Wei offices until they in turn closed on 30 September 1930. Under the terms of the Convention signed with China the Royal Navy continued to use the base at Wei Hai Wei until the mid-1930s.

BRITISH POST OFFICES IN JAPAN

Under the terms of the Anglo-Japanese Treaty of Yedo, signed on 26 August 1858, four Japanese ports were opened to British trade. British consulates were established at Decima (Nagasaki), Kanagawa (Yokohama), Hiogo (Kobe) and Hakodadi (Hakodate). The postage stamps of Hong Kong became available at the Yokohama and Nagasaki consulates during October 1864 and at Hiogo in 1869, although cancellation of mail did not commence until 1866 at Yokohama and Nagasaki or 1876 at Hiogo. Japan became a member of the UPU on 1 June 1877 and all of the British Postal Agencies were closed by the end of 1879.

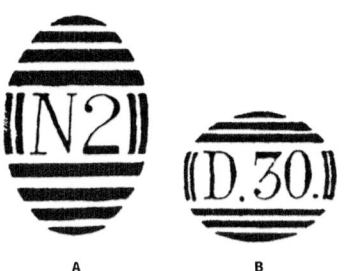

A	B

C

HAKODATE

A British consular office existed at Hakodate, but it was never issued with a c.d.s. obliterator or Hong Kong stamps. No British covers are recorded from this consulate prior to opening of the Japanese Post Office.

HIOGO

The Port of Hiogo (Kobe) was first opened to foreigners on 1 January 1868. The British Consular mail service at Hiogo commenced during 1869 to serve the foreigners at Hiogo, Kobe and Osaka. The cities of Hiogo and Kobe later merged to become the single city of Kobe. The consular office at Hiogo closed on 30 November 1879.

Type **B** ('D.30.') (*supplied* 1876) *used* 1876–1879

Type **D** (*supplied* 1876) *used* 1876–1879

Stamps of HONG KONG cancelled at Hiogo between 1876 and 1879 with postmarks detailed above.

1863–71. Wmk Crown CC (Nos. 8/19).

Z1	2c. brown	£6000
Z2	4c. grey	£4250
Z3	6c. lilac	£5500

Z4	8c. orange	£5000
Z5	12c. blue	£6000
Z6	18c. lilac	
Z7	24c. green	£4500
Z8	30c. vermilion	
Z9	30c. mauve	£6000
Z10	48c. rose	£9000
Z12	96c. brownish grey	£9000

1877. (Nos. 20/21).

Z13	16c. on 18c. lilac	

1877. Wmk Crown CC (No. 22).

Z15	16c. yellow	£7000

NAGASAKI

The British Consulate opened in Nagasaki on 14 June 1859, but, with few British residents at the port, the consular staff found it inconvenient to carry out postal duties so that few Nagasaki c.d.s. or 'N2' cancellations exist. The postal service was terminated on 30 September 1879.

Type **A** ('N2') (*supplied* 1866) *used* 1876–1879

Type **D** (*supplied* 1866) *used* 1876–1879

Stamps of HONG KONG cancelled at Nagasaki between 1876 and 1879 with postmarks detailed above.

1862. No wmk (Nos. 1/8).

Z15a	18c. lilac	£3750

1863–71. Wmk Crown CC (Nos. 8/19).

Z16	2c. brown	£2250
Z17	4c. grey	£2000
Z18	6c. lilac	£2000
Z19	8c. orange	£2000
Z20	12c. blue	£2000
Z21	18c. lilac	£7500
Z22	24c. green	£3500
Z24	30c. mauve	£3000
Z25	48c. rose	£4000
Z27	96c. brownish grey	

1876–77. (Nos. 20/21).

Z28	16c. on 18c. lilac	£3000
Z29	28c. on 30c. mauve	£2250

1877. Wmk Crown CC (No. 22).

Z30	16c. yellow	£3250

YOKOHAMA

The British Consulate opened in Kanagawa on 21 July 1859, but was relocated to Yokohama where it provided postal services from 1 July 1860 until a separate Post Office was established in July 1867. The British Post Office in Yokohama closed on 31 December 1879.

Type **A** ('YI') (*supplied* 1866) *used* 1867–1879

Type **D** (*supplied* 1866) *used* 1866–1879

Stamps of HONG KONG cancelled at Yokohama between 1866 and 1879 with postmarks detailed above.

1862. No wmk (Nos. 1/8).

Z30a	8c. yellow-buff	£450
Z31	18c. lilac	£180

1863–71. Wmk Crown CC (Nos. 8/19).

Z32	2c. brown	22·00
Z33	4c. grey	23·00
	a. Perf 12½	£550
Z34	6c. lilac	30·00
Z35	8c. orange	28·00
Z36	12c. blue	22·00
Z37	18c. lilac	£750
Z38	24c. green	30·00
Z39	30c. vermilion	75·00
Z40	30c. mauve	25·00
Z41	48c. rose	80·00
Z42	96c. olive-bistre	£5000
Z43	96c. brownish grey	£110

1876–77. (Nos. 20/21).

Z44	16c. on 18c. lilac	£350
Z45	28c. on 30c. mauve	£120

1877. Wmk Crown CC (No. 22).

Z46	16c. yellow	£150

POSTAL FISCAL STAMPS

1874. Wmk Crown CC. Perf 15½×15 (Nos. F1/F3).

ZF47	$2 olive-green	£225
ZF48	$3 dull violet	£170
ZF49	$10 rose-carmine	£2250

Stanley Gibbons
Stamp Catalogues

We have catalogues to suit every aspect of stamp collecting

Our catalogues cover stamps issued from across the globe - from the Penny Black to the latest issues. Whether you're a specialist in a certain reign or a thematic collector, we should have something to suit your needs. All catalogues include the famous SG numbering system, making it as easy as possible to find the stamp you're looking for.

Commonwealth & British Empire Stamps 1840–1970 (127th edition, 2025)

King George VI (9th edition, 2018)

Commonwealth Country Catalogues

Australia with Australian States & Dependencies (12th edition, 2022)
Bangladesh, Pakistan & Sri Lanka (3rd edition, 2015)
Brunei, Malaysia & Singapore (5th edition, 2017)
Canada (8th edition, 2024)
Cyprus, Gibraltar & Malta (6th edition, 2023)
East Africa with Egypt & Sudan (4th edition, 2018)
Eastern Pacific (3rd edition, 2015)
Falkland Islands (9th edition, 2024)
India (including Convention & Feudatory States) (6th edition, 2023)
Indian Ocean (4th edition, 2022)
Ireland (8th edition, 2023)
Leeward Islands (3rd edition, 2017)
New Zealand & Dependencies (7th edition, 2022)
Northern Caribbean, Bahamas & Bermuda (4th edition, 2016)
St Helena & Dependencies (6th edition, 2017)
West Africa (2nd edition, 2012)
Western Pacific (4th edition, 2017)
Windward Islands & Barbados (3rd edition, 2015)

Stamps of the World 2025

Volume 1   Abu Dhabi – Charkhari
Volume 2   Chile – Georgia
Volume 3   German Commands – Jasdan
Volume 4   Jersey – New Republic
Volume 5   New South Wales – Singapore
Volume 6   Sirmoor – Zululand

Great Britain Catalogues

2025 Collect British Stamps (76th edition, 2025)
2022 Channel Islands & Isle of Man (31st edition, 2022)
2024 GB Concise (39th edition, 2024)

Great Britain Specialised

Volume 1   Queen Victoria, Part 1 Line-engraved and Embossed Issues (1st edition, 2020)
Volume 2   King Edward VII to King George VI (14th edition, 2015)
Volume 3   Queen Elizabeth II Pre-decimal issues (13th edition, 2019)
Volume 4   Queen Elizabeth II Decimal Definitive Issues – Part 1 (10th edition, 2008)
           Queen Elizabeth II Decimal Definitive Issues – Part 2 (10th edition, 2010)

Foreign Countries

Arabia (1st edition, 2016)
Austria and Hungary (8th edition 2014)
Belgium & Luxembourg (1st edition, 2015)
China (12th edition, 2018)
Czech Republic and Slovakia (1st edition, 2017)
Denmark and Norway (1st edition, 2018)
Finland and Sweden (1st edition, 2017)
France, Andorra and Monaco (2nd edition, 2023)
French Colonies (1st edition, 2016)
Germany (13th edition, 2022)
Hong Kong (7th edition, 2025)
Italy and Colonies (1st edition, 2022)
Middle East (1st edition, 2018)
Netherlands & Colonies (1st edition, 2017)
North East Africa (2nd edition, 2017)
Poland (2nd edition, 2023)
Portugal and Colonies (1st edition, 2022)
Southern Balkans (1st edition, 2019)
Spain and Colonies (1st edition, 2019)
Switzerland (1st edition, 2019)
United States of America (8th edition, 2015)

STANLEY GIBBONS
THE HOME OF STAMP COLLECTING

BY APPOINTMENT TO HIS MAJESTY THE KING PHILATELISTS STANLEY GIBBONS LONDON

STANLEY GIBBONS | 399 Strand | London | WC2R 0LX
www.stanleygibbons.com

 /StanleyGibbons   @StanleyGibbons   @StanleyGibbons   @StanleyGibbons1856

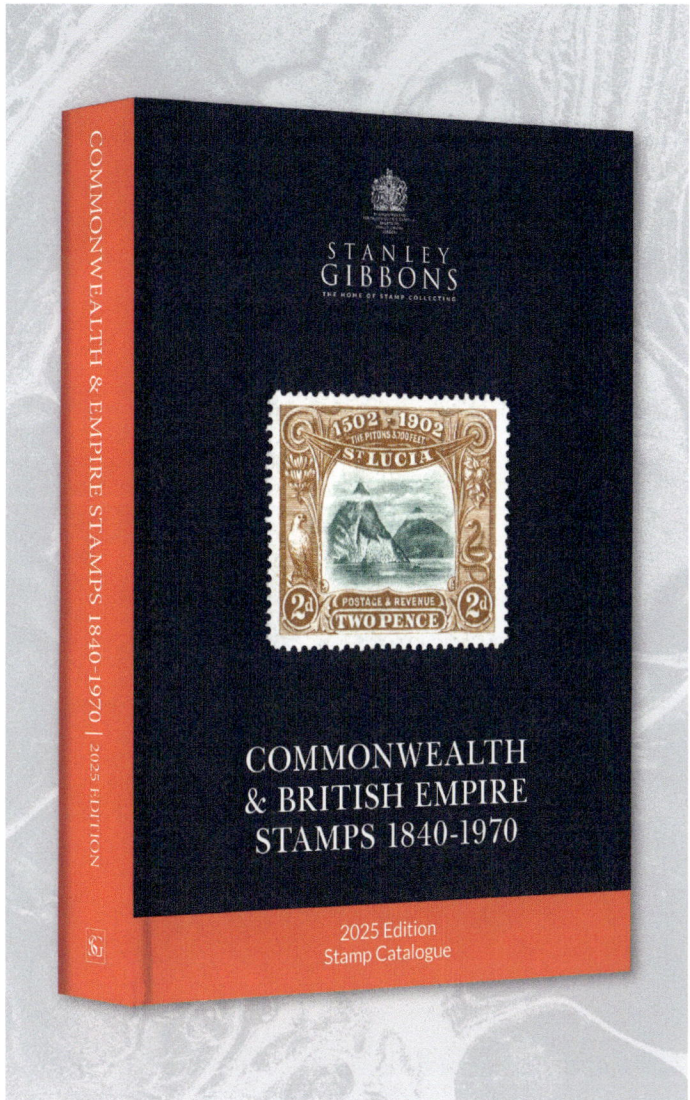

The King George VI Album Set

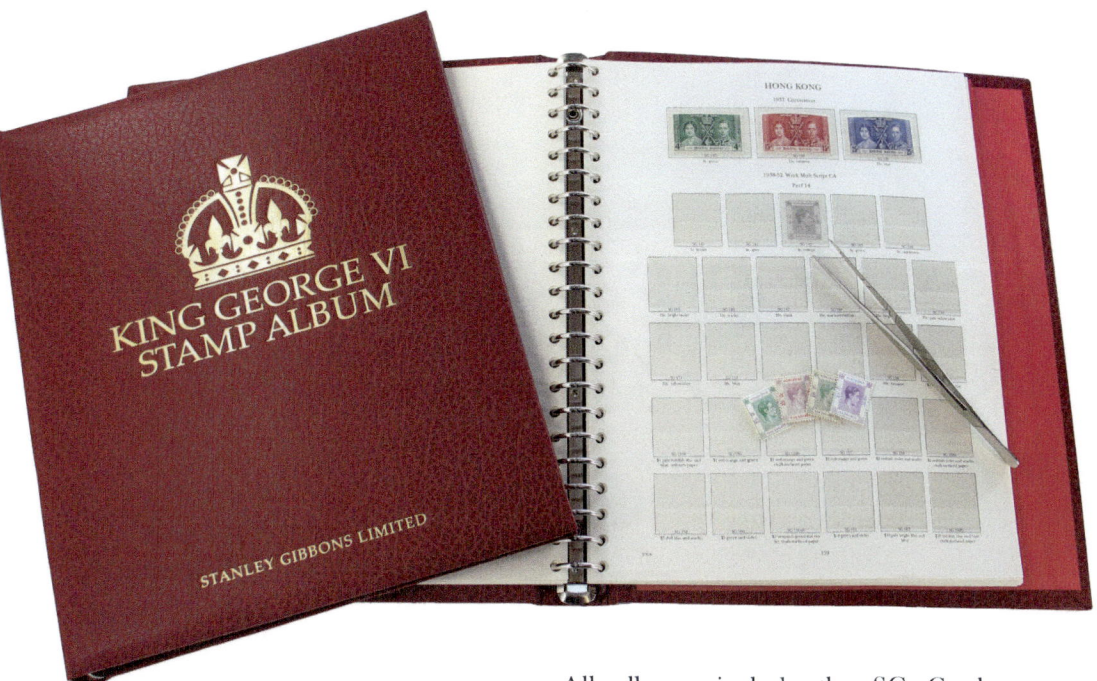

The King George VI 1936 - 1952 is presented in a six volume set of luxury padded binders, housed in three slipcases. All albums are handmade with a 22 Ring mechanism to securely hold your collection and comes supplied with a matching slipcase.

Pre-printed on cream acid free paper with spaces for all main SG numbers as per our Commonwealth and Empire stamp catalogue 1840 - 1970.

Covering all Postage, Air Due, Postal Fiscal and Offical Stamps. There are spaces for all perforation and watermark changes (including sideways but not inverted or reversed), different plates, Types and Dies, Shades and Varieties are not included.

All albums include the SG Catalogue numbers, Information Pages and many illustrations of Types and Dies are included to aid identifying the correct space for a stamp.

Indian States and Japan Occupation are not included in the main album but available separately.

All leaves are punched 22 Ring.
Leaf Size 222 x 280mm.

Available with clear mounts already affixed, or without mounts.

Product Code: RKG6
Standard (Without mounts): £479.00
Hingeless (With mounts): £716.00

Available from Stanley Gibbons customer service, or our distribution partners Dauwalders at www.dauwalders.co.uk